Series Editors:
Dario Castiglione (University of Exeter) and
Vincent Hoffmann-Martinot (Sciences Po Bordeaux)

political parties and interest groups in norway

Elin Haugsgjerd Allern

First published by the ECPR Press in 2010

The ECPR Press is the publishing imprint of the European Consortium for Political Research (ECPR), a scholarly association, which supports and encourages the training, research and cross-national cooperation of political scientists in institutions throughout Europe and beyond. The ECPR's Central Services are located at the University of Essex, Wivenhoe Park, Colchester, CO4 3SQ, UK

Typeset by ECPR Press
Printed and bound by Lightning Source

British Library Cataloguing in Publication Data
A catalogue record for this book is available from the British Library

Paperback ISBN: 978-0-9558203-6-6

www.ecprnet.eu/ecprpress

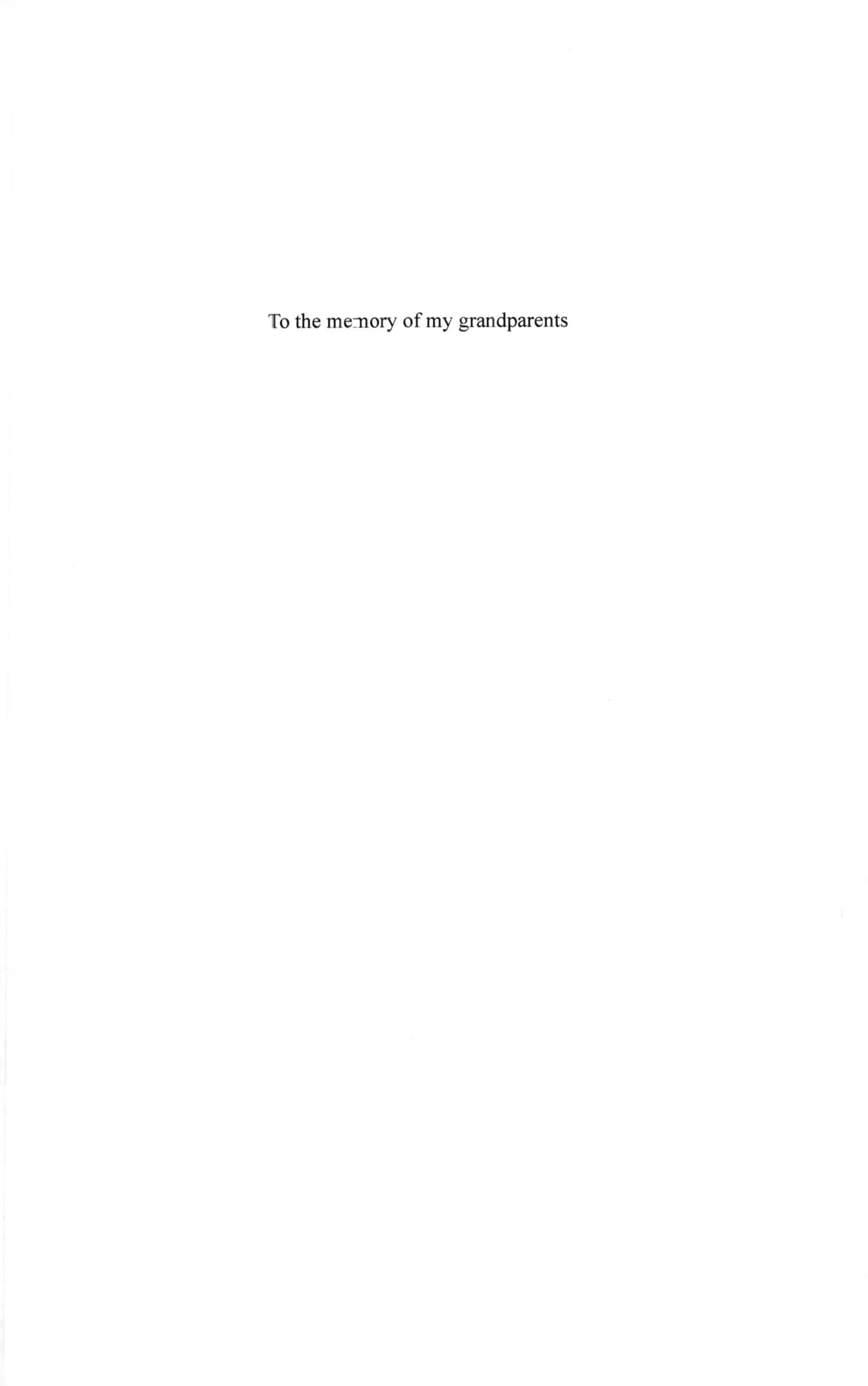

To the memory of my grandparents

Publications from the ECPR Press

ECPR Monographs:

Causes of War (ISBN: 9781907301018) Thomas Lindemann

Citizenship (ISBN: 9780954796655) Paul Magnette

Deliberation Behind Closed Doors (ISBN: 9780955248849) Daniel Naurin

European Integration and its Limits (ISBN: 9780955820373) Daniel Finke

Gender and Vote in Britain (ISBN: 9780954796693) Rosie Campbell

Globalisation (ISBN: 9780955248825) Danilo Zolo

Joining Political Organisations (ISBN: 9780955248894) Laura Morales

Paying for Democracy (ISBN: 9780954796631) Kevin Casas-Zamora

Political Conflict and Political Preferences (ISBN: 9780955820304) Claudia Landwehr

Representing Women? (ISBN: 9780954796648) Mercedes Mateo Diaz

The Personalisation of Politics (ISBN: 9781907301032) Lauri Karvonen

The Politics of Income Taxation (ISBN: 9780954796686) Steffen Ganghof

The Return of the State of War (ISBN: 9780955248856) Dario Battistella

Urban Foreign Policy and Domestic Dilemmas (ISBN: 9781907301070) Nico van der Heiden

Widen the Market, Narrow the Competition (ISBN: 9781907301087) Daniel Mügge

General Interest Books:

Parties and Elections in New European Democracies (ISBN: 9780955820328) Richard Rose and Neil Munro

Masters of Political Science (ISBN: 9780955820335) Edited by Donatella Campus and Gianfranco Pasquino

Please visit www.ecprnet.eu/ecprpress for up-to-date information about new publications

contents

LIST OF FIGURES AND TABLES

Figures

Tables

LIST OF ABBREVIATIONS

	English name	Domestic language name
Parties		
ALP/ FrP	Ander's Langes Party/Progress Party	Anders Langes Parti/ Fremskrittspartiet
Bp/Sp	Farmers' Party/Centre Party	Bondepartiet/Senterpartiet
DnA	Labour Party	Det norske Arbeiderparti
FDP	Free Democrats	Freie Demokratische Partei
FPÖ	Austrian Freedom Party	Freiheitliche Partei Österreich
H	Conservatives (Conservative Party)	Høyre
KrF	Christian People's Party	Kristelig Folkeparti
RV	Red Electoral Alliance	Rød Valgallianse
SF/SV	Socialist People's Party/ Socialist Left Party	Sosialistisk Folkeparti/Sosialistisk Venstreparti
V	Liberals (Liberal Party)	Venstre
Interest groups		
FoEn	The Norwegian Society for the Conservation of Nature/ Friends of the Earth Norway	Norges Naturvernforbund
LO	The Norwegian Confederation of Trade Unions	Landsorganisasjonen i Norge
NAF	Employers' Association of Norway	Norges Arbeidsgiverforening
NEKF	The Norwegian Electricians & Power Plant Union	Norsk Elektriker- og Kraftstasjonforbund
NBS	The Norwegian Farmers' and Smallholders' Union	Norges bonde- og småbrukarlag,
NHO	Confederation of Norwegian Enterprise	Næringslivets Hovedorganisasjon
NNN	The Norwegian Union of Food and Allied Workers	Norsk Nærings- og nytelsesmiddelar-beiderforbund

	English name	Domestic language name
NKF	The Norwegian Municipal Union	Norsk Kommuneforbund
Oslo RF	Oslo Shipowners' Association	Rederiforbundet i Oslo
RF	Norwegian Shipowners' Association	Norges Rederiforbund
YS	Confederation of Vocational Unions	Yrkesorganisasjonenes Sentralforbund
Others		
EC	European Community	Det Europeiske Fellesskap
EU	European Union	Den Europeiske Union
NRK	(Norwegian state broadcasting system)	Norsk Rikskringkasting

acknowledgments

This book started life as a significantly revised version of my doctoral thesis on political parties and interest groups in Norway. During the period of research and writing process, I have accumulated many debts to institutions and individuals who, in one way or another, have helped me.

The project could not have been conducted without the support and openness of the seven Norwegian political parties studied here. I am grateful to all the secretaries-general, party secretaries and other informants for their willingness to talk to me about party strategies and routines in relation to interest groups. Without all the party elite members who completed my pilot and final questionnaires, this book could not have been written. To the Norwegian Labour Party and the Norwegian Confederation of Trade Unions I owe a special debt of gratitude for granting me access to the minutes of their joint 'Co-operation Committee', and to the Norwegian Labour Movement Archives and Library, and the Constitutional Office of *the Storting*, for assistance in my search for written sources.

Several institutions have funded or in other ways made it possible to write this book. Above all, I have over several years enjoyed excellent working conditions at both the Department of Political Science, University of Oslo, and at the Institute for Social Research (ISF) in Oslo. In the spring term of 2004, the Department of Political Science at the Johns Hopkins University, Baltimore, Maryland, kindly hosted me as a visiting scholar. Finally, I wish to acknowledge the European Consortium for Political Research, and the ECPR Standing Group on Political Parties in particular, for their institutional support to young scholars.

Let me extend my warmest thanks to some of the many individuals whose views, comments and criticisms have aided me, and without which I should not have ventured into so wide a field. Sigurd Allern, Nicholas Aylott, Tim Bale, Jozef Bátora, Lars Bille, Tor Bjørklund, Flemming J. Christiansen, Robert Harmel, Knut Heidar, Elisabeth Ivarsflaten, Rune Karlsen, Richard S. Katz, Oddbjørn Knutsen, Ferdinand Müller-Rommel, Hanne Marthe Narud, Karina Kosiara-Pedersen, Riccardo Pelizzo, Thomas Poguntke, Jo Saglie, Hege Skjeie, Kaare Strøm, Lars Svåsand, Paul Thyness, Jack Veugelers and Steven Wolinetz have all read one or more chapters from, or papers based on, my research project and/or book manuscript, and have provided useful comments at various stages.

In particular, I would like to thank Tim Bale, Knut Heidar and Thomas Poguntke for their insightful and detailed comments on the entire draft manuscript. Together with Kaare Strøm, they have also offered me invaluable advice on how to transform a doctoral thesis into a regular research monograph. For the same reasons, I am deeply grateful to the book series' editors Vincent Hoffmann-Martinot and Alan Ware as well. A special note of appreciation is also due to Nicholas Aylott for useful theory discussions at various stages. Last, but not least, I would like to thank Rebecca Knappett and Mark Kench at the ECPR Press for their support during the entire production process.

Had I been wise enough to take into account all the criticisms and suggestions offered by my colleagues, the result would have been a better book. I must record my gratitude to them for their help while, of course, absolving them of responsibility for what is written here.

In conclusion, I would like to express appreciation to my supportive family, who have over the years stimulated my interest in politics and writing in many different ways. I dedicate this book to the memory of my grandparents. And finally let me thank Yngvar Bratvedt, my husband, for endless support, patience and enthusiasm throughout the journey!

Elin Haugsgjerd Allern
Oslo, November 2010

preface

Parties are mechanisms of power as well as social organisations. This means that fruitful research on parties can be designed both within a polity-embedded approach and from the perspective of broader social forces. Party organisations are the meeting point of polity and society. To explain party behaviour one will need to audit the balance between state, social and organisational factors. The individual facts will of course show variation between parties, over time and cross countries. Researching the relative importance of these factors is a major theme within empirical party research. One reason is that the facts are central to debates on 'what to do about the parties'.

This is a book for academics and scholars interested in political parties, interest groups and social movements – or Scandinavian politics. It should also appeal to a broader audience interested in the general debate on how parties and democracy have developed during the twentieth century. The crux of normative discussions on parties centres on the question of whether parties ought to be social forces or political agents in order to sustain democracy. Are parties the instruments of a 'political class', making democracy exclusively dependent of voters having the chance to 'throw the rascals out', or is democracy also a broader linkage between politicians and social forces and a society's citizens? Normative discussions feed into empirical research and open up the battleground for debates on institutional change and, more specifically, for 'party laws'.

Moisej Ostrogoski's classic *Democracy and the Organization of Political Parties* from 1902 is an early comparative discussion on parties in democracies. His description of the evolving British parties was that they became increasingly similar; they 'tend to become simple aggregates, drawn together, by the attractive force of a leader, for the conquest or the preservation of power'. Moreover, 'parallel with the separation of society from politics, are seen indications of the divorce of politics from principles'.[1] To nineteenth century liberals like Ostrogorski, parties as such were perceived as alarming. The literature of the last decades presents a stark contrast to this perception, not so much in empirical themes but in normative undertones. One example is the democratic concerns aired in the 'decline of parties' debate.

Elin H. Allern looks at Norwegian parties' relationship with interest groups and finds interest organisations still much present in party life, contrary to assertions of 'stateified' parties in contemporary western democracies. The state-parties

1. Ostrogoski, Moisej (1902: vol. I: 623): *Democracy and the Organization of Political Parties.* New York: Macmillan.

argument is that parties are increasingly losing their social base and increasingly becoming dependent on and integrated into the state apparatus. Taking an organisational perspective, and by emphasising the parties' autonomy as collective actors, Allern looks at the parties' structural and behavioural links to interest groups within turn of the century Norwegian parties. Her analytical framework is anchored in the general literature on political organisations and parties and developed for comparative use.

This is an innovative, methodologically rigorous and theory-driven study. Allern goes behind the formal aspect of party-interest group links, convincingly arguing that the realities of interaction and political influence are also embedded in informal relationships. The scaling down of organisational links has concealed the persistence of interest organisation impact. Her analytical focus is what explains these connections and what are their effects. The empirical analysis is based on organisational data, interviews with key informants and a survey of party elites to substantiate the analysis.

Allern's study is a rare modern study of an old theme, both within party research and more generally within the debate on the instruments and forces shaping democratic regimes. A major message to the current party debate is that exploring new trends, however exciting, should not make researchers forget about the old ones, at least not until it is clear that they can safely be left to the historians. This is certainly not the case here.

Parties' relationship to interest groups, or to so-called 'non-political organisations', is, in fact, the forerunner of the more fashionable interest in the new forces of civil society: the citizen action groups, the ad hoc groups, the new social movements or whatever the label is. These studies are all variations of a central question in democratic debates: are parties basically sustained within the political sphere, or are they also products of social forces?

Knut Heidar

part one
general introduction

chapter one | political parties, interest groups and democracy

> One of the paradoxes of political science around the world, particularly in liberal democracies, is that broad agreement exists on the importance of the relationship between political parties and interest groups but little research has been conducted on that relationship. Clive S. Thomas[1]

Recent decades have seen much discussion of the role and importance of political parties in established democracies. In practice, 'democracy' still means free and regular elections along some sort of party lines, but the capacity of parties to connect the citizenry with government agencies is questioned. Concurrently, greater attention is being paid to other types of intermediaries like organised interest groups, the mass media, business corporations and professional lobbyists. Nevertheless, political parties remain the only intermediary with direct access to public office. An important question therefore is whether and how today's political parties are connected to other organisations and collective actors outside government. However, whilst studies of parties and interest groups separately represent 'highways' of research, the relations between them have been largely overlooked by political scientists. This book throws new light on the topic by presenting an in-depth study of party-interest group relationships in Norway at the beginning of the twenty-first century.

PARTIES AND INTEREST GROUPS AS INTERMEDIARIES

The erosion of traditional bases of party support, the increase in issue voting and indications of weakened party organisations put the future of parties on the public agenda in the United States during the 1970s (Broder 1972), and later in Western Europe as well (Berger 1981; Lawson and Merkl 1988). More than thirty years on, political parties have not vanished from the scene. The rise of party elections and party organisations in new democracies during the end of the twentieth century has strengthened the argument that parties are not obsolete (see e.g. Puhle 2002: 58; van Biezen 2003a: 4). But it is widely agreed that their organisation and position in established democracies have changed significantly. The indications of decline of party organisations as intermediaries in democracy are numerous.

The decay of party membership since the heyday of the 1950s and early 1960s is well-documented (Scarrow 2002a; Mair and van Biezen 2001), as is the decrease in party identification (Dalton 2002b: 25–9). Popular confidence in parties is today generally low in Western democracies (Pharr, Putnam and Dalton 2000). In recent decades, the public has increasingly turned to various types of interest groups and ad-hoc protests to make its voice heard to the government (Dalton

1. Thomas (2001b: ix)

2002a, chs 3–4). No longer can political parties depend primarily on members to support their activities, and state subventions now constitute a major financial resource for party organisations (Nassmacher 2001). The major campaigning arena is not conventions, rallies or caucuses, but non-partisan national radio and TV channels. Also, grassroots within parties seem to have lost power, to the benefit of the party leadership and party groups in the national assembly (Katz and Mair 2002). In other words, 'the golden age' of the mass membership party is over in Europe (Kirchheimer 1966; Mair 1994; Ignazi 1996; Katz and Mair 1995), and it is often argued that party organisations are less able to provide political linkage – 'interconnections between mass opinion and public decision' (Key, quoted in Lawson 1988: 14) – than before (Gunther and Diamond 2001: 3–4; Schmitter 2001). Increasingly dominated by the elite, parties risk decline as channels – or agents – for popular demands (Kirchheimer 1966). Whatever the case may be, at least one significant piece of the puzzle is still largely missing: the relationship of parties with interest groups.

THE RELATIONSHIP OF PARTIES WITH INTEREST GROUPS

Historically, the political parties of Western Europe have used interest groups as a major instrument for communicating with their main constituencies (Poguntke 2002). In the late 19th century, interlocking links implying interpenetration of corporate and electoral organisations were established between socialist parties and trade unions (see e.g. Duverger 1954/1972; Padgett and Paterson 1991, ch. 5). Close relationships also existed between the agrarian parties and the farmers' unions (Duverger 1954/1972), and between religious parties and organisations (von Beyme 1985: 192). Later, conservative parties established stable alliances with, among others, business associations (Schmitter 2001: 82). In most West European democracies, parties grew to be '(...) threads of a finely woven web of communication which includes interest groups, social movements, and state bureaucracies' (Kitschelt 1989: 284). More specifically, the two-tier system between parties and particular interest organisations gave some groups more or less direct access to power.

Whether this particular pattern of relationships has been primarily positive or negative for democracy is open to discussion, with the conclusion depending partly on how one defines democracy and the role of parties in democratic political systems (see e.g. Wright 1971; Katz 1997). In any case, it shows that the relationship between parties and interest groups shapes the nature of democratic governance (cf. Schattschneider 1942, 1960; Neumann 1956: 412–13; Duverger 1954/1972; Almond and Powell 1966; Katz and Mair 1995; Thomas 2001c: 1). How party organisations behave towards interest groups indicate whether political parties are embedded in the organised parts of civil society, and may also tell us what kinds of interests and constituencies they primarily represent (cf. Puhle 2002: 61).

Even so, only limited research has been conducted on such links to date. Various passing references to the relationship between parties and interest groups exist (for example Wilson 1990, ch. 6; Berry 1997, ch. 3) and some have combined the study of parties and interest groups (see e.g. Beer 1965/1982; Duverger 1972;

Ippolito and Walker 1980; Kitschelt 1989; Müller-Rommel 1990; Yishai 1991; Selle 1997; Warner 2000; Thomas 2001a; Poguntke 2002), especially with respect to trade unions (see e.g. Harrison 1960; Kassalow 1963; Padgett and Paterson 1991; Minkin 1991; Piazza 2001; Quinn 2002). It is widely agreed that long-established links – like those between social democratic parties and trade unions – have declined in many cases (see e.g. Padgett and Paterson 1991: 177; Gunther and Diamond 2001: 3; Piazza 2001; Thomas 2001a). However, relatively few have systematically studied the *general* party-interest group dyad empirically (Warner 2000: 14; Thomas 2001a). Party-interest group relations have simply been taken for granted – across different political systems, institutional make-ups, types of party systems, and sectors (Thomas 2001c: 1ff).[2]

A possible explanation of this neglect is the fact that parties and interest groups are, to a certain extent, *alternative* institutions in democracy. Classical liberal theory distinguishes clearly between political parties and interest groups (Almond and Powell 1966). While parties operate within the realms of both public office and civil society, interest groups are primarily societal organisations that seek to influence public decision-making 'from without' (cf. Schmitter 2001: 71). Therefore, as suggested by Rokkan's (1966) distinction between numerical democracy and corporate pluralism, parties and interest groups play complementary roles in modern democracies. Indeed, they are also widely seen as more or less antithetical to each other's power as collective actors and to each other's importance as intermediary institutions (see e.g. Lawson and Merkl 1988; Mair 1995: 42; Dalton 2002b: 22): 'When political parties are strong, it is argued, interest groups are weakened; when interest groups are strong, political parties are weakened' (Wilson 1990: 156).

In practice, however, the distinction between the two types of organisations – or intermediaries – is less clear (cf. Yishai 1991: 99–100). First, as the historical interlinkages suggest, parties and interest groups may share long-term policy goals, and they often live in a mutually dependent relationship. Political parties are gatekeepers to political power and thereby potential targets for organised interest groups wanting to influence public policy. Interest groups, for their part, may provide parties with policy expertise, information about grievances and opinions of voters, financial resources, and organisational support. Second, a party may begin as little more than a 'mask' for an interest group (Key 1942/1964: 155). As Lipset and Rokkan (1967) showed, many European parties originally emerged from social movements, outside Parliament. Nevertheless, the emphasis has been on the functional difference, which has contributed to the separation of research on parties and on interest organisations (Thomas 2001c; Ronit 1998: 8; Beyers *et al.* 2008: 1119–20).

2. There is a literature on the relationship between interest groups and parties in authoritarian and especially communist regimes, but that topic is beyond the scope of this book (see Evanson and Magstadt 2001 for a brief review). For literature on parties and interest groups in democratisation processes and new democracies, see for example Morlino (1998), Warner (2000), Schmitter (2001), Thomas (2001e), van Biezen (1998; 2003a; 2005) and McMenamin (2004). In recent years, moreover, the topic of parties and non-governmental organisations in global politics has received attention: see for example Lawson (2002) and van der Heijden (2002).

This book represents one attempt to bridge the gap, starting from the party side of the relationship. The general objective here is twofold: to develop an analytical framework for studying party relationships with organised interest groups in civil society, and to foster empirical knowledge by reporting from an in-depth study of Norwegian political parties. Party organisations – not the relationship *as such* – are the objects of analysis here. The focus is on the parties' extra-parliamentary organisation and activity in terms of links – or lack thereof – with interest groups.

SPECIFIC GOALS OF THE BOOK

The book can, as whole, be described as a 'multi-stage rocket', theoretically and empirically. The first step, and the primary specific aim of this book, is to contribute to our knowledge about the *nature* of political parties' relationship with interest groups: *to what extent do Norwegian political parties have links with interest groups in the early 2000s – how are parties linked and with what organisations?* Numerous different links may connect a party with an external organisation. I concentrate on those that open up contact on political and organisational issues, such as permanent liaison committees and regular meetings between parties and interest groups. I argue that a full-scale analysis also needs to take account of informal links at the individual level.

In this part of the book, the over-all aim is to empirically explore the widespread (hypo)thesis that contemporary parties are characterised by fairly distant – or tenuous – relations with interest groups. Although the focus is on contemporary relationships, historical relations – such as the original alliance between labour parties and trade unions – serve as significant points of reference. I start by discussing the question of what might generally characterise this aspect of party organisation and behaviour today. During the twentieth century Western parties moved from being relatively closed communities to more open, professionally driven structures, due to such general developments in society as eroding class identities and the rise of new mass media (Duverger 1954/1972; Kirchheimer 1966). Against this background, elaborated in Chapter 3, it is often argued that the general incentives for close relationships with particular interest groups have now become relatively weak. For example, social democratic parties can no longer base their electoral support primarily on linkages with the traditional working class, but need to appeal to a new, internally heterogeneous middle class. Existing empirical studies indicate that parties historically closely linked with certain organisations have become more independent over time, but that this trend may not be uniform (cf. e.g. Padgett and Paterson 1991: 216ff; Thomas 2001e). The degree to which most established parties are today characterised by weaker relations with a wide range of interest groups, is a moot point.

True, political parties are autonomous actors, capable of being independent from their environment, not direct reflections of economic, social and cultural structures (van Biezen 2003b: 179). Institutions and structures constrain political parties, but different parties do not necessarily respond in the same way to similar environments. However, the literature emphasising system-level characteristics like cleavage structure and technology leads us to expect that party relationships with interest groups are in the early 2000s broadly similar – in the sense that major parties are generally characterised by fairly distant relationships, but links to a variety of interest groups. In recent years, it has even been indicated that the introduction of state subventions and increased ideological convergence between established parties have reduced the incentive for links into civil society in general (Katz and Mair 1995). Accordingly, as a specific alternative, it is suggested that political parties tend to have a distant relationship – if any significant links at all – with interest groups. This book explores these widespread hypotheses of homogeneity by studying parties operating within the same society and political system – i.e. Norway.

The second major question discussed – and the next step of this book – relates to *the shaping factors* of party links with the interest-group community in Norway: *what explain differences in party relationships with interest groups at particular points in time?* While most effort has been devoted to mapping, describing and categorising patterns of relationships, the aim of the study has also been to contribute to the debate on what shape this aspect of the organisation and behaviour of political parties. Under what more specific conditions do parties prefer, or end up with, close relationships with interest groups as opposed to distance or separation? When do parties seek links with multiple organisations, when do they prefer exclusiveness? As suggested above, parties are exogenously constrained by their surroundings and can be assumed to adapt instrumentally to their (shifting) circumstances. As the results of general developments in society do not necessarily imply similar incentive structures for all parties, such variables represent one set of possible explanatory factors of differences between parties. But I believe that both a look at the enduring institutional setting and more actor-oriented theory is needed if we aim to understand variations in contemporary party-interest group relationships.

Therefore explanatory assumptions and hypotheses focusing on parties as agents are developed, first and foremost in line with the tradition of *rational choice institutionalism* in studies of political parties. According to this 'soft' rational choice approach parties are assumed to be largely instrumental policy-seeking and office-seeking collective actors, but constrained by the political institutions within which they act (cf. e.g. Strøm and Müller 1999). Informed by economic theory on transaction costs, interaction between parties and interest groups is analysed as 'political exchange': Party-interest group links are not only about communication, but represent means by which the mutual exchange of resources are made more reliable and stable. A general cost-benefit model is developed, with emphasis on the party's calculations. Differences in party relationships with interest groups are generally expected to correspond systematically to variation in the costs and benefits (potentially) involved in links with interest groups.

However, this book also aims to explore how non-rational factors might, additionally, colour party-interest group relationships in the particular cases studied here. Parties are, I assume, above all goal-driven organisations, but they also represent collections of norms, routines, understandings and historical legacies. Therefore, I follow up by elaborating two alternative – yet not entirely mutually exclusive – analytical perspectives on party relationships with interest groups. Here the analysis leans on Angelo Panebianco's (1988) work on party organisations, but draws on more general theoretical schools within comparative politics as well: *historical* and *normative institutionalism* (cf. Thelen 1999; Peters 1999). Both schools question the importance of rationality, and emphasise other shaping factors or logics of behaviour. The aim is to clarify what parties' behaviour vis-à-vis interest groups would generally look like if it was not largely shaped by cost-benefit calculations and to be able take account of possible deviations from a rational course.

In each case, I briefly discuss if similar factors may also stimulate interest groups to prefer to relate to parties in different ways. Of course, a party cannot be linked with an organisation that does not want to have contact, and the intensity of links will depend on the choices made on both sides. The question of how the national political institutions might impinge on the relationship is addressed in a separate section, but not in detail as my empirical focus is on parties within one political system. I end up by generating several primary and secondary hypotheses intended to explain differences in party-interest group relationships at the organisational level. Later, the hypotheses are explored empirically as regards the Norwegian case. A full-blown test of them is not conducted, but a empirically sound exploration of *major differences* between Norwegian parties is provided.

The third, and final, question is: *what are the consequences of party-interest group links – do they matter for the political decisions made by political parties?* Presumably, the overall relationship with interest groups is an important characteristic of parties as intermediaries in democracy. However, as is shown in Chapter 4, the political significance of relations with interest groups cannot be taken for granted. For example, old links may be kept mainly for symbolic reasons, whereas new, weaker ones may be equally influential in practice. Thus, an additional aspect to examine empirically is whether links with interest groups actually affect the political decision-making of parties. This said, since the aim is mainly to check whether the links have substantial value – not to conduct a full-blown impact assessment – I choose to explore this aspect both theoretically and empirically before I address the issue of why parties' relationships with interest groups might possibly vary.

RESEARCH DESIGN: COMPARING MULTIPLE PARTIES IN ONE COUNTRY

The general research questions of this book are explored through a case study of the seven major Norwegian parties, i.e. those parties persistently represented in the Norwegian Parliament – *the Storting* – after the Second World War: the Centre Party (Senterpartiet, Sp), the Conservatives (Høyre, H), Christian People's Party (Kristelig Folkeparti, KrF), Labour Party (Arbeiderpartiet, DnA), Liberals (Venstre, V), the Progress Party (Fremskrittspartiet, FrP); and the Socialist Left Party (Sosialistisk Venstreparti, SV).[3] The unit of analysis is more precisely the

3. For the translation of Norwegian party names, I apply the terms used in Thomas T. Mackie and Richard Rose's (1991) *The International Almanac of Electoral History* and the Yearbook of *European Journal of Political Research* (Aalberg 2005). But for practical reasons, I occasionally refer to the 'Conservatives' as the 'Conservative Party' and the 'Liberals' as the 'Liberal Party'. Also, it should be noted that *Kristelig Folkeparti* itself has started to employ the label 'Christian Democratic Party', not the literal translation 'Christian People's Party' (Venås 2006 [telephone conversation], see also http://www.stortinget.no/english/alphabetic.html).

parties' central organisation. The key method is comparison at the party level: the parties' individual characteristics as regards their relations with interest groups are determined relative to each other (cf. Pedersen 2003: 86). The number of parties is relatively small, but as marginal parties without parliamentary seats have been excluded from the examination, the selection of parties – within Norway – should be fairly balanced on the whole. The choice does not necessarily mean significant variation in relationship with interest groups.

To be sure, I cannot make definite claims on the extent to which the results can be generalised beyond Norway. In general, as Gerring (2007: 42) puts it, 'theory testing is not the case study's strong suit'. Examination of the general impact of structural and institutional variables requires, of course, a cross-national survey. However, the research to be presented is indeed *implicitly* comparative, in the cross-country sense (Lijphart 1971), through the development of an analytical framework which can later be applied to parties in other countries. Embedded in abstract, middle-range theory, the study avoids getting caught up in particularities. Well-defined analytical, methodological and empirical components help us making a larger statement about party-interest groups relationships in contemporary established democracies.

As we shall see, a study of Norwegian parties and interest groups in particular has given us the chance to further explore how today's political parties are linked into the associational life in a society where such links have been strong historically, and where the social structure and other relevant system-level circumstances do call for the pattern of fairly distant, but wide-ranging relationships today. The general socio-economic and cultural developments have been significant by international standards. However, there are also enduring institutional features – such limited party finance regulation – generally stimulating party-interest group relationships in Norway (see Chapter 6). So Norway does not represent a 'crucial' case as regards the hypothesised patterns of party-interest group relationships (cf. Gerring 2007: 89); it is probably neither a least-likely nor a most-likely case of party distance to interest groups at the beginning of the twenty-first century.

Moreover, the study to be presented takes advantage of the specific benefits of a case study design. First, by studying parties in one single country we get beneath the 'surface' and may thereby contribute to a more comprehensive description of party relations with interest groups. Earlier research has focused on links regulated by party statutes; as explained in Chapter 4, this study looks beyond formal organisational structures. Such a strategy calls for closeness to the party organisation and its agents and a limited number of units of analysis (Ragin 1994: 49). Second, existing research has paid more attention to parties on the left than to parties on the right and focused on links with the parties' traditional associate (cf. ch. 2; see also Wolinetz 2002: 139), whereas concentrating on one party system makes it possible to compare – in-depth – a variety of party types and parties of different ideological origins along several dimensions. Third, this study enables us to come closer to identifying *some* of the more specific conditions under which parties may be likely to have close relationships with interest groups, more distant relationships, a narrow or wide-ranging network of links, or prefer to be almost detached from civil society (cf. Andersen 1997: 83; Yin 1994: 13). By looking at diverse political parties operating within identical system-level constraints, I am able to explore the possible impact of actor-oriented factors like differing goal orientations or dissimilar organisational histories by comparison.

The choice of supplementing a 'soft' cost-benefit model with alternative secondary explanatory factors, reflects the embracement of a fairly complex view of real-life politics. The design is open to the possibility of multiple and conjunctural factors, i.e. the influence of specific combinations of factors (Ragin 1987: 25, 36–42). A study of units within one country allows the analyst to move closer to decision-making processes and to pursue traces of party leaders' reasoning and calculations in ways not possible when the units of observations span many countries (cf. Mershon 2002: 26). Above all, this study is concerned with examining what factors shape Norwegian parties' relationships with interest groups. With an eye to future comparative research, however, I acknowledge that the more we nuance a parsimonious rational choice approach, the less generalisable the model is likely to be become. A modified and more complex cost-benefit model is not developed here.

Finally, the aim is *not* to identify necessary or sufficient causes – if such actually exist. Generally speaking, this work is oriented more towards descriptive than causal inference. I seek to better understand party-group relationships, but the explanatory ambitions are modest (cf. King *et al.* 1994). I do not try to reveal why discrete party decisions were made about links with interest groups. But despite its narrow focus on Norway, this book adds to our general knowledge in several ways. A typology of different relationships which can also be used in later studies across political systems – at least in a simplified version – is developed, and a multitude of theory-driven expectations, focusing on the party-organisational level, are explored – an examination which may provide the basis for future tests of hypotheses on a larger number of cases, across countries.

DATA AND METHODS: ASSETS AND LIMITATIONS[4]

The empirical analysis concentrates on the national party organisation, in which the highest authority is the national congress. However, since I have chosen to give priority to insight into day-to-day politics, the focus is on the central organisation and its top elite. Moreover, the study examines only the manifesto-making process – and not candidate selection or electioneering – in detail. This delimitation reflects the thematic emphasis on policy-making. The manifesto represents a party's systematic attempt to aggregate, prioritise and unify policy views.[5]

4. A more detailed description of the data material and methods can be found in Allern (2007), or it can be obtained by contacting the author.

5. Developing election programmes is an extensive organisational process in Norway. Usually, a manifesto committee, headed by a member of the top leadership, is responsible for making memos and a first draft, which is distributed and debated in the local party branches prior to the actual party congress. Activists at all levels are involved in a process that may go on for more than two years in Norway. A final proposal is recommended to the party congress by the manifesto committee, the national executive committee or the national council (Heidar and Saglie 2002).

Sources of Evidence

The empirical analysis is based on an original and extensive data material. The list of possible party-interest group links which is specified in Chapter 4, makes it clear that a party's closeness and range of relations can be measured at different levels of aggregation; by data on the party at large and by personal data (cf. Lazarsfeld and Barton 1951: 187ff). Thus, it has been necessary to collect data regarding sub-units within each party, e.g. on national executive committees, policy-making committees, and individual members of the party elite. I have collected and analysed relevant party documents (a list of documents is attached in Appendix A), personally interviewed key informants (a list of names is attached on Appendix A), and conducted a (web) survey among the entire populations of national party elites. Also the political significance of the links is explored on the basis of various sources: archival records, interviews with key informants and the survey. As regards explanatory factors, party documents (including income accounts), data from election studies, the elite survey as well as in-depth interviews serve as sources of evidence.

Identification of Key Informants and Respondents

The various key informants were all selected because they were assumed to be persons in positions with significant insight in the party's general relationships with interest groups, and they were primarily addressed as a source of factual information about the party as a whole by means of a semi-structured questionnaire (cf. Dexter 1970; Berry 2002). The population studied by means of a survey was limited to the formal national party elite. In line with the focus on the extra-parliamentary organisation, the survey did not address the parliamentary representatives.

The national party leaderships in Norway are composed of two main bodies: *the national council* (*landsstyret*) which meets only a few times a year and includes members of all province branches and sections of the party, in addition to the *national executive committee* (*sentralstyret*).[6] However, the emphasis on day-to-day politics made it reasonable to concentrate on members of the national executive, and exclude members of the national council from the survey. Moreover, party bureaucrats – not working solely with organisational and administrative matters in the party headquarters – were also included in the survey. The national headquarters are supervised by the executive committee and headed by the secretary-general or an elected party secretary, but are not formally an integrated part of the party organisational hierarchy. However, employed or elected staff members are involved in the parties de facto policy-making and political-strategic work on a daily basis. Therefore they were was also defined as a part of the national party elite.

The questions mostly concern the preceding year – which by and large means 2003. Respondents were asked to report possible links with with interest groups

6. This terminology is in line with the terms Svåsand (1992) applied in Katz' and Mair's (1992) data handbook.

belonging to several pre-defined organisation categories. The survey was conducted by means of a self-administered electronic set of questions on the Internet, a survey method which is only suitable if all respondents use e-mail and are familiar with Internet, like in the case of organisational elites (Dillman 2000: 355–6).

Validity, Reliability and Generalisation

By taking more than a 'snapshot' – mapping links at the organisational level from 2000 to 2004 – this research takes into account that relationships are not a static phenomenon, and may change abruptly. Ideally, one should also have interviewed organisation elites to validate the results. As will be discussed below, elite statements cannot be taken at face value. However, there is in practice a trade-off between such a strategy and collecting data from different levels of aggregation and party sources. By the latter *triangulation* (cf. Yin 1994: 91–3), a converging line of inquiry is developed, so that the data material can nevertheless provide a robust representation of Norwegian parties' relationship with interest groups.

Nevertheless, each source of evidence has, of course, to be critically examined individually as to validity and reliability, as well as in regard to the question of generalisation. In general, one should keep in mind that links with interest groups may be perceived as sensitive information for parties. Hence, it is not obvious that all relevant information is voluntarily revealed by the informants and respondents. Furthermore, information might be worded so to match the party's public image.

The issue of party goals and behavioural logics represents a particular challenge. Like individuals' motives, party objectives and values are mental constructions. Their existence can be assumed, but what actors say about their behaviour cannot be taken at face value. As Warner (2000: 74) points out: 'What actors say about what they are doing may be propaganda, or it may be that they misunderstand their own behaviour and thus misinterpret it; public pronouncement also may be only for public consumption.' Nevertheless, it is worth checking out the theoretical assumptions against which the actors – who are more familiar with their actions than others – think. Hadenius (1984) differentiates two main categories of potential indicators: political actors' written and oral statements about motives and other actions of which the motive is known. Use can also be made of more indirect indicators such as attempts of image building, criteria for success, electoral strategy and long-term ideological development (cf. Warner 2000: 74–5).

The issue of generalisation of the survey material should also briefly be mentioned here. As the questionnaire was sent to the entire elite populations of the seven parties studied, the problem of sampling errors is non-existent. The response rates vary between 50 and 76 per cent in most parties: the overall rate is 60 per cent, whilst the average is 59 per cent. The Liberals' response rate is only 29 per cent, and too low for the party to be fully included in the analysis. The general response rate among the remaining party elite members is, in contrast, indeed satisfactory: the average across parties is 64 per cent. For some individual respondents 2003 was perhaps an exceptional year, but it is assumed that such discrepancies are in total outweighed by similar instances in other parties.

Nonetheless, the survey results must be interpreted with caution. First, we must ask whether the non-responses are a problem. Those who did not reply do, by and large, not seem to differ systematically from the other party elite members in relevant respects (Allern 2004), but executive members – with positions in Parliament and government – are slightly 'underrepresented' in a few cases. The possible implications of this difference seem unclear, but will be discussed in due course. Second, despite the lack of sampling errors, variation between different parties' elite contacts with interest groups might be random for examle due to exceptional cirumstances – like sick leave – in one or more parties at the time of the research. Thus, only clear differences in percentages should be – and are – reported, and it is crucial to mention all incidents where even a few different answers would have influenced the results, the conclusions, significantly (see Appendix B for a more detailed discussion of these issues).

Analysis Techniques

The analysis techniques used vary according to the type of data under examination demonstrating how quantitative and qualitative techniques might be fruitfully combined in case studies. The documents have been explored by simple, qualitative content analysis by using references and quotes.[7] The in-depth interviews with eighteen different key party informants, and written correspondence with six (additional) others, include organisational facts that are summarised in tables. The survey is primarily analysed by means of frequencies and cross-tabulations. Since the analytical focus is not on individuals, but the party leadership and its staff, I have not controlled for variables like age, gender, etc. Such factors at the individual level may indirectly influence the variation between parties and also influence the probability of frequent contact with a particular group. But what is of interest here is to describe and compare the over-all behaviour of different party elite groups.

In order to provide comparability among and between parties, all data from the survey are presented as relative figures. Since the size of elite populations varies considerably, it is not reasonable to equal one person's organisational experience across parties. An individual elite member's experience from or contact with interest groups is most likely more significant for small elites than for large ones. In other words, what can be considered a weak or strong link will vary among parties; I assume it will take more individuals to create a strong link in a party characterised by a large elite group than in a party with a small elite. Nevertheless, it should be noted that the smallness of N implies that parties with particularly small elites (the Conservatives and the Christian People's Party) will more readily obtain higher scores in certain cases (cf. discussion above). In any case, I also regularly refer to the absolute figures, to make it clear that we are in fact dealing with small populations.

Since response rates also vary among parties, figures referring to 'all party

7. Archive studies of the Joint Co-operation Committee of the Labour Party and the Confederation of Trade Unions also include some quantitative elements – counting of numbers and topics discussed. These books of minutes are kept in closed files in LO' headquarters, but the party leadership and LO's leadership gave me access to all the reports from 1997–2004.

elites' are average numbers, I considered the option of weighting numbers according to the individual party elite's share of the total elite population, but concluded that the application of *averages* across parties was more in line with my analytical focus on the elites as (party) groups, not individuals. In this way, I avoided that the figures for 'all' became dominated by the largest parties.[8]

The analysis of closeness and range of relationships employs sociograms, in addition to tables of frequencies, inspired by the increasingly popular method of *network analysis* (see e.g. Borgatti and Everett 1997; Diani and McAdam 2003). In practice, this means that links are presented by means of paths linking graphic presentations of individual parties and different categories of interest groups. *The strength* of links is indicated by *different degrees of thickness* of paths. However, since this was a study of the party side of the relationships, and not the dyad as such, I could not use the software developed for network analysis. The sociograms in this analysis have therefore been developed manually.[9] The complete frequencies of personal overlaps and transfers for each party are included in Appendix D.[10]

PLAN OF THE BOOK

The book is divided into three main parts. The first section consists of the introductory chapter and Chapter 2. Chapter 2 starts by defining what is meant by 'political party' and 'interest group', and then present the Norwegian universe of political parties and interest groups.

Part two is made up by Chapter 3 to 6. Chapter 3 reviews the relevant literature and empirical studies on the topic. The main conclusion is that more knowledge is needed on the characteristics of contemporary relationships. Historically close relationships between particular parties and interest groups have declined, but it is not clear to what extent fairly distant relationships represent a general tendency, and whether parties are also linked with other interest groups. Up to now, empirical research has focused on old parties mainly on the left, and their changing relations with trade unions. Equally importantly, I show that there is no general agreement as to what defines a party's relationship with interest groups. Next, the review indicates that greater attention should be paid to what factors shape party relationships with interest groups, and more specifically what explains variations in party links – at a particular point in time or history.

Chapter 4 and 5 develop an analytical framework for comparative studies of

8. Only respondents who responded to the question under examination are included in the analyses, unless mentioned otherwise. Generally, if missing responses, or 'don't know' answers, can reasonably be interpreted as equivalent to a negative response, these are included as a separate category. Percentages have been rounded on the basis of standard rules in order to add up to 100 in all cases. This means that when rounding after decimals summed up to 99 or 101, the highest number – if such existed – was rounded up or down as necessary.

9. Network analysis studies the attributes of pairs of individuals or organisations (dyadic attributes), i.e. attributes of relationships between actors themselves (cf. Borgatti and Everett 1997: 243). In such an analysis, for example, the percentage basis of personal overlaps should be both elites, not only the party elite (see e.g. Osa 2003).

10. For complete *contact frequencies* for all parties, see Allern (2007) or contact the author.

such relations. In Chapter 4, a typology of party-interest group relationships is first generated, with suggestions for empirical indicators. Thereafter, the question of a general tendency versus variation in party relationships with interest groups is addressed, presenting alternative expectations as regards patterns of relationships. Finally, I turn to the topic of actual political significance of links with interest groups. The chapter concludes by further discussing the issue operationalisation. Chapter 5 deals with the issue of what shape party-interest group relationships. First, the perspective of rational choice institutionalism on political parties is elaborated and the cost-benefit model as regards party relationships with interest groups is developed. Second, I present the alternative theory perspectives as contrasts, and identify possible secondary explanatory factors. The chapter concludes by presenting hypotheses to be explored empirically.

Chapter 6 presents the case of Norway. It discusses to what extent Norwegian parties' relations with interest groups can tell us something about party-interest group relationships more generally. As a backdrop for the empirical analyses, the chapter first provides a general description – based on secondary sources – of party relationships with interest groups in the first half of the twentieth century. Next, relevant features of the Norwegian society and state are presented and discussed.

Part three comprises Chapters 7 to 14. Instead of jumping straight to the comparison of the various parties' links or lack thereof, the book first presents each party case in separate chapters. I start by describing the relations of Norway's dominant party in power since 1935 – Labour – and follow up with its traditional major antagonist, the Conservatives. Thereafter, the three centrist parties of the twentieth century are presented according to age: the Liberals, the Centre Party, and the Christian People's Party. I finish with the two parties established after the Second World War: Socialist Left and the Progress Party. This approach allows a richer and more nuanced description of individual parties' relationships, on which we can then base a broader comparison.

As a backdrop for the empirical exploration, the party's key developments in terms of ideology and voter profile are also briefly summarised. The description includes what we know about the development of its approach to interest groups in the second half of the twentieth century. To aid readers particularly interested in specific kinds of parties in terms of ideological origin, all parties are grouped in what are commonly agreed to be the prevalent ideological 'party families' in Western Europe. In Chapter 14, the analysis shifts from a party-based approach to a comparative perspective, analysing the relationships with interest groups by contrasting Norway's seven major political parties. A major empirical finding is that political parties have not withdrawn from the associational life, and that the relationships of political parties with interest groups do differ in Norway. The most common pattern is one of fairly distant relationships with numerous and various groups, but substantial diversity exists, and some parties have quite strong links to old associates.

Part three deals with the political significance and shaping factors of party links or lack thereof. Chapter 15 explores the significance of party links with interest groups in Norway. The analysis is restricted to some basic indications, but nevertheless argues that there is convincing evidence to indicate that the links – and the patterns of party relationships with interest groups – matter politically. The major conclusion of this part of the empirical analysis is that the links of political parties with interest groups are not merely symbolic and structural exercises in Norway. Also fairly weak links seem to affect party decisions, and make existing relations with a wide range of interest groups politically significant.

Chapter 16 looks into variations in party relationships with interest groups, and explores the utility of a rational choice perspective, through a comparative analysis of major differences in the patterns of relationships revealed. The book concludes that a cost-benefit analysis takes us a fair step forward. Parties do base their relationship with interest groups on rational calculations to a significant extent, and party differences do seem to correspond to variations in the costs and benefits (potentially) involved in links with interest groups. However, the cost-benefit model fails to account for all the observed variation. The impact of historical legacy, and accommodation to the values defining the party's original identity, seems to be the most fruitful additional explanations.

The final part of the book consists of Chapter 17, which summarises the major findings of the individual and comparative analyses. The book concludes with a discussion of the theoretical implications of these results, and indicates possible research questions for future studies.

chapter two | the universe of political parties and interest groups in norway

This chapter presents the population of Norwegian political parties and interest groups and begins by discussing what distinguishes an interest group from a political party, and more precisely what is meant by 'interest group' in this context. Next, the historical emergence and early development of Norwegian political parties and interest groups is described in the light of these definitions and taxonomies. While parties are portrayed in terms of their ideological characteristics, organisation and voter profile, a major distinction is made between interest groups seeking to advance the material benefits of their members and groups seeking to advance particular ideas or values.

POLITICAL PARTIES AND INTEREST GROUPS DEFINED

The notions of *parties* and *interest groups* concern the concept of *civil society*. Most definitions of 'civil society' refer to the public sphere and intermediaries which are neither the state nor the extended family (Scott and Marshall 2006). *Civil society* can be defined as 'the arena of uncoerced collective action around shared interests, purposes and values [that] commonly embraces a diversity of spaces, actors and institutional forms, varying in their degree of formality, autonomy and power' (CCS 2004). Civil society consists of participation in non-governmental, voluntary associations, mass media, professional associations and trade unions within the framework of the law. Broader understandings also exist and may, for example, include firms and other corporative bodies (e.g. McLean and McMillan 2003). It could also be argued that party organisations are themselves a part of civil society (e.g. Poguntke 2002: 44).

Hence, the distinction between parties and interest groups is, indeed, not crystal clear. Both parties and interest groups may serve as intermediaries – or buffers – between society and state; they both aggregate individual interests and preferences into collective demands and seek to influence the form and content of public policy. Both terms normally exclude entities like latent social groupings and totally unorganised groups of individuals. The difference between them concerns the foci of their main activity (Schmitter 2001: 70–1). Interest groups are often oriented towards a more narrow range of policy fields than political parties, but, above all, the contrast is about groups seeking public office and more or less organised attempts at influencing public policy from the outside (Peters 1999: 118; Beyers *et al.* 2008: 1119–20).

Parties may vary along several dimensions – in terms of, for example, ideology, organisational structure and origin, and voter profile (cf. Katz and Mair 1995). A common minimal definition of a *political party* is, however, '(…) any political group identified by an official label that presents at elections, and is capable of placing through elections (free or non-free), candidates for public office' (Sartori

1976: 63, see also Epstein 1967: 9). The distinctive characteristic of political parties is thus their role in territorially-based elections: 'They control the process of nominating candidates, who, if they win, occupy specified positions of authority, form a government, and accept responsibility for the conduct of public policy' (Schmitter 2001: 71).

Interest groups, by contrast, seek to affect public policy without competing in elections or being held publicly accountable for their policies (Schmitter 2001: 71). A common definition of an 'interest group' is: '(...) an association of individuals or organisations, usually formally organized, that attempts to influence public policy' (Thomas 2001c: 7–8).[11] Such groups may occasionally contest elections, and hybrids do indeed exist, but most likely it is only a matter of time before one must query whether a new party organisation has been established instead. The term 'interest' denotes a desire for a particular result or condition, be it a material object or a more abstract philosophical goal (Ippolito and Walker 1980: 270).[12] The term thus usually excludes organisations that are only exceptionally – or never – involved in politics, such as bridge or bowling clubs and self-help associations without any political agenda (*ibid*).

A great number of taxonomies exists in the literature distinguishing between different group categories, but a basis distinction is often made between 'groups seeking to advance the material benefits of their members and groups seeking to advance an idea or a value to which they adhere' (Yishai 1991: 22). This distinction between sectional and non-sectional groups is certainly not absolute, but in the former category of 'sectional groups', we usually find the classic economic interest groups, like trade unions and associations within business and industry. The second category of 'promotional groups' (or 'issue-oriented groups', 'citizens groups') consists of groups seeking a collective good, not selective benefits, and traditionally includes organisations like environmental groups and welfare groups seeking to aid the society at large (*ibid*: 22-24; Berry 1997: 29).

As mass membership is not a criterion in the applied definition, more or less professionalised 'advocacy organisations' or 'lobbying group' are included in addition to voluntary associations. It is also reasonable to assume that community-centred organisations like sports associations, young groups and associations for the elderly may be – or at least occasionally act as – 'interested parties' although they were not *founded* with the aim of influencing public policy. Moreover, as hinted above, interest groups – as defined here – comprise organised parts of social movements. It could be argued that 'special interest groups', 'social movement organisations' and/or 'civil society organisations' are distinct phenomena, but the distinctions are certainly not watertight (see Beyers *et al*. 2008: 1109).

However, *social movements* do have some distinguishing features worth mentioning. According to a common view, they try to exert influence on the behalf of a

11. Other common notions are 'pressure groups' and 'non-governmental organisations' (Grant 2003). However, since the non-governmental status is implicit and as 'pressure' entails a somewhat negative connotation in some cultural contexts, I prefer to leave these terms aside.

12. For a more detailed discussion of the definition of interest groups, see Baumgartner and Leech (1998: 25); Yoho (1998) and Beyers *et al*. (2008: 1109).

broader spectrum of the citizenry, both at home and abroad (Schmitter 2001: 71). So-called *new* social movements are those organisations and groups that emerged in the 1960s and 1970s and challenged the mainstream political agenda and political style of established democracies (Kitschelt 1986; Dalton *et al.* 1990: 4).[13] The concept is thus often restricted to groups representing people outside established institutions, attempting to change the economic, social or political structure by means of non-institutionalised forms of claim-making (Beyers 2008: 1110). Most importantly, 'social movement' is commonly defined as a *network* connecting formal organisations *and* individuals. Social movements also tend usually to lack clearly defined leadership (Thomas 2001c: 10). In the words of Diani (1992: 13), 'a social movement is a network of informal interactions between a plurality of individuals, groups and/or organizations engaged in a political and cultural conflict, on the basis of a shared collective identity'. Even a party might be incorporated in a social movement through links at the organisational or individual level with non-party groups (cf. Diani 1992: 15). As a whole, then, a social movement is not an interest organisation. But individual *parts* of social movements can be distinct organisations trying to induce public policy as an interest group. The need for this distinction is reflected in the notion of 'social movement organisations' (SMOs), which also includes hierarchical and highly routinised organisations that give meaning and direction to the movements (Dalton *et al.* 1990: 9).

To conclude, for the sake of simplicity, the concept of interest group applied in this book includes 'traditional' or 'sectional' economic interest groups (such as trade unions and business organisations) and 'non-traditional' or 'promotional' interest groups, including non-profit voluntary organisations (like cultural, faith-based and humanitarian organisations), advocacy organisations without members *and* organised parts of social movements (like international solidarity and environmental groups). But as the focus is on parties' relationship with civil societies' *associational life,* business firms, research-oriented think-tanks, media institutions, and professional lobbyists will not be regarded as interest groups in the context of this analysis.

To some extent, the term will be used interchangeably with 'interest organisation'. In all cases, we are talking about more or less organised groups that, technically, exist independently of the party organisation itself. So-called *ancillary, collateral organisations* are thus not regarded as 'interest groups'. Organisations such as, for example, 'Christian democratic women' are fully integrated in the party structure and know no independent membership (see Chapters 3 and 4). They are virtually synonymous with what Poguntke (2006) refers to as internal interest groups; organisations created through the organisational activity of the party itself, just like party-owned research centres and institutes for political training (Andeweg 1999: 11).[14]

13. For a detailed discussion on the difference between old and new social movements, see Dalton *et al.* (1990) and Diani (1992).

14. Yishai (1991: 100) has presented a distinction between different kinds of interest groups *within* parties: affiliated and non-affiliated. However, I consider it useful to reserve the term 'groups within parties' to organisations that are party-created organisational units, not external organisations.

THE EMERGENCE AND EARLY DEVELOPMENT OF NORWEGIAN PARTIES

This study concentrates on the seven Norwegian political parties that have been persistently represented in the Norwegian Parliament – the Storting – after the Second World War. For this reason, the Communist Party of Norway (*Norges Kommunistiske Parti*), the Red Electoral Alliance (*Rød Valgallianse*), as well as the Coastal Party (*Kystpartiet*), have been excluded from the analysis, whereas the Socialist Left (*Sosialistisk Venstreparti*) is included. The Greens (*Miljøpartiet De Grønne*) have never held seats in the Storting. Neither does the study deal with the former fascist-inspired National Socialists (*Nasjonal Samling,* established in 1933, and dissolved after the war), but it does encompass the more recent right-wing Progress Party (*Fremskrittspartiet*). The emergence and early development of the Norwegian party system – and parties in terms of key aspects like ideology, organisation and voter profile – is briefly described below.

The Rise of the Five-Party System

The birth of the Norwegian party system is usually dated back to approximately 1884, with the establishment of the Conservatives and the Liberals. The backdrop was the dispute that crystallised during the early 1880s around the struggle over constitutional reform and parliamentary democracy (granted in 1884), which finally led to the dissolution of the union with Sweden in 1905 (Urwin 1997: 38). The political conflict mirrored a fundamental disagreement between two sets of actors: on the one hand, the elites of the capital and national bureaucracy; and on the other, an alliance between a rural, populist-nationalist movement protecting traditional values, and a radical urban opposition to the political hegemony of the traditional *Embedsmannsstat* ('civil servant's state').

According to Stein Rokkan's model for socio-political cleavages, the establishment of the Liberals and Conservatives reflected both a territorial opposition between centre and periphery, and a socio-cultural conflict over language, between the established *riksmål* norm and the proponents of giving Norway a *new language* based on rural language (Rokkan 1967: 372; Valen 1992: 63).[15] But the Liberals brought together a wide range of groups and movements, and the party formation was far from predetermined (Leiphart and Svåsand 1988: 305). During the 1870s and 1880s, parliamentary representatives gradually organised into two different and stable groups. Parliamentary party groups were founded in the spring of 1883 (the Liberals) and in January 1884 (the Conservatives). Later, both established extra-parliamentary national organisations as well (Nordby 2000: 80–4; Mjeldheim 1984: 87), although the Conservatives remained loosely organised at the local level until after the Second World War (Tresselt 1977: 94).

The Liberals continued to unite numerous interests – including an urban liberal wing and a rural national democratic tradition – in one party with no clear ideological identity (Leiphart and Svåsand 1988: 307; Kirchner 1988a: 4). It has traditionally been classified as a conservative – not radical or progressive – so-

15. The language was called *landsmål*, and later *nynorsk*.

cial liberal party. Originally, the ideology heavily emphasised mass participation and democracy. The principle of freedom was supplemented by emphasis on the importance of equality (von Beyme 1985: 45; Kirchner 1988a: 2–4). The Norwegian Conservative party was characterised by the traditional conservative emphasis on private property and freedom (von Beyme 1985: 46). But in the wake of the industrial revolution, new conflicts emerged in the labour market, and the Conservatives approached business and industry interests as well as the employer segment (Rokkan 1967; Valen 1992). A strong incentive was provided by the rise of a working-class identity and interests, initially organised in trade unions supporting the Liberals and later represented by the Labour Party.[16]

After the introduction of universal suffrage in Norway in 1913, the functional-economic cleavage increasingly cut across the territorial-cultural axis. The Labour Party (DnA), founded in 1887 as an extra-parliamentary organisation of both trade unions and political associations within the labour movement, did not gain its first parliamentary representative until 1903. With regard to the industrial revolution, Norway was a latecomer in West European industrialisation: at the turn of the century only 8.5 per cent of the workforce was working under factory-like conditions. But between 1905 and 1920, Norway experienced a spectacular industrial growth (Heidar 1981: 2). In 1915, Labour reached voting parity with the Liberals and Conservatives. This initiated the 'three-party phase' of Norwegian political history (Svåsand 1990: 44–6).

DnA's original ideology was strongly characterised by co-operative ideas compared to the core policies of labour parties elsewhere (von Beyme 1985: 62–3). In 1918, opposition to syndicalism became more influential, and the Norwegian Labour Party grew more radical and less reformist than its counterparts in Denmark and Sweden (Elvander 1980: 38–9). After the Russian Revolution, it experienced a severe split caused by a decision (made two years previously) to join the Communist International in 1921. As in France, a majority adhered to the party, but in 1923 the Norwegian Labour Party left the Comintern. In 1927, it was once again united (Arter 2003: 75). However, the split had led to significant secession on the left, which led, in turn, to the formation of the Communist Party (Arter 1999: 54). Labour's first government was elected in 1928, although it lasted only two weeks. Since that time, DnA has remained Norway's largest political party in terms of share of votes. DnA returned to government in 1935 and stayed in power until 1965.

During the early 1930s, Labour abandoned its revolutionary profile. Although it was the party of the organised blue-collar workers, DnA also appealed to day labourers on farms, tenant farmers, smallholders, fishermen and forest workers, and especially those living in Northern Norway, the most economically under-

16. This brief summary ignores several party splits in the early years. Within a year after the party formation, the Liberals split several times. Based on a conflict along a religious cleavage, the fundamentalists were excluded from the parliamentary group and established the Moderate Liberals (*Moderate Venstre*), a party later incorporated in the Conservatives. After the dissolution of the union between Norway and Sweden in 1905, a new split occurred due to economic issues. The National Liberals (*Frisinnede Venstre*) was established in 1908 (Leiphart and Svåsand 1988: 305–6).

developed region of the country (Lorenz 1972: 82; Rokkan 1967: 403). Most industrial workers had themselves grown up on farms. The urban-rural, industrial-agricultural mix was therefore not difficult to justify (Martin 1974: 82). After a brief period of post-war radicalism, DnA and the other Scandinavian labour parties reverted to the pragmatic, Keynesian model of social democracy (Padgett and Paterson 1991: 25).

Through the alliance between smallholders, farm workers and blue-collar workers, DnA challenged other agrarian interests (Ohman Nielsen 2001: 9). The engagement of farmers in Norwegian party politics, however, dates back to the nineteenth century. A national organisation of farmers (*Norges Landmandsforbund*, called *Norges Bondelag* since 1922) opposing the social radicals among the Liberals had been established in 1896 when the agrarian sector was hit by economic difficulties (Steen 1988: 224; Christensen 1992: 9; Rovde 1995: 139). In the late nineteenth and early twentieth centuries, the Farmers' Union became an active participant in electoral politics. Consideration was given to establishing a separate farmers' party, but the issue of universal suffrage and union with Sweden discouraged such initiatives (Rovde 1995: 140–1; Aasland 1974: 275).

Until 1920, the Union's main tactic was to influence public policy through the major parties and by addressing the relevant parliamentary committees (Kristinsson 1991: 44; Rovde 1995: 137). Through those members who were also affiliated to a party the Farmers' Union tried to influence party manifesto-making and selection of candidates from within as well (Aasland 1974: 209; 213; 224). According to Ohman Nielsen (2001: 26), the Farmers' Union, in fact, spent twice as much on election campaigning for its preferred candidates as did, for instance, the Liberals in 1918. Based on the view that all parts of the agricultural community shared certain interests (Rovde 2000: 58), the Farmers' Union avoided taking sides on issues where farmers were divided (Kristinsson 1991: 44–5). In 1910, a clause declaring party-political neutrality had been added its statutes (Aasland 1974: 213–14). The strategy was to promote the establishment of a farmers' parliamentary group across party lines (Aasland 1974: 183). In 1906, forty Storting representatives had approved the political programme of the Farmers' Union, and eventually a parliamentary alliance of farmer representatives developed (for details, see Allern 2007: 96–7).

Throughout the following decade, however, the Farmers' Union was to give increasing consideration to the need for a separate agrarian party. Disagreement over import policy was the final catalyst that resulted in a split of opinion and a break with the established parties. The Farmers' Union favoured high grain tariffs, whereas customs duties were opposed by industrial and consumer interests in both the Conservatives and the Liberals (Aasland 1974: 215; 232–3; Rovde 1995: 208). Furthermore, an oppositional agrarian interest organisation was founded in 1913: the Norwegian Farmers' and Smallholders' Union (*Norges bonde- og småbrukarlag, NBS*) (Rovde 2000: 60).[17] Against this background, in 1920 the national con-

17. Increasing grain tariffs were equally unattractive to livestock producers and smallholders, who had a natural interest in keeping down the prices of grain and fodder (Kristinsson 1991: 44). The new organisation generally made demands for better working conditions for forest and agricultural workers (Christensen 1992: 7).

gress of the Farmers' Union voted to establish the Farmers' Party (*Bondepartiet*, Bp) (Aasland 1974: 225ff; Ohman Nielsen 2001: 39). Finally, the transition to proportional representation in multi-member constituencies in 1920 – and fragmentation of the party system – enhanced the conditions for successful party formation, and made it more difficult to play individual candidates off against each other (Christensen 1992: 8; Aasland 1974: 23; Ohman Nielsen 2001: 27).

Whilst the farmers' movement had originally been related to socio-cultural conflicts between the centre and periphery, the agrarian party mainly struggled for votes along the cleavage between producers and consumers of food in the commodity market (Lipset and Rokkan 1967: 44–6; Rokkan 1966; Rokkan 1967; Christensen 1992: 10). Norway's agrarian party regarded itself as an umbrella for farm interests and canvassed protectionism. Bp's social base primarily embraced larger landowners (Christensen 2001: 37–8). The party strongly opposed the egalitarian ideals of the labour movement. A focus on that which distinguished farmers' and workers' interests was an important factor that served to bind together the party's representatives in the Storting, whilst anti-socialism was a driving force in electoral campaigning (Ohman Nielsen 2001: 123–9). In the 1930s, the agrarian party attempted to establish a common political manifesto with radical right-wing groups (Christensen 2001: 39).[18] The party was furthermore marked by emphasis on Christian moral values (Madsen 2001: 314), but internally it was divided between cultural traditionalists and more pragmatic modernists. Hence, in Norway as in the other Scandinavian countries, a five-party system had materialised by the 1920s (Berglund and Lindström 1978).

Fragmentation of the Centre, Left and Right

In the centre, however, more fragmentation emerged, due to socio-cultural conflicts. From a comparative perspective, the religious homogeneity of Scandinavian countries did not lead to a general cleavage on the grounds of religion, reinforced by the orthodox Lutheran emphasis on the separation of religion and politics (Madeley 1994: 143). The Norwegian state church was formally strong, but its political role was limited (Karvonen 1994: 121). Christian circles preferred to seek support among individual candidates across party lines (Opdahl 1976: 74; Garvik 1983). However, the pietistic movements in south-western Norway, which earlier had splintered temporarily from the Liberals (Rokkan 1967: 391; Valen 1992: 64),[19] did not want the state to govern alone (Heidar and Saglie 2004: 48). Dissatisfaction with the moral profile of the political establishment increased over time. In 1919, Christian organisations established a committee charged with the task of evaluating the issues of a full-blown religious party (Garvik 1983: 18). Various cultural issues, which emerged on the public agenda during the 1920s, stimulated a protest

18. Association with the radical right was also due to the fact that the founder of Norway's Nazi party and prime Nazi collaborator, Vidkun Quisling, participated in the first Agrarian government between 1931 and 1933.

19. As early as 1907, missionary leaders founded the Church Party (*Kirkepartiet*), but it did not contest elections and was soon dissolved.

faction of the Lutheran laymen movement to form the Christian People's Party (KrF) in 1933, supported by a temperance movement that opposed the liberalisation of state alcohol policies (Rokkan 1967; Urwin 1997: 41; Lomeland 1971).

In contrast to its Swedish counterpart, KrF was not eventually reunited with the Liberals (Bjørklund 1983a: 25). In 1938, a national party organisation was formally established (Opdahl 1976: 13; Sæter and Åsheim 1985: 42). After the Second World War, KrF developed a national headquarters, and the number of parliamentary representatives increased from one to eight in 1945 (Korsvold 1974). KrF called itself a 'people's party' from the very beginning and grew to be a party that appealed across social classes, albeit not as extensively and successfully as its Christian Democratic counterparts in Europe (see Keersbergen 1994; Kalyvas (1996). KrF was a distinctly Christian party. While the continental Christian parties' origin was confessional, the Norwegian Christian People's Party represented first and foremost a territorially limited, Lutheran *opposition* to the supremacy of the Evangelical Lutheran state church hierarchy (Rokkan 1967; Madeley 2000; Madeley 1994).[20] Nevertheless, KrF soon changed from a pure protest party to being oriented towards Christian believers in general (Karvonen 1994: 131; Selle 1997: 156). Hence, Norway's pre-war party system was not stabilised before the 1930s. The establishment of the Christian People's Party meant that Norway deviated from the archetypal Nordic five-party model (Arter 1999: 50; Heidar 2004: 51; Demker and Svåsand 2005: 15).

In the 1960s, significant separation also occurred within the left wing of the political spectrum. As in other European countries, various citizen initiatives emerged and flourished in Norwegian politics in the 1960s and 1970s. By calling attention to issues such as environmentalism, feminism, the use of nuclear energy, social equality and alternative lifestyles, these new social movements challenged the 'frozenness' of Western European party systems (Müller-Rommel 1989). Alternative party formations trailed behind, representing the potential emergence of a post-industrial cleavage rooted in the new middle class (Poguntke 1993; Kitschelt 1994). First, new left-wing parties appeared in some countries where they competed with established communist and social democratic parties. Later, green or ecological parties attracted considerable support (Kitschelt 1988: 194). Whilst the latter type has been seen as the archetypal *new politics party* (Poguntke 1993: 6), others have seen both types of party as parts of one single family, for example by applying the label of *left-libertarian parties* (Kitschelt 1988: 194).

In Norway, a relatively significant Socialist Left Party (SV; called the Socialist People's Party (SF) until 1975) developed – but no significant green party. Like other new left parties in Western Europe, SV (SF) opposed the market place and insisted on solidarity and equality (Kitschelt 1988: 197). But the party foundation in 1961 was primarily based on an internal opposition to DnA's official foreign and security policies. The specific occasion preceding the party formation was

20. The laymen movement as a whole did not – like the Swedish one – break with the state church in Norway (Bjørklund 2001: 38). See Madeley (1994: 147) for a critical discussion of the characteristics of this movement in a religious, confessional context.

DnA's decision to modify its party manifesto in a way that was seen to allow the use of nuclear weapons on Norwegian territory under certain circumstances (Vasaasen 1990). In this sense, elements of new politics have been present from the beginning. SF, the predecessor of today's SV, gave priority to issues like anti-militarism, anti-nuclear power, anti-hierarchy, and solidarity with the Third World (Christensen 1996: 527).

Notwithstanding, SV (SF) was originally also supported by a leftist opposition within the trade union movement: one that disapproved of the post-war social democratic pragmatism and promoted '(...) nationalization of industry, state management, and a controlled economy' (Knutsen 1997: 247; see also Ersson 2005: 66).[21] Unlike the case of the other Nordic left socialist parties, a populist development of decentralisation and preservation of local communities became keywords in the late 1960s (Knutsen 1997: 232; Nyhamar 1990: 248). After the divisive debate over Norway's proposed entry to the European Union (then the EC) in the early 1970s, the anti-EC faction of Labour ceded and joined the Socialist People's Party together with the Communists for a few years (under umbrella of the Socialist Electoral Alliance). Despite electoral success, an attempt to unite the parties permanently did not succeed, but the manifesto of what was to become the Socialist Left Party, SV, formulated a more clearly Marxist manifesto in 1975.

However, the radicalisation was not to last. SV's party programme has, since the mid-1970s, decreasingly reflected a revolutionary perspective and increasingly accentuated social reforms and ecology (Aardal 1993, Knutsen 1997: 247–8; Ersson 2005: 66). The breakthrough of green issues in Norwegian election politics occurred in 1973 (Aardal 1993: 98–9). According to Gundersen (1996), environmental issues were thereafter partly de-ideologised, but environmental attitudes experienced a breakthrough in public opinion in the late 1980s (Aardal 1991). SV became the Norwegian left-libertarian alternative to link the values of 'new politics' with a traditional leftist emphasis on equality (Kitschelt 1988; Knutsen 1997). The fact that the DnA leadership had excluded the original dissenters and party founders – arguing that internal factionalism was illegal according to party statutes – gave rise to a less centrally organised, hierarchical party structure (Svåsand 1994: 111).

As a direct result of the EC issue and referendum in 1972, divisions also occurred among the non-socialist parties. Opponents of EC membership among the Liberals dissented and created a new party,[22] and in 1973, a new party also developed on the extreme right wing. The non-socialist government in power since 1965 had not formulated policies which resulted in tax exemptions, but rather an increase in the level of taxes and duties. In protest, the Conservative party

21. In 1969, the youth organisation left SF and founded a Maoist-Leninist communist party (*Arbeidernes Kommunistiske Parti*, AKP (m-l) in 1973, which has later contested elections through the Red Electoral Alliance (*Rød Valgallianse*). In 2007, AKP and RV established the party *Rødt ('Red')*.

22. The new party was named the Liberal People's Party (first the New People's Party), but was reunited with the Liberals in 1988. A few dissenters nevertheless established yet another liberal party, called the Liberal People's Party from 1992.

member Anders Lange initiated a one-man show called the 'Anders Lange's Party for a Strong Reduction in Taxes, Duties and Public Intervention' (ALP), which received 5 percent of the vote and four parliamentary seats in 1973 (Andersen and Bjørklund 1990: 196; Svåsand and Wörlund 2005: 254).[23] Later – after the sudden death of Lange in 1974 – ALP was to be transformed into a permanent party organisation, changing its name to the Progress Party (*Fremskrittspartiet*, FrP) (Harmel and Svåsand 1993; Heidar and Saglie 2002). It has been consistently represented in the Storting since the 1981 elections.

Hence, FrP has a populist legacy, in terms of loose organisation, charismatic leader and anti-elite profile (Taggart 1995; Andersen and Bjørklund 2000: 200–1). It emerged as a neo-liberal party, and is seen an example of the New European Right. Those who argue that the New Right indicates the rise of a new value-based cleavage – cutting across the traditional left-right axis – often call these parties *the radical right* (Inglehart 1971, 1977; Kitschelt 1995). Others highlight the populist element – scepticism towards political elites and a belief in popular government – and refer to *the populist right* (Betz 1998). According to Mudde (2007), one should distinguish between *populist radical right parties* and others, like *non-radical right populists* and *non-populist right*. Radical right populist parties combine non-egalitarian values with nativism and authoritarianism (*ibid*: 26),[24] whereas nonradical right populists are primarily neoliberal (*ibid*: 47). Core FrP issues have traditionally been economic liberalisation and privatisation of public services, and later a more restrictive immigration policy. But FrP is not rooted in the historical European right-wing extremism. Fascist and Nazi parties have never been successful in Scandinavia (Andersen and Bjørklund 2000: 193; Widfeldt 2000: 486). The Norwegian Progress Party is, like its Danish equivalent, traditionally characterised as a borderline case of the extreme or radical right (Ignazi 1992: 13–15; Kitschelt 1995: 121; Ignazi 2003: 157), and Mudde (2007:19) characterises FrP as a non-radical right populist party (see Chapter 13 for further discussion of this issue).

NORWEGIAN ASSOCIATIONAL LIFE: MAJOR DEVELOPMENTS

Several kinds of interest groups – both sectional and promotional organisations – predate political parties in Norway. As explained above, some have even initiated new party formations.

At the beginning of the nineteenth century, locally organised humanitarian and cultural bodies were established (Kvavik 1976: 35–6). The first wave also saw the establishment of broad social movements in the middle of the nineteenth century

23. A common explanation for the immediate success is that the preceding referendum about membership in the European Community had divided the electorate, weakened old voter loyalties and thereby created more volatile voters (Svåsand and Wörlund 2005: 254).

24. Radicalism is defined as opposition to some key features of liberal democracy, and 'most notably political pluralism and the constitutional protection of minorities' (Mudde 2007: 25), whereas nativism is an ideology that 'holds that states should be inhabited exclusively by members of the native group and that nonnative elements are fundamentally threatening to the homogenous nation-state' (*ibid*: 19).

(Wollebæk and Selle 2002: 57). The labour movement, the temperance movement, the Lutheran laymen's movement, the language organisations, and the sports associations all developed during the 1840s and 1850s.

The Norwegian Missionary Society (*Det Norsk Misjonsselskap*) was founded in 1842, the Norwegian organisation of the Red Cross (*Røde Kors*) in 1864. Labour associations emerged around 1850, and national unions developed during the 1890s. At the turn of the century (1899), the Norwegian Confederation of Trade Unions was born (*Landsorganisasjonen i Norge, LO).* To begin with, the recruitment to LO was urban and crafts-based. Norway industrialised rapidly, but primarily after the dissolution of the Union with Sweden in 1905 (Elvander 2002: 120). In 1905, the iron and metal workers and the graphical unions joined ranks (Heidar 1981: 1–2). In 1923, the LO Convention passed a decision to shift from organisation along craft lines to one with an industrial focus.

Other labour market organisations emerged in the mid-nineteenth century (Kvavik 1976: 35–6). By the turn of the century, several national federations had been established. The Norwegian Confederation of the Craft Industry (*Norges Håndverkerforbund*) was launched in 1886, the Employers' Association of Norway (*Norges Arbeidsgiverforening*) in 1900. In 1896 the Norwegian Farmers' Union (*Norsk Landmandsforbund*, later *Norges Bondelag*) was founded. The Norwegian Shipowners' Association (*Norsk Rederiforbund*) was established in 1909.

In their early days, the organised interest groups were not much involved in electoral politics, but towards the end of the century their political pressure increased (Torgersen 1984: 44–5). The period between 1884 and 1900 is commonly described as the breakthrough of organised interest groups in Norway: 'on the basis of national organisations, and by having the threat of separate party formation in reserve, interest groups exerted a constant pressure on existing parties (...): from candidate selection to the final voting in the Storting' (Danielsen 1964: 349–50, my translation). However, as the party organisations were consolidated, political parties replaced special interest groups at the core of politics (Torgersen 1984: 46–8).

Early in the twentieth century, the Norwegian organisation interest-group community became more fragmented and specialised. The real growth of national organisations is a twentieth-century phenomenon (Kvavik 1976: 38). A large portion of white-collar employees were organised in independent, non-partisan organisations. Youth and women established separate associations (Wollebæk and Selle 2002: 59). Social and humanitarian organisations flourished. The precursor of Norway's environmental movement – the Norwegian Society for the Conservation of Nature/Friends of the Earth Norway (*FoEN – Norges Naturvernforbund*) – was founded in 1914. The years from 1905 to 1920 were a golden age for special interest groups in Norwegian politics (Fuglum 1989: 86). The change of electoral formula from indirect multi-member district plurality system to a majority-plurality two-round system in single-member districts in 1906 increased the interest groups' need and opportunity to influence elections. In the new system, interest group representation was no longer secured by ticket-balancing, but interest groups could field their own candidates – or threaten to do so – unless the other candidates gave in to their policy demands (Mjeldheim 1978: 176–8). Furthermore, the loose organisational character of most existing parties in the first decade of the twentieth century meant that there were opportunities for extensive and influential 'lobbyism' (Espeli 1999: 79–80).

After the Second World War, the number of cultural and leisure-oriented organisations – associations that do not necessarily qualify as interest groups – increased significantly in the wake of welfare developments (Wollebæk and Selle 2002: 79–80). More importantly, as in the rest of Western Europe, various 'new' social movements developed during the 1960s and 1970s: environmental, feminist and peace groups which challenged the mainstream political agenda and working methods of conventional and established political institutions and organisations (Dalton *et al.* 1990: 4). One example of these new social movement organisations is Norway's Nature and Youth (*Natur og Ungdom*, a member of Friends of the Earth) founded in 1967.

In the 1970s, also professional organisations and staff unions were united in national federations like the Confederation of Vocational Unions (*Yrkesorganisasjonenes Sentralforbund*) and the Confederation of Academic and Professional Unions in Norway (*Akademikernes Fellesorganisasjon*). Throughout the 1980s and 1990s, the social movements from the later nineteenth and early twentieth century were gradually replaced by the organised interest groups related to leisure activities and sports, but also new kinds of groups oriented towards welfare and economy, nationality and health (Wollebæk and Selle 2002: 79–80; Selle and Tranvik 2004: 88–90). The environmental movement found expression in more pragmatic, less anti-establishment organisations (Gundersen 1996; Strømsnes and Selle 1996). On the other hand, the anti-globalisation movement – an example of which is the Norwegian branch of Attac – has, at times, been an influential force since the 1990s.

Hence, today the Norwegian interest group community consists of a wide range of different kinds of groups, including both 'sectional' and 'promotional' groups. The voluntary sector is small in terms of paid jobs, but 'Norway ranks among the countries with the highest proportion of members in the population' (Selle and Tranvik 2004: 83; see also Tranvik and Selle 2005: 856). Hallenstvedt and Trollvik (1993: ix) report that there were more than 2,300 nationwide, voluntary – non-governmental and non-commercial – organisations in Norway at the end of the twentieth century.

CONCLUSION

Norwegian parties have for long been faced with a sizeable community of social organisations. Indeed, interest groups predate political parties in Norway, and some parties emerged from social organisations.

By the end of the 1920s, the Norwegian party system had become a stable structure reflecting several long-lasting cleavages. The left-right economic cleavage continued to dominate, and the party system was characterised by stability: a polarised system with the two major parties, Labour and the Conservatives, obtaining electoral support of 40 per cent and 30 per cent of the vote respectively

(Valen and Katz 1964, Valen 1992; Heidar 2005). According to Rokkan's seminal triangular model of political conflicts in Norway, parties and interest organisations were primarily organised around three poles along the economic-functional axis: labour, capital and agrarian interests (Rokkan 1966: 93).

As we shall see in Chapter 6, such patterns of overlapping interests were also reflected in – more or less – close relationships between particular parties and interest groups in general, while the parties which emerged after the Second World War behaved somewhat differently towards the interest-group community. However, before presenting the historical background of Norwegian parties in this sense, we need to clarify how party-group links can be systematically compared and studied. What insights has been provided by existing research as regards party-interest group relationships in general? This is the question to be discussed in the next chapter.

part two
framework of analysis

chapter three | parties and interest groups: overlooked relations of democracy?

This chapter presents and discusses the major insights that existing studies have provided into the relationship between parties and interest groups. First, major contributions from the scholarly literature taking party organisations as the starting point are reviewed. Second, the chapter briefly examines the research emphasising interest groups. Here the argument is that more knowledge is needed on the nature of parties' contemporary relationship with other organisations. Formerly integrated relationships have in some cases declined significantly, but how distant the relations have become, and to what extent variation exists, is not a settled question. To what extent and how parties are linked with those organisations which are not their traditional associates is also a fairly moot point. Next, the review shows that more attention should be paid to the factors that shape a party's relationships with interest groups.

THE RELATIONSHIP OF POLITICAL PARTIES WITH INTEREST GROUPS

In recent decades, considerable effort has been devoted to investigating long-term party change, including some studies on the development of the relationship between parties and interest groups. However, before taking a closer look at this research, let us see what the scholarly literature on party development in the early years of mass politics has to offer. As will become clear, research on party relationships with interest groups has not been a growth area in political science, but the topic has long-established roots in party research in the West (Key 1942/1964).

In Retrospect: Integrated, Class-based or Confession-based Relationships

After the introduction of mass suffrage and consolidation of national party systems, elections grew to be the domain of organised political parties (see Duverger 1954/1972; Epstein 1967). However, this is not to say that interest groups vanished from electoral politics. In the United States, most interest groups did not 'encroach on the parties' dominance of the electoral process' but 'co-operated with parties to achieve their policy goals' in the early stages of democracy (Thomas 2001d: 86; see also Hrebenar *et al.* 1999). In Western Europe, several parties emerged from social movements in opposition to the political establishment, and some political parties were even formally founded – and later largely controlled – by interest groups. A major example is the trade unions' establishment of the British Labour Party (Duverger 1954/1972; Panebianco 1988).

Party-Interest Group Relationships as Manifestations of Political Cleavages

As far as the *nature* of party links with interest groups is concerned, a reasonable starting point is the sociological literature which dominated political science in the 1950s and 1960s. Here both political parties and interest groups are seen as manifestations of underlying social cleavages. Pairs of parties and interest groups articulate similar interests through the corporate and electoral channels respectively. In Rokkan's classical triangular model of political conflicts in Norway (Scandinavia), parties and interest groups are primarily organised around three poles along the 'economic-functional' axis: labour (trade unions and a social democratic party), capital (business organisations and a conservative party) and agrarian interests (farmers' unions and an agrarian party) (Rokkan 1966: 92). Similar patterns were found also elsewhere. Many West European parties originated from social movements in the nineteenth century, and maintained close relationships with their organisational origin (Lipset and Rokkan 1967).

However, in his triangular model, Rokkan does not specify *how* the relationship between parties and interest group(s) materialised. It could be argued, as Sundberg (2003: 90–1) does, that the model implicitly includes some sort of organised co-operation between the party and the associated interest group. Success in elections and public decision-making requires co-ordinated action. Moreover, Lipset and Rokkan (1967: 15) themselves emphasised that some parties – especially the labour and the church movements – from early on developed a network of social organisations themselves: for example youth organisations, sports clubs and leisure associations (see also von Beyme 1985: 191–2; Poguntke 1998: 159; Luther 1999: 4, 8). Yet, there has been more emphasis on the differing foci of parties and interest groups than on the elaboration of the organisational structure of their interlinkages (Rokkan 1966: 105). Party elites are themselves, it was argued, capable of producing voter alignments by establishing parties as independent poles of attraction over time (Lipset and Rokkan 1967: 3), but party organisations were – as in classic political sociology – analysed largely as 'transmission belts' to the state for well-defined interests (Warner 2000: 18). A parallel view has appeared in traditional functional analyses. Here parties are interpreted as performers of certain systemic functions like interest aggregation, responding to the demands of 'their' interest groups (La Palombara and Weiner 1966; King 1969). Once formed, a close relationship is more or less 'on autopilot' (Warner 2000: 18). The question of why parties may later choose to loosen such a relationship is thus also neglected.[25]

Links with Interest Groups as a Distinguishing Feature of Party Organisations

More informative studies, in both regards, are provided by those who have analysed the early development of parties *as organisations*. According to scholars like Duverger (1954/1972) and Epstein (1967), sociological factors play

25. An exception is, in one sense, the literature on the labour movement which emphasises the dilemma of unions when the social democratic party is in power, and to a certain extent the literature on the Church and the rise of Christian Democratic parties (see Warner 2000: 18).

an important part, but so does the parties' pursuit of votes in competitive elections. Consequently, the organisational aspect is made more explicit. In Duverger's seminal work on European political party organisations, links with interest groups are a focal point. A key finding is that the social base and organisational structure primarily distinguished the *mass party* of the twentieth century from the originally predominant *cadre party* – the caucus of notables of the late nineteenth century (Duverger 1954/1972). Another distinctive feature of the mass parties was their relationship with organisations in civil society.

The socialist mass party emerged outside the national assemblies on the basis of trade union movements, co-operatives and friendly societies (Duverger 1954/1972: 24–7, 17, 75). The party organisation represented the tool of a rising working class who lacked political rights, financial resources and actual influence. Its fundamental unit was the branch with its members (*ibid*: 25, 63), but the firm social roots were also manifest in close relationships with trade unions. The unions financed the socialist parties – or more specifically Labour parties – which were seen as the political wing of the trade unions in their respective countries.[26] According to Duverger, the strongest links were manifested by parties with an indirect structure – parties whose members were collectively, not individually, affiliated through the trade unions.[27]

The early British Labour Party was the prime example of unions linked through collective membership (Duverger 1954/1972: 5–7; Panebianco 1988: 89). National trade unions affiliated their memberships, or significant proportions of them, to the party organisation (Minkin 1991). A large union might pay party dues for a million members, thereby gaining considerable power within the party (Epstein 1967: 147). Affiliated members could not participate in constituency party meetings, but affiliated unions had the right to attend the annual congress, with votes proportional to their financial contributions (Koelbe 1987: 255). Consequently, the highest decision-making organ was dominated by the unions' allotting of votes as a single unit ('bloc vote'). The trade union representatives were in the majority on the National Executive Committee (see Padgett and Paterson 1991: 182; Jordan and Maloney 2001: 30; Quinn 2002), and played a decisive role in candidate selection (Denver 1988: 52–3). A similar relationship could also be found in Australia and New Zealand (Epstein 1967: 148; Truman 1980). In fact, according to Rawson (1969: 314), the Australian Labour Party came closest to the ideal type, if the archetype is defined in terms of the effects of collective union membership on the party organisation as whole.

The labour parties of Sweden and Norway were established before the national

26. According to Rawson (1969: 313), the formal affiliation of trade unions to the party organisation distinguished labour parties from socialist, social democratic and communist parties.

27. The idea of an indirect party presupposes that there is no party community distinct from the social group. Hence, there is a conflict between this 'indirect' party structure and the mass party's characteristic membership organisation (cf. Webb 1992: 11–12). Even though the unions also functioned as party branches, this does not necessarily imply that all union members felt like being party members as well. According to Panebianco's (1988: 56) interpretation, archetypal mass parties were, by definition, autonomous organisations *vis-à-vis* unions.

confederations of unions, but also developed collective membership – at the local (branch) level. In practice, the weight of the unions in Scandinavia, financially and in terms of membership, apparently approximated that of British unions. National unions made large grants to the national party and, as in Britain, furnished much of the campaign apparatus at election time (Epstein 1967: 149–50).[28] Most importantly, the guaranteed representation of the Confederation of Trade Unions (LO) in the national party executive provided formally interconnected organisational structures at the national and federal levels (Allern *et al.* 2007). Ironically, according to Padgett and Paterson (1991: 182), in Britain there was no formal relationship between the Labour Party's extra-parliamantary organisation and the Trade Unions Congress (TUC), since the trade union movement was highly fragmented. In contrast, the Scandinavian trade union movements were characterised by comparatively strong internal cohesion (Sundberg 2003: 93; Padgett and Paterson 1991: 179).

Duverger further identifies two other kinds of indirect parties in the early twentieth century: the Catholic parties and agrarian parties (Duverger 1954/1972: 5–7; see also von Beyme 1985: 191). Whereas the labour parties were based upon a single social class, Catholic parties could bring together different social classes, each of which retained its own organisations. Accordingly, Catholic parties were not only dependent on the Church and religious organisations, but appeared as federations of Catholic workers' unions and co-operatives, peasants' associations, associations of industrialists and others (Duverger 1954/1972: 6; Rawson 1969: 313; von Beyme 1985: 192). In the deeply divided societies often termed 'consociational democracies', organised pillars developed between major parties and organisations that shared the same identity of their respective subcultures (Kitschelt 1989: 28), so these parties have, in order to ensure maximum loyalty to each segment, also been characterised by a particularly high number of party-created ancillary or auxiliary organisations (Lipset and Rokkan 1967: 15–16; Luther 1999: 4, 8; Poguntke 2006: 396). By contrast, the organisational network of the agrarian parties was comparatively moderate. These parties were primarily made up of farmers' unions and agricultural co-operatives (Duverger 1954/1972: 6).

The bourgeois parties primarily represented the upper classes, and normally could start out with sufficient financial resources and easy access to public office. But in systems with universal suffrage, the cadre parties had to follow the example of the mass parties if they were to retain their influence over time, according to Duverger (1954/1972: xxvii). In the early 1950s, when he published the first edition of his book, non-left parties were trying to incorporate supporters in formal organisations (Scarrow 2002a: 94). Duverger concluded that liberal and conservative parties would continue to adapt to the mass party model in order to maintain electoral support. Duverger (1954/1972) concluded that liberal and conservative parties would continue to adapt to the mass party model in order to maintain elec-

28. In fact, Valen and Katz (1964: 316) suggest that precisely the *local* character of the collective membership *strengthened* the power of trade unions: Union activists attended the party congress as delegates from party branches and were thereby able to show more political flexibility; avoiding adaptation to unrealistic views for symbolic reasons.

toral support, and it turned out that their organisational adaptation actually encompassed establishment of links with particular interest groups.

According to von Beyme (1985: 191), liberal and conservative parties used contact with peasants' associations, lodges, middle-class citizens' associations and other similar organisations 'to compensate for lack of internal organization'. However, they preferred a looser form of affiliation. Some liberal parties in Europe have had close ties to certain trade unions, and later, white-collar groups, but these links were never well-developed (Kirchner 1988b: 480). Eventually, bourgeois parties formed more stable alliances with employers' and business organisations, and professional associations as well (Schmitter 2001: 82). The Christian Democratic parties established after the Second World War in Europe avoided any indirect, class-based structure (von Beyme 1985: 194), but the Catholic Church formed alliances with such parties in the post-war era (Warner 2000).

Indeed, formal affiliation of other organisations was not a widespread phenomenon in Europe in the first half of the twentieth century, not even among socialist parties (Duverger 1954/1972: 13–14). As indicated above, collective membership developed primarily when the party was established before the unions. Moreover, the direct structure dominated in countries with a more fragmented and divided trade union movement. In predominantly Catholic nations such as France and Italy, trade unions have always been less strongly linked with political parties than in Great Britain or Scandinavia, and the principal trade unions were originally most closely aligned to communist parties (cf. Padgett and Paterson 1991: 184).[29]

Eventually, indirect parties also opened up for individual memberships (Duverger 1954/1972: 9–17). Exactly how parties may be linked to the aligned interest groups when there is no collective membership has not been elaborated (Duverger 1954/1972; Rawson 1969: 316; von Beyme 1985), even if it should be noted that Duverger (1968: 455–8) distinguishes between no links, formal or informal subordination of interest group to party, formal or informal subordination of party to interest group, or egalitarian (permanent or ad hoc) co-operation between interest group and party elsewhere. The general literature on socialist parties has more specifically shown that individual parties and interest groups could be closely connected through for example liaison committees, leadership and membership overlap and interchange, and a wide arena of common collective activities (see Harrison 1960; Kassalow 1963; Elvander 1980; Koelbe 1987: 256; Padgett and Paterson 1991: 177–85; van Biezen 2003a: 23). Most importantly, however, Duverger (1954/1972) identifies two key aspects of party relationships with organised groups in civil society, apart from power relationships: how *close relations* they have, and *with what interest groups.*

29. Epstein (1967: 152) adds a third category to the list: the American example, in which there is no connection to a socialist working-class party and only non-structural connections to middle-class parties – usually the Democratic Party. While Padgett and Paterson (1991: 179-85) distinguish between the British model, the Swedish way, the West German and Austrian model and finally, the French and Italian. Kitschelt (1994: 225) groups the British and Austrian Left together, argues that Sweden and Germany represents an intermediate pattern, whilst the leadership of socialist parties in France, Italy, and Spain has been more autonomous of trade unions.

As regards what *shapes* party relationships, Duverger's approach is fairly inductive, but he points to correlations and strong regularities. He suggests that electoral competition would mean convergence of party organisation and behaviour after the introduction of universal suffrage. Whether the core organisation – or core organisations – are formally affiliated or not appears, as indicated above, to be correlated to the national cleavage and organisation structure, the constituency's need for resources, and, in the case of collective membership, whether the party or the interest group was established first. Rawson (1969: 315) also argues that a key variable is whether the party's origin is external. If an organisation has been involved in the formal founding of the party, it is more likely to accept or demand formal affiliation. The fact that Norwegian and Swedish unions were affiliated only at the local level reflects that the Labour Party was established before the Confederation of Trade Unions. The Danish case, where the trade union movement developed earlier and collective membership has never existed (Bille and Christiansen 2000), is an exception that he relates to influence from Germany and the tradition of guilds, among other factors (Rawson 1969: 326).[30] Later von Beyme (1985), who supports Duverger's basic distinction between collective affiliation and other kinds of links, has emphasised the significance of party ideology. For example, he argues that the syndicalist and anarchist elements in Latin socialist parties called for a territorial base, whilst the British model was in line with the country's tradition of guild socialism. Nevertheless, neither Duverger (1954/1972) nor Rawson (1969) nor von Beyme (1985) explore systematically under what more specific conditions a party is likely to have distant or close relationships with interest groups, and when a party is likely to favour exclusive to inclusive links.

Towards the Twenty-first Century: Dissociation from Core Organisations?

Since the mid-1970s, there has been a general shift towards the analysis of (continuing) change in many different facets of parties as organisations (Mair 1997; Luther 1999: 5). Followers of Duverger's rather inductive approach to parties have devoted considerable effort to disproving the thesis of the 'modernity' of the mass party. It is argued that social, technological, cultural and political developments have made this party model obsolete for parties organising for fierce electoral competition (Katz and Mair 1995; Harmel 2002: 125).[31] The debate encompasses numerous organisational and behavioural aspects, often depicted as a historical sequence of various party organisational archetypes. Here we concentrate on the most discussed ones – the *cadre party* or the *mass party,* which can be seen as a

30. As will become clear in Chapter 6, however, the choice of local collective membership in Norway is quite certainly also correlated to the fact that some unions were still dominated by liberals at the time of the establishment of a confederation.

31. The classic sociological approach is today most important in studies of electoral change and voting behaviour. Functionalism is, on the other hand, generally criticised for emphasising stability and the functionality of institutions over change and conflict. More radical criticisms have pointed to its tautological character: the fulfilment of the different functions is seen as a necessary condition for the maintenance of a given political system. Functionalist perspectives lack testable hypotheses (Montero and Gunther 2002: 10).

contrast to the *catch-all people's party* and *the cartel party* (Kirchheimer 1966; Epstein 1967; Panebianco 1988; Katz and Mair 1995). To some extent, the debate includes both the issue of what generally characterises the relations of today's parties with interest groups – compared to old patterns – and what are the shaping factors of party relationships with interest groups. [32]

The Nature of Party Relationship with Interest Groups: The Catch-all Alternative
As early as 1954, Kirchheimer introduced the concept of the *catch-all party* in an analysis of the decline in policy differences between major West German parties. According to a recent study of Kirchheimer's complete work, the background of the catch-all thesis was what Kirchheimer saw as the vanishing of principled opposition within parliament and society, and the reduction of politics to '(…) mere management of the state' (Krouwel 2003: 23). The result was collusion between political parties and the state. Kirchheimer's third concern was with the professionalisation of party organisations and the personalisation of electoral politics. Altogether he worriedly envisaged political apathy and erosion of the classic separation of powers (*ibid:* 24).

No longer did parties accentuate the expression of interests through a sharp interest profile: instead they emphasised a 'brokerage role' by seeking support among numerous and different segments. Even though we should not read the 'catch-all' notion literally, such parties differ from each other '(…) only enough to make themselves recognisable' (Wolinetz 1991: 116). The emphasis on political leaders with media appeal required parties dominated by organisational elites, and a more catch-all approach to electoral campaigning indicated a weakening of organisational ties to specific social classes. By accentuating shared interests and values between different social segments (Kirchheimer 1966: 186), the parties' original roots in structural and cultural cleavages would decline.

With collective identities about to erode, voters had become easy to lose; and this made communication with the surroundings outside the party's subculture much more important. As a consequence, collateral and other closely tied organisations turned into interest groups with weaker party links. Even if old allies were still organisationally integrated, their roles had changed: 'Instead of a joint strategy towards a common goal there appears an appreciation of limited if still mutually helpful services to be rendered' (Kirchheimer 1966: 192–3). In a more pluralist society, both parties and interest groups prefer independence and less binding links, Kirchheimer argued:

32. In accordance with the predominant usage in the literature, 'model' and 'type' will be used interchangeably, albeit as Sartori (1993) and van Biezen (2003b) reminds us, a true model embodies an explanatory claim and thus requires the identification of underlying mechanics. The party models, in contrast, are categories of a typology. It could be objected that only the cartel party was first developed as an ideal type (cf. Wolinetz 2002: 146), and that the typologies developed later vary as to the basic criterion of classification (Gunther and Diamond 2001). Nonetheless, in my view, the problem of comparison is limited when it comes to links with interest groups. As in the case of the mass party, the relationship with organised interest groups is highly relevant for the catch-all and cartel parties alike.

> The party bent on attracting a maximum of voters must modulate its interest-group relation in such way so as not to discourage potential voters who identify themselves with other interests. The interest group, in its turn, must never put all its egg in one basket. That might offend the sensibilities of some members with different political connections. More important, the interest group would not want to stifle feelings of hope in another catch-all party that some move in its direction might bring electoral rewards (1966: 193).

Major political parties would rather seek access to numerous and different interest groups to secure electoral support via interest-group intercession (Kirchheimer 1966: 190–1). As in government, a party does best, at least in the long run, when it can discover solutions that will work for all interest claimants concerned (*ibid*: 194). Likewise, Rawson (1969: 331–3) argued in the 1960 that the decline of working-class consciousness had made the formal affiliation of trade unions perhaps a hindrance rather than a benefit to the labour parties, whilst the increasing competition from non-partisan white-collar unions for party attention would make the formal links less valuable for the trade unions themselves. The main exceptions from the "catch-all thesis" were small regional parties (like the South Tyrolean People's Party), parties with very narrow ideological claims (like the Dutch Calvinists), parties based upon a limited programme of action (like the Danish single-tax Justice Party) or based on the demands of one particular professional category (like agrarian parties) (Kirchheimer 1966: 187–8). Neither did Kirchheimer believe that social democratic parties in small democracies, like the Norwegian and Swedish Social Democrats, would become catch-all parties due to their traditional majority status. But over time both the Scandinavian agrarian parties and social democratic parties have considerably broadened their political profile (Sundberg 2001; Christensen 1992).

Kirchheimer (1966) thus described the change in party relationships with interest groups as a general trend in Western democracies, but he did not really present a systematic collection of data along the relevant variables. Later attempts to test his hypothesis empirically have paid considerably more attention to the internal organisation of parties than to their external relations (see Katz and Mair 1994). But some comparative case studies and single-case studies exist. They indicate that parties historically closely linked with certain core organisations have become more independent, but the trend may not be uniform. The decline of the integrated relationship between labour parties and trade unions is particularly well-documented across countries (cf. Padgett and Paterson 1991: 216; Thomas 2001e).

Some parties – like the Belgian and Dutch social democratic parties – abolished collective membership just after the Second World War (Epstein 1967: 148). Recently, the best-known example of decline – yet not termination – is perhaps seen in the reforms of the British Labour Party. Webb (1992: 53) concluded that there had been no substantial weakening in the organisational linkage between Labour and its affiliated unions since the early 1960s. But over time the number of affiliated unions has decreased (Webb 1994: 114–15), and throughout the 1990s the trade unions' formal voting power in the party's decision-making bodies was reduced. For example, bloc voting in leadership elections was abolished and the party ended union participation in parliamentary candidate selection (Quinn 2002: 223). The concurrent elimination of Clause Four, which committed the party to the socialist objective, from the party's constitution strengthened the symbolic importance of these changes (Jordan and Maloney 2001: 31; Katz 2001: 73).[33] Other recent examples of significantly weakened party-trade union links are found in Scandinavia (Sundberg 2003), and in Australia and New Zealand (Katz 2001: 74).

However, indications of continuity, and variation, also exist. Padgett and Paterson (1991: 220) emphasised in the early 1990s that the pace of change in the labour parties' relationship with trade unions seemed to differ from country to country. In the case of Israel political parties and interest groups, Yishai (1991: 134) shows that some interest groups have strengthened their links with political parties over time. A comparative study of the Scandinavian labour and farmers' parties from the late 1990s concludes that both party types had less close relations with the respective unions than before, but that agrarian party links with farmers' unions had weakened the most (Sundberg 2001, 2003). Aylott (2003) reported that the change in party-union relationship in the case of Swedish Social Democrats has been patchy at the local level. In fact, it seems that the Danish Social Democratic Party and trade unions have grown further apart than their Swedish and Norwegian counterparts (Allern *et al.* 2007).

A broader comparative survey of thirteen European and Latin American countries also indicates that the degree of change varies (Thomas 2001a). Within the context of a common analytical framework, various country case studies are offered. The comparison is based on a typology – explored further in the next chapter – which refers primarily to degrees of ideological affinity, of organisational links or lack thereof, and variation in strategies between parties and interest groups. For example, it is argued that British group relationships have developed in a more autonomous direction, whilst parties dominate interest groups in the case of Italy. Interestingly, Thomas (2001e: 270) summarises that there is a clear tendency to the decline of the historical links between social democracy and trade unions in democracies that have had strong left-wing governing parties (as in Britain, Sweden, Israel, and even in a relatively recent democracy like Spain), but that there is no general trend towards weaker links with traditionally closely linked affinities. He concludes that there exists no single pattern of party-interest group relationships within or across countries today, although the links between political parties and interest groups in general seem rather weak (Thomas 2001e: 272; see also Wilson 1990: 159; Yishai 1991: 128, and Selle 1997: 156–60). However, the structure of the country-based analyses varies to some extent and the study does not attempt to examine the various aspects of party-interest group relationships in any detail. It is also relevant to ask whether the documented degree of heterogeneity is related to the fact that the concept of relationship applied is very broad (see Chapter 4).

In contrast, Poguntke (1998, 2002) concentrates on 'organizational linkage' – organised ways of linking citizens' preferences to elite decisions – in his com-

33. For in-depth studies of the relationship between the British Labour Party and the trade union movement until the 1990s, see Minkin (1991); Webb (1992) and Quinn (2003).

parative study of parties in eleven European countries.[34] He identifies three kinds of organisational environments through which a party can be linked with voters: party membership organisation, collateral organisations and new social movements (Poguntke 2002: 47; see also Poguntke 2006). Collateral organisations are defined as organisations with an exclusive relationship with a specific party based on a broad commonality of interests, which either exist independent of and mostly prior to a political party (e.g. religious interests, economic interests and ecological interests), or are created by the party itself. The strength of 'ties' with collateral organisations is measured on the basis of the number of party decision-making bodies to which the given organisation enjoys access, and in terms of different methods of selecting representatives and variation in voting rights, i.e. the number and intensity of ties (Poguntke 2002: 53).

The overall conclusion, regarding the period from 1960 to 1989, is that such links help parties to stabilise their electorates and points to tremendous stability in ties to collateral organisations over time. Such connections have far from eroded even if the membership figures in collateral organisations have declined (Poguntke 2006: 403). First, the number of such organisations per party has generally remained fairly stable (Poguntke 2000: 155). Second, their formal rights (the total linkage value) *vis-à-vis* party decision-making bodies have not changed much (Poguntke 2002: 55). Equally interesting, an underlying trend is that the difference between the relations of original cadre parties and of mass parties has decreased, in line with Duverger's evolutionary hypothesis. By the end of the period examined, the traditional elite parties had even stronger ties to collateral organisations than did the mass integration parties, although the (former) cadre parties averaged fewer organisations per party (Poguntke 2002: 55; Poguntke 2000: 157). There are national differences in the number of organisations and total linkage value, but such patterns persist over time. For example, countries with a traditionally high level of collateral organisations, like Austria, still have a relatively large number of organisations today (Poguntke 2000: 157). Regarding the strength of such ties, it is hard to say whether the differences between countries primarily follow ideological or organisational lines, or if specific national patterns actually exist (Poguntke 2000: 175).

But does the revealed overall stability mean that Kirchheimer's hypothesis is challenged? In his most detailed analysis, Poguntke addresses the important difference between party-created and external interest groups. As hypothesised (Poguntke 1998: 177; Poguntke 2000: 169), he finds that '… on average, external collateral organizations have become less relevant over time whereas internal collateral organizations have increased at roughly same rate' (1998: 176–8). In particular, he argues that the access of external organisations to the national executive committee has weakened, and party-created organisations have been developed to compensate for this. Thus, Poguntke's study also supports Kirchheimer's hypothesis of weakened party links with the traditionally associated *interest groups*,

34. The following countries were included: Austria, Belgium, Denmark, Finland, Germany, Ireland, Italy, the Netherlands, Norway, Sweden, and the UK. The complete analysis is only published in German (Poguntke 2000).

although there seem to be few cases where close relationships with parties and unions have actually been severed (Poguntke 2002: 59).

As for the new parties, their ties to other organisations are, as he expected, generally weak compared with the traditional relationships. New social movements are not tied to parties through guaranteed access to decision-making bodies. Indeed, the entire new social movement sector has preferred formal independence from political parties, concludes Poguntke (2002: 54–6). In this sense, he echoes Kitschelt (1989: 231) and others who see the new 'green' or pro-environmental parties as linked to social movements primarily at the individual level. Poguntke further argues that green parties and movements have grown apart as the new parties have '(...) been drawn in to the normal party political game of negotiation and compromise' (2006: 402).

However, Poguntke's comparative study does not map the *strength* of new parties' informal ties to other organisations. Systematic comparative data on such party ties to external groups are almost non-existent (Poguntke 2006). So the degree to which established parties have opted to establish weaker (informal) connections with a broad range of interest groups remain largely unexplored as well. As indicated above, lack of formal affiliation does not necessarily mean complete separation from other organisations. Party organisations have, for example, been linked into the interest-group community through joint committees, and through their leaders' and members' memberships in other social organisations (see Valen and Katz 1964: 312 and Kvavik 1976: 95). In recent years, Heidar and Saglie (2002) and Pedersen (2003) have demonstrated that Scandinavian parties still enjoy such links at membership and activist level. Based on interviews with the secretaries-general of Norway's seven major parties in the 1990s, Selle (1997) showed that a couple of parties had started to invite some external groups to become involved in the making of party platforms (see also Allern 2001; Heidar and Saglie 2002). Parties' links into civil society have not necessarily eroded: they may primarily have become shallower (cf. Webb 1994: 128–9).

In any case, more research, both at the organisational and individual level of political parties, is needed to describe more precisely the degree of distance (or closeness), within and across countries. The extent to which political parties approach the pattern of relationship with interest group depicted by the *catch-all party* type is still a largely unsettled question. In recent years, it has in fact been suggested there is no longer reason to believe that parties emphasise links with a wide range of interest groups as a replacement for old alliances. Writing some thirty years after Kirchheimer, Katz and Mair (1995, 2002) have observed that parties have become more elite-driven and dominated by their parliamentary groups, and suggested the transformation of catch-all parties to yet another organisational form: *the cartel party*.

The Nature of Party Relationship with Interest Groups: The Symptoms of Cartelisation

Cartel parties are characterised by their interpenetration of party and state, and the relative weakness of links to civil society. The change in party organisation reflects a new systemic element: the rise of party competition that imitates the functioning of the oligopolistic market. State subventions now often constitute a major financial and material resource for political parties. Frequently tied to prior party performance, these subsidies help to ensure the maintenance of existing parties and pose barriers to the emergence of new groups (Katz and Mair 1995: 15). In short, the state 'is invaded by the parties, and the rules of which are determined by the parties, becomes a fount of resources through which these parties not only help to ensure their own survival, but through which they can also enhance their capacity to resist challenges from newly mobilized alternatives' (*ibid:* 16). Additionally, all major parties – except for extreme fringe parties – have in practice access to office. Because of the absence of great policy battles in recent decades, winning and losing make less difference to the political objectives of a party (*ibid:* 22). Hence, the conditions have become ideal for the formation of a cartel. The result is, in effect, interparty collusion (Pelizzo 2003: 40; Katz and Mair 2009: 757) – as presumably hypothesised by Kirchheimer already in the 1960s. A major indicator is convergence along the old left-right axis (Katz and Mair 1996: 530, but see also Blyth and Katz 2005; Katz and Mair 2009: 755, 761).

Within a cartelised party system, parties do not primarily make demands on the behalf of social groups. They are professionalised organisations weakly rooted in civil society (Katz and Mair 1995: 23; Katz and Mair 2009: 761). As Mair (1997:102–3) points out, even though parties are still key actors which present and aggregate 'demands from civil society to the state bureaucracy, they increasingly function as agents of that bureaucracy'. Hence, the cartel thesis implicitly suggests that today's political parties generally have tenuous relationships with interest groups. The interest groups themselves are the primary source of possible contact: 'Instead of parties making demands on the state on behalf of particular groups in civil society, these groups find that they themselves need to make demands on the party/state' (Katz and Mair 1995: 23). Although there may, for example, remain some formal links between trade unions and social democratic parties, not only do the unions deal directly with the bourgeois parties when these are in power, but they also deal with the social democratic parties when in power in much the same way. Conversely, 'social democratic parties may find themselves defending anti-union policies apparently made necessary by circumstances beyond their control' (Mair 1997: 103–4).

However, Katz and Mair (1996: 531) emphasise that parties do not 'conspire' to give themselves privileges. Most importantly, a cartel cannot prevent the emergence of external challenges so new parties do occur (Katz and Mair 2009: 757). Thus, the cartel party strategy would rather be to try to incorporate successful new parties into the cartel itself, as '(…) attempts of exclusion may prove counter-productive, offering to the excluded neophytes a weapon with which to mobilise the support of the disaffected' (Katz and Mair 1995: 24; 1996: 531). As the catch-all party led to the conditions that produced the cartel party, the emergence of the extreme right parties is interpreted as a reaction to the rise of party cartels in Western democracies. Not being former mass parties, these new parties will follow a somewhat different organisational path than the old ones. Hence, differences in the relationship with civil society will still exist; although it remains unclear exactly how new parties are linked with interest groups.

The cartel party thesis soon became much discussed. Kitschelt (2000: 150–1) maintains that the cartel thesis lacks the adequate micro-foundations of political action that could accurately characterise the relationship between voter, elected politicians, and appointed government officials. Most importantly, it is argued that extensive party competition still exists (see Koole 1996; Kitschelt 2000). According to Kitschelt, the main reason is that inter-party co-operation involves a prisoner's dilemma: each participant has an incentive to defect from the co-operative arrangement that all participants wish to maintain. The further parties distance themselves from their voters, the more the cartel's members realise an incentive to defect '(...) in order to reap extraordinary electoral success by catering to the voters' preferences rather than those of the cartel member' (2000: 168). It would take extremely powerful sanctions to keep parties in the cartel. As state subventions often are distributed according to the distribution of votes, the parties are still motivated to embrace popular positions in order to gain support. Kitschelt argues (2000: 175) that parties can rely less and less on those material and solidarity incentives to voter preferences that maintained voter loyalty in the age of mass party organisation (see also Koole 1996; Puhle 2002: 77; Wolinetz 2002: 149, 160).[35]

According to Yishai (2001: 670–1), cartel parties are vulnerable and have therefore already experienced a need to reincorporate society into politics. More specifically, she describes the rise of *post-cartel parties* in Israeli politics – parties with a strong orientation to civil society, seeking to exploit the electoral potential of marginalised groups by promoting partial identities and granting legitimacy to social groups. In other words, separation from civil society does not seem to be a successful strategy in the long run. Therefore the question is whether parties at the beginning of the twenty first century have in fact chosen emphasis on links with various external organisations in line with Kirchheimer's thesis, or whether they are instead marked by tenuous relations with, or are virtually detached from, the interest-group community.

Why Parties Are Linked With Interest Groups in A Specific Way or Prefer General Detachment

As for *what shapes* the parties' relationship with interest groups, the literature in the wake of Duverger's mass party thesis primarily points to factors that are meant to explain long-term, gradual change. Nevertheless, the literature already outlined also suggests that in each historical period certain system-level trends create a particular incentive structure that calls for specific types of relationships at particular points in history. In this sense, it indirectly proposes explanations for contemporary relations as well.

Kirchheimer's (1966) article has later been interpreted as some sort of prediction for future development, but he also attempts to explanation the rise of catch-all parties. According to the catch-all party thesis, the most important system-level trends after the Second World War have been the growth of a new middle class,

35. Recently, Katz and Mair (2009: 759) have agreed that cartels are threatened by defection, but maintains that the problem is 'more akin to the tragedy of the commons, in which short-term maximisation by each would foreseeably lead to ruin for all' (*ibid.*763-64, see also Blyth and Katz 2005).

the weakening of traditional class conflicts, and the rise of the new mass media. The decline in the relationship between social democratic parties and trade unions has been linked more specifically with purported post-industrialisation, the programmatic adaptation of labour parties to 'new politics' issues like environmental issues, and the globalisation – or at least internationalisation – of national economies. All these macro-economic changes have, in various ways, rendered trade unions less useful as political allies for social democratic parties (cf. Piazza 2001: 416–9).

The cartel party thesis argues that party transformation does not derive solely from societal changes, but is also stimulated by changes in the relationship between parties and the state. State subventions to parties and ideological convergence are key factors explaining why parties in general will withdraw from civil society. Later, fiscal limits, economic globalisation and the decline of Keynesianism[36] have been identified as major factors to explain why cartelisation is a rational party strategy (Blyth and Katz 2005: 40–1; see also Katz and Mair 2009: 754). To varying degrees, these structural and institutional features are explicitly assumed to stimulate today's parties to prefer a certain type of relationship with interest groups. In Chapter 4, their potential relative impact is discussed further.

To date, little attention has been paid to those environmental features that might modify the impact of the general circumstances in society and state on contemporary party-interest group relationships. The focus has been on what might explain differences between parties at different points in time. Duverger (1954/1972) looked at his time period as representing a distinct incentive structure that virtually compelled all major parties to organise and behave in a particular way. Kirchheimer certainly also followed an evolutionary logic in describing the emergence of the catch-all party. Such theses are inherently questionable because they ignore the dynamics of party organisation: the future – and 'the end' – seems already to have arrived.[37] Those mechanisms that actually generate party changes are not described in any detail. An underlying premise, inspired by Anthony Downs' *Economic Theory of Democracy*, is that parties are collective actors that change their organisational structure and behaviour in order to attract a maximum share of the vote (Kirchheimer 1966: 195). But the autonomy of parties as organisations is, in practice, limited. The underlying mechanism is the impact of electoral competition. Parties competing in the same systems, and responding to the same financial and electoral regimes and to similar structural and technological constraints, are likely to converge (Harmel 2002: 122; Wolinetz 2002: 139; Heidar and Saglie 2003: 219).

Succeeding contributions therefore explicitly distance themselves from determinist conclusions based on sociological reduction (see Epstein 1967: 19; 1980:

36. Keynesianism is, in simple terms, the body of economic thought highlighting the need for an interventionist role of the state in stimulating aggregate demand through monetary and fiscal policy in order to reach full-employment equilibrium (Padgett and Patterson 1991).

37. This phrase is borrowed from Allardt's (2001: 22) comment on the lack of time perspective in political sociology in the 1940s and 1950s.

361). In presenting their cartel thesis, that said, Katz and Mair (1995: 6) argue that the development of parties in Western Europe has reflected a '*dialectical* process (...) in which each new party type generates a reaction that stimulates further development, thus leading to yet another party type, and to another set of reactions, and so on'. The party models presented by them are polar types to which contemporary parties may approximate more or less closely. They do not inevitably characterise the course of every specific party. Particular circumstances, such as state funding, favour different models in different political systems (Katz and Mair 1996: 532). According to Mair (1997: 108) inter-party collusion is particularly strong in political systems with a tradition of intra-party co-operation. To assume that particular patterns of party-organisation relationships will characterise an entire historical phase, only to be followed by its displacement as the prototypical party by a different type in a subsequent period, is to misapply the recent contributions within this tradition (Montero and Gunther 2002: 14–15).

Katz and Mair also primarily describe and explain historical stages of party development (Katz and Mair 1995: 8; Mair 1997: 96). Scant attention is paid to the foundation, structure and behaviour of new parties, although it may well be argued that what matters for the party's initial formation is not necessarily what is influential for established parties. Accordingly, it could be argued that most party types reflect models of party change, more than models of party organisation *per se* (van Biezen 2003b: 178). Hence, the usefulness of this literature can be questioned if one aims at also explaining the *variation* in the relations of today's parties with interest groups, and not only a possible general tendency (cf. Panebianco 1988: 265).

First, even if general societal features affect the incentive structures of all parties, there are also more specific external stimuli, such as possible variation in the behaviour of old core voters, that might merit investigation. Second, Thomas (2001e) interestingly shows that constitutional, legal and political structures such as executive-legislative relations also influence party-interest group relationships. Specific historical factors also seem to shape the course of development in some countries. Chapter 5 includes a discussion of what seem to be the most promising institutional constraints to explore further in empirical research. Third, it could be more strongly highlighted that parties are autonomous actors who may shape their relations with interest groups independently of environmental trends and developments. In recent years, the respective leaderships' freedom of action has been more strongly emphasised in existing empirical research on parties and interest groups.

Kitschelt (1994: 212) suggests that parties with a relatively loose internal structure have more successfully adapted to environmental challenges than others. Poguntke (2002) argues that loosening of links with external collateral organisations is not the most preferred option in all cases. Severing ties such as formal affiliation of trade unions is politically a highly visible act and may provoke adverse reactions from some sections in the party. An abrupt change of external relations may also send an exaggerated signal as regards the party's re-orientation to the public. Hence, parties will normally choose the gradual 'hollowing out' of such links, rather than cutting them straight away (Poguntke 2000). In conclusion, he indirectly suggests that mutual benefits still outweigh the problems in many cases (2002: 59).

In Aylott's (2003) study of the relationship of the Swedish Labour Party with the trade unions, a key question is whether the benefit of such ties outweighs the costs to the party organisation in question (see also Yishai 1995 in Thomas 2001c; Allern *et al.* 2007). Among the most advanced contributions so far, based on rational choice theory, is Carolyn Warner's (2000, 2003) comparative study of the relationships of the Catholic Church with political parties. Warner (2000: 18, 23) emphasises that once formed, an alliance between a party and an interest group is not 'on autopilot', and presents an *exchange model* based on economic theory. The focus is on interest groups, but also the parties' strategic behaviour is briefly discussed. The key argument is that Christian Democratic parties after the Second World War calculated the costs and benefits of forming an alliance with the Church as an interest group, and chose such a relationship only if it generally benefited the party in its pursuit of votes and access to office. In a case study of the modernisation of the British Labour Party, Quinn (2002, 2003) presents a similar political exchange argument as regards the formal power of the trade unions within the party organisation.

In the case of the British labour movement, Minkin (1991: 653–4) finds that non-instrumental factors also matter: a 'movement consciousness', organisational 'rules' of unity and the shared historic project of ameliorating working people's conditions for life significantly constrain party relations with trade unions today. Likewise, Widfeldt (1999: 11) argues that non-socialist parties in the Nordic countries have usually tried to play down their contacts with interest groups, not least because they, for ideological reasons, do not want to seem involved in special interests.

These factors and other potential endogenous sources of variation in the relations of political parties interest groups, such as historical constraints like the formative phase of an long-established relationship to a specific organisation (Panebianco 1988) are elaborated on in Chapter 5. For the present, let us simply conclude that more systematic insight is needed into why parties might be characterised by rather different relationships with interest groups at particular points in time, both across and within countries (cf. Warner 2000: 14).

THE RELATIONSHIP OF INTEREST GROUPS WITH POLITICAL PARTIES

Although this book focuses on the party side of the relationship, a few words are in order on the insights provided by the literature that focuses primarily on interest groups. Complete explanations of parties' links into civil society can hardly be provided if one ignores the interest-group side of the relationship.

Corporatism versus Pluralism: Neglect of Party Organisation

By and large, the literature on interest groups has paid little attention to relations with political parties. The familiar distinction between pluralist, corporatist and elitist systems entails different views on the role of political parties (Yishai 1991: 3–18), but party organisations are not at the core of empirical analyses of interest-group politics. Although students of interest groups increasingly acknowledge that 'interest groups are only one facet in a complex geometry' (Warner 2000: 19), few have looked systematically at relations with political parties (but see Yishai 1991; Baumgartner and Leech 1998; Wilson 1990; Berry 1997; Maisel and Berry 2010). Interest groups are more often studied as self-sufficient bridges between the governed and the government (Warner 2000: 18), and to a certain extent at the expense of parties (cf. Lawson and Merkl 1988).

Two major bodies of literature on interest groups are based on the theories of pluralism and corporatism. So far, the focus in both scholarly traditions has been on the relationship with the government or the state as a whole. Studies of how interest groups try to influence public decision-making have documented interaction of interest groups with representatives, committees, the cabinet and civil servants (see Lijphart and Crepaz 1991; Marsh and Rhodes 1992; Christiansen and Rommetvedt 1999; Blom-Hansen and Daugbjerg 1999; Uhrwing 2001; Coxall 2001; Ciegler and Loomis 2002). However, neither pluralists nor corporatists have paid much attention to parties *as such*. For most pluralists, parties and interest groups are distinct units that play different roles in the political process. The significance of pluralism in interest groups for democratic governance is emphasised (Wright 1971).[38] Interestingly, a Norwegian exception is a study from the mid-1970s of labour market organisations which showed that a majority of elected officials hold or had held party offices and the headquarters' staff did have contact with party organisations and parliamentary groups, although to varying degrees (Egeberg 1981; see also Lægreid and Roness 1997: 175).

Although parties establish corporative arrangements, and may disagree on the need for such arrangements, they have seldom been important to analyses of corporatism. The major issue – especially in Europe (Mahoney and Baumgartner 2008: 1254–55) – has rather been whether corporatism exists or not (Warner 2000: 20). The corporatist literature has therefore largely ignored the question of party-organisation links. The tripartite relation of government, business and labour has been at the core of this type of research (Sundberg 2003: 89). In the corporatist perspective, 'party' is thus '(...) used synonymously with *governing* party and not with parties in general' (Thomas 2001c: 10).

At the Turn of the Twentieth Century: Towards Increased Party Attention

Along with the decrease in formal corporative structures in Western Europe, and the increase in more informal lobbying during the 1990s, parties have attracted more attention in recent studies on interest groups (e.g. Yishai 1991; Christiansen and Rommetvedt 1999; Bindekrantz 2005; Svennsson and Öberg 2002). Particularly in the United States, there is a growing literature on party-group relationships (e.g. Berry 1997, Wilson 1990; Thomas 2001c).[39] Attention has increasingly been paid

38. For a review of the development of the pluralist approach, see for example Baumgartner and Leech (1998).

39. See Maisel and Berry, forthcoming, for an overview. For a comparison of the development of American and European literature on interest groups see Mahoney and Baumgartner (2008).

to the involvement of interest groups in electoral campaigns through, for example, financial support and endorsements of parties and candidates (see Ippolito and Walker 1980; Hrebenar *et al.* 1999; Ciegler and Loomis 2002; Rozell *et al.* 2006).

In a study of all interest groups in Denmark published in 2005, contact with party organisations appears as a part of the organisations' repertoire, although it is not as widely used as other means like contacting parliamentary committees, ministers, public committees, and the media (Bindekrantz 2005: 702). A survey of the attempts of various Norwegian elite groups, including interest-group leaders, of influencing political decisions indicates that party organisations at least interact with other actors in national politics as a response to external requests (Gulbrandsen *et al.* 2002: 220). The importance of parties is also emphasised in some contemporary policy-network studies. A central element in the idea of powerful 'issue networks' is that boundaries between government and interest groups can be less relevant than boundaries between different policy communities (Wilson 1990: 157; Daugbjerg and Marsh 1998; Peters 1999: 115–16). Most importantly, parties and their strategies can prove to be significant components of these power relations in public policy-making (Kasa 2000).

Nevertheless, little specific attention has been paid to the links between parties and interest groups *outside* government agencies (cf. e.g. Beyers 2008).[40] The general literature on new social movements like environmental groups emphasise the tendency of movement groups to be non-partisan (see Dalton 1994). Interestingly, new social movements like environmental groups, which emerged as opponents to the establishment, are often sceptical to parties in general (Dalton 1994: 227–8; Poguntke 2006: 401; but see Young 1996). In addition, empirical research shows that single-issue organisations and social movements *generally* tend to regard government and parliaments as more promising for their activities than political parties (Dalton 1994: 227; Poguntke 1998: 159). According to Dalton (1994: 229–31), neither group characteristics nor the external environment seem to affect the relationship. For example, the availability of green parties does not facilitate party contact, and even if some movements have contributed to the establishment of new parties, well-organised links with such parties are rarely a part of their strategy (see Young 1996).

However, studies showing that political parties and movements as interlinked at the individual level also exist (Kitschelt 1989; Dalton 1994: 220; Goldstone 2004: 342). In the case of the West German peace movement, Schmitt (1989: 591–2) finds that not only the elite of the Greens' party but also other party leaders are affiliated to such social movement organisations. Kriesi and van Praag (1987: 383) show that the peace movement is not cut off from traditional political organisations but has extensive membership overlap with parties, and especially with the parties on the left. This indicates that it is also worth further exploring the

40. Warner (2000: 21–2) notes the relevance of another body of literature applying economic theory to 'the role of interest groups in economic growth and government regulations', but concludes that neither does this literature encompass the party organisation in its empirical analyses. It ignores the fact that individual politicians are constrained by institutions like parties.

relationships of established parties with anti-establishment groups.

In the growing literature on social movement networks in politics links with parties have not been major objects of analysis (see Diani and McAdam 2003, but see Goldstone 2003). But the social network perspective may well have theoretical elements of relevance to offer. Here, individuals or organisations are characterised, for example, by the density of their links with others (see Diani and McAdam 2003). Schwartz (2005) has recently described party linkages with other organisations and groups as 'networks'. By referring to examples from Canadian and US politics, she argues that links with interest groups are '(...) basically either tight or loose, each with the potential for positive and negative consequences', depending upon shifting environments (*ibid*: 56). She considers linkage as essential to the vitality of political parties, but emphasises, like the literature on long-term party change, that these are ongoing processes: parties sometimes sever old relations, at other times they establish new links.

Finally, it should be noted that Thomas' (2001a) comparative study and Warner's (2000) recent analysis of the Catholic Church after the Second World War represent particularly valuable exceptions. From the perspective of interest groups, there are two key questions: under what circumstances is a binding link the preferred solution? And why does an organisation prefer to cultivate the relationship with multiple parties or with only one? Kirchheimer suggested that interest groups *generally* hesitate about linking themselves closely with a specific party. Thomas (2001c: 18) highlights the importance of the organisation's formative phase, ideology and leadership in this regard, but the emphasis is on social, political and institutional constraints. Thus, the possible implications of interest groups as autonomous actors are not well developed.

As mentioned, Warner (2000) has developed a cost-benefit model, which will be returned to in Chapter 5, which is undoubtedly a highly valuable supplement to Thomas' analysis. The major conclusion is that in the post-war period the Catholic Church abandoned alliances when the party failed it on a key issue of concern, when the changed context made it more advantageous to be independent, and when the association became costly for its representation (*ibid*: 213). However, the fruitfulness of her approach to interest groups *in general* remains to be discussed and examined empirically. By and large, the literature on interest groups and social movements has so far treated organisations separately from political parties (cf. Beyers *et al*. 2008: 1119–20).

CONCLUSION

A key issue in the debate on the development of political parties in established democracies is to what extent parties are still linked into civil society. In the first half of the twentieth century, West European party organisations were firmly embedded in particular social segments by, among other things, close relations with particular interest groups. The example *par excellence* is the traditionally intimate relationship between socialist parties and blue-collar trade unions.

Since the 1960s, however, it has been argued that socio-economic and technological development have made exclusive and close relations less useful for both sides (Kirchheimer 1966). It is now widely agreed that the relationships between social democratic parties and trade unions are more distant than they once were. Some scholars have even argued that we have entered yet another era in which parties have weak links into civil society in general (Katz and Mair 1995).

Nevertheless, there has been little empirical study of party relations with organised interest groups outside Parliament. Until recently, the topic has largely been ignored both by party scholars and by students of interest groups. Recent studies indicate that a certain variation in the strength of old links exists between parties in different countries, but there has been a bias in empirical research towards social democratic parties and their traditionally integrated relationship with trade unions. The degree to which established parties have replaced old links with less binding ones, and to what extent they have opted to establish (weaker) connections with a broad range of interest groups, is an area that would merit further study.

Equally important, there is no general agreement as to what defines a party's relationship with interest groups. The literature on long-term development identifies degrees of closeness or distance as a key dimension, but the indicators applied in empirical research vary. In Sundberg's project and Thomas' study, finances and data on overlapping memberships are included as a part of the dependent dimension, whilst Poguntke has focused on 'organizational linkage' through collateral organisations and new social movements. Then again, Warner (2000: 103–5) defines a relationship exclusively as a 'contract' of endorsement and exchange of benefits. Such differences in conceptualisation are of paramount importance. For example, finances and ideology can be seen as external to the relationship if the focus is on contact about political and strategic issues, whereas a broader definition implies that a relationship can exist without any direct organisational involvement between the two sides.

Studies on long-established links for contact tend to concentrate on what are often called 'formal ties'. In his concluding remarks, Poguntke (2002: 59) asks whether the measure of linkage through formal collateral organisations overestimates stability, '(...) because it is not very sensitive to gradual change in the substantive effectiveness of a given organizational connection'. Likewise, emphasis on guaranteed access to decision-making bodies does not take account of the fact that informal links can also be of substantial interest in practice. In the next chapter, the case will be made for a focus on links that open up for contact in political and organisational issues, but with the inclusion of different kinds of such links. In none of the comparative studies previously mentioned is actual contact between parties and interest groups systematically investigated. Moreover, with the exception of Poguntke's study of correlation to volatility, little has been written on the actual significance of party-interest group relationships (cf. Thomas 2001e: 287–8). Therefore, this book includes a suggestion for multifaceted conceptual tools with which one can empirically map and compare party relationships with interest groups systematically.

The question of what factors shape and explain this aspect of party organisation and behaviour has neither been systematically explored in the scholarly literature. Emphasis has been on system-level trends that might create convergence in parties' long-term development, and thus a general tendency in their relations with interest groups. With a few notable exceptions, the exogenous constraints that may lead to more differences between parties within and across nations have mostly been ignored. Nor have factors endogenous to the party organisation received much attention in this context. In sum, relatively little work has as yet explored the conditions under which parties and interest groups choose to establish links, or opt for distance or separation.

In the next two chapters, an analytical framework for comparative, synchronous studies of all three aspects is proposed: the extent to which parties are linked with interest groups, the (possible) significance of their relations with other organisations, as well as the question of why parties approach specific or different patterns of relationships.

chapter four | the nature of party relationships with interest groups

To what extent are contemporary political parties linked with interest groups? In this chapter, the first part of an analytical framework for comparative studies of political parties and their relationships with interest groups is developed. The concentration is on parties and interest groups in established democracies.[41] Several aspects of the nature of party relationships are addressed.

The discussion starts by exploring and delimiting the concept of party-interest group relationships: what is the difference between having and not having links with an interest group for a political party, and how may parties' relationships with interest groups vary? The aim is to develop an analytical tool that will enable accurate description and categorisation of the nature of parties' relations across a range of party organisations and national contexts at particular points in time. Subsequently, the question of whether a predominant pattern of party relationships with interest groups exist today will be examined. What would such a general tendency specifically look like in the early 2000s? Next, the possible consequences of party relationships with interest groups are critically discussed: can we generally expect the links to be politically significant, and in what way? Thus, as explained in the Introduction, the issue of political significance is explored *before* the issue of why parties' relationships with interest groups might possibly vary is addressed in Chapter 5. Finally, it is also suggested how we can go about studying the associated research questions empirically.

CONCEPTUALISING PARTY RELATIONSHIPS WITH INTEREST GROUPS

What constitutes the relationship of a political party with interest groups? In the scholarly literature, individual parties and interest organisations are described as involved in relationships by being 'aligned', 'interlinked', 'tied' and 'connected'. However, what this actually means is open to debate. In the most general sense, relationships between parties and interest groups might even be characterised by *lack of* connections (cf. Thomas 2001c: 19). But more specifically, the notion of 'relationship' usually refers to how parties and interest groups are in fact connected as organisations, behave towards each other or deal with each other. In the same ways as the term 'linkage', 'relationship' entails a connotation of interaction or contact (cf. Lawson 1988: 14). If there is no actual contact, there is separation.[42]

However, sometimes 'relationship' is used in a highly abstract and broad sense,

41. For literature on parties and interest groups in democratisation processes and new democracies, see Chapter 1, footnote 2.

42. The definition is considerably narrower than Lawson's (1980: 3) concept of *linkage* as '(...) substantive connection between rulers and the ruled'. Linkage implies, as mentioned initially, '(...) interconnections between mass opinion and public decision' (V.O. Key, quoted in Lawson 1988: 14).

for example by pointing to a degree of ideological affinity. In addition to some sort of organisational integration or contact, the transfer of finances and other resources is also commonly included (see Kvavik 1976; Wilson 1990; Sundberg 2003; and Allern and Heidar 2001). Von Beyme (1985: 191) suggests that a major distinction embraces loose co-operation, contact mainly limited to party finance and election campaigns, and organisational integration through collective membership of party members. Yishai (2001) argues that party links with 'civil associations' have historically had three manifestations: ideological overlap, party use of social organisations to provide social services, and economic support from civil associations.

In contrast, Verge (2009) distinguishes between three different party strategies towards interest groups: competition, penetration and collaboration. In the case of social democratic parties, Kitschelt (1994: 225) emphasises trade union control of leadership appointments and consequently places emphasis on power relations, as does Mavrogordatos (2009) by making a distinction between independence, group dependence, party dependence and interdependence (cf. Duverger 1968: 455–8). Thomas (2001c: 20–1; 2001e: 281–4) differentiates between the integration model, the dominant party model, the cooperation/proximate ideology model, the separation/pragmatic involvement model, non-involvement model, competition/rivalry model, and the conflict/confrontation model.[43] In this way, he describes relationships in terms of differing degrees of ideological affinity or adversity, of organisational links or lack thereof, as well as in terms of strategies and power relations between parties and interest groups (Thomas 2001c: 19).

Hence, the relationship of political parties with other organisations is a multidimensional phenomenon, and how to study it is open to debate. When the starting point is parties intermediary institutions, however, it will be argued that 'relationship' can *primarily* be understood in terms of *links providing contact* between parties and interest groups as organisations. Since the aim is not only to describe relationships but also to explain variation in such links, it seems furthermore reasonable to focus on a narrow, sharp concept of relationships. Even though party strategies and power relations are relevant aspects that might indeed be correlated with the links for contact, they reflect alternative dimensions analytically. In this book, the key question is to what extent parties do actually interact with external organisations, and not whether parties prevent establishments of interest groups or if interest groups primarily dominate parties or vice versa. For similar reasons, it seems logical to treat aspects like ideology and finances as potentially significant independent variables, rather than elements in the relationships *as such* (cf. Kitschelt 1989). For interest groups, various forms of support can represent resources to offer parties in exchange for better access to decision-making party bodies and elites. For parties the prospect of financial donations might accordingly constitute an incentive for opening up intensive contact with specific interest groups. A 'strong' organisational link is most likely to be based upon ideological overlap, but ideology is not an equivalent to it.

The assumed correlations between different aspects of party-interest group re-

43. The models are based on contributions from Yishai and Thomas and Hrebenar (1995, see Thomas 2001c), as well as from Wilson (1990).

lationships must, in any case, be studied empirically. Hence, it can be argued that *a relationship consists of links that connects interest organisations to the party's members, decision-makers and/or decision-making bodies, i.e. links that open up for contact and potentially provide communication about information, know-how, opinions and policy views between parties and interest organisations*. Thus *links* are those *means by which a party and an interest group may communicate* such as, for example, corporate membership, joint committees, leadership overlaps or regular elite contact (see Table 4.1 for a specification). In order to avoid confusion, 'links' will only be referred to, and not for example 'ties', whereas the term 'relations' will be used instead of the more general term 'relationship' when useful.

Next, the question is how the extent of parties' relationships with interest groups may vary between parties. According to the relevant literature on long-term party change outlined in Chapter 3, parties have probably developed in the direction of having fairly distant and wide-ranging relations over time. It will be argued that the underlying dimensions of *closeness* and *range of relationships* are also suitable analytical tools in comparative studies of political party links into the interest-group community today. The two dimensions refer to fundamental yet different aspects of a party's relationships: How strongly (rather than loosely/tightly) is the party linked and with what organisations?

In the following sections, what constitutes the links is discussed in further detail. First, however, it should be noted that the *strength* of links refers to 'technical' aspects like formal status, not substantial value in terms of political significance. In line with the book's focus on the national extra-parliamentary organisation of parties, possible links with lower party levels and the parliamentary group will not be included in the discussion. Moreover, the issue of what *part* of the party that is relatively most important for relations with interest groups cannot be addressed *per se*. Instead the focus is on considering if and how the extent (strength) of national extra-parliamentary links is likely to vary across political systems and parties.

Closeness of Relationships

As shown in Chapter 3, there is no general agreement about the distinguishing feature of truly close relationships as regards links for contact. Duverger (1954/1972) emphasises the existence – or lack – of collective membership: the strongest links are manifested by parties with an indirect structure. He also makes a distinction between formal and informal links (Duverger 1968), but does not systematically elaborate on the alternative ways parties can be linked with interest groups. Schwartz (2005: 40) differentiates among affiliation, alliances and co-optation. But she does not specify what an alliance is in practice, and co-optation describes the tactic when a group is completely incorporated in the party in order to prevent the rise of a competitor. Wilson's (1990: 159–60) distinction between close integration, the model of non-partisan interest group (i.e. separation) and the intermediate category of political or bipartisan interest groups also fails to systematically capture degrees of closeness in the relationships as defined above.

Poguntke (2006: 397–8) argues that parties may have more or less close relationships with collateral organisations. As mentioned in Chapter 3, these can in the most powerful way be corporately linked to the party (through collective membership), through being formally affiliated (through guaranteed representation in decision-making bodies) or informally linked (through exclusive negotiations) based on a broad commonality of interests. As long as ancillary organisations are excluded, this classification is certainly useful when trying to measure fairly or very close party-interest group relationships in terms of links for contacts. There is obviously a fundamental difference between organisations that are, according to the party statutes, partly incorporated in the party structure, and formally independent groups.

However, when the aim is also to map more distant party relationships, Poguntke's scheme has limitations in terms of usefulness. Certainly, parties can have a fairly close relationship with an interest group without links like collective membership and formal affiliation. Historically, there are, for instance, many examples of trade unions that have been strongly linked with a social democratic party without being incorporated in the party structure (Padgett and Paterson, 1991: 179–85). Poguntke's notion of a 'independent' or 'informal' collateral organisation acknowledges this, but emphasises exclusiveness and permanent exchange (van Biezen, Mair and Poguntke 2009),[44] and includes an ideological element in terms of a 'broad commonality of interests' (Poguntke 2006). Hence, he does not provide a conceptual tool which *specifies non-statutory links for contact* between parties and interest groups in the organisational sense.

The distinction between formal versus informal links is not sufficient as it ignores different qualities of non-statutory links. It is true that relations not regulated by party statutes are less formal than those which are. As Poguntke (2006) points out, integration of interest groups into the party structure establishes a special relationship. But we need to recognise that there can be quite 'official' contacts with groups which are not written into the party rules. In other words, the relationship between formally autonomous parties and interest groups is not necessarily unofficial and badly organised, and non-statutory links may constitute significant structures for contact (cf. Minkin 1991: xv). Therefore, a more useful basic distinction can be made between *overlapping organisational structures* – such as corporate membership – on the one hand and *inter-organisational links* for contact – such as liaison committees – on the other.

Next, it must be recognised that significant links can also materialise outside well-organised settings. In his study of ecological parties and new social movements, Kitschelt (1989: 231–3) differentiates between movements connected to a party by links with the party at large, and those linked through selective com-

44. van Biezen, Mair and Poguntke (2009) distinguish between two major types of collateral organisations: 'First, mass organizations which are either fully independent of political parties or maintain corporate links with them (e.g. through collective membership); and second, affiliated or ancillary organizations which are characterized by a partial or even complete membership overlap with a specific party'. External interest groups are mostly to be found among the so-called mass organisations.

munication, i.e. interaction between individual elected officials.[45] In this way, he shows that the individual level also matters in the relationship of parties with interest groups, and points to ways less organised parties may be linked with interest groups. Such links are more contingent upon political circumstances and leadership personalities (Poguntke 1998: 156–7), and create a less binding, more flexible relationship (cf. Schwartz 2005: 44). Nonetheless, as long as they act as official representatives, party and organisation elites still take part in organised, or formal, contact. In other words, organised links may materialise both at the organisational level and at the individual level.

Instead it will be argued that purely informal contact – contact not officially reported to the respective decision-making bodies – is a separate and weaker kind of link. Actual personal overlaps represent another genuinely informal kind of link. Although there may be a tacit norm for representation of interest groups, such representation is still not official: the elite member is elected as an individual. In fact, in some cases care is taken to ensure that the two hats worn by the same person are not to be mixed up (Yishai 1991: 131).[46] To conclude, we may distinguish fundamentally between the following classes of a party's links with (individual or categories of) interest organisations, referring to decreasing degrees of closeness:

- overlapping organisational structures (i.e. statutory links);
- inter-organisational links for contact;
- unorganised (informal) links for contact.

'Class' or 'kind' is used instead of 'type of links' because 'type' is usually used to refer to special compounds of attributes. Classifications are an ordering resulting from one criterion (Lasswell and Barton 1951: 169). The distinction serves as a tool for classifying species (parties, i.e. their relationship with interest organisations) in a way that systematically highlights relevant differences or similarities (Scarrow 1996: 28). However, it should be noted that the various classes of links are not necessarily mutually exclusive: Even if a party is linked to an interest group through, for example, corporate membership it might also have inter-organisational links with this organisation. Hence, in terms of closeness to particular (types of) interest groups, the primary question to be settled is what the *maximum level of links for contact* is.

45. More precisely, Kitschelt (1989: 231) distinguishes between arms-length relations, selective communication, organised ties, and clientelism. The first category denotes a minimum of contact, the others increasing density of communication and co-ordination. The problem is, however, that the categorisation is not one-dimensional albeit presented as such. The issue of arms-length relations implicitly refers to frequency of contact, whilst clientelism denotes a situation where the movement organisation tries to shift the burden of protest mobilisation to the party (Kitschelt 1989: 232–3). Kitschelt also adds that 'cultural interpenetration' – a continuous flow of symbols and ideas – may compensate for weak organised ties (1989: 246). However, ideological overlap is not treated as an indicator of links in this context since the major phenomenon to be explained is parties' links for contact with interest organisations.

46. However, if applying a more crude measure – by only including major links like corporate membership, liaison committee and leadership overlap – it could be argued that a tacit norm of representation in the party executive indicates a degree of institutionalisation (cf. the notion 'institutional tie' employed by Aylott, Allern and Christensen 2007).

Table 4.1 specifies what kind of links each category denotes in practice. The list is not exhaustive; but it is extensive and based on the review of existing literature (see Duverger 1954/1972; Valen and Katz 1964; Schmitt 1989; Kriesi and van Praag 1987; Kitschelt 1989; Padgett and Paterson 1991; Quinn 2002; Poguntke 2002, Poguntke 2006; Sundberg 2003). In line with the focus on external and organised groups, it does not include joint management of agencies (such as educational organisations and newspapers) or party-internal, informal sub-groups (see Valen and Katz 1964: 313–5; Kvavik 1976: 97). Moreover, the list has deliberately been restricted to *the national level* of extra-parliamentary party politics, and it concentrates on how a relationship materialises *in connection with the party's central organisation*: organised links for contact within the frame of interest organisation bodies or arrangements are not systematically included (only indirectly through contact reported at the individual level). Nor do the indicators assess the presence of party leaders in interest-group elites. On the other hand, personal *transfers have been included,* and not only *overlaps* – that is, respectively, the extent to which party elites hold positions in interest groups and the extent to which the elites have held such positions previously. Due to capacity constraints, it is not always possible to be an official or staff member in two organisations simultaneously, and former positions are also likely to open up more contact today.

Next, the question is how we can measure *the general degree of closeness* between a party and an interest group based on information about such links. As noted above, the major distinction regarding the closeness (or distance) of a relationship concerns whether the contact takes place by means of overlapping organisational structures, exclusively in inter-organisational settings or only informally. Next, the question is how many, what kind of – or alternatively, how intense – links that exist within each principal category.

A high number of links within the class of overlapping organisational structures and inter-organisational links, indicates a higher degree of closeness, but the degree of closeness is still dependent on the specific form: the existence of a permanent joint committee or agreements about regular meetings would certainly indicate stronger links than occasional invitations to party arrangements.[47] For various reasons, however, it is not possible to summarise the links into an additive, weighted index – not even within each class of links. Firstly, since collective affiliation is a fundamentally different kind of link from guaranteed access to decision-making bodies (Poguntke 2002: 50). Secondly, because the existence of one kind of link (like a joint committee) may reduce the needs for links (like meetings outside party bodies) within other categories, thereby making an addition less meaningful. Indeed, permanent joint committees can nearly be seen as a functional equivalent to statutory links because their abolition may politically be almost as costly as a rule change implying the end of previously guaranteed access to a decision-making body.

47. The individual sub-category of links may itself be more or less intense, but it is beyond the scope of this study to assess the strength of each individual kind of links in this sense. For example, an individual interest group may have guaranteed access to few or many party bodies. See Poguntke (2002: 52–3) for a quantitative measurement of strength of this kind of link. I choose not to apply this formula since I include a greater number of indicators than Poguntke does.

Table 4.1: Sub-groups of links providing contact with interest organisations at the national level

Overlapping organisational structures	Inter-organisational links for contact	Unorganised links for contact
National/local collective affiliation (membership) of an interest organisation* Guaranteed access to the party's national decision-making bodies (representation regulated by party statutes)	*Organisational level* Permanent joint committee(s) Temporary joint committee(s) Joint conferences Written or tacit agreements about regular meetings and representation Formal invitation to the party congress Formal invitations to party meetings, seminars, and conferences Specific dialogue seminars/ hearings *Individual level* Formal meetings and other forms of contact between official representatives	Various forms of unofficial contact between individual representatives and spokesmen Actual personal overlaps in – or transfers to – the party's central organisation**

* Local collective membership is included although it is not *per se* a national feature. The reason is that collective membership at the local level indirectly implies a potentially strong formal 'bottom-up' link to the national party organisation and it is regulated by national party statutes.

** Regular memberships are not included, as the focus is on links opening up for contact between parties and interest groups, i.e. the organisational level or decision-making elite level.

Instead, we should to take into account how intense the links measured at the individual level are (by means of survey data). The existence of inter-organisational links does not automatically mean that a given interest group is more strongly connected with the party in terms of personal overlaps and transfers. There is not necessarily a strong correlation between the strength of, for example, organised links and the actual frequency of contact with various types of interest organisations. Party elites may also be involved in unofficial (informal) contact with interest group representatives. Moreover, it is hard to find out exactly which interest groups (or interest group categories) the party is linked to through, for example, inter-organisational links such as hearings on specific policy issues.

Table 4.2: Types of relationships in terms of closeness

Maximum level of links for contact	**Frequency of actual contact**	
	Regular	Occasional
Overlapping organisational structures	*Integration*	*Fictitious integration*
Inter-organisational links	*Alliance*	*Organised ad hoc relationship*
Unorganised links	*Informal partnership*	*Issue-based contact*

Finally, and ideally, we should examine whether the party elite members actually do initiate some of the meetings themselves. The contact reported might, in theory, be primarily the result of interest group initiatives, and thus not a valid indicator of the party's attempts to establish an inter-organisational or informal links in terms of more or less regular ad hoc meetings. However, in order to assess and compare parties' *overall* degree of closeness we also need a cruder, summarising measure. By combining the *maximum level of links* for contact and *the frequency of actual contact*, we might distinguish six major *types of relationships in terms of closeness*: integration, fictitious integration, alliance, ad hoc relation, informal partnership, and issue-based contact (see typology in Table 4.2). The frequency variable is of course in reality in a scale, but is dichotomised here for the sake of simplicity. Below, I will discuss what reasonable threshold values for regular and occasional contact are. *Integration* represents the maximum degree of closeness whilst *issue-based contact* represents the lowest, approaching (virtual) *separation.* An *alliance* might be closer than fictitious integration in practice, whilst an *informal partnership* is ranked above the type of an *organised ad hoc relationship.* In each case, it is important to bear in mind that individual relationships are not a static phenomenon, and some aspects of a relationship may change abruptly. Ultimately, we must ask whether a party's general relations with interest groups are characterised by one or several types of relationships.

Range of Relationships

Closeness is not the only major dimension along which a party's overall relationship – the total network of links – with interest organisations may vary. A party's *range of relationships* with interest organisations concerns the scope of its relations with the interest-group community, and can be defined as a combination of the *total number of organisations* (the quantitative aspect) and the *political variety of interest groups included* (the qualitative aspect).

In a comparative perspective, such figures are somewhat context sensitive, depending on the size of the organisation society as a whole. A proportional measure is thus needed, but defining a high proportion of possible links precisely is, of course, not a straightforward task. Hence, it could be argued that the range of a party's relationships is primarily about the political variety of interest groups included in the network of links. Truly wide-ranging relations are not cleavage-based, and may include links with organisations representing several conflicting sub-cultures and both old and new interest groups. Since all parties need to set some priorities due to capacity constraints, however, it seems reasonable to allow for some variation between parties in terms what links across cleavages exactly mean. A single party can hardly establish significant links with the entire community of interest groups. A reasonable assumption to make is that an individual party will give priority to organisations associated with the same political issues as the group with which it traditionally had a close relationship. This is because parties tend to benefit from competition when putting their core issues on the political agenda and therefore will be most interested in support from groups within these fields. Hence, for example, a labour party should be associated not only with industrial unions but also with white-collar unions and business organisations to be characterised as a party with wide-ranging relationships – in addition to numerous links with groups from other policy fields. In sum, networks of party links with interest groups will largely be overlapping and not polarised. Since the qualitative aspect of range may also vary between national contexts, however, further specification in terms of specific organisation categories or types is not useful – or possible – at a general level.

Taken together, the closeness and range of relations depict a party's general configuration, or pattern, of relationships with interest groups. However, they cannot be easily combined and used to crystallise *archetypal* patterns of party relationships with interest groups. Whereas the degree of closeness refers primarily to relationships with individual organisations, range describes the total network of a party's links. A party might in theory be more strongly linked with some organisations than others, for example by having rather a close relationship with its old ally while simultaneously trying to establish weaker links with other interest groups. Nevertheless, it could reasonably be hypothesised that there is some sort of correlation between the two dimensions. For example it is difficult to imagine that a party would have as close a relationship with numerous and perhaps conflicting organisations as some social democratic parties used to have with trade unions. Moreover, if different parties are expected to be linked with the same interest groups, it is hard to see that these parties and organisations can be involved in integrated relationships. To a certain extent, integration entails exclusiveness, and breadth a certain distance.[48] As shown in Chapter 3, a mass party was characterised by having integrated organisational structure with its organised *classe gardée,* and significant relationships with few others. Similarly, in line with the catch-all thesis, it makes sense to assume that a wide-ranging network of links tends to mean generally rather distant relationships.

48. Perhaps the combination is functional in a totalitarian one-party system. Here a single party monopolises political power and may penetrate civil society in general. But here focus is on parties in established democracies.

A GENERAL PATTERN OF RELATIONSHIPS TODAY?

Having conceptualised parties' relationship(s) with interest groups, the question of what might generally characterise this aspect of party organisation and behaviour today is now examined.

In order to identify, select and aggregate relevant grievances, communicate and transform them into public policies, parties need stable means of communication (Poguntke 1998: 158). Interest groups can provide party elites with a fairly clear picture of relevant grievances among relevant segments of their electorate. Intra-organisational processes of interest aggregation have already identified those demands which seem most important to a majority of the members (Poguntke 2002: 46). As will be elaborated in Chapter 5, political parties may approach interest groups to get votes, monetary support and organisational assistance, while interest groups in turn need parties for legislation and policy rewards (Warner 2000: 29, 99; McLean 1987: 70; Schwartz 2005: 44). But as shown in Chapter 3, numerous scholars have argued that the results of general socio-economic developments make some patterns of relationships more attractive – and hence more likely – than others in the early 2000s.

As early as the 1960s, Kirchheimer (1966) hypothesised that, faced by a plural society, most parties would distance themselves from old allies and prefer to be linked with various interest groups in order to secure significant electoral support (see also Panebianco 1988: 266–7). The general assumption underpinning this argument is that a high level of political conflict and ideological diversity is likely to stimulate specific groups and parties to ally whilst relatively weak collective class identities and cleavages are not (cf. Rokkan 1966; Thomas 2001c: 273, 275). In the following section, the literature on party relationships with interest groups – emphasising structural changes in the economy and the electorate – is presented in further detail. If a predominant pattern actually exists, what would it more specifically look like in the early 2000s?

Contemporary Party-Interest Group Relationships

After the Second World War, the advanced industrialised economies have shifted from being based on industry towards an emphasis on the service sector. A new, more extensive and pluralist middle class has emerged, and the traditional, manual working class has declined relatively in size. According to Kitschelt (1994: 8–39), this socio-economic development has altered voter preferences in a way that is particularly challenging for social democratic parties. Policy changes have been necessary to maintain a strong position, and links with the trade unions have become an obstacle to efficient adaptation. The decline of Keynesianism after the international economic recession in the 1970s, which followed the oil price crisis in 1973–74 – and later the wave of 'neo-liberalism' as presented in the policies of Thatcher and Reagan – has put social democracy on further trial (Padgett and Paterson 1991; Taylor 1993; Piazza 2001).

Moreover, traditional blue-collar unions organise less of the workforce than they used to. The new middle class is gathered elsewhere and is sometimes hostile towards the old trade union movement (Koelbe 1992). During the 1980s and early

1990s, union density fell on average in advanced industrial societies (Wallerstein and Western 2000: 357–8), a development which Piazza (2001) more specifically connects to the process of globalisation, i.e. the increasing importance of international trade and investment to national GDP. He presents evidence that union density is negatively affected by globalisation and has not been significantly related to the recent success of centre-left parties: '(...) organized labour is not the electoral (or workplace) force as it used to be' (Piazza 2001: 426).[49] In brief, the social democratic parties no longer have the vote-mobilising potential in traditional voter groups that they used to. Close relationships with trade unions do not seem very attractive even if the attachment to strong unions have been argued to still be an electoral asset for social democratic parties (see Kunkel and Pontusson 1998).

In economies based on a large public sector, the dilemma for social democrats is especially pronounced. Voters employed in public administration and services are highly unionised, but often in employees' organisations outside the traditional trade union movement. Besides, unions with core members in declining sectors like heavy industry may easily develop militant preferences, in turn making them even less attractive to social democratic parties (Howell 2001: 16–18). Moreover, the growth of the public sector has complicated the process of centralised wage bargaining and contributed to decline of corporatism in recent years (Hernes 1991: 247–55; Wallerstein and Western 2000). If the degree of corporatism is positively correlated to closeness of party-interest organisation relationships as suggested by Padgett and Paterson (1991: 178, 192), the development strengthens the likelihood for distant relations between some parties and interest organisations. Later, the growing power of the European Union has increased the potential for conflict for parties that promote policies unpopular with unions. In recent decades, there has been a significant rise in income inequalities in Western countries (Atkinson 1999), and it has been argued that immigrants represent a new lower class (for example, see Østerud 2005). Throughout Europe, social democracy has been accused of scrapping the core values of the labour movement (Allern *et al.* 2007).

Neither are middle-class voters easily persuaded to cast their votes for the centre-right in the early 2000s. For example, liberal and conservatives parties today face a middle class largely employed in the public, not the private, sector in some countries. Likewise, the share of employees in primary-sector industries has declined throughout Europe, not least in the Nordic countries (ILO 2002a), a development which has stimulated agrarian parties to seek support not only among farmers but also among a wider range of voter groups (Arter 2001). The religious parties in Western democracies have, for their part, been challenged by the consequences of increased secularisation. Growth in the proportion of voters not affiliated to a church means greater leeway for polarisation, but has not resulted in a more significant religious cleavage (Knutsen 2004a: 82). According to Inglehart

49. Piazza (2001) argues that he hereby explains de-linking of the relationship between labour parties and unions, but it should be noted that he does not operationalise the relation in terms of organisational links. The dependent variables measured are 'left party power' and 'the policy orientation of the primary centre-left, social-democratic party(ies) with regard to social democratic values' (p. 420).

and Norris (2004: 201–7) religious identities have been progressively weakened, and denominational differences play a less significant role in electoral politics. Hence, relatively few voters are likely to be recruited primarily on the basis of religious values, as reflected in the fact that support for religious parties has fallen in most post-industrial nations (*ibid.*: 208).

In other words, major political parties that aim to attract enough voters to get into office generally take a risk if they rely primarily on the support of a particular social class, segment or confessional group. Having a close relationship with a particular interest group therefore seems to offer more disadvantages than benefits in general. Elections today are best described as a highly competitive 'chase' for elusive voters (Rohrschneider 2002). Independently, the rise of the new mass media is assumed to have made strongly organised bureaucratic structures like traditional membership and collateral organisations less attractive to parties in general (Kirchheimer 1966; Panebianco 1988). The fact that the party membership figures have diminished may have further strengthened the party leadership's need for contact with external circles to stay informed about the grievances and policy views of various sub-cultures and parts of the electorate. Thus, the general social and technological conditions suggest that parties today rather prefer fairly distant relationships with a wide range of interest groups to very close relationships with particular interest groups.

Finally, the literature emphasising the importance of system-level trends for long-term party change has in recent years implicitly questioned the general interest of political parties today in being linked with societal organisations. Katz and Mair (1995) have – through their cartel party thesis – argued that we have entered yet another era in which parties have distanced themselves from civil society in general. The professionalisation of political parties has increased the party leadership's freedom to interact with various groups, but the state has, for example through public subventions, become a fount of resources through which major parties enhance their capacity to resist opposition and new challengers (Katz and Mair 1995: 16). Moreover, the Western fiscal crisis, the decline of Keynesianism, the rise of 'neo-liberalism' and economic globalisation are all supposedly reflected in the absence of major policy battles between established parties alternating in government. The result, they argue, is, in effect, inter-party collusion (Blyth and Katz 2005; Katz and Mair 2009).

As shown in Chapter 3, the foundation for the cartel argument is disputed. Above all, it is argued that extensive party competition still exists (see Koole 1996; Kitschelt 2000). As relevant as this criticism might be, the focus is here on the organisational symptoms. Although the study to be presented provides an indication of how much system-level conditions matter, the aim is not to put the micro-foundation of the cartel thesis on trial, nor to explore the extent to which a cartel of parties actually exists. As will become clear, the empirical analysis will mainly explore the impact of factors at the organisational level. So most importantly, according to Katz and Mair (1995), today's parties are not heavily dependent on external support from, for instance, organised interest groups. They are professionalised organisations that are only weakly rooted in civil society.

However, it should be added that one way to cope with new challengers is by incorporating new issues in the party manifestos and trying to approach, if not integrate, the associated interest groups. Since poorly organised movement groups are weak interest aggregators, the vote-stabilising potential is limited (Poguntke 2002: 48), but the electorates' rational for voting for new and small parties may at least decrease by means of such contact. Thus, on the basis of the cartel argument we would expect that political parties tend to have fairly weak links with interest groups in the sense that they do not put emphasis on establishing well-organised links for such contact. The increased dominance of parliamentary groups has probably made party organisations less attractive targets for interest organisations too.

As demonstrated in Chapter 3, existing empirical studies indicate that parties historically closely linked with certain organisations have declined over time, but that this trend may not be uniform (cf. e.g. Padgett and Paterson 1991: 216; Thomas 2001c; Allern *et al.* 2007). The degree to which established parties are today characterised by weaker relations with a broad range of interest groups is a moot point. But the common emphasis on system-level characteristics leads us to expect – expressed in the terminology developed above as regards closeness and range – that *political parties tend to have organised but not very strong links – organised ad hoc relationships – with a wide range of interest groups today*. Alternatively, it is suggested that *parties tend to mostly have distant relations – informal issue-based contact – or to be nearly separated from the interest-group community in general*. On the whole, then, party networks of links are expected to be largely overlapping and not polarised within a given system. Both expectations imply that the *old pattern of close relations with particular interest groups belongs to the past*, and that a *predominant pattern in terms of closeness and range of party relationships exists*. Implicit, but also to be examined as regards Norwegian parties, is the general assumption of correlation between the closeness and range of party relationships with interest groups.

However, it is important to emphasise that parties are seen as autonomous – largely instrumental – actors that are even capable of acting upon their context themselves (cf. van Biezen 2003b: 179). The described patterns are not expected to be uniform. Hence, the arguments do imply that national variations in relevant system-level characteristics may breed a few cross-national differences in patterns of relationships. For example, the social bases of politics vary across political systems despite general social trends in advanced industrial societies (Wolinetz 1991: 120). Political cleavages or dimensions still shape West European party systems, with the exact conflict structure varying across nations (Karvonen and Kuhnle 2001). Within one society, many conflicts co-exist, but only a limited number reach the public sphere, whilst the specific nature of these conflicts is to a certain extent the result of strategic choices made by political elites (Schattschneider 1960). Accordingly, the extent to which parties altogether are characterised by a polarised or overlapping network may differ to some extent between systems, if links actually exist. Or if civil society is well developed and strong, parties are seen as more likely to depend on interest organisations than in countries with a weak associational life (Chhibber 1999: 233). Also, it has been argued that the enduring, national institutional setting – the state structure – may limit the range of options available to parties (cf. Thomas 2001c). Finally, parties do in any case need to make themselves distinct and hence may not want to put *all* – and similar – organisations on an equal footing. The point is that numerous scholars have hypothesised that a *predominant* pattern of relationships will exist both across and within political systems – and disagree somewhat as regards what a general tendency would look like today. A major aim of this book is to carefully explore this issue – or conventional wisdoms – empirically as far as Norwegian parties are concerned.

New Right, Left and Green Parties: Similar or Special?[50]

This said, new parties, that is above all new right, new left, and green parties, are often identified as probable exceptions to the fairly general rule as these have been established as a *reaction* to 'old politics'. Katz and Mair (1996: 531) emphasise that a cartel cannot prevent the emergence of external challenges. The fact that the organisations of larger and established groups (trade unions, employers' associations) have developed relationships with the state themselves makes it even more likely for new interest groups and parties to be founded in opposition to the political establishment (Katz and Mair 1995: 23). Thus, even though old cleavages and conflicts have become diluted, the rise of a new and cross-cutting cleavage in European politics – whether it be called materialist/post-materialist or libertarian/authoritarian – suggests that a few parties are still inclined to be involved in a close relationship with a particular kind of organisation (Dalton *et al.* 1984; Inglehart 1990; Kitschelt 1994; Kitschelt 1995). Moreover, these new parties might well be considered 'political outcasts' by numerous interest groups. This would mean that relatively few requests for contact are made *to* such parties from interest groups in general.

However, it has also been argued that significant differences are likely to exist between the new parties based on, among other things, ideology. According to the 'new politics' literature on party formation, the typical *new green parties or new left parties* are party organisations emphasising participatory values through grass roots participation and relations to social movements. The more extreme of these parties did completely 'flatten' their organisations and banned leadership positions and opened up party gatherings to non-members. In this way, they have given rise to a new model of party organisation: *the new politics party* (Kitschelt 1989; Poguntke 1993; Harmel 2002: 125). Over a longer time period, party competition for votes might have 'normalised' these parties organisationally, making them look more like traditional mass membership parties. However, this does not necessarily mean that they now approach the pattern of relationships with interest groups as described previously (cf. Chapter 5). Indeed, they are usually assumed to be characterised by unorganised links, in line with the anti-establishment profile, but still have significant relationships with movement organisations like environmental groups (see Kitschelt 1989; Poguntke 2006).

---

50. Indirectly, this section – as did the conclusion of the previous one – touches upon the issue of what features might explain differences in patterns of relationships. But the general debate as regards explanatory factors will be dealt with in Chapter Four. Here the focus is on the general issue of homogeneity vs heterogeneity.

In contrast, the relationships of *new right populist and radical right populist parties* have traditionally been associated with charismatic leadership and centralisation of power, not organisational linkages into civil society (Panebianco 1988; Taggart 1995, Ignazi 1996; Pedahzur and Brichta 2002; Kitschelt 2006). Often these parties are sceptical of party politics in general, aiming for a more direct connection between government and the governed (Betz 1998: 4–5).[51] They have typically been characterised by weak party organisation and distant relationship with civil society organisations. To paraphrase Herbert Kitschelt (2006: 286), they may have 'movement appeal' but do not use to 'create or display social movement practices' themselves. Instead some of them might rather seek electoral support on the basis of professional 'market research', in line with the so-called *business-firm party*, modelled on the leadership-dominated (but not radical) populist right party *Forza Italia* in Italy (Krouwel 2006). A softer, more traditionally organised version is Harmel and Svåsand's (1993) concept of *entrepreneurial issue parties,* with reference to the Danish and Norwegian *Progress Parties* (*Fremskrittspartiet)*. Such parties are also creatures of their leaders, not of social movements, but they emphasise specific political issues in the message the leaders create, whereas for '(...) other charismatic parties the leader *is* the message' (*ibid*: 68). However, neither of these party types are marked by organisational links into civil society.

Many recent studies point to the 'crucial importance of party organization for the electoral success of populist radical right parties' in general (Mudde 2007: 264, see also Carter 2005: 64). Indeed, strong membership-based organisations have developed in numerous cases over time.[52] Moreover, existing single case studies include examples of populist or radical right parties characterised by significant links with particular interest groups: for instance, the French *Front National*'s enjoys informal links with a *sous-société* of sympathising organised interests such as right-wing farmers (Birenbaum 1992: 220).[53] Yet very little empirical information is available as regards the organisational features of new populist radical right or right populist parties (Mudde 2007: 264), and it is widely alleged that the general norm is that these parties have weak roots in civil society (Harmel and Svåsand 1993; Carter 2005: 64; Kitschelt 2006).

Hence, the general literature on parties established in the second half of the twentieth century, leads us to expect that *new parties are distinctively different from old parties as regards the pattern of relationships with interest groups*. Moreover, it is suggested that new left, green and right parties *are distinctively*

51. Extreme-right parties questioning the legitimacy of democracy in general, are thus excluded. For a discussion of the question of which real-life parties that belong to these party groups, see Mudde (2007: 41).

52. A key question in light of this development is whether, contrary to conventional wisdom, charismatic leadership of parties and institutionalisation can go hand in hand (cf. Mudde 2007: 263). However, I leave this question to the elaboration of explanatory perspectives in Chapter 4.

53. A less relevant example in this context is the former agrarian but now radicalised *Swiss People's Party* (Mudde 2007: 58), which has been characterised by a particularly close relationship with Swiss *Farmers' Association* (Schneider and Naumann 1982: 288); see also Barney and Laycock (1999: 324).

different from each other: while *new left-wing and green parties tend to have informal but significant links – informal partnerships – with social movement organisations, populist radical right and right populist parties are hypothesised to be usually characterised by lack of significant links with interest groups.*

SIGNIFICANCE OF PARTY RELATIONSHIPS WITH INTEREST GROUPS

Can we generally expect the relationships or links to be politically significant? If they are, in what way will they most likely matter? A major reason for studying party relationships with interest groups is the view that links with externally organised interests – or lack thereof – is an essential characteristic of parties as intermediary institutions. A party's choice of links – external relations – involves the role as gatekeeper to political power. In the same way as the size of party membership and the characteristics of internal decision-making structures, the relationships with interest groups tell us something essential about individual parties' roots in civil society (Poguntke 2002; 2006). Moreover, the links constituting relationships can be seen as manifestations of the party's constituency and represented interests. Hence, the notion of close relationships entails a connotation of political consequences. Indeed, 'strong links' are often seen as equivalent to 'politically influential' links.

If parties purposely establish relationships with interest groups, there is reason to believe that they do in fact take account of opinions articulated by means of these links. Interest groups can, through parties, affect short-term and long-term policy-making, electioneering, and candidate selection and thereby the parties' internal distribution of power and electoral performance. However, in the following section the focus is on the *assumed impact on the outcome of parties' policy-related decision-making*. It cannot be taken for granted that party links with interest groups actually imply interconnections between party decisions and organisations in more than a metaphorical sense. Thus, assessing the political significance provides a test of whether existing relationships have substantial value.

Significance of Closeness

The first question is whether the dominance of weaker links implies limited impact of individual organisations, whilst close relationships mean more influential interest groups. The various classes of links with interest groups reflect differing degrees of closeness to the parties' internal decision-making processes. According to Poguntke (2002: 47), formal affiliation of other organisations leads to penetration, whilst other links between organisational elites are based on reaction to pressure. Overlapping organisational structures imply that organisations gain direct access by formal representation in decision-making and consultative bodies. Thus, this kind of relationship provides the interest group with formal power within the party organisation (cf. Poguntke 2006: 397). If a party's relationships with interest groups are predominantly inter-organisational, the individual organisation has more limited possibilities for direct influence on a party's decision-making, but might be involved in almost binding contact and decision-making in practice. Informal contact among individual elite members represents the most distant form of contact.

However, the correlation between the degree of closeness and the extent of interest-group influence is not necessarily 'proportional'. Firstly, the impact of interest groups can be truly significant also through informal contact with party representatives (see Thomas 2001d: 97). In fact, based on experiences from the USA, Wilson (1990: 167) has argued that 'the more formalized the structure of the party, the more its insulation from interest group'. Secondly, truly close relationships have historically been based on the perception of a common constituency and shared values. Thus, party-interest group contact in such cases is probably also often about co-ordination and co-operation, not necessarily attempts to make the party change its policy views. Thirdly, at times, strong links are perhaps even established in order to regulate conflict, not to make the interest group more powerful (cf. Elvander 1980: 175–6) Finally, it is reasonable to assume that parties also more strongly influence interest groups in close relationships.[54]

Nor can the intensity of contact be interpreted as a robust indicator of interest-group power without further discussion, even though achieving access to decision-makers and interest groups' impact on policy decisions are usually empirically related (see Baumgartner and Leech 1998: 128). Organisations that have regular access to politicians and party staff are most likely more influential than organisations with limited contact, but particularly frequent contact at a certain point in time may also reflect intensified conflict between a party and an organisation. In times of political tension, as indicated above, the need for debate naturally increases between actors that are usually linked.

Equally important, contact between party and organisation elites might in theory primarily fill a symbolic, not meaningful, function. As members may be recruited in order to provide party with legitimacy (cf. Katz 1987), parties establish evident links with interest groups primarily in order to signal that their party is an 'open' organisation which is willing to listen to non-party actors. This does not necessarily mean that the party elites follow up by giving interest groups the chance of actual political influence (cf. Uhrwing 2001: 15). As will be elaborated later, parties may in theory choose to relate to interest groups in a specific way primarily in order to reflect particular norms for what is considered suitable party behaviour in democracy. Hence, the major question is to what extent the impact of various interest groups varies systematically according to differences in closeness of relationships or not.

Significance of Range

Second, we should explore whether parties with a wide range of links also are influenced by equally diverse interests independent of the closeness of individual relationships. If a party has a wide-ranging organised network, then its underlying long-term objective is perhaps to make the party manifesto reflect the interests of a wide range of social and cultural segments. In that case, there is reason to believe that the party will in fact adapt to a variety of interest-group preferences to a greater or lesser extent.

54. Indeed, it is reasonable to argue that in a truly close relationship, the degree of mutual influence is high. But as in the rest of this study, I concentrate on the party side.

However, if the main intention is simply to indicate openness towards society, some interest groups might be ignored even if they enjoy a significant link for contact. For example, it could be argued that the parties are more inclined to listen to organisations that address policy fields where the party organisation and its elite have little prior knowledge: the need for ideas is simply greater. Or it could be that a party might more readily make use of information within policy fields and on social segments with which the party elite and organisation are already familiar. A key finding in organisation research on learning and innovation is that an organisation's learning capacity is limited at both the organisational and individual level. According to Cohen and Levinthal (1990: 374–5), the absorptive capacity is a function of prior related knowledge: 'prior knowledge permits the assimilation and exploitation of new knowledge'. Thus, the question is whether the range of a party's relationships is of more substantial than symbolic value in practice.

THE ISSUE OF OPERATIONALISATION

How should we go about exploring these questions empirically? In this book, we shall concentrate on comparing the relationships of parties with parliamentary representation within individual countries, and more specifically parties and interest groups in Norway. But mapping parties' relationships with *all* existing interest groups within one single system is hardly possible. Therefore, the empirical analysis to be presented is limited to the exploration of relationships with various *kinds* of interest groups according to their thematic foci, such as trade unions, business organisations, religious organisations, and environmental groups. A complete list of organisation categories is attached in Appendix C.

The choice of grouping is based on two considerations: first, the need to distinguish between interest groups associated with old and new cleavages. For example, employers' organisations must be separated from employee groups (for details, see below). Second, I wanted to make the number suitable for application in a survey, which means that it could not be too large.[55] Consequently, the distinctions made are not perfect: some categories are broader than others, and not all relevant group differences are explored in detail. Hence, it is important to discuss the methodological implications of these choices when analysing the data. For example, for a party it might be easier to be registered as having extensive, frequent contact with a broad category of interest groups than a narrow one, simply because there are more organisations to choose from.

The previous conceptualisation made clear that party relationships with interest groups need to be measured at different levels of aggregation: by data about the party at large and by personal data (cf. Lazarsfeld and Barton 1951: 187). Due to the multi-dimensional, rich assessment of both closeness and range of party relationships with interest groups absolute measures cannot be developed. The

55. If the empirical study had included comparison across countries, the choice of organisation categories had to be even further discussed. To some extent, the categories are sensitive to the national context. For example, 'language organisations' represent in a Norwegian context a highly relevant category mirroring an old socio-cultural cleavage, but are probably not of interest as a separate category in all other countries.

final assessment will depend on both qualitative and quantitative data, and, at the end of the day, at the summarising effort of the researcher. Regarding the *degree of closeness*, the conceptualisation implies that we must first find whether links exist in the form of overlapping organisational structures, and next, inter-organisational links for contact – and how many and what kind of such links a given party has. Second, links at the individual level will need to be assessed. As noted above, parties can both be quite strongly linked with interest groups by means of personal overlap and flows, and through unorganised links for contact at the individual level. In all parts, we may have a closer look at the manifesto-making process to substantiate the description further. But the examination of whether the party elites actually do initiate meetings themselves is, however, only included in the comparative analysis.

Assessing the *strength* of personal overlaps and transfers is not a straightforward task. The famous *bloc vote* of trade unions in the case of the British Labour Party implied union control over a majority of the votes in the party's decision-making bodies. However, it seems unreasonable to let such extreme – and historically unusual – degrees of leadership overlap be the threshold for what can be considered as a relatively strong link between one party and one single interest group in general. The analysis therefore distinguishes three levels – *weak, medium* or *strong* – depending on whether less than 10 per cent, between 10 and 20 per cent, or more than 20 per cent of the national elite hold/have held office *and/or* are/have been staff members in an organisation within the category in question.

Next, the extent of the individual party elite members' actual contact – formal as well as informal – must also be checked at the aggregate level. A separate survey item addresses the extent of formal (official) as opposed to informal contact in general.[56] Four frequency categories can be identified: *weekly or more* often, *monthly*, a *few times a year* and *never*. Exact assessment of how strong links these frequencies represent requires comparison with other parties: we need to compare the size of elite shares with more or less frequent contact. But if a *majority* of the party elite has monthly contact with a specific kind of interest groups, this can be seen as a considerable extent of regular contact, since we cannot consider all organisations to be potential contacts for everyone. Accordingly, the following distinction can be used when comparing the strength of links with different organisations in each party case: *weak, medium* and *strong,* depending on whether 50 per cent or more had contact *never*, *at least a few times,* or *monthly* or *more often*, respectively. As regards the relationship typology, this means that a majority of the party elite must have contact monthly or more often with the interest group category in question for the party to pass the threshold for 'regular contact'.

The *range* of a party's relationships has both a quantitative and qualitative side. In the numerical sense, range can be measured as a proportion based on

56. In practice it is hard for respondents to distinguish official meetings clearly from unorganised contact in relation to individual organisations and categories. Therefore, it has not been possible to separate the frequency of organised (formal) and unorganised (informal) contact in relation to *each* organisation category.

survey data: the number of organisation categories to which the party is linked, divided by the maximum number of organisation categories to which a party might be linked (according to the list in Appendix C). But should all links, measured at the individual level, be taken into account?

On the one hand, in small populations, what one individual does or does not might well be important for the party as a whole, especially if he or she happens to be the party leader or secretary-general. On the other hand, with a low threshold comes the risk of blurring substantial differences between the networks' political profiles: most parties can be expected to be contacted themselves by various interest groups. Also, it seems highly unlikely that, when an organisation has well-organised links for contact – or shared leaders or staff – with a party, this will result only in occasional contact with a small share of elite members. Therefore, the total network of links does not include what is defined as weak links in terms of frequency. In other words, cases where *less than a majority* of the elite has *occasional* or *regular contact* are excluded in this part of the empirical analysis. However, one should also take account of whether the strength of links vary significantly between interest groups categories, as such differences could indicate that a narrower inner circle exists in a given party network.

In order to assess the qualitative aspect of the variety of represented interests, non-quantitative judgement is needed, and as argued above, the evaluation probably needs to be somewhat context sensitive. In the Norwegian case, studied in depth, a wide-range of relations can be defined as links that cut across the socio-economic class cleavage which is reflected in the ideological left-right dimension, the territorial and sectoral cleavages expressed through the centre-periphery and the urban-rural dimension, respectively, and the cultural cleavages which are mirrored by a moral-religious dimension. In recent decades, it has also been discussed whether new conflict dimensions have emerged related to issues or fields like immigration, environmentalism and globalisation (Aardal 2007). But there is no doubt that the dominant dimension of political contention over the past half-century has been the left-right axis (Narud and Strøm, forthcoming).

As regards the left-right axis, the territorial dimension and the sectoral cleavage, the most relevant interest groups are employers', business and trade organisations, the traditionally blue-collar trade unions and other employees' organisations, primary-sector organisations, client organisations, humanitarian and social aid organisations and community-centred organisations according to previous research (e.g. Heidar and Saglie 2002: 273). As regards the moral-religious dimension, relevant groups include Christian and missionary organisations, temperance organisations, language organisations, non-Christian religious organisations, and organisations promoting non-religious philosophies of life (*ibid.*). Organisations associated with 'new politics' are, above all, environmental groups, internationally-oriented organisations (e.g. peace organisations), feminist groups and organisations for politically less powerful groups like immigrants and refugees. However, it should be noted that agricultural organisations, temperance organisations as well as language groups no longer represent large voter groups.[57] Whereas organised groups for and against EU membership do not mirror one particular cleavage and cut across several parties (Heidar and Saglie 2002: 127).

Nor is it evident what *politically significant links* – in terms of influential interest groups – mean in practice. A first indication of the actual political significance of parties' links with interest groups can be provided by looking more closely at the content of the parties' contact. Some meetings and correspondence with interest groups might be fairly trivial and non-political in character, while contact in other cases may be marked by real attempts to influence decision-makers (Svensson and Öberg 2002: 305). In substantial terms, the contact may involve a party's attempts at getting more know-how, seeking political support for its own views, its endeavours to identify political preferences among interest groups, practical co-operation between allies, as well as organisations' attempts at politically influencing party decisions (cf. Heidar 1988: 150).[58] Obviously, contact about factual information suggests a less potent link than contacts involving active attempts at influencing political decisions. On the other hand, seeking facts and know-how does not necessarily reflect trivial contact or lack of political significance as it might well mirror the technocratic norm generally characteristic of public policy-making in Western societies in general (Fischer 1990). Through expert knowledge provided by interest groups, politicians try to enhance their capacity to solve various societal problems, and through fact-based arguments, rather than moral reasoning, interest groups influence policy-making (Uhrwing 2001: 259–60). Moreover, expertise knowledge and moral (or ideological) reasoning are not necessarily mutually exclusive, and facts can be used to support other types of arguments.

Finally, we need to explore whether the organisations with which parties interact actually influence the final political decisions, that is lead the party to formulate a policy proposition differently than the party would have done without the contact. This is of course a very difficult task. We should bear in mind that a change in a party's policy preferences corresponding to the stands of a given organisation does not necessarily mean that interest groups have caused this change. The party may have reached a similar conclusion independently, or other actors may have had an impact, for instance through mass media. A party may also adapt to the preferences of interest groups without entering into direct contact. Hence, a full exploration of this subject requires examining a great number of possible intervening factors and calls for in-depth policy analyses of specific policy fields.[59] In a more tentative general analysis, however, we may rely on evaluations by parties' and organisations' representatives concerning the general influence of various

57. The language question has in recent times been more or less absent from the political debate.

58. The distinction partly parallels Oliver and Meyers' (2003:176) concept of 'network ties' among social movements: communication of information, influence and joint action. Focusing on organisations' influence on parties (and not vice versa), I do not, like Oliver and Meyers, regard joint action as an extreme case of (mutual) influence, but as a case of co-ordination of joint activities.

59. For a review of the literature on measuring power and influence, see Baumgartner and Leech (1998: 58).

(kinds of) interests groups on the given party's political decisions. Thus the major analysis will be confined to a restricted number of indicators based on interviews with key informants and survey data. A critical approach to such data is, of course, necessary: the informants' responses cannot be taken at face value. In the end, the interpreter must base the analysis on his or her evaluation of the credibility of each informant's responses (see Hermansson 2004: 53).

CONCLUSION

This chapter has sought to develop an analytical framework for comparative studies of the nature of today's political parties' relationships with interest groups. It has also elaborated indicators of ways of being linked with interest groups, as well as the operational definitions of consequences of relationships.

First, the rather fuzzy concept of 'relationship' was discussed. It was argued that 'relationship' entails a connotation of actual contact, and thus can usefully be limited to links that enable contact with interest groups, although it is useful to note that such links can materialise in numerous ways. Inspired by the literature on long-term party development, the concept of party relationships was developed on the basis of two key dimensions: closeness and range of relations. As a heuristic device to the complex task of mapping overall degrees of closeness and distance in extra-parliamentary relationships, a typology of six archetypal relationships was suggested based on the variables of maximum level of links for contact and frequency of actual contact: integration, fictitious integration, alliance, organised ad hoc relationship, informal partnership, and issue-based contact. Various kinds of specific links were also specified. Furthermore, it was argued that there is likely to be a correlation between the two dimensions: a party with close relationships will tend to have a rather narrow-ranging network of links.

Second, this chapter elaborated the literature on party-interest group relationships emphasising structural changes in the economy and the electorate. It was noted that numerous scholars have argued that contemporary parties are to a large extent characterised by fairly distant relations with a range of interest groups, or generally tenuous links. Third, the case was made for examining the consequential aspect of parties' external relationships. The notion of close relationships implies a sub-text of political significance, but such effects cannot be taken for granted. Finally, it was discussed how these questions can be explored empirically. In the remainder of this book, Norwegian political parties' relationships with interest groups will be studied in light of these research questions. However, first, one major theoretical question remains: how can we best explain possible differences in party relationships, within and across countries, today? This topic is addressed in the next chapter.

chapter five | what factors shape party relationships with interest groups?

Political parties are constrained by the social surroundings within which they act, and differences in such structures might explain how parties' relationships with interest groups vary, not least across countries. This chapter further explores the question of what might shape party-interest group relationships, beyond general structural characteristics. So far, limited attention has been paid to the possible impact of party agency and institutional framework on such links. Therefore, in this chapter, the options parties face as autonomous actors *vis-à-vis* interest groups and the possible impact of the national institutional setting, are further discussed. As will become clear, more knowledge on both aspects is probably needed if we want a better understanding of party links with interest groups.[60]

INTRODUCTION

Political parties are, by definition, organised attempts to seek power through elections and they are autonomous actors who may behave differently under similar social circumstances. In Europe, they are firmly organised, and a 'dominant coalition' (Panebianco 1988) usually exists, even though real-life parties are not unitary actors. Faced by a universe of interest groups, party agencies can be assumed to carefully evaluate their need for links with various kinds of interest groups in light of the general party missions. Moreover, they operate within a larger framework of political institutions and national regulations.

Accordingly, parties and interest groups will be looked at from the perspective of *rational choice institutionalism* on political parties. Parties are assumed to be largely instrumental policy-seeking and office-seeking actors, but constrained by the political institutions within which they act. Despite the individualistic basis underpinning their arguments, rational choice oriented scholars, for example Kenneth A. Shepsle, have developed to study institutions and how institutions constrain political behaviour (see Peters 1999: 43–62 for an overview). More specifically, the aim is to evaluate empirically specific statements about real world party-interest group relationships derived from a 'soft' rational choice model (cf. Laver 1997: 4).

However, this does not mean that the assumption is that non-instrumental behaviour is generally missing in politics (cf. Miller 2000: 536). Parties are, it is assumed, above all goal-driven organisations, but they also represent collections of norms, routines, understandings and historical legacies. Therefore, two alternative

60. Although this book is not examining party relationships across countries, the framework should take account of such differences: as a whole, the study of Norwegian parties is implicitly comparative.

analytical perspectives on party relationships with interest groups are explored, based on *historical* and *normative institutionalism.*[61] Both these schools question the importance of rationality, emphasise other shaping factors or logics of behaviour, and are to some extent echoed in contemporary party literature. Although no distinct alternative institutional theory on party politics exists (Peters 1999: 112), it will be argued that in *both* cases we might lean on Angelo Panebianco's (1988) analyses of party organisations. In this way, the framework will help us to avoid theoretical biases by further clarifying what parties' behaviour *vis-à-vis* interest groups would generally look like if it is not shaped by cost-benefit calculations. Moreover, the specific theory elements of the alternative perspectives are used to identify some secondary explanatory hypotheses to be explored empirically. Hereby, we may find out to what extent non-rationalist factors additionally colour party-interest group relationships in Norway.

Despite major differences, the distinction between the three literatures is not watertight (see Miller 2000: 536; Thelen 1999: 370–1; Olsen 2009). The *primacy* of the rationalist perspective is emphasised but without entirely dismissing the possible relevance of 'historical' and 'normative' factors. This said, the aim is certainly not to solve the major theoretical problem of fitting '(...) different motivations and logics of action into a single theory framework' (March and Olsen 2004: 19). Focusing on parties in a single country, the study is, above all, concerned with explaining variation between Norwegian parties in particular. As ever, the more we nuance a parsimonious rational choice approach, the less generalisable the model is likely to be become. Therefore, each theory approach is first presented as an alternative on its own terms. Second, the cost-benefit model is specified by developing hypotheses to be explored empirically, and how this perspective can be informed by the other schools is discussed. What secondary hypotheses on possible deviations from a rational course can be generated in light of the alternative perspectives?

For now it suffices to note that all three perspectives belong to the 'new institutionalism(s)' in political science due to their common concern for how institutions shape political strategies and outcomes (Thelen and Steinmo 1992; Hall and Taylor 1996; Peters 1999; Thelen 1999).[62] Therefore, this common potential source of cross-national diversity in party relationships with interest groups is outlined in a separate section towards the end of the chapter. Besides, one must generally bear in mind that the aim is to offer explanations for differences in *the overall pattern of party relationships with interest groups*: to which degree parties opt for

61. It is common to distinguish between rational choice institutionalism, historical institutionalism and sociological institutionalism in comparative politics (Thelen 1999). However, in line with Peters (1999: 110), I choose to use the term normative institutionalism on what is sometimes called sociological institutionalism in political science (Hall and Taylor 1996), to make clear that I concentrate on the literature which is most specifically concerned with political behaviour (i.e. the March and Olsen's version of institutionalism).

62. For an overview of the different schools within 'new institutionalism', see for example Hall and Taylor (1996), Peters (1999) and Olsen (2009). For 'old' institutional theory on political parties, see for example Duverger (1954/1972).

closeness with different kinds of interest groups, and to what extent they seek to be linked with a wide range of interest groups. Finally, even though contact at the elite level reflects individual choices, it is assumed that major differences between parties' total elite behaviour is somehow connected with leadership decisions and hence collective cost-benefit calculations.

RATIONAL CHOICE INSTITUTIONALISM: A COST-BENEFIT MODEL

One of the basic tenets of classic rational choice theory is the principle of methodological individualism, which holds that social phenomena can be explained in terms of the individual actions of which they are composed.

General Assumptions

Individuals are seen as driven by the wants that express a fixed set of 'preferences': 'Economic man' calculates what is best for him given the constraints and the available information about the conditions under which choices are made. 'Social structure' is thus seen as chains of interconnected individual actions, not autonomous forces (Scott 2000). Social interaction is analysed as exchange relations, and political action is assumed to be largely motivated by the search for a reasonable balance of benefits over costs. '"Rational people" are motivated by their urge to fulfil their desires' (Laver 1997: 18), and 'a "rational" individual (...) adopts a strategy that selects the course of action that most effectively fulfils his or her desires' (*ibid*: 20).

Collective action is incorporated by the definition of collective actors as agents reducible to the actions of individuals. Accordingly, political organisations can be analysed as decision-making apparatuses through which individual preferences become aggregated and transformed into an agreed policy (Scott 2000). By defining individual actors, such as party leaders by their institutional positions rather than personal preferences, rational choice theory has imported structural features into explanations of individual acts. One can refer to political organisations as a '(...) shorthand for aggregates of individual actions that take place within such bodies' (Quinn 2003: 4). Due to systemic constraints like electoral competition, individual politicians cannot seek individual interests only (Sartori 1976: 25). Among other things, alliances enable individual politicians to 'tender for much larger political services contracts, far beyond the scope of any individual entrepreneur' (Laver 1997: 85–7). In general, rational choice theorists see the development of organisational forms and institutions as the result of actors' attempts to reduce transaction costs in their exchanges with other actors (Pierson 2000).

Over the past decade, significant efforts have been made to develop a broad theory on political parties based on this general analytical perspective. Following the classic work by Anthony Downs (1957), electoral politics is depicted as a political marketplace: competing and power-seeking parties offer candidates and policies to the electorate in return for their votes. Parties, that is permanent alliances between individual politicians, are seen as tools to reduce transaction costs in politics; 'search and information costs, bargaining and decision costs, policing and enforcement costs' (Müller 2000: 113). Within this general framework, alternative models of competitive party behaviour have been developed in different fields of research. Strøm (1990) and Strøm and Müller (1999: 5–9) succinctly sum them up as the office-seeking party (e.g. Riker); vote-seeking party (e.g. Downs) and the policy-seeking party (e.g. De Swaan), whereas they themselves emphasise that political parties are driven by *multiple* goals: political leaders value all the above-mentioned goods, and try to maximise legislative representation (i.e. votes), in order to pursue the chance of holding office as well as the realisation of policy. Pure vote-seekers, office-seekers and policy-seekers are unlikely to exist (Strøm and Müller 1999: 12). Also, maintaining party organisation and internal unity is sometimes presented as a fourth party goal (Sjöblom 1968: 73–87), but Müller and Strøm (1999: 282) consider party identity and unity to be mainly a '(...) shorthand for future electoral considerations' (see also Kitschelt 1994: 50, 212).

This more nuanced, yet parsimonious, party and goal concept is the one applied in the following discussion. The goals are not mutually exclusive, nor are they completely independent of each other. Parties in competitive systems must pursue votes in order to win office and carry out their programmes (Poguntke 2002: 44). Yet, it can be argued that party leaders '(...) rarely have the opportunity to realize all their goals simultaneously' (Strøm and Müller 1999: 9). Sometimes they experience trade-offs and need to give priority to one goal over others. For example, a party may need to sacrifice policy views, or sometimes prospective votes, in order to gain access to office through entering into a coalition with other parties (Strøm 1990: 572–3). Therefore, as a heuristic device, we can distinguish between parties that are *primarily* vote-seeking, policy-seeking and office-seeking (Strøm and Müller 1999; see also Harmel and Janda 1994: 387). But unlike the pursuit of office and policy, votes are normally pursued instrumentally, not intrinsically, as votes are hardly valuable in their own right (Strøm and Müller 1999: 10–1). Hence, office-seeking serves as the major alternative to policy-seeking as a party's primary goal (see further specification below).[63]

Also, these recent efforts to apply 'soft' rational choice theory to party politics assume that the institutional environments of political parties significantly constrain their behaviour by making specific strategies appear more efficient and attractive than others to party elites (Strøm and Müller 1999; Müller 2002). Moreover, parties can be seen as being more than mere aggregations of the issue-stands of their individual candidates. Whereas Downs (1957: 28) viewed parties as 'teams of men', Schlesinger (1984; 1991), Strøm (1990) and Strøm and Müller (1999) see parties as formal structures of various levels of individuals not always sharing the same interests and goals (see also Poguntke 2002: 44; Katz and Mair 1993: 594–601). Party leaders are involved not only in an exchange with voters, but also with the party members, who need to be compensated for their contributions. As a consequence of one of the intrinsic problems of collective action,

63. Trade-offs between office and votes may occur (Müller and Strøm 1999: 281), but as specific decisions will not be examined empirically, I content myself to distinguish between office-seeking (by means of votes) and policy-seeking parties.

i.e. that many people who stand to benefit from a given collective action will nevertheless often refuse to join (Olson 1971), policy promises will often be insufficient and voters will need extra incentives for joining. Shared policy views are not sufficient reason for making a contribution (Schlesinger 1991: 16–9; Katz 2002: 100–1). Since the time-lag between contributing finance/labour and receiving compensation is great, members may reasonably ask themselves whether party leaders are in fact willing and able to compensate them for their 'investments'.

A common way to overcome this problem of *imperfect information* and *non-simultaneous exchange* is to provide the actors with enforcement mechanisms like agenda-control powers and ex-post sanctions, i.e. to decentralise policy decisions and leadership accountability (Strøm 1990: 577–9; Strøm and Müller 1999: 16; Müller 2002: 249).[64] In other words, intra-party membership democracy is a way to decrease transaction costs in the exchange of finances, labour and policy between party leaders and members (Quinn 2002: 209). Internal rules and party organs make the supply of policy promises more credible in the eyes of the party activists. Party organisations allow the monitoring of the other party activists and office holders to ensure that they pursue the collective goal (see Müller 2002: 314). Thus, one assumes that the formal leadership controls the party and may act as a unitary, instrumental actor, but that the leadership's freedom of action is significantly constrained by the internal party organisation (Strøm and Müller 1999; Müller 2002). With these specifications in mind, we can now look at how parties are likely to approach interest groups seen from the perspective of rational choice theory on party politics.

Parties-Interest Group Relations as Shaped by Exchange[65]

In line with the analogy of the market, we can generally presuppose that party relationships with interest groups is based on, or shaped by, the instrumental exchange of various 'goods'. In brief, political parties need support for votes, monetary support and organisational assistance, while interest groups in turn need parties for legislation and policy rewards (Warner 2000: 29, 99; McLean 1990: 70; Schwartz 2005: 44; Allern *et al.* 2007). Just as collateral organisations stabilise party electorates (Poguntke 2002: 57–8); establishing relationships with external interest groups can serve as a way of increasing or maintaining electoral support as organisation elites may try persuade their members to vote for specific parties and support parties' headquarters with financial donations and labour (Allern *et al.* 2007). The size of these benefits might in general be influenced by existing structural

64. This is line with Mancur Olson's (1971) argument that free-rider problems related to public goods can be reduced or solved by offering extra, selective incentives to participate and facilitating condition co-operation, among other things.

65. As will become clear, my argument is informed by the theory framework of articles on the Scandinavian labour movements co-authored with Nicholas Aylott and Flemming Juul Christiansen (Allern *et al.* 2007, Allern *et al.* 2010). A major difference is, however, that this chapter is more detailed and specific in several respects, included the issue of potential costs, the possible variation in parties' goal priorities and alternative explanatory factors.

constraints (for instance, employment patterns), but costs and benefits *specific* to parties and groups are emphasised here.[66]

Compared to political parties, interest groups have been described as policy maximisers in general (Berry 1997; Schlesinger 1984; Quinn 2002). Party leaders, in contrast, assess the costs and benefits of having more or less close relationships with interest groups for the pursuit of access to office and maximisation of policy by means of votes. For parties, the potential costs, besides invested time and generally reduced freedom of action, include potential drawbacks like repelling other voter groups and limiting the party's coalition possibilities. Moreover, strong links with particular interest groups involve the risk of making policy promises that collide with other, and perhaps more important, policy preferences. For interest groups, alienating members and limited possibility to 'seeking out the highest bidder' among all parties are probable disadvantages, in addition to the costs of invested resources (cf. Kirchheimer 1966: 193; McLean 1990: 70; Warner 2000: 165–6). Close relationships might also increase the risk of conformity, making both sides less able to adapt to changing circumstances (Schwartz 2005: 54).

Hence, links for contacts between parties and interest groups can be envisaged as shaped by a mutual exchange of resources. Differences in party relationships – strength of links – with interest groups will thus reflect variations in the involved balance of costs and benefits. Parties and interest groups that do not have much (less) to offer each other in terms of 'goods', i.e. cases where the costs of being (closely) linked are likely exceed the benefits for each actor, are assumed to be interconnected by significantly weaker links, if any links exist at all. Once formed, however, close relationships do not go 'on autopilot', as political-sociological approaches risk suggesting (cf. Warner 2000: 18, 23). As '(...) in any marriages of convenience, conflict between an interest group and its chosen party always lurks in the background and occasionally becomes manifest' (*ibid*: 116). Even in the European labour movements, the basis for close relationships soon become a pragmatic alliance in addition to overlapping long-term policy objectives (cf. Taylor 1993: 134). As Minkin (1991: xiiii) phrases it utilising the British case: 'Politics was always both a necessary instrument and a problem for the unions'. The size of benefits and costs involved may fluctuate and change over time.

When the exchange of resources occurs efficiently, we may expect close party-group relationships, in terms of overlapping structures or strong inter-organisational links, to be maintained. But when 'one side in the exchange can no longer produce the goods that the other side seeks, or if those goods become less valuable to the recipient, we assume the institutional links will become weaker, as the costs (....) of being closely linked are likely to exceed the benefits for each actor' (Allern *et al.* 2009). Accordingly, a breakdown in the equilibrium of utility-maximising

66. There is also the potential for support once a party is in office and is implementing public policies. For example, co-operation with the workforce may breed industrial appeasement (Howell 2001: 13). Moreover, the amount and quality of information communicated is also relevant, and like party members, organisation members might serve as partisan ambassadors. But none of these benefits are considered as separate goods here for the sake of parsimony, and as the aim is, ultimately, to identify easily testable propositions (hypotheses).

approaches of the involved actors is likely to advance the erosion of already existing close relationships (cf. Bates *et al.* 1998: 8; see also Hall and Taylor 1996: 942–6).

Transaction Costs and Problems of Exchange

In recent years, primarily from the perspective of interest groups, some theorists have promoted an approach more explicitly based on theories of the transaction costs of economic exchange (see Coase 1937; Williamson 1979; Williamson and Winter 1993). Warner (2000) explicitly takes as a starting point that, in 'new institutional economics', a business firm is more than a mere production function. Firms are instead seen as governance structures in which certain, frequent transactions are organised more efficiently (at lower cost) than in the market. Major examples of transaction costs that firms seek to reduce are search and information costs when browsing the market, costs related to bargaining of acceptable agreements, and the costs of making sure that the other party sticks to the terms of a contract (Pierson 2000; Miller 2000).

As a consequence, services provided at a lower cost internally will be produced by the demander itself instead of being contracted for on the 'spot market' (Williamson 1979). More specifically, it is argued that if the goods and services which are traded cannot easily be used elsewhere if an agreed exchange is not fulfilled, these assets are specific and the exchange is vulnerable to attempts to renegotiate contracts. Therefore, such exchange is more efficiently organised in firms through 'vertical integration'.[67] It is also maintained that leaving an established relationship is difficult and costly, and acts as a disincentive to exit (Warner 2000: 30). When actors commit themselves to a structure which they expect will continue to exist, the costs of choosing other options increase (Pierson 2000: 490).[68]

Warner's argument is that interest groups are similar to this concept of the firm. Interest groups may choose to incorporate the supplier (the political party) or create an equivalent (a new party) in order to obtain the product, instead of frequently 'buying' it in the 'market'. To the extent that most benefits exchanged by an interest group and a political party are '(...) specific to their particular relationship, one might expect to find the group creating its own party or taking over an existing one' (Warner 2000: 29–30).[69] Warner emphasises that whereas the establishment of new parties is quite rare, a similar mechanism can lead both interest groups and political parties to establish *enduring alliances* – 'contracts of exchange' – in order

67. Moreover, frequency of trade and the exact level of market uncertainty (as regards demands and supply) also influence the likelihood of incorporation (Williamson 1979), but these factors are probably less relevant in a political context. Parties and interest groups are not involved in direct trade and the size of the 'political market' is more limited than economic markets.

68. The costs of leaving an established relationship is often named 'sunk costs' or 'opportunity costs' (Warner 2000: 30).

69. For example, Warner (2000: 29) points to finances as an asset which is specific to a relationship since it is difficult to redeploy once invested. Thus, if a group must support a party financially to succeed, is has specific assets invested. In contrast, it is easier to suddenly prevent the party from using its organisational facilities.

to decrease transaction costs such as the problem of making party leaders keep their policy promises (Warner 2000: 28–30, 100–5). As in the political exchange between party leaders and members (cf. Strøm and Müller 1999: 16–8), key problems are imperfect information and non-simultaneity.

However, unlike other scholars using similar theory on party organisations, Warner (2000: 163–4, 97) does not explicitly depict links as an *organisational* phenomenon to overcome problems of enforcement. Whereas, in contrast, Quinn (2002) assumes that parties, seen as analogous to business firms, incorporate interest groups in their organisational structure in order to guarantee stability in the provision of monetary support and labour. For their part, interest groups join such 'institutionalised frameworks' to make the parties' supply of policy more reliable. If interest groups anticipate that parties will break promises, for example by implementing other policies than previously offered in government, they may undersupply resources like labour and financial support. Hence, it might also be useful for parties to establish 'credible compensation mechanisms' with interest groups.

Specifically, Quinn (2002) suggests that in the case of British Labour and trade unions, the formal affiliation, representation and voting rights of the trade unions have provided greater stability and reliability in the party's and the unions' exchange of finances, labour and policy. Inter-organisational links like permanent liaison committees may fill a similar function. Hence, particularly close relations between parties and interest groups can be seen as 'aggregations of rules with members (…) agreeing to follow those rules in exchange for such benefits as they are able to derive from their membership within the structure' (Peters 1999: 47).

However, the concern here is with the *general* relationship of parties with interest groups, not only links that constitute 'institutionalised frameworks'. Weaker links, and relations with groups that are not necessarily strongly organised themselves, are also studied. Therefore, the cost-benefit analysis needs to discuss under what circumstances different parties (elites) (and interest groups [elites]) will choose differing *degrees of closeness*, in terms of classes and specific kinds of links and clear differences in intensity of contact. In addition, the issue of the parties' *range of relationships* needs to be addressed separately. So in the remainder of this section, a broader and thus 'softer' cost-benefit model is instead further specified. Variation in types of transaction costs and the degree of asset specifics is not at the core of this analysis. Nor is the concept of 'credible compensation mechanisms' discussed in further detail. As party organisations are the objects of analysis, the primary focus is on the party side of the relationship.

A General Cost-Benefit Model

Establishing close relations with one or more interest groups is a way to make the exchange of resources such as the supply of votes, monetary support and policy rewards more reliable. Faced by a set of interest groups, it is assumed that a party assesses the voting record of organisation members, membership size and the amount of monetary and organisational resources to be provided. As a result, differences in party relationships with interest groups will vary systematically according to the benefits that can be provided to the party by various interest groups.

The fewer benefits provided to a party from a specific kind of interest group, the less likely it is that the party will opt for a close relationship with that organisation and the more likely it is to prefer a fairly or very distant relationship (*ad hoc based relationships* of *issue-based contact*). If, on the other hand, benefits for the parties' pursuit of goals are significant, a close relationship, such as an *integrated type* or an *inter-organisational alliance* is more likely to be chosen. But as this degree of closeness creates a more binding exchange, parties are unlikely to be linked with *many* interest groups in this way. In fact, a feasible trade-off is probably a fairly narrow range of relationships. If a party receives large amounts of resources from a specific segment, it does probably not receive as much from competing interests.

Also, according to rational choice theory, parties will evaluate the benefits in light of what they have to 'pay' for its support (Warner 2000: 184) – above all, in terms of *the risk of repelling significant voter groups* and/or *coalition partners* and *policy sacrifices*. Hence, we assume that these specific and variable costs involved in a relationship must be lower than the benefits for parties to choose strong links instead of opting for greater distance. However, while the resources supplied by interest groups may, indirectly, benefit office-seeking and policy-seeking purposes in a similar way, parties' evaluation of the costs is likely to depend significantly on goal priorities. All parties will calculate the usefulness of (strong) links with interest groups in light of their party's ideological orientation (cf. Warner 2000: 184). Truly close relations, identified by overlapping organisational structures, presupposes some kind of consensus on basic policy issues. But parties are probably willing to sacrifice its policies to different degrees depending on how strongly they emphasise access to office (spoils) as valuable *per se*. Their willingness to stay in a close relationship with a 'friendly' associate that actually repels significant voter groups is likely to depend on how highly they value policy-seeking compared to office-seeking.

Nevertheless, for the sake of simplicity, a distinction between office-seeking and emphasis on policy as 'ideological purism' is the only distinction made in what follows: it is assumed that most parties are willing to compromise with interest groups to participate in government on a regular basis, either because access to office may allow more of the party's ideological preferences to be implemented as public policy or because they value spoils *per se* (cf. Allern and Aylott 2009). At the same time, the assumption is that some parties are not interested in participating in government and that they virtually avoid seeking office by, at least temporarily, cultivating their role as an ideologically 'pure' opposition party.[70] The distinction is, obviously, reductionist, but it is parsimonious.[71] Also, it largely avoids seeking to attribute goals on the basis of observed behaviour and thereby running the risk of tautologically arguing that behaviour is thus shaped by preferences

70. The underlying motive for this choice might, of course, vary. Some 'anti-establishment' or 'anti-system' parties may simply not want to assume responsibility for public policy in general, while others parties fear that office-seeking entails the danger of 'exterminating' themselves given that access to office would usually mean joining a coalition government.

71. For a discussion of different meanings of 'policy pursuit', see Strøm and Müller (1999: 7).

(Hadenius 1984: 153; 24; Sjöblom 1980: 162–5). It is simply assumed that 'office-seeking parties' (as defined here) tend to avoid relations involving costs that make a relationship in sum *decrease* the chances of getting access to office on a regular basis, while 'ideologically purist' parties might be willing to accept overall limited usefulness for office-seeking as long as the links generate resources that support its ability to articulate policy views. The distinction also implies, of course, that some parties are willing to sacrifice less of its policies to receive benefits from interest groups than others, but as discrete policy decisions are beyond the scope of this study, that aspect is left aside here.

In any case, if no interest group offers especially valuable benefits to any party, it can be hypothesised that parties will generally have weak links with interest groups, but perhaps relationships with more and various interest groups if the relevant links prove sufficiently useful. The more organisations from which a party can receive some benefits, the more likely it is to establish relationships with a wide range of interest groups. If interest groups are generally not attractive target groups for a party, the party leadership will probably rely on other sources and methods. However, a party may also establish links in order to generate more resources in the future. According to general rational choice theory, the *threat* of costs or *promise* of rewards may motivate actors just as much as the reward or the punishment itself (Scott 2000). As argued earlier, closeness in terms of links for contact is likely to *increase* the chances for actually obtaining significant benefits: for example, a party can establish links with a group with the aim of improving its reputation among organisation members. Here it is not easy to decide what came first – a close relationship, or significant benefits. But the assumption is that there must be a significant potential for exchange of valuable resources for a party to get involved in close relationships.

Nor is it obvious if the status as party in power or opposition influences the calculation. On the one hand, governing parties perhaps do not need close relationships as much as parties in opposition do, because they have access to corporative structures and expertise. Moreover, governing responsibilities are difficult to combine with binding interest group co-operation. New parties, in contrast, may need strong links to grow (cf. Schwartz 2005: 53–5). On the other hand, it might be that (prospective) governing parties will tend to cultivate links with interest groups more assiduously since they are particularly concerned about implementation assistance (cf. Minkin 1991: 639–41, 648). The point is that if parties and interest groups are enmeshed in fairly close relationships, they in fact receive, or are likely to receive, significant resources compared to the costs involved.

Finally, the question is whether we also need to look into the internal power structure of the party organisation in question. Internal power relations may influence the choices party leaders make as regards links with interest groups. It is, for example, possible to argue that a party leadership will hesitate to establish new links or abolish old relationships with interest groups if the choice entails the risk of severe internal conflicts. Even though party members seem to have lost power in recent decades, grassroots and mid-level activists still have a say in European parties.[72] In studies of discrete party *change*, internal resistance has been shown to slow down the pace of change (Harmel and Janda 1994). Yet, again for the sake of parsimony – and since the aim is not to look at particular decisions concerning links with interest groups – the analytical focus will be on the party leadership (cf. Warner 2000). As we shall see, the other theory perspectives put stronger emphasis on intra-party relations.

Relations According to Interest Groups

Before turning to the alternative explanatory perspectives, a few words are in order concerning the interest-group side of the cost-benefit model, even if parties are the units of analysis in this book. It seems evident that a party cannot be linked with an interest group that does not want to have contact, and the strength of party links will certainly depend on the interest groups as well (Warner 2000). If a cost-benefit analysis of the party side does not reveal a systematic pattern, a brief look at the perspective of the interest groups may provide another piece to the puzzle.[73]

Under what conditions do interest groups seek or maintain a close relationship, with one or multiple parties? Presumably, the primary aims of these organisations in politics are to maximise their memberships (if relevant) and to promote the special interests of their members or a particular cause (cf. Allern *et al.* 2007). Parties may recommend organisation membership and provide interest groups with not only valuable information about the political process, but also access to office and policy rewards. Even though many organisations formally are politically neutral, '(…) they represent interests with which parties are strongly concerned in their platforms and policies (…)' (Valen and Katz 1964: 312).

Through a more well-organised relationship with specific parties, interest groups get more reliable access to legislation, they may 'pre-programme' politicians and improve their own chances for policy rewards (Warner 2000: 98). In this way, links with parties may enhance an interest organisation's ability to offer benefits to its members, in particular collective benefits (Allern *et al.* 2007). For groups that are not in opposition to the establishment as a whole, well-established parties with regular access to government stand out as particularly attractive. Also, a party may contribute to increased memberships in interest organisations through compulsory or suggested affiliation for party members.

However, closeness is also associated with a potential increase of drawbacks. An intimate relationship with only one party may well seem disadvantageous as long as parties combine several interests and organisations work for one interest group. Although European trade unions have shown that it is to some extent possible to combine close relationships with one party and non-partisan participation in public policy-making (Wilson 1990: 160), interest groups are likely to hesitate before putting all their eggs in one basket (Kirchheimer 1966: 193): a close rela-

72. This argument could be related to the fact that strong leadership accountability often means emphasis on core policy (Strøm and Müller 1999: 18).

73. For a more detailed elaboration of costs and benefits for interest organisations associated with party-interest group relationships, see Warner (2000), but also Neumann (1956: 412); Wilson (1990); Quinn (2003); and Schwartz (2005).

tionship with one party may lead to a loss of credibility with others (Wilson 1990: 160), and perhaps even with the parties currently in power (Schwartz 2005: 44). As Dalton (1994: 238–9) points out, groups may pursue differing issues, depending on which party is in power. Furthermore, closeness entails the danger of becoming a political hostage to particular public policies (cf. Heidar 1981: 8), and there is the risk of directly repulsing (potential) members and supporters voting for other parties (Warner 2000: 102).[74]

Hence, according to rational choice theory on the exchange between parties and interest groups, organisation elites will calculate whether the (potential) benefits (members, policy rewards, and access to office) compensate for potential drawbacks. In brief, it can be hypothesised that an interest group is most likely to prefer a fairly distant relationship (if any at all), if association becomes relatively costly for the group's reputation or if a party has failed on a key issue of concern (cf. Warner 2000). Maintaining overlapping organisational structures is probably an option only if the party can deliver favourable policies that its competitors cannot match.

HISTORICAL INSTITUTIONALISM: THE IMPACT OF CONTEXT AND HISTORY

How would the less deductive school of historical institutionalism approach the issue of political parties' relations with interest groups?[75] The aim is here not to generate a wholesale alternative explanatory perspective. The idea is to further clarify what non-instrumental behaviour *vis-à-vis* interest groups would look like, and to lay the foundation for a secondary hypothesis that might help us to take account of possible deviations from a rational course.

General Assumptions

Traditionally, the argument outlining the core difference between rational choice theory and historical institutionalism is centred on whether preference formation is treated as exogenous or as endogenous. Historical institutional theory maintains that not only strategies but also the goals that the actors pursue are shaped by the institutional environment, which is defined as being not only the formal setting, but also informal procedures, routines and norms (Hall and Taylor 1996: 938–9). Thus, the basic goal preferences of political actors need to be explained by historical and context-sensitive analyses (Thelen and Steinmo 1992: 8–9). But most important in this context, historical institutionalism takes as a starting point that there will generally be more than one way to achieve an actor's ends, and it is (more)

74. It is widely agreed that such risks have increased within the labour movement in recent decades (see Howell 2001), and also characterises new social movements like environmental groups (Dalton 1994). Moreover, it has been reported that movement organisations like the Greenpeace and Amnesty International consider a non-partisan image as a precondition for their own fund-raising capacity (Poguntke 2002: 48).

75. As will become clear, the outline is primarily based on historical institutionalism as described by Hall and Taylor (1996), Thelen and Steinmo (1992); and Pierson (2000). The literature known as 'historical institutionalism' is diverse, so what follows is certainly not a complete outline.

strongly emphasised that real-life organisations are only boundedly rational: political actors do not have all the necessary information to be utility-maximisers (Simon 1985). As in normative (sociological) institutionalism, political actors are argued to be better described as rule- or routine-following 'satisficers' rather than utility-maximisers (DiMaggio and Powell 1991: 9; Thelen and Steinmo 1992: 8).

Whether political actors can manage to create institutional arrangements that increase the credibility of mutual commitments over time is also questioned. Pierson (2000) argues that it is relatively difficult to measure what is exchanged in politics, since the goals are more diffuse, and there is a much looser coupling between actions and outcomes in politics. Furthermore, the efficiency-creating mechanisms so central in market economy – 'competition' and 'learning' – are fairly weak elements in politics: '(…) poor performance (...) is not always easy to identify or to attribute to a particular source' (*ibid*: 488). Therefore, it is argued, politics must be analysed as a dynamic process which might produce unintended consequences (Thelen 1999: 382–3).

Moreover, historical institutionalism emphasises that institutional arrangements and organisations are hard to change in politics. Indeed, as shown above, rational choice theorists have increasingly acknowledged that exiting from an institutionalised arrangement is costly and uncertain, but historical institutionalism puts particularly strong emphasis on institutional 'stickiness'. More specifically, '(…) the policy choices made when an institution is being formed, or when a policy is initiated, will have continuing and largely determinate influence over the policy far into the future' (Peters 1999: 63). The logic is called 'path dependency', and calls for research into historical developments when explaining patterns of behaviour in politics today (Thelen and Steinmo 1992; Pierson 2000). General operative forces are mediated by contextual features that are often inherited from the past (Hall and Taylor 1996: 941). Actors adapt their strategies to the institutional frame within which they act, thereby strengthening the logic of the system itself. Such positive feedback mechanisms may lead to the survival of solutions even after they have become disadvantageous for the actors involved (Thelen 1999; Pierson 2000: 492). Traditionally, historical institutionalism has been less precise than rational choice institutionalism as to exactly how institutions affect behaviour (Hall and Taylor 1996: 950; Thelen 1999: 370). Presumably, institutions change radically only when critical junctures occur, and the historical development moves onto a new path (Thelen 1999: 387).

Applied to party politics, the electoral market mechanism described by party scholars informed by rational choice theory would be seen as an unrealistic assumption. It would be emphasised that the number of competing parties are naturally limited – and the competition not free – for example due to electoral thresholds (cf. Ware 1979). Hence, informed by Pierson's argument, a historical-institutional perspective on party politics would hold that limited success in pursuing primary goals does not readily lead to modification in party strategy in terms of organisation and political behaviour. Rational choice theorists have in recent years made the difference less stark by for example admitting the possibility of multiple party goals (cf. Thelen 1999: 374–5). However, although parties seek access to office and realisation of policy, historical institutionalism would suggest that party leaders might also have other primary goals, for example intra-party democracy, and that the preferences taken for granted by rational choice theory need to be *explained* by historical and contextual analyses.

In the existing literature on political parties, similar arguments are, above all, articulated by Angelo Panebianco. Panebianco (1988: 6–9) takes as a starting point that parties are organisations which do not generally act as unified benefit-maximisers. They are themselves complex institutions in which party leaders are embedded. Moreover, Panebianco (1988: 58) emphasises that a party's characteristics '(...) depend more upon its history, i.e. how the organization originated and how it consolidated, than upon any other factor (....). Every organization bears the mark of its formation, of the crucial political-administrative decisions made by its founders, the decisions which "moulded" the organization'. The strategic options of today's leadership are restricted by previous choices and structures of conflict following previous choices. Political parties, and especially well-established ones, are therefore an inert mass, in which radical transformational changes seldom occur (Harmel and Janda 1994, but see also Kitschelt 1994: 212). For fundamental changes to occur, such as change of ideology and relationship with external organisations, electoral shocks and alternation of leadership (or of 'dominant coalition' which is often the de facto leadership) are needed (Harmel and Janda 1994; Panebianco 1988: 58, 243-4).

Party-interest Group Relationships: A Historical Perspective[76]

According to historical institutional theory, we will obviously not expect party relations with interest groups to be largely marked and shaped by cost-benefit calculations of party leaders in the light of specific goals.[77] The chain between establishing links with interest groups and the goals that parties pursue more or less instrumentally is considered to be too long, and the current political context and events may lead party leaders to give priority to different objectives within a specific period of time. What is dysfunctional for one party may well be profitable for another, and competition and learning are held to be limited in politics. Hence, there is no such thing as an 'ideal way' of being linked with interest groups for parties (or vice versa), and variation between parties is deemed to be not mainly due to differing cost-benefit analyses.

In addition to the current political context and events, a major source of variation between party relationships with interest groups according to historical institutionalism is instead historical choices and structures. Borrowing Warner's (2000: 40) words, the relationships that political parties have with interest groups might have been placed on different trajectories which prove hard to leave. Therefore, contemporary party-interest group relationships can be expected to reflect his-

76. As will become clear, the nature of this perspective makes a specific paragraph on the interest group side of the relationships less necessary.

77. If we can identify primary goals which correspond to variation in interest-group relationships, the priority needs to be explained.

torical differences including traditional organisational routines. Relationships between parties and interest groups which were once integrated, or institutionalised, are legacies of historical processes. A close relationship between particular parties and interest groups may exist even if it is now 'dysfunctional' or 'inefficient'.

According to Panebianco (1988: 51–9), the presence or absence of an external sponsor organisation is an important part of a party organisation's genetic model that continues to shape its relationship with interest groups. Consequently, parties that were once heavily dependent on an external sponsor do not reach the same level of autonomy as parties whose resources are not controlled by others. The party functions as the 'political arm' of the sponsor group and is, in the main, externally legitimated. As a result, the freedom to adapt to changing societal circumstances is more limited in these cases. Hence, it can be assumed that parties that were originally dominated by an external organisation are today less likely to be characterised by a wide range of more distant relationships than the case with originally more independent ones. More generally, it can be argued that an old history of close relationships with interest groups also entails a legacy that makes the costs of reversal high for both parts and constrains the current leadership's flexibility to adapt to contemporary social and political conditions (cf. Thelen and Steinmo 1992; Warner 2000: 134). The links may even be reinforced – by the parties' and interest groups' adaptation to their internal logic – and thereby outlive the circumstances that gave rise to them (cf. Thelen 1999). So when trying to explain contemporary patterns of relationships we need to look at the parties in retrospect to detect possible historical paths. Seen from the perspective of historical institutionalism, variation in party interest group links today are assumed to mirror historical differences in closeness to particular groups (cf. Allern *et al.* 2007).

NORMATIVE INSTITUTIONALISM: THE IMPORTANCE OF NORMS AND INSTITUTIONALISATION

Another theoretical perspective which can help us to put the cost-benefit analysis of party relationships with interest groups in perspective is 'normative institutionalism'.[78] This approach is above all associated with the work of March and Olsen (see 1984; 1989). It has been criticised for making amorphous statements which are hard to disprove (see Peters 1999: 98), but it is worthwhile exploring what one can expect to shape parties' relationship with interest groups based on this contrast to rational choice theory. Despite the usual emphasis of party researchers on the role of political parties in democracy, there has as yet been little reference to this type of institutional theory but, as will become clear, similar ideas can be found again in the literature on party organisations.

78. Normative institutionalism is rooted in sociological institutional theory, but, according to Peter's (1999: 110) comparative review of the new institutionalism(s) puts stronger emphasis on political behaviour and the active shaping of institutions.

General Assumptions

A basic assumption embraced by normative institutional theory on political organisation and behaviour is, as in historical institutionalism, that political actors do not generally behave as rational utility-maximisers of well-defined goals. Political organisations or institutions are assumed to have multiple intentions, which are not necessarily consistent, and often ambiguous (March and Olsen 1989: 65–6). Political organisations are also seen as much more than formal structures; they represent complex systems of values, attitudes, understandings, and routines which socialise individual behaviour and shape leaders' decisions about specific aims and tools, organisational reform and political behaviour (cf. March and Olsen 1984; March and Olsen 1989: 21–6; Peters 1999: 26; March and Olsen 2004; Olsen 2009).

In the party literature, emphasis on such internal dynamics, in addition to instrumental goal-seeking, is, above all, articulated by Panebianco (1988). Indeed, Panebianco puts strong emphasis on historical legacy, and does *not* refer to 'normative institutionalism' himself. But, he includes similar elements (cf. Hermansson 2004: 33–7). Like Michels (1911/1962), Panebianco (1988: 53–4) maintains that parties are established, structured and initially managed in order to realise certain goals (values, interest and policy views) shared by their founders. But this 'official aim' does not continue to inform its choices in terms of simple policy-seeking through elections. Anchored in party manifestos, the party's original core values and ideas – the features making the party distinct from other parties – become a part of the organisational structure itself.[79]

Party ideology conceals the distribution of selective incentives and is seen a key source of collective benefits provided to party members because it maintains the *party identity* in the eyes of its supporters (Panebianco 1988: 11). Thus, party leaders' freedom of action is strongly limited by more than the party members' formal rights to control their leaders. Despite shifting circumstances, a party's strategic choices also need to take account of what is seen as the party's *raison d'être*: to gain and maintain legitimacy, the party leadership – or the *de facto* 'dominant coalition' – needs to accommodate the strategies to the party's original political purpose. Indication of means improves the leaders' ability to function as a 'symbolic centre of identification'. If a political strategy fails and loses credibility, the party identity suffers (cf. Panebianco 1988: 41). But equally important, any leader who, by proposing a new political strategy, puts into question the historical perception of what justifies the party's existence risks being seen as illegitimate. 'Party activities which blatantly contradict the official goals often result in unacceptable organizational costs' (Panebianco 1988: 11).

However, Panebianco (1988: 6–7, 17, 240) adds that the significance of a party's ideological origin, which may be summarised as its identity, will decrease over time. After a phase of institutionalisation, party organisations change from what Selznick (1957) defined as rational organisational tools, to *institutions.* Institutionalisation is commonly defined as 'routinisation' of party organisation

79. Cf. Selznick (1957) on 'the institutional embodiment of purpose'.

and behaviour (Harmel and Svåsand 1993: 35; Levitsky 2009: 317).[80] Panebianco (1988: 55–60) also offers indicators of routinisation, such as the development of a centralised party bureaucracy, but more broadly defines institutionalisation as the state where the party becomes valuable in and of itself.[81] The party organisation, he argues, decreasingly sees itself as the representative of a social group or an ideology, and there ensues a shift of balance from formal (official) to informal goals. The prevailing collective goal, and the party leadership's key task, then becomes simply to ensure that the party survive fierce electoral competition (Panebianco 1988: 8–9). But this does not mean that the parties transform into unitary vote- or office-maximising collective actors. The freedom of 'dominant coalitions' is still, to some extent, limited by numerous competing stakeholders and by the collective party identity (*ibid:* 18–9).[82]

Furthermore, based on normative institutionalism in general, it could be argued that at another level parties as collective actors are constrained by general institutional norms of democracy towards political parties. Organisations are expected to accommodate or conform to societal rules or ideas of what defines the *class* of institution to which they belong (cf. March and Olsen 1984). Thus the survival of political organisations like parties depends on their ability to fulfil the democratic normative expectations (March and Olsen 1995: 190; Peters 1999: 112). Some are taken for granted and can in practice render the cost-efficient options of action out of the question – leaders instead follow the *logic of appropriateness* (March and Olsen 1984; 1989). In fact, it is suggested, choices made by political organisations (or more precisely their leaders) may well be irrational and subject to myths (see Meyer and Rowan 1977; Di Maggio and Powell 1983).

Related arguments, varying in levels of explicitness, can be found in the scholarly literature on political parties. In most established democracies, parties are basically seen as organisations whose *common* 'raison d'être is to create a substan-

80. Harmel and Svåsand (1993) distinguish between three phases of institutionalisation: identification, organisation and stabilisation. The first concerns development of a public message, the second deals with development of organisational routines and capacity, and the final is about development of reputation and relations with other parties. For an overview of different definitions of party institutionalisation, see Pedahzur and Brichta (2002).

81. More precisely, according to Panebianco (1988: 54) institutionalisation is about '(1) the development of interest related to the organization's preservation (…), and (2) the development of diffuse loyalties'. Hence, institutionalisation in this sense both requires introduction of selective incentives to individuals (like career possibilities) and collective incentives (of identity) to members and core voters, and illustrates that there are not water-tight boundaries to rational choice theory. What is a relatively strong degree of institutionalisation may vary over time. Panebianco (1988: 267) paradoxically concludes that during the second half of the twentieth century a rather uniform process of de-institutionalisation of parties have taken place in terms of the decline of the strongly organised mass parties.

82. As Levitsky (2009: 319) points out, 'routinization and value infusion are distinct organizational phenomena that do not necessarily occur together'. However, the major point here is that parties' original ideology are suggested to become less important over time due to focus on party survival. Moreover, it is assumed that close relations between parties and interest groups require a minimum of organisational structure on both sides.

tive connection between the rulers and the ruled' (Lawson 1980: 3). Attention to democracy in party platforms is spread across the ideological spectrum (Kittilson and Scarrow 2003). Democratically functional party institution is one that is able to connect citizens to the state and public opinion to public policy (Peters 1999: 112). However, of most interest to us are the factors that may contribute to *differences* in party behaviour. Alternative normative expectations regarding democracy and parties may well co-exist within one and the same society. As individual actors in politics, parties play multiple roles (cf. March and Olsen 2004: 9). The social development towards increased interest pluralism may have led to a heightened emphasis on the governing role of political parties (Katz and Mair 1995), through mediation between various voter groups, at the expense of interest representation and made the *catch-all party* model culturally 'normal'.[83] But the leaders of party organisations within a single system can, over time, choose to emphasise the expectations associated with different models of democracy to varying degrees. Whilst some parties – or ideological party 'families' – clearly support the idea that the major role of parties is efficient interest representation, others highlight the governing role of political parties in democracy, i.e. orientation towards the society as a whole (cf. Wright 1971). The former norm is also identified as the 'representation' mission of parties (Harmel and Janda 1994: 377).[84] The latter corresponds to pluralist liberal democratic theory. Here parties are supposed to cross-cut the major ideological and social cleavages of society and thus not serve as an advocate for specific social groups (Katz 1997: 60). In a certain sense, emphasis on the governing role also echoes Edmund Burke's concept of parties as bodies '(…) of men united for promoting by their joint endeavours the national interest upon some particular principle in which they are all agreed' (quoted in Ware 1996: 5).

Party-interest Group Relationships as Accommodation to Identity and Norms

What does this alternative understanding of party politics imply for party relationships with interest groups? In general, normative institutionalism would not expect party-interest group relationships to be primarily based on cost-benefit calculations. Instead, party relations are assumed to reflect accommodation to party identity and norms. More specifically, parties are largely expected to vary according to ideological origins and normative conceptions of democracy.

83. Such a phenomenon can be referred to as 'isomorphism' or diffusion of institutionalized myths' within a 'field of organizations' according to the sociological organisation theory (see Meyer and Rowan 1977; DiMaggio and Powell 1983). But note that it could be argued there is a basic difference between March and Olsen's 'logic of appropriateness' and the theory of an organisational field. The former describe conscious accommodation to norms through conviction and the other a less deliberate adaptation to conventions and organisational myths driven by an assumed need for legitimacy in the environment (Bátora 2006: 38). Thelen (1999: 386) describes the isomorphism in organisational fields as some sort of a path dependency: 'political actors extract causal designations from the world around them (...)'.

84. It might, as Harmel and Janda (1994: 377) themselves do, be presented as a separate party goal, but in this context it functions as a normative expectation.

First, the assumption that party ideology becomes part of a constraining organisational structure means that a party which was once established as an organisational tool for a particular class, social group or cause will probably continue to view its relationships with other organisations in the light of this original 'ownership'. If strong links with an associated interest organisation once existed, party members might still see this political strategy as a symbol of the party's basic rationale, as a confirmation of the party identity, and leaders who try to modify can expect to encounter significant resistance. Party elites are, to a certain extent, 'prisoners' of their historical political strategies in relation to interest groups (cf. Panebianco 1988: 41). The argument echoes von Beyme (1985: 193–5) who pointed to the historical correspondence between party ideology and type of party membership: for example the British model of collectively affiliated unions was in line with the country's tradition of guild socialism

Hence, parties are more likely to be marked by closeness to particular interest groups, which were a traditional associate, than parties which were originally established more independently of well-defined interests. In these cases, the party ideology, as an indication of party identity, will probably make it less easy to loosen old relations and establish links with other groups as these might be historical or new opponents to their original ally. For instance, social democratic parties might see 'unity' and 'solidarity' within the labour movement as a whole as a way to ensure that their official goals not get lost. Or to put it differently, party-union links – and union friendly policies – might function as means by which the party leaders' improve their ability to serve as a 'symbolic centre' of party identification.[85]

In contrast, centre-right parties are often concerned with what they see as cross-class, national interests and might therefore consider strong links with particular interest groups as being at odds with the party's collective identity. In some cases they even have an anti-ideological nature which might, as von Beyme (1985: 50) has argued, serve to make adaptation to new political items easier. Thus, seen from a norm-based perspective, originally class-based, confession-based or issue-oriented political parties will less readily adapt to, and therefore less likely be characterised by, the pattern of weaker links with a wide range of interest groups than will parties established with a cross-class or in other ways 'catch-all' orientation.

However, according to Panebianco's (1988) argument, the process of institutionalisation will weaken the importance of the party's original political aims and associated values over time. As a consequence, if parties emerged as the organisational tool for a specific group, well-established, i.e. strongly institutionalised, parties are more autonomous from this environment than newly established ones. If the party was created by a charismatic leader, institutionalisation would

85. Along similar lines, Minkin (1991) explains why the British party-union alliance has survived over time: informal norms have regulated party union behaviour and weakened the conflict potential. For example, the value of union autonomy from the state has led to the 'rule' that British Labour governments should not hinder the unions' pursuit of industrial interests, whilst unions in return should not punish the party if it fails to deliver the public policies they prefer (see also Quinn 2003).

instead involve, or lead to, a transfer of loyalties from the leader to the organisation (Panebianco 1988: 53–4). So, it can also be hypothesised that old, i.e. the most strongly institutionalised, parties tend to have a more distant relationship with originally associated interest groups, and are more likely to have a wide-ranging network of links, than are parties that have been recently established as an organisational tool for a particular social group or cause. For example, as mentioned in Chapter 4, new left and green parties, which focus on hitherto-ignored social interests, have been argued to follow what Kitschelt refers to as 'logic of constituency representation': they model their organisation on the ideas and practices of the social movements (Kitschelt 1989: 67). Ideological reservation may thus, for example, 'dictate' new left and green parties away from exchange with professional and economic interest groups (cf. Kitschelt 1989: 245). Meanwhile, different kinds of populist right parties' relationship with interest groups have, with a few exceptions, been described as traditionally more distant than all others as the leadership's legitimacy is primarily based on the leader's charisma and not on organised links into civil society (see Ignazi 1996; Gunther and Diamond 2001: 11; Hopkin and Paolucci 1999). True, also newer parties have, by the early 2000s, institutionalised to some extent in the sense that they have become more firmly organised, mainstream-like party organisations (see Harmel and Svåsand 1993: 77). Yet, they are significantly younger than the parties established before the Second World War. Hence, if links originally existed, new parties are less likely to have distanced their associates by the early 2000s, according to this argument. Pedahzur and Brichta (2002) argue that the successful organisational development of some 'charismatic parties' questions Panebianco's definition of institutionalisation as autonomy from the charismatic leader. However, this question will not be further explored until the explanatory analysis in Chapter 16.

Second, in line with the idea of 'logic of appropriateness', it can be suggested that parties establish links with interest groups that correspond to the normative democratic expectations of parties. Moreover, parties may prefer wide-ranging and distant relationships by arguing that this is what 'modern' parties in Western democracies do. But most importantly, different views on what is the primary role of political parties in democracy may well give rise to variation in relationships with interest groups. In a norm-based perspective, not all options are necessarily available to all parties. Some parties may simply prioritise their image and practice as an 'open' or 'embedded' organisation more than others. Parties that advocate social representation of groups will probably have tried to compensate for what they have lost (old parties), or never gained (new parties) in membership by cultivating organised and informal links with interest groups (cf. Poguntke 2000, quoted in Puhle 2002: 74–5). By contrast, according to a norm-based perspective, parties that emphasise the governing role through interest mediation, thereby espousing pluralist values, will probably try to signal this view by maintaining greater distance from interest groups in general.

With regard to the range of relationships, a systematic difference can also be expected for matters of principle against this background. Although pluralist societies make it hard to define interest representation as the articulation of particular group interests, and all parties are involved in interest mediation, emphasis on interest articulation nonetheless calls for a certain level of distinctiveness for major parties. Thus, according to this perspective, it might seem illegitimate, or 'inappropriate', for such parties' organisations to treat all kinds of interest groups on equal terms. Instead, they may choose to demonstrate a certain profile by limiting their networks. Accordingly, parties that primarily endorse the governing role of parties can reasonably be expected to deliberately discriminate less between different groups according to the perspective based on normative institutionalism.

The Relations According to Interest Groups

Even though theorists do not depict party-interest group relations as exchange, a brief look into the normative cores of interest groups is also required if when trying to explore the importance of such factors. First, it might be suspected that variation in the general role perception of interest groups may contribute to variation between parties' external relationships. Despite the existence of general norms for non-party intermediary institutions, it has been argued that interest groups in Western societies also define their major mission in society in various ways (cf. Warner 2000: 74). Whereas some interest groups see themselves as a complete *alternative* to parties, other groups regard their organisations as full-blown political actors who appropriately interact closely with particular political parties.

Historically, for example, some trade unions came to be engaged in a broad range of policy issues, whereas other employees' organisations have regarded partisan commitment as '(…) inherently undesirable because it is incompatible with the professional status of the group' (Wilson 1990: 160). For various reasons, new social movements are often sceptical to parties in general (Kitschelt 1989; Dalton 1994: 227). Indeed, involvement in movements does not exclude activity in conventional politics in practice (Goldstone 2004), but it could be argued that the social movements' anti-establishment identity calls for more distant relationships and a certain concentration on specific parties. According to Dalton (1994: 232), some environmentalists feel that parties avoid the fundamental questions they raise, and therefore are more a part of the problem than the solution. New groups like the environmental movement '(...) exercise a political role that is partially in conflict with the norms of partisan politics' (Dalton 1994: 232).

Interestingly, in recent years it has been argued that the European trade unions have begun to develop into little more than 'insurance companies', whose survival depends increasingly on the supply of selective incentives. If union members identify themselves less and less as members of the historical labour movement, and increasingly see themselves as individual employees, they may come to dislike the exclusive co-operation of their union with a particular party, or even the use of trade funds for political purposes at all (Poguntke 1998: 158). In any case, on the basis of a norm-based perspective on parties, it can generally be assumed that differences in party relationships with interest groups are connected with the role perception endorsed by various organisations. Parties are not likely to convince interest groups that embrace supra-partisanship as an institutional norm to take part in truly close relationships.

POSSIBLE IMPACT OF NATIONAL POLITICAL INSTITUTIONS

As part of the 'new institutionalism(s)' in political science, all the above-mentioned theoretical schools are also concerned with how national political institutions shape political strategies and outcome. Such enduring, possible constraints on parties' relationships with interest groups *in general* are further specified based on general theory and existing empirical research. The following list is not exhaustive and more specific assertions will have to be generated for use in empirical research. However, as this book will use such variables only to describe the case(s) of Norwegian parties, the outline is confined to a few general assumptions. Institutional variation is, of course, mostly to be found between rather than within countries (Strøm and Müller 1999: 24). In line with the basis in rational choice theory, the emphasis is on the utility aspect of links with interest groups, but other types of correspondence will also be indicated.

The *institutional make-up* of the political system imposes a general constraint on party organisations. The systemic context represents important incentive or disincentive structures for party organisation and behaviour. Both the institutional setting of representative and policy-making institutions and direct and indirect state regulations limit the range of strategic options: 'Institutions rule out some types of behaviour and make others more or less likely by influencing the costs and benefits that a party can expect when following a certain course of action' (Müller 2002: 252; see also Chhibber 1999: 9). Alternatively, institutions may colour preference formation by functioning as expressions of the democratic expectations that parties are supposed to meet (Thelen 1999; Peters 1999), and hereby make some types of party behaviour more likely than others. [86]

As to party relationships with interest groups, *the state structure* is probably the most relevant part of the institutional setting. A federal structure – in contrast to a unitary state – confines the development of strong national party organisations for numerous reasons. Above all due to the transfer of power to local levels, parties generally tend to allocate resources at the sub-national level, at the expense of national activities, in federal systems (Müller 2002: 253). The example par excellence is seen in the loosely organised, non-programmatic parties of the USA, where the structure of government allows fifty diverse states to regulate the political parties (Foster and Muste 1992: 12–13). Instead of integrated relationships with particular interest groups like trade unions, US electoral politics are characterised by a large number of organisations attempting to influence candidate selection and party manifestos from outside (Key 1942/1964; Rozell *et al.* 2006). Accordingly, it can be hypothesised that well-organised links between national extra-parliamentary parties and organised interest groups are less likely in federal states. Parties need freedom to take account of local variations, and they do not have the necessary organisational capacity at the national level.[87] Moreover, the

86. For a general discussion of how institutional framework can constrain the strategic options of parties, see Müller (2002).

87. Wilson (1990: 166–7) argues that the weak degree of formalisation of American parties as membership organisations make them easy to influence for interest groups. American political parties possess few resources themselves and are strongly dependent on external support.

political culture of local autonomy in federal states may limit the extent to which centralisation of party organisations and their relationships with interest groups will be seen as legitimate in a democratic perspective.

However, the correlation is not necessarily strong in either case. Germany is an example of a federal state that has well-organised parties and historically fairly close relationships between parties and interest groups (see Padgett and Paterson 1991: 180–2). A less radical proposition is that federal systems promote a greater variety of relationships than do unitary systems, especially if party organisations are loosely structured (Thomas 2001e: 274–5). According to Wilson (1990: 161) unitary states encourage interest groups to rely on technocratic lobbying because the centralisation of power makes decision-makers less open to the mobilisation of political force.

Parliamentary government – as opposed to separation of power – is another major institutional constraint that can promote some patterns of relationships more than others. According to Thomas (2001e: 274–5), parliamentary government has tended to encourage alliances between specific parties and interest groups, whilst separation of power has been associated with supra-partisan interest groups. When numerous power centres exist, it might be risky for interest groups to be strongly linked with one specific party (Wilson 1990: 162). Interest groups must always cultivate access to both branches, so they will hesitate to favour one party's candidates before elections (Rozell *et al.* 2006: 14–5). However, frequent alternation in government and minority government may weaken the differences between the two institutional settings in this regard. In such a parliamentary environment, interest groups cannot base their influence on friendly relationships with one party only. Parties that are out of power may have very little impact on the executive (cf. Thomas 2001e: 274–5; Selle 1997: 159).

As regards *direct state regulation*, the type of electoral system is obviously a relevant variable of which to take account. Electoral laws can help or hinder parties in their pursuit of all major goals (Müller 2002: 264). They influence parties' freedom of manoeuvre and might thus indirectly affect the usefulness of various ways of being linked with interest groups. Proportional multi-member systems (PR) and low thresholds open up for small fringe parties in contrast to single-member plurality systems (SM). PR systems therefore complicate the pattern of party competition, and make parties even less concerned with winning elections and more policy-seeking than in SM – or two-party – systems (Thomas 2001e: 275–6). As Berry (1997: 47) points out, green parties have emerged in Europe, whereas environmentalists in the United States have found themselves left with the option of engaging as a non-party actor in elections (see also Thomas 2001e: 275–6).

Accordingly, the advantage of a catch-all approach to voters appears limited in PR systems, especially if the threshold is low: parties risk splinter movements among ideologically-motivated members at the extremes (cf. Rokkan 1966: 92). Thus, it is possible to argue that having links with a wide range of interest groups is less useful in multi-party (PR) systems than in two-party (SM) systems. Parties with a limited range of rather close relationships are more likely to be found in the former than the latter setting. Moreover, it could be argued that a proportional system reflects the democratic value of interest articulation, whilst plurality systems promote aggregation (Katz 1997). In a two-party system, the normative standard is more likely electoral victory and access to office. In a proportional, multi-party system, a 'successful party' is rather one that can sustain its commitments to major constituencies (Peters 1999: 123). In consequence, the electoral system may define a particular range of relationships with interest groups as more in accordance with democratic values than others, and in this way constrain the choice of party leaders, seen from a normative perspective.

State funding of parties is another institutional regulation likely to affect parties and party competition. Whereas empirical research thus far has generally questioned the actual importance of this regulation (Pierre, Svåsand and Widfeldt 2000, Müller 2002: 263), it is highly relevant for the issue of links with interest groups. As Katz and Mair implicitly suggest (1995), the *size* of public subventions may create various incentive structures for party relations to civil society. Parties that receive generous support may be less enthusiastic about the benefits of close relationships with interest groups than parties in systems where public subventions are more modest (cf. Thomas 2001e: 276).

Indirectly, the *legal and constitutional regulations of interest groups* can also play a part (Thomas 2001e: 276–7). The extent of regulations varies between countries, and particularly regulated are the American parties and interest groups (*ibid:* 84). Such rules can impinge on the financial contributions donated by interest groups to parties (Müller 2002: 269), and hence on the incentive for parties to seek to establish well-organised and more binding links.[88] Moreover, from a normative perspective, regulations may signal that a certain distance between parties and interest groups is generally to be recommended in a democracy. Thus, it can be hypothesised that cross-national variations in closeness of parties to interest groups to some extent reflect differences in national structures of party finance. According to Shefter (1977: 414), the parties' power to disburse selective benefits to their constituencies represents a similar possible constraint: where parties were more divorced from the state apparatus and could not strongly develop patronage, they tended to develop a mass organisation and strong links with interest groups.

The existence of *corporatist arrangements* – interlocking arrangements between the government apparatus and organised interests (Padgett and Paterson 1991: 190) – is also a regulative limit to party organisation and behaviour (Müller

88. However, it should be noted that although the American system limits private financial contributions, it has been unable to place limits on campaign expenditures. Hence, parties and interest groups have tried to finds ways around the regulations. One particular result is the independent political action committees (PACs) attached to an interest group whose purpose is fund-raising for candidates (Thomas 2001d: 85; Conway *et al.* 2002). It can also be added that prohibition of political advertising on television may limit the need for party fund-raising among interest organisations. TV ads represent an expensive form of political communication. In many countries broadcasting of political ads is pervasive, but differences in regulations exist (Kaid and Holtz-Bacha 1995). In Norway and Sweden, for example, broadcasting of advertising is generally forbidden (NOU 2004: 25: 122–6).

2002: 269). This model of politics has in fact been said to undermine political parties as such, since more power is located in corporate arrangements (Yishai 1991: 10). For example, Kristiansen (1991: 139–40) argues that the need for a pure farmers' party decreased in Norway when interest organisations came to play a more active role in public policy-making. Parties become less attractive target groups for interest organisations, which call for fewer links between parties and interest groups in general. On the other hand, corporatist structures tend to favour major interest groups. Hence, numerous organisations are left with the option of seeking access to political party parties (cf. Selle 1997: 159). Strong corporatism may also enable parties to win and maintain office more efficiently. Even when out of government, parties may influence public policy through their associated interest group(s) (Müller 2002: 269; see also Thomas 2001e: 276), and strong corporatist arrangements have often been associated with close party-union relationships (e.g. Padgett and Paterson 1991: 178, 192). Hence, we can hypothesise that corporatism will promote party-interest group contact, but not wide-ranging relationships. Recently, however, it has alternatively been argued that a close relationship between social democrats and unions is detrimental to corporatism in polarised political environments as unions might be 'tempted to seek direct political influence instead of bargaining with employer organizations' (Anthonsen *et al.*, forthcoming).

Finally, based on the perspective of normative institutionalism, it can be argued that the prevailing *national political culture* may temper the impact of party specific values, and enable more cross-national variations. Parties operating in systems where ideals of interest articulation are strong may experience a relatively greater pull to create links with organised interest groups, than parties in political cultures where such values are less prominent. Similarly, a positive attitude towards government legitimises links between civil society and the state through parties in general, whereas scepticism toward the state can adversely affect it (Thomas 2001c: 16). Hence, democratic norms may also, in theory, give rise to national variation in party-interest group relationships.

SUMMARY OF PERSPECTIVES

Table 5.1 summarises the factors that have primarily been suggested to explain variation in the relationships of parties with interest groups, as well as the concept of 'party' on which the alternative analytical perspectives are based. Social, economic and political conditions and national political institutions are presented as macro-level constraints that all perspectives see as relevant in one way or another. But as general structural and institutional differences exist mostly between countries, the remainder of this book concentrates on factors at the organisational level. The focus will be on the possible interplay between the party organisation and those parts of the environment that might cause differences within party systems.

A party, or multiple parties, cannot behave largely in line with all the models simultaneously, but as argued above, the distinction between the three alternative literatures is not watertight if the differing basic, general assumptions are ignored.

Table 5.1: Explanatory perspectives on variation in parties' relationship with interest groups – distinguishing and shared elements[1]

	Rational choice perspective (RC institutionalism)	Historical perspective (Historical institutionalism)	Norm-based perspective (Normative institutionalism)
Concept of party	Party as rationally organised tool for maximisation of office and policy by means of votes	Party as a more boundedly rational organisational tool with endogenous aims	Party as collections of norms, rules, routines, understandings, in addition to formal structure and goals
	Accent on formal leadership, constrained by intra-party democracy	Accent on the party as a carrier of an historical legacy as organisation	Accent on complex internal dynamics and party values
Emphasised (endogenous & exogenous) factors (meso level)	Strength of benefits provided by the interest group and size of associated costs for party goals Variation in primary goal	Variation in primary goal, but contingent upon political and institutional context Historical trajectories (paths) of parties' relationship with interest groups	Differences in organisational identity (ideology) Degree of institutionalisation (age) and of internal conflicts Variation in views on democracy and party models
Shared (exogenous) factors (macro level)	*Social, economic and political conditions:* Economic and social structure Strength of cleavages/political conflicts Degree of cultural pluralism etc. *National political institutions:* Parliamentary government vs separation of powers Federalism vs unitary state (state structure) Legal regulations of interest groups Size of state funding Electoral laws (proportionality versus plurality) National political culture		

1 The explanatory factors at the system level are presented as shared elements between the perspectives as they are at least partly overlapping if the broader arguments are ignored. However, there is little doubt that political culture is a distinguishing feature of normative institutionalism, whilst the size of state funding is emphasised most strongly by a rational choice perspective.

For example, 'soft' rational choice theorists could argue that cultural norms make some strategies less attractive than others in specific contexts (Thelen 1999: 376). Even if historical legacies do not seem well-suited for explaining why a party established links with new groups (cf. Peters 1999: 68), rational choice scholars have increasingly acknowledged that long-established 'institutional frameworks' with interest groups might be hard to leave (cf. Warner 2000: 40). Indeed, work within rational choice exists that embraces a more historical view of institutions (Thelen 1999: 379). Finally, alternative behavioural logics such as following 'norms of appropriateness' may exist even if parties are *largely* instrumental goal-seekers (cf. March and Olsen 2004: 19).

Starting with the rational choice perspective makes it possible to assess the relative significance of other factors as accounting for deviations from a rational course (cf. Weber (1978: 6) on the rationalist ideal type). I do, of course, not aim to identify the exact conditions under which norms are likely to preclude rational goal-seeking behaviour. The question generally addressed is: Do party-interest groups relationships *by and large* vary in line with the expectations of rational choice theory? And, to the extent that the cost-benefit model is not able to explain variation in party-interest group relationships, what does? Historical constraints? Specific contextual/political events? Or do a few parties – or parties under certain conditions – seem to accommodate to identity and norms?

In what follows, hypotheses to be explored empirically are derived from the theoretical statements and empirical assertions presented above.[89] The major question to be discussed is what patterns between variables we would expect based on a general cost-benefit model as regards party-interest group relationships. This is the *primary* general idea to be specified. Second, specific elements from the alternative perspectives are used to identify some *secondary hypotheses* concerning other shaping factors. The list of expectations is not exhaustive, but it enables a first empirical exploration. In either case, it is important to differentiate between links as a result of party action and links that mirror initiatives by interest groups. However, perspective of interest groups will be briefly addressed only in the concluding section of the empirical analysis in this book (see Chapter 16), as our main focus is on the party side of the relationships. The inclusion of numerous interest groups makes it necessary to restrict the analysis to various categories of organisations – blue collar trade unions, environmental groups and the like – not individual units.

---

89. In the words of Harmel and Janda (1994: 279), *propositions* in a theory are 'empirical assertions that are intended to be tested against data' but ones which employ 'abstract concepts that need to be made more concrete before they can be tested in practice', by means of translation into parallel *hypotheses.* As I explicitly refer to the specific terminology and indicators developed in Chapters 4 and 5 of this book, it could be argued that the assertions that follow are hypotheses, whereas previous empirical assertions are propositions. This being said, the distinction is not water-tight here and aspects of the subsequent assertions need to be made more concrete in due course in order to enable empirical exploration

THE COST-BENEFIT MODEL: HYPOTHESES TO BE EXPLORED

Based on the cost-benefit model developed above we generally expect intra-party debates on party-interest group relationships to be characterised by calculations as to the usefulness for the party's pursuit of party goals (office and policy by means of votes). A cost-benefit model looks at party relationships with interest groups as results of deliberate reasoning and choices. Limited active and utility-oriented decision-making would weaken the empirical support for the cost benefit model in general. However, we cannot put much emphasis on how party leaders discuss party-interest group relationships as they might present their approach in normative terms, while making actual decisions based on cost-benefit considerations. So even though we should keep in mind that different logics of actions might be good approximations under specific conditions (March and Olsen 2004: 17–23), the major question is whether variation between party relationships with interest groups primarily follows differences in the actual balance of costs and benefits for parties' goal-seeking. If the various possible correlations are generally strong, this would strengthen the rational choice perspective.

We are, of course, not able to compare the parties' possible relationships with all individual interest groups in-depth in one empirical analysis, not even in a single-country study. First, the question is what can explain that a party choose to have a close relationship with a specific kind of organisation, while others prefer a more distant relationship? Based on the discussion above we may hypothesise: *A party with a relatively close relationship with one kind of interest group tends to be provided with significantly more benefits (votes, financial resources, organisational support) for the pursuit of goals (office and policy) by the given organisation(s) than other parties receive.*

However, as argued above, truly close relations probably presupposes significant overlap in policy views. Thus, basic ideological differences may call for different preferences as regards potential 'partners' for the closest types of relationships. Therefore, a relevant question to separately explore is why parties relationship with their traditional associate vary: *A party with a relatively close relationship with its traditional associate(s) tends to be provided with significantly more benefits (votes, financial resources, organisational support) for the pursuit of goals (office and policy) by the given organisation(s) than parties with more distant relations receive.*

In both cases, we also assume that *the costs of the relatively close relationships – integrated relationships or alliances – with interest groups, in terms of the risk of repelling other voter groups and/or coalition partners and policy sacrifices, tend to be fairly limited in general (compared to benefits).* In sum, the benefits tend to exceed the costs of closeness for a party with strong links to a particular interest group. Next, we open up for exploration of some variation in cost assessments based on the parties' primary goal (as defined above): *The less useful a close relationship with a given interest group is for achieving executive office, the more likely office-seeking parties are to choose distance, whereas 'ideologically purist' parties tend to accept such costs.*

However, to also give a crude indication of whether parties' *overall* relationship with the interest groups seem to vary according to how useful such links generally appear to be, we shall secondly have a look at major characteristics of parties' closeness/distance from the interest group universe as a whole, and variation in range of party relationships. On the one hand: *A party with relatively close relationships with interest groups in general tends to be provided with more benefits (votes, financial resources, organisational support) from different interest groups than are parties marked by general distance from the interest-group community.* On the other hand: *A party with a relatively narrow range of relationships with interest groups tends to be provided with significant benefits from comparatively few organisation categories, or particularly great benefits from one specific interest group.* Obviously, the cost-side is hard to explore in such a summative kind of analysis. Still, it seems reasonable to assume that *'office-seeking parties' are more likely to have a wide range of links than 'ideologically purist parties'.*

HISTORICAL STRUCTURES AND NORMS: SECONDARY HYPOTHESES

As regards possible deviations from a largely rational course *vis-à-vis* interest groups, parties can first be expected to mirror historic patterns relationships and recent developments in the political context. Above all, the following secondary hypothesis can be formulated based on *elements* of the historical perspective, given that party organisations might to some extent be limited by their prior actions and structures in relation to interest groups: *A party that used to have a relatively close relationship – nearly an integrated relationship – with a specific kind of interest group is less likely to have a fairly distant relationship with its old associate(s), and a wide-ranging network of links with others, than are parties that used to have more distant relationships historically.*[90]

Informed by elements from a normative perspective, the following secondary hypothesis can be added, assuming that value-based constraints and accommodation to norms do exist: First, *a party that was originally established independently of well-defined interests is more likely to be marked by relative distance (more or less organised ad hoc contact) from its old associate(s), and a wide range of links, than are parties originally established to promote the interests or a particular social group or cause.* Second, an *institutionalised (old) party tends to have a relatively distant relationship (more or less organised ad hoc contact) to the originally associated interest group(s), and a relatively wide-ranging network of links, compared to new parties established as organisational tools for a particular social group or cause.* Third, *a party with relatively close relationships with one or more kinds of interest groups tends to emphasise interest representation most, whereas a party characterised by relative distance from the interest-group community tends primarily to promote its governing role.* Fourth, a *party with a relatively wide-ranging network of links with interest groups tends to emphasise*

90. For the sake of simplicity, a separate hypothesis is not derived from the assumption that current political events might impinge on the relationship as well.

its governing role, whilst a party characterised by a relatively narrow range of relationships tends primarily to promote interest representation.

However, it is important to note that these secondary hypotheses are not necessarily mutually exclusive. Indeed, some of the factors might perhaps be reciprocally reinforcing. Thus, it will not necessarily be possible to decide precisely what secondary explanations that receive most empirical support or whether some are in fact refuted. As a whole, the analysis will be oriented more towards descriptive than causal inference. The aim is to examine whether matching patterns exist.

CONCLUSIONS

This chapter has set out some actor-oriented theoretical building blocks that can be used in empirical studies of party-interest group relationships. More specifically, a cost-benefit model concerning party-interest group relationships was developed based on the school of *rational choice institutionalism*. By contrasting this with a historic and normative perspective, informed by *historical institutionalism* and *normative institutionalism*, the aim was to clarify what parties' behaviour *vis-à-vis* interest groups would generally look like if it is not shaped by cost-benefit calculations. Whilst rational choice theory is well-developed in relation to political parties, the other two 'new institutionalisms' are not that often explicitly echoed by students of party politics. However, it was argued that they are both relevant for, and to some extent also used in, studies of political parties.

In addition, the specific theory elements have been used to identify some alternative secondary explanations of party-interest group relationships to take account of possible *deviations* from a rational course. From this, explanatory hypotheses to be explored empirically were derived in conclusion. The next task – after having mapped the similarities and differences of party-interest group relationships in Norway – is to see whether the empirical evidence as regards variation along the dimensions of closeness and range, more or less, matches the patterns described above. But first, the subsequent chapter reflects on whether a study of Norwegian party organisations and their relations with interest groups can tell us anything about party-interest groups relationships more generally.

chapter six | the case of norway: historical relationships and contemporary circumstances

To study parties of various ages, organisational origins and ideological profiles in depth, this book empirically concentrates on parties in one single country. More specifically, it brings to light the current state of party relationships with interest groups in Norway. For Norwegians, this is probably a welcome account. For those particularly interested in Scandinavian politics, there should at least be a recognisable aspect of the analysis. But can the state of Norwegian parties tell us anything about party relationships with interest organisations in established democracies more generally? This question will, in different ways, be discussed below. As we shall see, a study of Norway gives us the chance to explore how today's political parties are linked into the associational life in a society where such links have in fact been strong historically. On the other hand, as society and state, Norway is probably neither an example of the least-likely nor a most-likely case of party distance from interest groups at the beginning of the twenty-first century.

NORWEGIAN PARTIES AND INTEREST GROUPS: HISTORICAL BACKGROUND

As discussed in the previous chapter, various aspects of party history may throw light on relations with interest groups today. To provide the necessary background, the major known characteristics of the parties' historical relationships with interest groups in Norway will be summarised below.

Historical Relationship of Norwegian Parties with Interest Groups

In the early years of party politics in Norway, interest groups emphasised political neutrality, and parties were loosely organised. Towards the end of the ninteenth century, however, a rapprochement took place.

Old Parties and Interest Groups

The Labour Party, established in 1887, was initially made up of local political associations and trade unions. The first successful modern trade unions had been dominated by liberals (Elvander 1980: 38), but a social democratic association of unions was established in 1885 (Bull 1985: 383). Furthermore, the Liberals eventually developed an anti-socialist image (Bjørnson 1990: 228), and liberal unions become gradually extinct (Bull 1985: 442). When the Norwegian Labour Party (DnA) was founded in 1887 its purpose was just as much to operate as the central organisation for trade unions as to fight for political interests as a party (Bull 1985: 440; Elvander 1980: 38). But the relationship between the political and corporate wing was not without friction, and in 1899, the Scandinavian Labour Congress initiated the establishment of the Confederation of Trade Unions (LO).

With the creation of LO, a division of labour within the labour movement was established. Whether the Federation should be widely engaged in political issues divided various LO leaders during the first decades (Terjesen 1999: 13), but Norwegian trade unions were of the moderate brand, '(...) leaving 'pure politics' to the party' (Heidar 1981: 2). DnA was to concentrate on general social reforms, and leave the issues of salaries and labour conditions to LO (Bjørgum 1999: 33). The fact that some union leaders were still liberals made formal affiliation of national unions or the federation as a whole, as in the British case, unfeasible. According to Bull (1985: 404), the Danish and the German labour movements served as models for the Norwegian social democrats and unionists, but as Duverger (1954/72) has pointed out, parties that had been established as national organisations before the confederations of unions tended generally to avoid formal affiliation. In any case, voluntary collective membership of union clubs was established at the local level (Maurseth 1987: 47). Individual members had to opt out if they did not want to be affiliated to DnA. Most local trade unions clubs made the decision to sign up with their entire, or parts of their, membership to the local party branch (Zachariassen 1966: 34). To ensure a reciprocal flow of members, it was a constitutional rule (§14) that all party members 'should' join an LO-affiliated union if possible (Martin 1974: 80).[91]

At the national level, the party and the unions were linked by guaranteed, mutual representation in executive bodies. Two members of Labour's national executive committee automatically had seats in LO's executive committee (*sekretariatet*) and vice versa (Bull 1985: 461). DnA was seen as the political wing of the trade unions. During the party splits of the 1920s, the formal representation came to an end and the LO Congress asked the unions to abolish collective membership in Labour (Bjørgum 1999: 43). But after the party was reunited (without the Communists) in 1927, DnA and LO continued to be interlinked through collective membership of union members and de facto representation of LO leaders in the national executive committee (Millen 1963: 125–6; Galenson 1968: 155–6; Eliassen 197; Martin 1974: 77). As a norm, the LO leader, the deputy leader and several heads of major national unions held seats in the party's national executive committee (Millen 1963: 125). In addition the LO leader has usually headed the important Election Committee at the Labour Party Congress (Skjeie 1999). Party leaders were also invited to attend meetings of LO's general council, although without the right to vote (Martin 1974: 76). A permanent joint committee including the top leadership of LO and DnA was also set up: *Samarbeidskomiteen mellom DnA og LO* ('The Co-operation Committee between the Ap and LO') (Skjeie 1999: 108). Joint meetings for consultation and deliberation were to be arranged (Zachariassen 1966: 32). The economic crisis of the 1930s put the unity of the la-

91. No historical analysis revealing the relative size of individual and collective party members exists. However, it has been documented that from 1906 to 1920 the number of party branches and members was more or less equal to the number of union branches and members respectively (Zachariassen 1966: 34–5).

bour movement on trial, but the Norwegian trade unions avoided the split between communists and social democrats so common in Southern Europe.

Thus, the Norwegian labour movement is a major European example of a historically close and almost *integrated relationship* between a social democratic party and trade unions (Elvander 1980; Sundberg 2003: 93, Padgett and Paterson 1991: 179). In contrast to the British case, unions could not 'buy' representation in provincial and national party by enrolling a large number of their members. It has never been possible for a union to nominate directly and elect members to the Storting (Martin 1974: 77). Norway's unions have never been formally represented at the DnA party congress, as they were in Britain, Australia and New Zealand (see Chapter 3). Nevertheless, local collective membership and strong *inter-organisational links* existed.[92] Finally, it should briefly be noted that the relationship was associated with significant corporate support of DnA; by means of transfer of membership dues and financial donations to DnA from LO, shared professional staff or party activists on the LO payroll, the union-owned labour press and joint sources of funding like the People's House movement (*Folkets Hus-bevegelsen*) (Millen 1963: 125–7; Epstein 1967: 150; Martin 1974: 77; Maurseth 1987: 49, 64).

The older Norwegian *Conservatives* (Høyre, H) had originally more diffuse roots. It emerged, as described in Chapter 2, as an elite party for civil servants and was first founded as a parliamentary group (Torgersen 1984: 44). However, the development of DnA and the introduction of mass suffrage, as Duverger (1954/1972) suggested, paved the way for an ideological and organisational transformation. From about the turn of the nineteenth century, organised interest groups – like the teetotallers and religious organisations – started to put significant pressure on the nomination process and parliamentary deliberations (Danielsen 1964: 349–55; Fuglum 1989: 86; Aasland 1974: 276). In the 1920s, it could be argued that a non-socialist labour organisation (*Norges borgerlige Arbeiderorganisation*) became a collateral organisation of the Conservatives through representation at the party convention (Danielsen 1984: 84). Through its members, the Farmers' Union tried to influence both the party manifesto and the candidate selection of the Conservatives. Due to overlapping membership and leadership between the party and the union, the Farmers' Union was seen as being fairly close to the Conservatives in its early years (Aasland 1974: 213–14).

In contrast, at this point, business and industry were not pleased with the way the Conservatives and the Liberals protected their needs (Torgersen 1984: 46). As the conflict within the labour market intensified, the Conservatives grew to be a secular, urban party for self-employed citizens and the business community. In accordance, the party organisation also gradually established links with business and trade organisations in general and with the Employers' Association of Norway (*Norges Arbeidsgiverforening*, NAF) in particular. However, the emphasis on party independence implied no guaranteed access to party bodies or joint committees. The relationship was based on informal contact and personal overlaps (Kaartvedt

92. Hence, in accordance with the terminology developed in Chapter 3, I disagree with Martin (1974), who concludes that the party-union relationship has been primarily informal.

1984; Danielsen 1984; Selle 1997). A secret fund-raising business organisation 'against bolshevism' called 'Our Country' (*Vort Land*) reached a formal agreement with the Conservative Party's national executive committee in the 1920s, but a crisis soon emerged in the relation with the party in government (Danielsen 1984: 174–8; Ohman Nielsen 2001: 99–100). Eventually, the experience spurred the Conservatives to establish a dues-paying mass-membership organisation.

In 1947, a new secret donors' cartel, called *Libertas,* was launched by businessmen to support the liberal, business-oriented faction within the Conservatives and other non-socialist parties. Its founders argued, from the perspective of business and industry, that the policies and the working methods of the more moderate and ideological tradition with origins in the 'civil servant state' were not sufficiently efficient (Sejersted 2003: 68; Kvavik 1976: 100). Libertas was kept formally separate from the individual business and industry organisations through an umbrella structure, but financial support was given to conservative – of which some were party-owned – newspapers and the party organisation before the Second World War (Sejersted 2003: 71–4; see also Heidenheimer and Langdon 1968: 107; Kvavik 1976: 100–1;). At its inception, Libertas also aimed to establish its own organisation for political agitation, and several 'information institutes' for shipping, trade, industry and the like were launched. But this strategy proved to be in conflict with the Conservative Party leader's preference for secrecy (Sejersted 2003: 69; Valen and Katz 1964: 310).[93] Hence, we can hypothesise that the Conservatives' pre-war relationship with the business, trade and employers' organisations belonged to the type of an *alliance* or *informal partnership.*

Liberal parties have, in contrast, often been characterised by absence of significant links with interest-group associations (Kirchner 1988b: 479). Yet, interestingly, the Norwegian *Liberals (Venstre, V)* represented an exception in the early years. Although it rallied voters around so-called national interests, the party was fairly close to the farmers', language and teetotallers' movements in the late nineteenth century (Rokkan 1967; Mjeldheim 1984; Selle 1997). By the turn of the century, an extra-parliamentary electoral organisation had developed both nationally and locally (Nerbøvik 1984: 33). Through shared leaders, the party and the movements overlapped to some extent (Mjeldheim 1984: 384, Fuglum 1989: 91–2). Although the Farmers' Union was originally closer to the Conservatives, its membership also included liberals. In 1919, some individual parliamentary representatives from the Liberals even gave their formal approval to the action programme of the Farmers' Union, which naturally caused tensions with the Liberals' parliamentary group (Aasland 1974: 195). Moreover, the founders of the major feminist organisation also belonged to the liberal milieu (Blom 1984: 46). Members of the language movement tried to influence party decisions informally from within (Fuglum 1989: 86; Bjørklund 1984: 183). Although the temperance movement was officially neutral, many of its members and leaders belonged to the Liberal Party (Mjeldheim 1984: 384; Øidne 1984: 161). Additionally, by means of spe-

93. In 1948, Libertas was made publicly known by the Labour Party newspaper (Sejersted 2003: 67). I will return to the consequences of this change for the relationship in Chapter 8.

cial committees at various levels, the party collected money among individuals, companies and associations within the business community (Tresselt 1977: 35; Danielsen 1984: 102).

Hence, the Liberals' relationship with associated social movement groups never included overlapping organisational structures and well-organised links as did the labour movement. Most likely, assuming frequent contact, the historical relationships were probably closer to an *informal partnership* than an *alliance*, and experienced momentous tensions in the first half of the twentieth century. The broadening of the Liberals' constituencies from the rural areas to the cities made them vulnerable to fragmentation (Lipset and Rokkan 1967: 18). Frequent conflicts and frictions characterised the liberal conglomerate of diverging opinions and alliances (Nerbøvik 1984). For example, the party did not have a clear stand in issues concerning alcohol policy in the late nineteenth century (Mjeldheim 1984: 385). The parliamentary group as a whole did not acknowledge individuals' approval of the agrarian programme (Aasland 1974: 201; 214–16). After the Farmers' Party and the Christian People's Party were established as the informal, political instrument of the Farmers' Unions and the Christian organisations respectively, the Liberals declined and became less heterogeneous (Ohman Nielsen 2001: 48). By the same token, its basic character of being a 'movement party' weakened. As an organisation, the Liberals increasingly emphasised and developed their profile as an advocate of national interests.

In 1920, the Farmers' Union (*Norges Bondelag*) founded the *Farmers' Party* as its own political wing (in 1959 renamed the *Centre Party*, Sp). After the establishment of a separate electoral organisation at the national level, the Farmers' Union gained guaranteed access to the party's national executive committee. A co-operation agreement implied that party programme should reflect the union's programme (Leirfall 1989: 21). In exchange, the union donated money to the party each year. However, the apparently *integrated relationship* was gradually disbanded. In 1938, financial donations came to an end and the party launched a separate membership organisation and the separation process entered a final phase through revised party-union settlements (Rovde 1995: 321).

The party launched a separate membership organisation in 1938, and the co-operation agreement was abolished after the Second World War (Rovde 1995: 227; Ohman Nielsen 2001: 351). In contrast to the Labour Party, neither a liaison committee nor joint conferences were established. In 1946, the Farmers' Union, once again, wrote political autonomy into its preamble (Steen 1988: 225). The personal overlaps between decision-making bodies, however, remained extensive (Rovde 1995: 227–8; Ohman Nielsen 2001: 318, 351). Hence, as in other Nordic countries, the party-union relationship within the farm movement has, after the establishment of a separate party organisation, been less close than the corresponding case within the labour movement (Sundberg 2001: 180). Probably, it soon moved in the direction of an *alliance* or perhaps rather an *informal partnership*.

The *Christian People's Party* (KrF) emerged from the Lutheran laymen's movement (Lomeland 1971). Most of its founders were officials in Christian organisations – the Western Norwegian Free Church Association for Home Mission

(*Det Vestlandske Indremisjonsforbund*), founded in 1898, and the Norwegian Lutheran Mission Corps (*Norsk Luthersk Kinamisjonsforbund*, later *Norsk Luthersk Misjonssamband*) from 1891 (Lomeland 1971: 86). From 1933 to 1945, there was a shift of dominance from VIMF towards the more conservative and more national Lutheran Home Mission Agency of Norway (*Det Norsk Lutherske Indremisjonsselskap*), which had been founded in 1868 within the Lutheran Church of Norway (from 2001 called *Normisjon* also including the former *Santalmisjonen*) (Opdahl 1976: 46; Bjørklund 1983a: 29). KrF party leaders also had been involved in the temperance movement (Valen and Katz 1964: 320; Opdahl 1976: 44).

In 1945, seventeen out of KrF's eighteen executive members and parliamentary representatives were concurrently or formerly active members in religious organisations or the Church. A formal rule dictated that all officials should profess Christianity (Sæter 1985: 228). Affiliation to the major home mission organisations dominated, and most missionaries were still local leaders or members of the national executive committee (Opdahl 1976: 44). Later, more members of the Oxford Group (later 'Moral Rearmament'), which was composed of mainly middle-class Christians in the capital, and employees (clerics) of the Church of Norway joined the party. KrF was becoming less and less a party for people active in mission organisations (Bjørklund 1983a: 32–3; Madeley 1994: 147–50). On the whole, the party organisation appeared to be an informal instrument for Christian organisation elites. Similarly, during election campaigns the organisations functioned as opinion leaders and communication channels for the party (Bjørklund 1983a: 30; Opdahl 1976: 53). For instance, one major Christian organisation asked all Christian voters to emphasise Christian values when choosing between parties in 1933 (Lomeland 1971: 121). Prior to the general elections in 1945, Christian organisation leaders signed a public appeal openly encouraging voters to choose the Christian People's Party (Opdahl 1976: 59; Bjørklund 1983a: 30), and the party campaign was supported by various religious leaders (Madeley 1994: 149–50).

However, Norway's Christian organisations were not collectively affiliated to the party, as religious organisations in other European countries were to 'their' parties (Lucardie and ten Napel 1994). Christian organisations were neither formally represented in party bodies, nor linked through liaison committees. Some have claimed that financial support was raised at missionary meetings, but Opdahl (1976: 38–9) concludes that there is no clear evidence of this assertion. The organisations preferred separation of religion and politics at the organisational level (Selle 1997: 156), in line with the original Lutheran approach. The relationship between the Christian People's Party and various religious organisations might have approached an *informal partnership* more than an organised alliance. Furthermore, the post-war KrF was not characterised by links with trade unions and employers' organisations, unlike the case of the Christian Democratic parties in Europe (van Kersbergen 1994: 37), and KrF has not established a truly wide network of collateral organisations like the continental Catholic parties, besides the ones most parties include, like a women's organisation and youth organisation (Bjørklund 1983a: 35; Lipset and Rokkan 1967: 15).

To sum up, before the Second World War, all major Norwegian parties had a fairly close relationship with a particular interest group, or a specific segment of other organisations. Although we do not know the frequency of actual contact, it is not unreasonable to assume that most parties had either an *alliance* or *informal partnership* with their traditional associate. However, variation existed in the closeness of the relationship. Through local collective membership of trade unions, the political and corporate wing of the labour movement was almost integrated organisationally. The overlapping organisational structures between the Farmers' Party (later Centre Party) and the Farmers' Union, in contrast, ended just after the war (cf. Valen and Katz 1964: 312–15. Interestingly, Valen and Katz (1964: 309–10) conclude that only trade unions took a clear partisan stand before the elections in 1957.

Party relationships with other interest groups, including the range of their network links, are less documented. Of course, all parties had some contact with various groups when in public office. Subscribing to the doctrine of mixed economy and pluralism, even Norway's social democrats had in some way to come to terms with organised capital and white-collar confederations (Padgett and Paterson 1991: 186). Valen and Katz' (1964) local community study of the post-war era indicate that party leaders, halfway into the twentieth century, were members of various kinds of interest groups. However, there is little doubt that party links into the interest-group community outside the Storting clearly reflected their roots in relevant cleavages. The historical accounts suggest that their relationships outside their sub-culture were fairly distant and limited. Above all, Labour had a distant relationship with the civil service and employers' segment, whilst the Conservative Party was almost completely separated from the trade union movement (Torgersen 1984: 48). The Farmers' Union and Party primarily articulated the interests of large-scale farmers, and the Christian People's Party concentrated on Christian circles. By and large, we may conclude that Norwegian parties generally approached the pattern of *close relationships with particular interest groups* before the Second World War.

A certain exception is found in the Labour Party's relative closeness to smallholders, forest workers and fishermen from the 1930s and onwards. Due to a rapid but late process of industrialisation, it was acknowledged early on that the party needed to consist of more than its original core voters (Lorenz 1972: 82). From the 1920s and 1930s, Labour attracted support outside urban areas among smallholders, fishermen and forest workers (Rokkan 1967; 403; Steen 1988: 250). Although no formal co-operation agreements developed, the party was linked with smallholders' and fishermen's organisations through ad hoc meetings and overlapping memberships (Steen 1988: 304–5; Valen and Katz 1964: 314). In 1939, the DnA party congress decided that membership in one of these organisations was to be obligatory for party members employed in agriculture and fisheries (Steen 1988: 303–4).[94]

94. As in Sweden and Finland, the hardships of the 1920s resulted in a historical 'crisis agreement' in Norway between the Labour Party and the Farmers' Party in the 1930s: In 1935, Bp supported DnA's package of social security reforms through which all citizens were included in the redistribution of public goods (old age pension, unemployment insurance (etc.). In return, the Labour Party provided measures for agricultural protection). However, the agreement did not lead to a more permanent red-green alliance in Norway as in Sweden (Christensen 2001: 38).

New Parties and Interest Groups

Since the 1960s, the Norwegian party system has been increasingly coloured by the *Socialist People's Party* (SF; Socialist Left Party from 1975, SV) and since the 1970s, also by the Norwegian *Progress Party*. As shown in Chapter 2, the Socialist People's Party emerged as a splinter group of the Labour Party. A key strategy was to cultivate links to the trade union movement. Collective membership was not established with any union, but a special party-union committee was responsible for the contact with the trade unions from the very beginning. According to the party's annual reports, party activists devoted much time mobilising a left-wing opposition within LO and its unions in the 1970s (Socialist Left Party Annual Reports 1977–81). At the top elite level, almost half of the party executive members also held positions in the trade unions during the 1960s, but generally at the local level (Haaversen-Westhassel 1984: 102–5).

At the same time, the party founders belonged to an opposition to the Labour Party's foreign and security policies, and SV was forcefully supported by the anti-nuclear groups and opponents to the Vietnam War (Christensen and Midtbø 1998: 2). SV's members were involved in for example peace groups and feminist organisations (Selle 1997: 157). A little less than a third of the party executive members held positions locally or nationally in international solidarity groups in the 1960s. Few, if any, executive members were office holders in the women's movement (Haaversen-Westhassel 1984: 102–5). The party organisation also pre-dated new social movements. It could well be argued that SV primarily *built bridges* to – and did not emerge from – external organisations. Whereas the Socialist People's Party had primarily been seeking access to trade unions, the successor established links with movement organisations. According to Selle (1997: 158), these links were originally more issue-oriented than strongly cleavage-based.

In any case, SV grew to be characterised as a meeting place for feminist women's organisations, anti-EC groups, international solidarity groups and later the radicalised environmental movement (Selle 1997). According to its annual reports, the party had links in particular with the Association of Norwegian Women (*Norsk Kvinneforbund*); with Bread and Roses (*Brød & Roser*), a radical feminist group; and with various solidarity organisations in the late 1970s. The SV party leadership apparently regarded contact with various movements as an important task for the party organisation as such to develop (Socialist Left Party Annual Report 1977–79: 23–5). The party encouraged its members to seek top positions in various organisations, such as Women for Peace (*Kvinner for fred*) and No to Nuclear Arms (*Nei til Atomvåpen*). In some groups, party activists from the Socialist Left were elected to the executive bodies (Selle 1997: 157). However, in contrast to the old Labour party and the Centre Party – but in line with the liberal and Christian case – SV's relationships with interest groups did not involve overlapping organisational structures and well-organised links. By no means did SV control the various organisations with which it was associated. The social movements of the 1960s and 1970s did not represent a potential source of financial support, and they preferred to be politically neutral (Socialist Left Party Annual Report 1977–79; Alldén 1980: 53). Hence, SV has no history of a 'legal marriage' with either the old trade union movement or the 'new' social movements.

In contrast, the New Right party, FrP, has a populist legacy (Andersen and Bjørklund 2000: 200–1). As other '(radical) populist right' parties, FrP was founded as anti-party (Hainsworth 2000: 9), and not on the basis of an organised social movement. The founding father was a dog kennels owner and former member of the Conservatives who had been affiliated with the right-wing Patriots League (*Fedrelandslaget*) in the 1930s (Svåsand 1998a: 78). He opposed the regular model of party organisation, and presented the first party manifesto on a single sheet of paper (Harmel and Svåsand 1993: 77–8). As a loosely organised 'entrepreneurial party' (see Chapter 4), the early Progress Party was originally characterised by lack of organisational roots in civil society. It soon established a permanent party organisation but was not embedded in any organised interest group (Selle 1997: 157).

To conclude, Norway's political parties all have a specific historical legacy to be taken account of when analysing their current relations with interest organisations. Even if most parties had a special relationship with the organisation(s) associated with their location in the cleavage structure, in practice the degree of closeness to this interest group has varied.

CONTEMPORARY CONDITIONS: THE NORWEGIAN SOCIETY AND STATE

Can the state of Norwegian parties tell us anything about party relationships with interest organisations in established democracies more generally? Research indicates that differences in pattern of relationships exist between countries (Thomas 2001e). The aim is not to test hypotheses of such variation, and no specific claims can be made as to whether the results are generalisable beyond Norway. However, a description of the national context enables us to discuss if there are any characteristics of this context to suggest that the overall pattern of Norwegian party relationships with interest organisations is exceptional in one way or another.

Social Structure and Other Societal Circumstances

Comparative political research on Norway has emphasised such national peculiarities as the relative strength of the periphery, the cross-cutting, territorial cleavage in the Norwegian party system, the corporatist mode of government and the egalitarian political culture. In addition, the latent issue of Norwegian membership in the European Union, which in connection with two post-war referendums has de-activated the traditional left-right axis, but temporarily reinforced the territorial dimension and the socio-cultural conflicts (Valen 1999: 106).

This picture is, however, increasingly an 'outdated stereotype' (Østerud 2005: 705). Recently, the Norwegian Power and Democracy Project[95] concluded that the country is undergoing deep-seated structural changes weakening the special characteristics of its political system. Changes in Norwegian capitalism have come

95. In 1997, the Storting decided to launch a power and democracy study to analyse the state of Norwegian democracy at the dawn of the twenty first century. An independent steering committee of five researchers was appointed (see Østerud and Selle 2006: 45, note 1).

to challenge the traditionally strong degree of co-operation between labour and capital, and the consensus on universal welfare systems. Today, there is a bigger concentration of firms with international affiliations. The state is still an active part of the economy, but increasingly as a market actor (Østerud and Selle 2006: 28). In other words, Norway is no longer as good an example of a specific kind of polity as it once was.

But, what is primarily of interest here, are those systemic features that are assumed to clearly affect party-interest group relationships. Let us start by having a closer look at the Norwegian social structure. Although coherent and systematic comparative evidence cannot be found along all the relevant variables, there can be no doubt that the general socio-economic development has, in a comparative perspective, been substantial in Norway after the Second World War. In the 1960s, Kirchheimer (1966: 185–8) argued that Scandinavia's social democrats had less incentive to widen their voter appeal than their sister parties because they had been enjoying majority status for decades. Since then, however, significant changes have taken place in the electorate.

The decline in the primary sector, the weakening of traditional heavy industry, and the rapid expansion in the service industries, have radically changed patterns of employment. According to the Norwegian Election Studies, the size of the Norwegian electorate belonging to the traditional manual working class has declined from about 44 per cent in 1965 to 19 per cent in 2001. The proportion of voters in the civil service, administration and similar sectors (*funksjonærer*) has increased from about 29 per cent to 59 per cent during the same period of time (Berglund 2003: 117). Comparative data from the late 1980s showed that the number of manual workers in the workforce, or the percentage of the workforce employed in industry, was lower in Norway than in many other West European countries (Kitschelt 1994: 42–3). Norway's industrial development, which was centred on the oil and gas industry, gave rise to few traditional working-class environments (Lindström 2005: 96).

Norwegian election studies also show that the proportion of voters working in the primary sector has radically decreased since 1965, from 19 per cent to 3 per cent (Berglund 2003: 117). This means that the social basis for the economic-functional axis in Norwegian politics has radically changed or weakened since Second World War. Only 3 per cent of the workforce is engaged in agriculture, forestry and fishing.[96] In this sector Norway mirrors the development of the rest of Europe, although in several countries, especially in Southern Europe, the share of employees in agriculture, forest and fisheries is significantly higher. In 2001, 4 per cent of the Norwegian workforce was employed in agriculture, as against about 12 per cent in Spain and 17 per cent in Greece (ILO 2002a: 144).

Hence, Norwegian political parties seem indeed to be faced by a social structure that does not make focus on old constituencies attractive for electoral purposes. The Norwegian pattern of employment clearly demonstrates that the Centre Party and the Labour Party can no longer generate significant electoral support

---

96. Source: Statistics Norway, the Labour Force Survey, see http://statbank.ssb.no/statistikkbanken/.

by appealing solely to their traditional core voters. True, there has never been any direct correspondence between socialist electoral support and the proportion of blue-collar workers. According to Kitschelt, changes in class structure account for a minuscule share of left party votes (Kitschelt 1994: 41–3). However, *working-class dispositions* provide a key for understanding, and class structuring of the vote has declined significantly over time in Western Europe, including Scandinavia and Norway (Franklin *et al.* 1992; Knutsen 2004b: 72). Listhaug (1997: 80–3) observes a 20 per cent decline in socialist support from the working class (skilled and unskilled workers, including farm labour) between 1957 and 1989. Secondary attributes like union membership have proven more resistant, but still have a declining influence on party choice (Kitschelt 1994: 45; Berglund 2003: 122–5). In economies based on large public sectors, the dilemma for social democrats has been particularly great. Also in Norway, large and attractive voter groups of employees in public administration and services are organised outside the trade union movement (Stokke 2000; see also Chapter 16). As far as the Norwegian Centre Party is concerned, Berglund (2003: 127) argues that experiences from primary industry during the early days of the party still play a part, but the strategy of concentration on mobilising traditional social classes has limited electoral potential.

A similar development can be seen in relation to other traditional cleavages. There are still regional variations in electoral support to political parties in Norway (Valen 2001), but urbanisation has weakened the potential number of voters mobilised in the periphery, also in recent years. In 1990, 70 per cent of the population lived in urban settlements. In 2005, the share was 77 per cent.[97] Hence, relatively few voters can be gained on the basis of a rural profile today. The core voters of the Christian People's Party, and originally the Liberals, have also decreased in number. The share of voters who belong to religious organisations or are active teetotallers had declined to about 8 per cent of the electorate by 2001 (Berglund 2003: 117). Increased secularisation has not opened up a more significant cleavage in Norway (Knutsen 2004b: 82). Furthermore, immigration is reflected in a culturally more diverse society, albeit only to a fairly limited extent: in 2005, 8 per cent of the Norwegian population was not born in Norway.[98]

More importantly, the socio-cultural cleavage related to religion and moral issues has become a weaker explanatory factor of party support, albeit not as weak as sometimes suggested (Berglund 2003: 136). Inglehart and Norris (2004: 202) show that religion is weakened as a predictor of ideological orientations, and more so in Norway than many other countries. The level of electoral volatility is relatively high (Dalton *et al.* 2002: 41). Hence, by and large, all old parties have been stimulated to identify more various 'target groups' and try to create wider demographical profiles. One way to increase the potential for success is by having links with a wide range of interest organisations (Kirchheimer 1966). Also, this overview suggest that the societal changes in Norway have been significant by international standards, and make fairly distant and wide-ranging relationships with

97. Based on figures from Statistics Norway, see http://statbank.ssb.no/statistikkbanken/.

98. Source: Statistics Norway, see http://statbank.ssb.no/statistikkbanken/.

interest organisations indeed seem likely and even more likely than in some other cases (cf. Strøm and Svåsand 1997: 23; see also Kitschelt 1994: 42–3).

More specific features should also be noted. Due to the fact that Norway's Labour has not been divided by religion or ethnicity, and the Communist Party has been relatively weak, the social democratic competitive environment differs from those of labour movements on the European continent. Martin (1974: 75) argues that this makes Norway a good case for study of the impact of *socio-economic* circumstances. However, Kitschelt (1994: 58) maintains that for social democratic parties severe competition from religious and communist parties, and the low degree of class voting have been positively correlated with electoral success since the 1970s and 1980s (*ibid:* 61). One probable explanation, Kitschelt suggests, is that the lower the degree of working-class support, the more the party enjoys strategic flexibility (*ibid:* 56). Hence, despite significant social change, DnA has perhaps had generally less readily established links with interest groups across classes than many of its continental counterparts.[99]

Furthermore, the Norwegian party system, despite the decline of old conflicts, is still based on numerous and cross-cutting conflict dimensions (Heidar 2005). In recent decades, major long-established parties have increasingly found themselves challenged by significant competitors on the flanks (cf. Wolinetz 1991: 120). Norway has the lowest post-materialist or left-libertarian mobilisation in all Scandinavia (Knutsen 1990), but the political significance of this axis is considerable (Knutsen 1989). In Norway, support for both the new Socialist Left Party and Progress Party has increased over time. In the 2001 elections, FrP and SV together received about 31 per cent of the vote.[100] This indicates that the existence of fringe parties may stimulate the old Norwegian parties – and DnA in particular – to take account of new social segments and interests groups, to a greater extent than with parties in systems where there are no such competitors.

Finally, Norwegian parties have – like other Western parties – been challenged by the rise of non-partisan broadcast media (Østby 1997). The establishment and steady increase of public subventions to parties have further decreased the need for close links into civil society (Katz and Mair 1995). Historically, Norwegian political parties have been poor organisations, dependent upon membership dues, contributions from individuals and donations from friendly organisations. Today, however, the situation is quite different. Indeed, the level of state subventions of parties is high in the Nordic countries (NOU 2004: 58). Public subventions to parties were instituted in the year of 1970, and between 1970 and 2004, public funding increased from about NOK 55m to 148m (adjusted figures, approx. €6.9m to €18.6m) (ibid: 25). Figure 6.1 contrasts the size of donations from interest groups with the parties' total revenues from 1998 to 2004. We see that the total sum of do-

99. Kitschelt (1994: 51) also refers to close links with trade unions as one of the constraints on the party's strategic flexibility. Here, however, links with unions are, like the electoral strategy, regarded as a matter of choice; the degree of closeness to unions is what is to be explained in this analysis.

100. Source: Statistics Norway, see http://statbank.ssb.no/statistikkbanken/.

nations has been rather stable, reaching approximately NOK 18m (€2.3m) in years of general elections.[101] Yet we also note that monetary support from interest groups represents only a limited share of total party revenues. This makes the utility of the total support from interest groups to parties seem fairly limited in general.

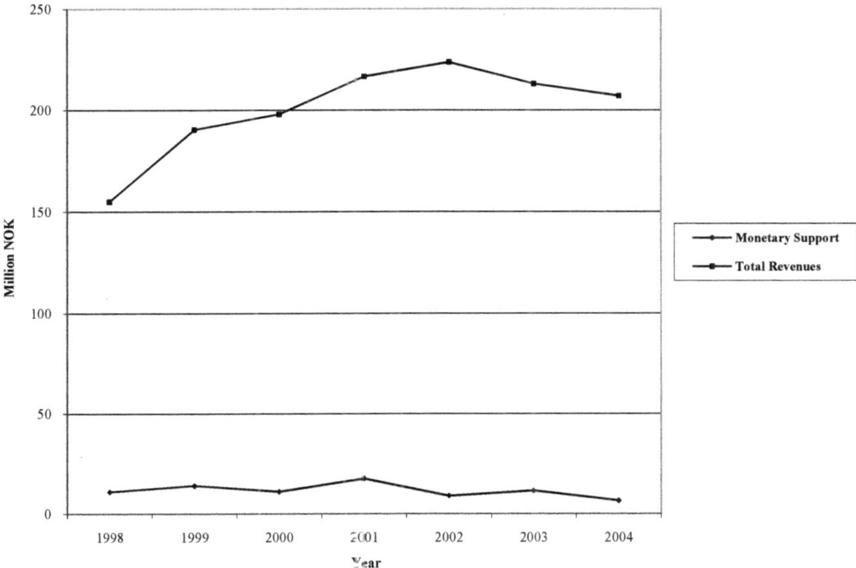

Figure 6.1: Revenues, parties' central organisations. Total monetary support from interest groups and total party revenues, 1998–2004. Nominal figures (NOK)[1]

1 It was not possible to identify the relevant figures from SV's accounts from 1998, 1999 and 2000, but the figures were provided by the current Finance Manager Hilde Longva (Longva 2005 [e-mail correspondence]).

Source: Parties' income accounts.

Pierre, Svåsand and Widfeldt (2000: 17–18) find no systematic correspondence between development of membership numbers and the introduction of public subventions. The development of the state subvention regime does not preclude the possibility that parties may find additional support from specific interest group sufficiently attractive. But if parties put strong emphasis on their *relative* need for financial donations as regards relationships with interest groups, the high level of public funding could make it more likely that Norwegian parties have, in general, fairly distant relationships with interest groups.

101. The amounts in Euro are based on an exchange rate of about 7.9 NOK for 1 EUR (22.03.06).

Political Institutions and Regulations

In terms of *institutional setting*, Norway is a fairly decentralised but unitary state characterised by parliamentary government (Lijphart 1999). Hence, the state structure makes national relationships with interest organisations relevant, as well-organised parties exist at the national level, in contrast to the case in federal states like the United States. According to Wilson (1990: 161) a unitary structure may, however, encourage technocratic lobbying more than exchange with parties due to the concentration of power. Likewise, the parliamentary government makes it more risky for interest groups to be closely related to a specific party, especially in the case of majority governments. In a parliamentary system, the opposition risks having very limited impact on the executive (Thomas 2001e: 274–5). In any case, Norwegian parties have much in common with other parties elsewhere. There exist few countries that are characterised by both a federal structure and separation of power (Lijphart 1999). Moreover, increased frequency of minority governments has weakened the difference between the two institutional settings in this regard.

In contrast, *direct* and *indirect regulations* make Norway – or indeed the Scandinavian countries – a more special case. The electoral formula of list proportional representation (PR) is mirrored in the multi-party system and makes a cross-social segment approach to interest groups less useful in general. Parties risk electoral tradeoffs between voter groups (see Kitschelt 1994: Thomas 2001e: 264). Moreover, PR systems are associated with the norm of interest articulaton, not interest aggregation. Alternatively, it can be argued that PR systems produce more competition between parties for group support, and therefore reinforce the need for links with a wide range of organisations. In any case, this type of institutional constraint is shared by most other Western countries (Lijphart 1999). In contrast, political advertising is prohibited in Norway (Ot.prp.nr. 84 (2004–2005)), and the regulation of party finances is – in a comparative perspective – limited, as in the rest of Scandinavia (Nassmacher 2001). Until 1998, there were no requirements concerning access to income accounts until 1998 (Pierre *et al.* 2000: 12). Hence, interest groups have long been able to finance parties in secret and without restrictions, and private financing is still legal (Ot.prp. nr. 84 (2004–2005)). Such rules increase the incentives for parties to have close relationships with interest organisations despite generous public subventions to parties. According to Shefter (1977), the lack of ability to disburse selective benefits to constituencies has also historically paved the way for links with interest organisations in Norway.

As far as other regulations are concerned, the degree of corporatism – the extent to which large-scale corporate organisations with powerful vested interests are involved in the economic, social, and political decision-making process – is still, despite their decline and the increase of lobbyism following an increasing role of parliaments in public policy-making (Christiansen and Rommetvedt 1999; Østerud and Selle 2006: 33) fairly strong in Scandinavia, particularly in Norway (Lijphart 1999: 181). Norway usually ranks high on measures of centralisation, encompassment and collective bargaining in international comparison (Dølvik and Stokke 1998: 127), and the Norwegian political system has been regarded as a primary example of corporate pluralism (Rokkan 1966; Kvavik 1976: 29;

Selle and Tranvik 2004: 84–6).[102] Also organisations outside the labour market are linked with the state apparatus. Voluntary organisations do not rely heavily on public subventions in Norway, but like corporate groups they take part in institutionalised arrangements for exchange with the government (Selle and Tranvik 2004: 84–6). Also new social movement organisations like environmental groups are included in such arrangements.

Exactly how corporatist arrangements influence party-interest organisation relations is a fairly open question, but it has quite convincingly been argued that corporatism nurtures such relations in different ways, despite the general assumption that it acts to undermine political parties in general (e.g. Yishai 1991: 10, but see Anthonsen *et al.*, forthcoming). Party organisations deal with election manifesto-making and candidate selection, and these are relevant activities for interest groups independent of how public policy-making takes place. According to Padgett and Paterson (1991: 192, 187), unified labour movements opened the possibility of Scandinavian corporatism, may have strengthened the dependence between the trade unions and the social democrats (Sundberg 2003: 88), whilst corporatism decreased the distance between social democracy and business organisations. Moreover, not all interest groups have access to corporatist bodies and are left with the option of trying to induce political parties (Egeberg 1981; Selle 1997: 159).

Whatever the case may be, the closeness of groups outside the labour market to the state has made Selle and Tranvik (2004: 88) conclude that Norway's interest-group community lacks '(...) a self-understanding as sector in its own right' and powerful, autonomous sub-groups. Anti-establishment groups in Norway seem less critical towards established political parties than social movements in other European countries (cf. Bortne *et al.* 2001: 20). In sum, the historical closeness between civil society, parties and the state may call for a generally high level of contact between parties and interest groups in Norway. There is a political culture of state-friendly organisations, and Norwegian party organisations have historically emphasised the norm of having strong links into civil society.

Many of the interest groups have been based on mass memberships and internal democracy, in contrast to their more bureaucratic continental and US counterparts (Wollebæk and Selle 2002: 13), but recent decades have seen a development in the direction of local groups, more flexible organisational structures and increased centralisation and professionalisation. A bifurcated interest-group community is set to emerge (Strømsnes and Selle 1996; Selle and Tranvik 2004: 91), which increasingly introduces contracts both towards public authorities and with regard to their volunteers. In this sense, the national administrative capacity of interest groups to interact with party organisations is relatively strong today (Selle 1997: 160–1), but whether the national organisations are manifestations of civil society can be questioned (Østerud and Selle 2006: 35–6).

102. The first central wage agreement was arranged in 1907 (Terjesen 1999: 13). Centralised income agreements and their incorporation into public decision-making have later been seen as a part of the so-called *Scandinavian or Nordic model*, which also includes consultation of corporate organisations and close links between labour parties and blue-collar federations of trade unions (Arter 1999: 145–6).

CONCLUSIONS

The primary question in the following sections is to what extent Norwegian parties are linked with interest organisations in the early 2000s. What are the present characteristics of party relationships with interest groups? When we embark on the explanatory analysis, the historical backdrop and legacies previously outlined may prove useful. Before the Second World War, the parties in Norway approached the pattern of close relationships with particular interest organisations – but to varying degrees. However, the main question discussed here has been if such an analysis is of interest beyond the borders of Norway and Scandinavia. The national context may generally influence relationships in a specific direction.

Clearly, any case contributes to a largely unexplored field of research. A study of parties and interest groups in Norway provide us with the opportunity to examine how parties are linked into the associational life in a society where such links have been strong historically, and where the social structure and other relevant system-level circumstances indeed call for fairly distant, but wide-ranging relationships. We have, for example, seen that the socio-economic development has been significant by international standards in Norway. Thus, it can even be argued that the general pattern of relations described by the literature on long-term party organisational change seem more likely in Norway than in many other countries. On the other hand, the inverse argument can also be put forward in certain cases: for example, that for DnA it is less easy to emphasise cross-class appeals than for many other social democratic parties in Western Europe.

The traditionally peculiar features of the Norwegian polity, such as a strong periphery, have weakened over time. National political institutions like the state structure and parliamentary government make Norway similar to many other Western countries. However, there are also institutional features to suggest that the general level of contact between parties and interest groups is relatively high in Norway. Above all, despite the recent decline of corporatist arrangements, corporatism has made links with the state a regular procedure for interest organisations, and thereby perhaps also rendering links with parties more widespread. The positive attitudes of various interest organisations toward government also legitimise links between civil society and the state through parties in general (cf. Thomas 2001c: 16), and – one might add – the small size of the Norwegian community makes certain overlaps between parties and interest organisations unavoidable. To conclude, Norway does not represent a 'crucial' case (cf. Gerring 2007: 89); it is probably neither a least-likely nor a most-likely case of party distance from interest groups at the beginning of the twenty first century. But due to the contextual similarities as well as the differences, this analysis should be of interest to more people than those particularly interested in Norwegian or Scandinavian politics.

The empirical analysis that now follows concentrates on what is to be considered the 'dependent dimension' of this study as a whole: *to what extent, and more specifically, in what way Norwegian parties are linked with interest groups in the early 2000s*? First, each party is examined in depth in separate chapters, to indicate how closely or distantly individual parties are related to various kinds of interest groups, and to enable preliminary assessment of each party's range of relationships. These chapters start by assessing the closeness of parties to interest groups. Thus, the first question discussed in the in-depth analyses is the type of relationship. Is the party equally close or distant to all organisations?

Next, how wide-ranging are the party relations with interest groups? Does the party have numerous relationships, independent of traditional cleavages? Due to the relative complexity of the dimension of closeness, considerable attention will focus on this relational aspect. Instead of analysing the range aspect when studying every kind of link in particular, a brief analysis is presented at the end. Based on existing literature, each chapter starts by presenting the given party's key developments in terms of ideology, voter profile and approach to interest groups in the second half of the twentieth century as a backdrop to the empirical description of contemporary party-interest group relations. However, the aim of these introductions to Chapters 7 to 13 is simply to provide party-specific background information for those not familiar with recent party developments in Norway. They are not meant to identify the factors that shape contemporary patterns of party-interest group relationships.

Thereafter follows the cross-party comparison of party relationships with interest groups, and the analysis particularly addresses the question of a general trend versus diversity. Neither the relative closeness nor range of relationships with various interest groups can be fully assessed before the cross-party comparison in Chapter 14. As no absolute measurements exist, only a comparative analysis of contact frequencies at the individual level can tell us exactly what relatively close and wide-ranging relationships are. So here the key question of whether there is in fact significant variation among the five Norwegian parties established before the Second World War, or whether structural and other system-level circumstances are mirrored by one single predominant pattern, is examined. Do these parties by and large have equally strong or weak links with interest groups? Are the total networks of links generally wide-ranging and overlapping, or are they polarised? If differences exist, do they seem to reflect party-related differences in the results of structural developments? Finally, the question is whether the relationships of the new, post-war parties – Progress Party and the Socialist Left – with interest groups are in fact different.

part three
party relationships with interest groups: comparing characteristics

The aim of this section is to map the relationship of Norwegian parties with interest groups today by presenting the parties' values along the dimensions of closeness and range. The chapters deal with the two dimensions of party relationships in turn, and in both cases the chapters are organised in line with the step-wise measurements presented in Chapter 4. Instead of jumping straight to the comparison of the various parties, the section first presents each party case in separate chapters.

To recapitulate: each chapter starts by presenting the given party's key developments in the second half of the twentieth century as a backdrop to the empirical description. The assessment of closeness – to the various categories of interest groups and in general – primarily distinguishes between overlapping organisational structures, inter-organisational and unorganised links for contact with interest group. The strength of the given class of links is measured and presented in turn. The first two are – if existent at all – primarily described in terms of number and kind. Thereafter follows a description of unorganised links and actual elite contact – i.e. links measured at the individual level. Here, personal overlap and flows are first looked at. A basic distinction is made between weak, medium or strong links. Second, the frequency of elite contact is explored, again differentiating between weak, medium and strong links. As indicated, for the sake of simplicity, these frequencies include both informal and formal contact and will, therefore, also partly assess the intensity of organised meetings with various groups. But, at the start, a separate survey item addresses the extent of formal (official) as opposed to informal contact in general.

Finally, a party's overall closeness to/distance from (various kinds of) interest groups is more crudely assessed in light of the typology presented in Chapter 4, by combining the maximum level of links and the actual frequency of both formal and informal contact. As previously explained, a majority of the party elite must have contact monthly or more often with the interest group category in question for the party to pass the threshold for 'regular contact'. Moreover, at both the organisational and individual party level, we look at the manifesto-making process to substantiate the description further. But the examination of whether the party elites actually do initiate meetings themselves is, however, only included in the comparative analysis.

The empirical measure of the parties' range of relations will – as explained in Chapter 4 – be somewhat cruder. In the numerical sense, the general dimension of range is measured as the number of organisation categories to which the party is linked, divided by the maximum number of organisation categories to which a party might be linked. But this assessment of the total network of links does not include what is defined as weak links in terms of frequency (see above). Also, the strength of links across group categories is compared to see whether a 'inner circle' exists in a given party network. In order to assess the qualitative aspect of the variety of represented interests, non-quantitative and somewhat context and party sensitive judgement is needed. Truly wide-ranging relations cut across traditional cleavages, and may include links with organisations representing several conflicting sub-cultures and both old and new interest groups (see Chapter 4 for specification as regards the Norwegian case).

chapter seven | the labour party: seeking wide network yet closeness to trade unions

Our journey through the landscape of Norwegian political parties and interest groups starts with an in-depth examination of the dominant party in terms of the number of years in power after the Second World War. The Labour Party (DnA) emerged as a radical socialist party in the late 1880s, and is the party that historically has had the most long-lasting close relationship with an interest group in Norway by means of a nearly integrated relationship with the trade unions organised in LO.

BACKDROP: TOWARDS A DE-IDEOLOGISED CROSS-CLASS PARTY?

In terms of ideology, DnA has undergone a political transformation since its withdrawal from the Comintern (von Beyme 1985: 62–3). After the Second World War, internal policy debates in Norway's Labour Party came to have less and less to do with the great questions of socialism. By the 1950s, the social democrats of Norway had come to terms with reformed liberal capitalism and DnA's ideological distinctiveness had been significantly reduced (Torgersen 1962: 161; Heidar 1993: 63). Despite a brief period of radicalisation in the 1970s, ideology has been marginalised in election campaigns. As in the rest of Western Europe, political competition has revolved more and more around administrative competence (Nyhamar 1990: 207, 540; Katz and Mair 1995).

As argued in Chapter 4, the decline of Keynesianism after the international economic recession in the 1970s, challenged the practical solutions of social democracy throughout Europe (Padgett and Paterson 1991: 49–50). The independence of the Central Bank became an important tool for limiting price instability (Lijphart 1999: 234). State control over credit policy and capital movements weakened, and active labour market policies declined. Radical ideological changes in European labour parties trailed behind in the next decades (Arter 2003). During the 1970s, the Norwegian Labour Party, as the party in power, intervened more directly in the central negotiations of wage settlements between employers and employees in order to control the level of inflation through active income policies. For example, tax reductions and raise in child benefits were offered in return for modest wage increase. But in the 1980s, wage settlements were again left to the labour market. When in 1981 the Norwegian Labour Party significantly revised its programme of principles, this marked the beginning of a decade of gradual ideological change. In the 'freedom debate' in the late 1980s, DnA addressed such vital questions as the right balance between state and markets and between the public and the private sectors (Heidar 1993: 64–7; Arter 2003: 91).

The party leadership argued that greater variation in policy approaches was needed, and that consumer interests should have primacy over what benefited producers in trade unions (Heidar 1993: 62, 66). The party '(...) had to be demonstrably more than a union party' (Taylor 1993: 138). Some describe this development, and similar, more abrupt processes in other countries, as policy adjustments that were necessary in order to maintain the core values of social democracy – or as an innovation of a 'third way'. But it is widely argued that Europe's social democratic parties have shifted substantially in the direction of 'neo-liberalism' and greater political pragmatism (cf. Arter 2003: 97; Heidar 2005: 820). This shift has included increased awareness of the possible contributions of the voluntary sector in solving social problems (Selle 1997: 161). Yet it should be added that DnA appears more leftist, and less de-ideologised, than many other European social democratic parties from a long-term perspective (Lindström 2005: 92; Knutsen 1998a: 82–84).[103]

In recent decades, the rise of new political conflicts – whether labelled postmaterialism or referred to as libertarian versus authoritarian values – have further challenged Norwegian social democracy (Knutsen 1990; Knutsen 2004b: 76; Heidar 1993: 67–8). Environmental policies, to which DnA had formulated responses by the 1990s, have become a major contentious issue. But as late as 1989, DnA devoted a small part of its manifesto to environmental concerns compared to other Norwegian parties (Knutsen 1997: 243, 249). Moreover, Klarén (2000: 110) finds that DnA was the last Scandinavian labour party to dedicate a separate section to environmental policies. According to Kitschelt (1994: 291), DnA has done its best to prevent elections from '(...) re-centring around the left-libertarian versus authoritarian axis rather than the dominant distributive economic dimension'.

Nevertheless, in recent elections both the Socialist Left Party (SV) and the Progress Party (FrP) have won votes at the expense of Labour in Norway (Heidar 2004; Aardal 2003a: 35). Furthermore, the wealth from North Sea oil has paradoxically created an additional dilemma for Norwegian social democrats confronted by new protest parties: how to prevent the low unemployment-high wage economy from overheating and not repelling voters by limiting public expenditure (cf. Arter 2003: 92). Finally, it should be noted that affiliation to the North Atlantic Treaty Organisation (NATO) and European Union (EU) has at times shaken the party to its roots (Lindström 2005: 100). According to surveys among Labour members, Norway's social democrats today represent a coalition of conflicting political interests, values and attitudes (Heidar and Saglie 2002; Heidar 2005: 822). Thus, as has been the case with many other West European labour parties, DnA has moved somewhat to the right on the ideological left-right axis, but it is not characterised by a particularly distinct neo-liberal social democratic ideology in the early 2000s.

Heterogeneity also characterises DnA's constituencies. The growth of a new, secular middle class has opened up alternative paths of electoral recruitment for

103. According to Elvander (1980: 174), DnA de-radicalised its political profile more strongly than its Swedish counterpart after the Second World War. Compared to the Swedish Labour Party, Lindström (2005: 92) argues that the aforementioned difference in ideological orientation has become less clear over time.

social democratic parties throughout Europe (Padgett and Paterson 1991: 36; Kitschelt 1994). The Norwegian Labour Party tried to transform itself from a pure working class party to a broader people's party before the Second World War by appealing to smallholders, farmer workers, tenant farmers and fishermen (Lorenz 1972: 82). After the war, the party's agricultural policy continued this by emphasising small-scale agriculture (Steen 1988: 305–7), but DnA increasingly focused on salaried employees in general (Berglund 2003: 124). As in the case of the other Nordic social democratic parties, '(...) the strategy has been to mobilize broad sections of the less privileged in the urban as well as rural areas' (Heidar 2004: 44).

In the early 1950s, an internal party committee concluded that the Norwegian labour movement should no longer 'downgrade' intellectual workers and technocrats. While the wages and working conditions of industrial workers had improved significantly, civil servants, administrators, clerks and the workers in similar sectors were lagging behind in welfare developments. In 1953, 'salaried employees' was used as a term in Labour's party manifesto for the very first time. The party's constituency officially included 'the workers and officials, smallholders, fishermen, craftsmen and the small-scale businessmen' (Bergh 1987: 44, my translation). Gradually, more attention was also paid to women as a specific social segment (Lønnå 2000: 117–8). Until the mid-1960s, many Norwegian feminists had been Labour's opponents, accusing the Social Democrats of stimulating patriarchal economic structures (Lønnå 2000: 117–8). However, there was considerable disagreement as to whether the party should actively pursue a white-collar constituency *in addition* to its industrial-worker base. Over time, the view gained ground that the party needed to take account of tensions among voters even if Norway's social democrats perceived both groups as belonging to one category (Martin 1974: 85). At the 1987 DnA party congress, the party secretary explicitly addressed the rising level of tension among old and new voter groups, between the trade unionised, metalworking section of the party and the new 'public class' of salaried employees (Heidar 1993: 62, 66). However, the extent to which the party has followed up the strategy in practice is questionable. According to Lindström (2005: 101), Norway's social democrats seem to be 'agnostics' in regard to class consciousness.

In any case, and most importantly, Labour's attempts to reach broader voter groups have succeeded only in part. DnA still has some support among farmers, albeit decreasingly so (Knutsen 2004b: 68–9). With the exception of higher administrators in the private sector, there have been no significant differences between the support of lower civil servants, administrators, clerks etc. (*funksjonærer*) and that of workers with regard to the Norwegian Labour Party since 1973, according to the Norwegian Election Studies (Berglund 2003: 124). Since the 1970s, more women have tended to vote for socialist parties than men (Listhaug *et al.* 1995: 279; Knutsen 2004b: 75). Employees in the public sector are generally also inclined to vote for socialist parties (*ibid*: 74). However, using a more nuanced concept of occupational groups, Knutsen (2004b: 71) argues that support for DnA declines *abruptly* as one moves from the category of workers to the service sector. Moreover, the correlation between higher education and DnA support is negative (Berglund 2003: 124). The political opinions of social democratic voters are still associated with old core issues. DnA mobilises voters primarily along the economic left-right axis, and its voters are among the least 'green' electorates in Norway (Knutsen 1997: 254; Aardal 2003b: 86–7).

The Labour Party's approach to the Norwegian interest-group community has also changed after the Second World War, but the main period of change has been in recent decades. For a long time, a fairly integrated relationship with the trade unions continued to be DnA's distinguishing feature. As a reaction to the wartime Nazi occupation, LO included a statement on union freedom in its constitution (Bergh 1987: 58–61), but its relationship with DnA did not change.[104] LO's leadership accepted the DnA government's long-term aim of stability in the labour market and its policy of limited wage increases (Elvander 1980: 1974; Bjørgum 1999: 46). In 1949, 41 per cent of DnAs party members were still collectively affiliated (Bergh 1987: 58–61). In the 1950s, around 15 per cent of the members of the party's executive committee (including deputy members) were also part of the LO Secretariat (Allern and Heidar 2001). In 1957, the LO Chair stood as a candidate for the Storting and unions demanded greater representation of trade unionists in Labour lists (Valen and Katz 1964: 308). Labour continued to maintain a distance from employees' organisations not affiliated to LO. The party leadership distinguished between on the one hand, 'legitimate' supplements (such as the Norwegian Engineers' Organisation), on the other hand 'scab organisations' ('yellow unions') (such as the Federation of Local Government Employees) which were seen as having been created '(...) just in order to split and destroy the labour movement' (Terjesen 1995: 88, my translation).

But attempts to dissolve these challengers failed. Having accepted the pluralist society and a mixed economy, social democrats came to terms with a more fragmented organisational landscape and organised capital (Padgett and Paterson 1991: 186; Terjesen 1995: 63). The rather loosely organised relationship with smallholders continued, and instead of trying to make social democrats leave the Farmers' Union, Labour attempted to stimulate links with large-scale farmers. Also, the rise of the Christian People's Party strengthened the role of religious organisations outside the state church. Presumably, therefore, a greater focus on Norway's Christian circles became a priority as well (Bergh 1987: 52–4). Moreover, Labour's 'freedom debate' of the 1980s explicitly raised the question of whether a close relationship with the trade unions was compatible with the aim of being a party for more than trade unionists (Heidar 1993: 66).

As in Sweden, collective party membership in trade union clubs was phased out during the 1990s (Allern and Heidar 2001; Poguntke 2002; Sundberg 2003; Aylott 2003). In 1989, it was suggested that the party redefine the collective membership by making it possible for union clubs and branches to enrol some or all their members as individuals (Arbeiderpartiet 1989: 14). In 1992, the party con-

104. The Joint 'Co-operation Committee' remained, and the party executive additionally put in place a union-party committee responsible for organisational issues (Bjørgum 1999). Altogether, these arrangements were a part of the party's effort to mobilise support in the trade unions to confront the challenge from the Communist Party after the Second World War (Bergh 1987: 79–80).

gress adopted a proposition of abolishing the collective membership by the end of 1997 (Heidar and Saglie 1994: 131). Furthermore, Heidar (1993: 71, 74–5) and Selle (1997: 154, 161) describe DnA from the mid-1980s as a more open party which had started to invite some external organisations to contribute to its manifesto-making. In 1994, social movements – and others – were invited to discuss the general challenges of social democracy (*Dagbladet* 31.01.94 and 03.02.95; Andersen 1995: 5). In 1996, the concept of *Samråd* (literally 'consultation') was introduced. Both the party in government and the extra-parliamentary party organisation invited organisations related to youth, religion, sport, professions and environmental issues and other groups and individuals to dialogue meetings with party representatives (Bråten 2003 [interview]).

Taken together, these latter developments portray a party that has aimed to open the door to a rather wide-ranging network of inter-organisational links with the interest-group community. What then is the situation in the early 2000s?

RELATIONSHIPS WITH INTEREST GROUPS TODAY

Party documents from 2000 to 2004 confirm the impression of a party seeking access to a relatively wide range of interest groups. In 2002, an internal committee concluded that DnA should concentrate on appealing to salaried employees within the private and public sector, to more young voters, and also to people with higher education. In order to pursue this goal, developing dialogue with white-collar employees' organisations, sports associations and humanitarian organisations, the environmental movement, parents' groups, religious circles, ethnic minorities, business associations and organisations of the elderly has been defined as a key method (Arbeiderpartiet 2002a: 18–19; Kolberg 2002: 12–13).

Nevertheless, we should note that DnA's organisational evaluations and strategy documents highlight the relationship with LO in particular (Biannual Report 1990–92: 29; Arbeiderpartiet 1994; 2002a). The forms of co-operation with trade unions have been critically discussed in recent years (Arbeiderpartiet 2002a:19; Kolberg 2003 [interview]), but DnA concluded that relative closeness to the trade union movement is still an attractive strategy on the whole. At the 2002 party congress, the relationship with LO and its unions was on the agenda, but the conclusion was *not* to weaken the existing links. Earlier, the LO congress had once again approved its official relationship with the Labour Party (see also LO 2005).

When addressing the party congress, the party secretary emphasised independence, openness and orderliness, but in fact argued that the relationship ought to be strengthened in practice, both nationally and locally (Kolberg 2002: 11–12). However, within the Labour Party there is also a faction that wants to weaken the relationship, regularly arguing that DnA's closeness to LO hinders contact with other employees' organisations (see *Arbeiderbladet* 11.03.98; Gerhardsen (2002); *Aftenposten* 07.08.04; *Dagsavisen* 17.06.03). At the congress, however, there was limited active opposition to the party secretary's viewpoints, and the delegates concluded by passing the following statement:

> The Norwegian Labour Party wants to continue the binding co-operation with the LO on the basis of a shared view on society and common ideology, elements

which are fundamental for the co-operation. (...) Labour will also have an open dialogue with other employees' organizations and groups engaged in people's everyday life and social issues in general (Arbeiderpartiet 2002b).[105]

The question is whether the dual strategy has thereafter been translated into practice. Let us start by looking at the closeness of Labour's relationships with interest groups.

Closeness of Relationships

Overlapping Organisational Structures

Formally granting the leaders of an organisation guaranteed access to the party's executive bodies is among the strongest links a party can have with an interest group. At the national level, until the party splits in the 1920s, DnA has been linked only with LO in this way. Today, local collective membership no longer exists (Labour Party Statutes 2000–04). Instead, further 'trade branches' are to be established within local party organisations, i.e. party branches organised at work-places (Biannual Report 1996–98: 66). However, union clubs *themselves* cannot affiliate with the party through the aggregate of individual memberships, as they can in Sweden (Aylott 2003).[106] The formal organisational structures of DnA and interest groups are no longer overlapping: the party and the trade union movement are not two arms of a single body. The question is to what extent DnA nevertheless has inter-organisational links with the trade union movement, and whether there are also similar links with other organisations in the early 2000s.

Inter-organisational Links for Contact with Interest groups

As explained in Chapter 4, inter-organisational links for contact come in various forms. Existing links with interest groups are summarised in Tables 7.1 and 7.2. For practical reasons, the status regarding LO and other organisations within the labour movement is first elaborated, followed by a discussion as to what extent social democrats are linked at the organisational level with other organisations.

The standing Joint Co-operation Committee between Labour and the Confederation of Trade Unions is DnA's most prominent organised link for contact with LO. Despite internal debate, no fundamental changes have been made in its composition and function.[107] The committee has remained a consultative forum, in which party and LO top leaders meet regularly to discuss and elaborate a broad

105. Interestingly, the party secretary's speech presented this choice as made in advance: 'Together with LO, we have concluded that our co-operation shall continue' (Kolberg 2002: 11).

106. It can furthermore be noted that DnA's youth organisation ceased to be LO's youth section in 1995.

107. After the evaluation, the 'Co-operation Committee' was 're-established', but the only change made is that one more representative is included from LO since the LO Chair decided not to be re-elected tothe party's national executive committee in 2002 (see below). In addition, it was decided that members of the Joint Committee cannot be members of prospective joint committees with individual unions and vice versa (Kolberg 2003 [interview]).

Table 7.1: Labour Party inter-organisational links with LO and labour movement organisations 2000–04[1]

	Existence	If yes, what kind:
Permanent joint committee	Yes	Exists between DnA and LO, between DnA and the Norwegian Union of Municipal and General Employees (*Fagforbundet*)) and with LO unions that organise civil and military personnel in the Norwegian armed forces.
Temporary joint policy committees	Yes	The Co-operation Committee with LO establishes temporary committees from time to time.
Joint conferences	Yes	Regularly arranged with LO.
Written or tacit agreements about regular meetings	Yes	With individual unions.
Invitation to party congress	Yes	LO and other organisations from the labour movement are normally invited as guests.
Invitations to party meetings, seminars and conferences	Yes	LO, unions and other labour organisations are invited, primarily to seminars and conferences.
Specific dialogue seminars and hearings	Yes	A monthly joint seminar including representatives from LO, individual unions, DnA's parliamentary group, headquarters, possible cabinet members etc. is arranged. Non specific, formal hearing of the election manifesto in LO, but meetings with union representatives are arranged throughout the process.
Meetings outside party bodies	Yes	Such meetings take place on a regular basis.

1 A comparative study of the Scandinavian social democratic parties from 2008, confirms that no major changes have been made to the relationship with LO since 2004 (Allern *et al.* 2010).

Sources: Various party documents (see Appendix A) and Jota (2003, 2004 [interviews]), Kolberg (2003, 2004 [interviews]), Bjerke (2003 [interview]) and Bråten 2003 [interview])

range of political and organisational issues. The committee includes the party leader, deputy leader(s), party secretary, the headquarters' party-union adviser, parliamentary leader and prime ministeral candidate (if he/she is not also the party leader), the chair and deputy-chairs of LO, LO's chief treasurer, two leaders from LO's mid-level (cartels)[108], and the leaders of the two largest LO unions. In addition, the chief economist of LO attends the meetings and is currently the com-

108. Cartels are organised across national union borders according to its affiliation to sector and, within the public sector, in line with administrative level.

mitte's secretary (Arbeiderpartiet 2003a: 1–2).[109]

The agenda of the 'Co-operation Committee' is broadly defined: 'The committee shall discuss major issues and developments concerning the party and the union movement' (Arbeiderpartiet 2003a: 2).[110] Temporary sub-committees are established from time to time, discussing such major topics as 'restructuring of public companies' and 'modernisation of the public sector' during the 1990s (LO-DnA 1996; Labour Party Biannual Report 1998–2000: 47). Furthermore, joint conventions between the party and the trade union movement are arranged regularly (see Labour Party Biannual Reports 1994–2004).[111]

Equally interesting, Table 7.1 shows that DnA has written agreements with some individual unions about regular meetings. There are twenty-four unions organised in LO, varying in membership from less than 1000 to nearly 300,000 individuals.[112] With the largest union, the result of the merger of the former Norwegian Municipal Workers' Union (*Norsk Kommuneforbund*) and the Norwegian Health and Social Union (*Norsk Helse- and Sosialforbund*) into the Norwegian Union of Municipal and General Employees (*Fagforbundet*), DnA has a written co-operation agreement (Biannual Report 2002–04: 39).[113] During the negotiations preparing the organisational fusion of the two unions in 2003, the relationship with Labour was a contentious issue since the Health and Social Union was strictly non-

109. When Labour is in government, the Joint Committee also regularly invites ministers and state secretaries (from Labour) to report on current political issues, or union leaders to present their organisation's opinions on relevant matters (Jota 2003 [interview]).

110. The 'Co-operation Committee' has recently assumed responsibility for practical matters such as joint conventions from the so-called Party-union Committee, which was dissolved in 1992. This also applied to the local level. Joint committees are to replace local party-union committees (Labour Party Biannual Report 1992–94: 40; LO-Aktuelt 1996: 19). By 2004, there were local joint committees in nearly every county and in more than ninety municipalities (Jota 2003 [interview]). For the record, the parliamentary party-union committee was also dissolved during 1993, but regular meetings continued to take place (Biannual Report 1992–94: 73). The agenda of the Co-operation Committee will be revisited in Chapter 15. For summaries of the questions discussed, see Labour Party Biannual Reports 2000–04 and LO's Annual Reports from 2000–04.

111. An old tradition of mutual secretary conferences was re-established in 1996. It should also be noted that the women's organisation of DnA regularly arranges conferences and seminars with the trade union movement (Biannual Reports 1994–2002).

112. For a complete list of unions in English, see http://www.lo.no

113. The agreement, which was accepted by the party's national executive committte in 2003 (Biannual Report 2002–04: 39), dates back to 1979, when DnA made a formal co-operation agreement with the Norwegian Municipal Union (*Norsk Kommuneforbund*, NKF) and the Electricians & Power Plant Union (*Norsk Elektriker- og Kraftstasjonforbund, NEKF*). The Municipal Union founded a party-union committee, which included two secretaries from the party headquarters. An annual party-union conference was initiated and local joint committees established. The agreement was re-established in 1986 as a settlement of general party-union co-operation. After the introduction of a new Local Government Act, the agreement was once again revised in 1997. The new 'contract' gave the union representatives access to party meetings and affirmed that both parties were committed to mutual exchange of information about political issues. The union representatives had to be members of Labour and did not have the right to vote (Arbeiderpartiet/NEKF/NKF 1997; Arbeiderpartiet 2003b).

partisan (Nielsen 2002; *Klassekampen* 12.09.02). But the Union of Municipal and General Employees adopted the co-operation agreement of the former Norwegian Municipal Workers' Union after only small adjustments (Jota 2004 [telephone interview]).[114] Consultative party-union committees between DnA and the new union exist at the national level, regional and local levels and joint conferences are to be arranged. The Labour Party is committed to discuss all issues relevant for the members of the Union of Municipal and General Employees in the given party-union committee before they are settled in decision-making bodies, including public budgets (Arbeiderpartiet 2003b; Biannual Report 2002–04).[115] However, union representatives are no longer invited to internal party meetings, i.e. to Labour's party groups in the municipal assemblies (Jota 2004 [telephone interview]; Jota 2004 [e-mail correspondence]).

Other unions, such as the Officers' Union of Norway (*Norges Offisersforbund*) and the Norwegian Union of Social Educators and Social Workers (*Fellesorganisasjonen for barnevernpedagoger, sosionomer og vernepleiere*), have publicly argued that LO should weaken its links with DnA, as many LO members vote for other parties than Labour. Some critics suggest that equal links ought to be established with the Socialist Left Party, whilst others prefer a strictly non-partisan and independent trade union movement (see *Milnytt* 09.03.02; *Befalsbladet* 5, 2002; *Dagsavisen* 20.12.04 and 08.04.05). Nevertheless, DnA also has a party-union committee for defence policy with the LO unions that organise civil and military personnel in the Norwegian armed forces (Jota 2004 [telephone interview], Jota 2004 [e-mail correspondence]).[116]

In addition Labour invites LO, its individual unions and other labour movement organisations to the party congress, party conferences and so forth as guests (Party Congress Books of Minutes 1998–2002; Kolberg 2004 [interview]), and it is common practice that the LO chair formally addresses the biannual party congress in plenum. According to Svåsand, Strøm and Rasch (1997: 101) informal rules 'dictate' that union officials must be included in the delegations of the provincial party to the party congress. Also, the old practice of the LO chair heading the election committee at the party congress continued in the early 2000s

114. The old Electricians & Power Plant Union no longer exists, and the new Electrician and IT Workers Union did not join the Union of Municipal and General Employees' agreement with DnA. However, this is due to 'natural causes': few municipal employees are organised in this organisation anymore (Jota 2003 [interview]).

115. The national committee consists of one representative from the party's national executive committee, two from Labour's municipal faction in the Parliament, the municipal secretary from the headquarters, the leader for the Internal Municipal Committee, four representatives from the union's working committee and one union secretary (Arbeiderpartiet 2003b). Meetings take place about once a month. Locally, the agreement opens up for different forms (Jota 2003 [interview]; Jota 2004 [interview], Jota 2004 [e-mail correspondence]).

116. In addition to union representatives, the party-union adviser and the Labour Party parliamentary spokesman for defence issues attend the meetings, which are arranged 'when needed" (Jota 2004 [interview], Jota 2004 [e-mail correspondence]).

(Arbeiderpartiet 2005a).[117] Moreover, LO unions officially invite their members to social arrangements during the convention (Kolberg 2004 [interview]). But trade unions are not collectively represented as they are in the British Labour Party.[118]

Moreover, Table 7.1 shows that the 'Co-operation Committee' monthly invites LO, its unions, the parliamentary group, the party headquarters, any cabinet members, state secretaries and political advisers and externals to 'breakfast meetings' about current political issues (Labour Party Biannual Reports 1994–2004; Kolberg 2003 [interview]). Ad hoc meetings outside party bodies represent another kind of inter-organisational link. For example, the largest union in the private sector – the industrial United Federation of Trade Unions (*Fellesforbundet*) – prefers more ad hoc oriented meetings to formal agreements (Kolberg 2003 [interview]). As explained in Chapter 4, the strength of this sub-class of inter-organisational link will be further assessed below on the basis of individual data.

The in-depth examination of how the 2001–2005 Manifesto was prepared confirms the impression of strong links with trade unions at the organisational level. The programme is normally not formally on the agenda in the 'Co-operation Committee', which emphasises the election manifesto as a formally autonomous party product (Jota 2003 [interview]).[119] But at least one representative of LO is by common practice a member of DnA's manifesto committee (Jota 2003 [interview]; Bråten 2003 [interview]; Labour Party Biannual Reports 1994–2002; Arbeiderpartiet 2005b). In written reports, the 'Co-operation Committee' elaborates political issues of relevance for manifesto-makers. More importantly, the manifesto committee, or its secretary, is usually in contact with LO and its unions several times throughout the process (Bjerke 2003 [interview]; Bråten 2003 [interview]). Before the local elections in 2003, LO and DnA even presented a joint political manifesto (DnA-LO 2003). To summarise, the Labour Party has indeed strong inter-organisational links with the trade union movement. The party secretary summarises the result of the recent internal debate over the relationship with LO in this way: 'One could in fact conclude that this [the party-union] co-operation is now better organized and substantially stronger than it has been in years' (Kolberg 2003 [interview].[120] What is the situation with regard to interest groups outside the labour movement?

117. The practice was suspended in 2007, but this may be due to exceptional circumstances as the then chair had been first compelled to resign after a long-term conflict with an employee in LO's headquarters (Allern et al. 2009).

118. In 2000, 39 per cent of the congress delegates were former or current officials in LO or LO unions (Heidar and Saglie 2002: 279).

119. This is also the case with respect to LO's platform.

120. Including links at lower levels would not have altered the picture noticeably. As Aylott (2003) has shown in the case of Sweden, links seem rather strong at the municipal level: local party-union committees exist, trade branches are established after the abolition of collective membership (Jota 2003 [interview]), and a majority of Labour's members are affiliated to LO (Heidar and Saglie 2002: 275).

Table 7.2: Labour Party inter-organisational links for contact with other interest groups than LO 2000–04

Permanent joint committee	No	
Temporary joint policy committees	No	
Joint conferences	No	
Written or tacit agreements about regular meetings	No	
Invitation to the party congress	No	
Invitations to party meetings, seminars and conferences	Yes	Interest groups outside the labour movement are invited to certain party conferences.
Specific dialogue seminars and hearings	Yes	Dialogue seminars with other interest groups take place occasionally. The manifesto committee is in contact with interest groups during the manifesto-making process, but no formal hearing with organisations in general was arranged in the early 2000s.
Meetings outside party bodies	Yes	Such meetings are arranged on a more or less regular basis

Sources: Diverse party documents (see Appendix A) and Jota (2003, 2004 [interview]) and Kolberg (2003, 2004 [interview]).

The links with the Norwegian Fishermen's Association and the Norwegian Smallholders' Union are not what they once were. These organisations no longer think of themselves as being close to DnA and the labour movement (Selle 1997: 154), and the party elite started to question these relations as early as the 1950s (Bergh 1987: 52). Yet strategy discussions indicate that the DnA's leadership aims for the party organisation to have contact with various interest groups. Table 7.2 summarises the existing kinds of inter-organisational links for contact with organisations outside the labour movement. Primarily, Labour is linked with other organisations by regularly inviting them to speak at party conferences. According to the biannual reports, a number of conferences and seminars are arranged between party congresses (Biannual Reports 1994–2004). Interest groups occasionally participate as speakers and guests (Kolberg 2004 [interview]).[121] Organised contact with other groups also takes place through sporadic dialogue seminars and more or less regular meetings between organisation representatives and party leaders, policy-making committees or staff (Kolberg 2003, 2004 [interview]). Although the term has nearly disappeared from the party's official vocabulary, the practice

121. Labour representatives also regularly attend seminars arranged by interest groups (Biannual Reports 1994–2002).

of *Samråd* (dialogue meetings) has continued to a certain extent. For example, the party leadership met with various Christian organisations, Islamic circles and employees' organisations during 2003 and 2004 (Kolberg 2004 [interview]). Separate meetings with policy-making committees and headquarters staff are also arranged – such contact is explicitly defined as an organisational norm by the party secretary (Kolberg 2004 [interview]).

Ad hoc meetings are arranged with the professionals' Confederation of Vocational Unions (*Yrkesorganisasjonenes Sentralforbund*, YS) besides LO. On the other hand, the two other major employees' confederations – the Federation of Norwegian Professional Associations (*Akademikerne*) and the Confederation of Higher Education Unions (*Utdanningsgruppenes Hovedorganisasjon* (from 2001, now the Confederation of Unions for Professionals, *Unio*) – were not specifically mentioned by any informant (Jota 2003 [interview]); Kolberg 2004 [interview]). Correspondingly, Foss (2005: 77) finds that the headquarters of *Akademikerne* reports meeting with DnA's parliamentary group, but has almost no contact with central organisation of the party. Hence, the practice of consulting external organisations seems to have limitations at the *organisational level.*

A closer look at recent manifesto-making processes only partly modifies this preliminary conclusion. Heidar (1993) and Selle (1997) observed that DnA opened up this major organisational activity from the 1980s and onwards, but my examination of DnA's manifesto-making in the early 2000s does not support the description of a party that systematically consults interest groups. According to the party secretary, the practice has never been systematic *hearings* in the sense of written invitations to numerous kinds of organisations. What DnA introduced in the 1990s was the general concept of *Samråd* (Kolberg 2004 [interview]). After the 1997 general elections, Labour established a separate policy-making secretariat, which was responsible for drafting the manifesto debate prior to the party congress of 2000. As previous manifesto-making committees (Nyhamar 1990: 49; Andersen 1995: 5), it concentrated on experts and professionals from a range of sectors (Bjerke 2003 [interview]), but also met with different interest groups. Moreover, Labour indirectly opened up for external contributions by establishing an open web page about the manifesto-making process. Furthermore, the secretariat, which was later abolished, reviewed written comments sent to the party from interest groups on their own initiative (Allern 2001: 24–5). Prior to the party congress in 2001, party conferences were arranged, to which some interest groups – like environmental and humanitarian organisations – were invited in addition to LO. However, no collective routine for formal invitations to interest groups in general had developed before the 2001–2005 Election Manifesto was made (Bråten 2003 [interview], Bjerke 2003 [interview]).

Unorganised Links for Contact with Interest Groups and Frequency of Actual Contact

No doubt Labour has some well-organised links with interest groups, but primarily with the trade unions organised in LO. Does this tendency also characterise links measured at the individual level? First, Labour might be linked, in an unorganised fashion, with interest groups through *top elite members who hold or have held office, or who are or have been staff members at the national or local levels in various interest groups.* The survey conducted among members of the DnA national party executive and political advisers at headquarters in 2003/2004 maps the top elite's actual overlaps with and transfers from interest groups. All together, it reveals that a majority – about 80 per cent – of the Labour elite are current or former representatives or staff members in one or several interest groups. Figure 7.1 shows the share of Labour's top elite who hold or have held office, and the percentage that is or have been staff members in various organisations (see Appendix D for complete frequencies).

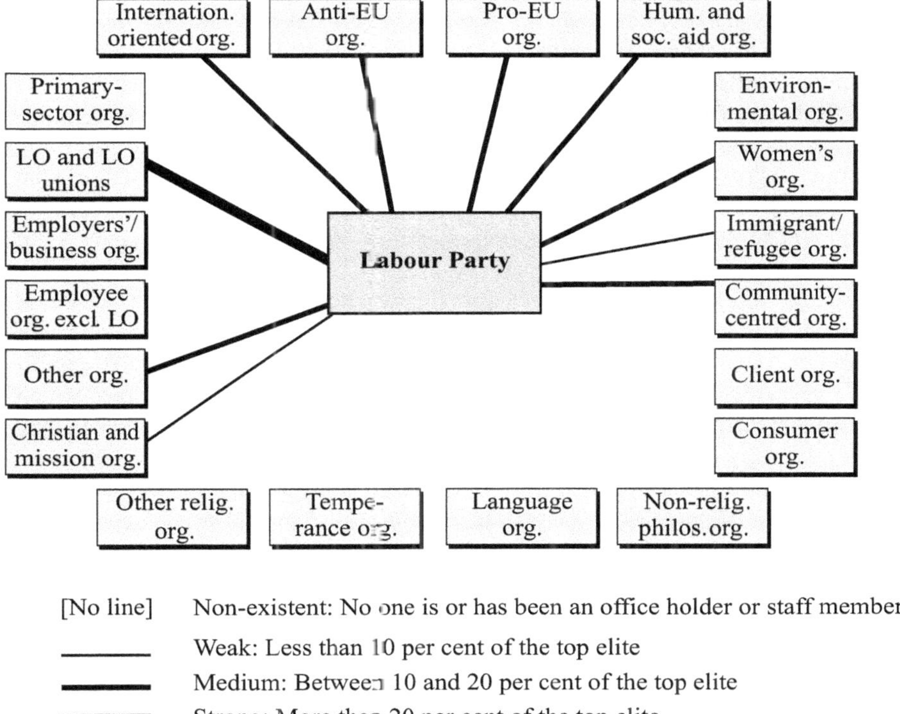

Figure 7.1: Labour Party links by top elite members who hold or have held office/who are or have been staff members at the national or local levels in various interest groups 2003/2004.[1] *N = 21*

1 If a respondent is/has been an official and also is/has been a staff member, the answer is registered only in the 'official category'.

Again, we start by assessing the particular link with LO and its unions. The party leader himself/herself has been recruited from various circles, but the trade union movement has traditionally been an important pool of potential Labour activists and leaders. The formal statute requirement that all party members 'shall' be members of an LO union was relaxed as early as 1969 (Martin 1974: 81), and in 2000 an internal party committee suggested deleting the paragraph (§12) that recommends LO membership for DnA members. However, the proposal was rejected, and informal rules still 'dictate' that LO and its unions should be represented in the party's executive committee. Figure 7.1 shows that trade union experience does indeed characterise the current Labour Party elite in Norway.

At the time of the research, 14 per cent of Labour's elite – 3 out of 21 – were currently officials in LO or LO unions locally or nationally. An additional 19 per cent had been LO union officials locally or nationally *before* they were elected to the party's national executive. On the other hand, more detailed analyses show that only 10 per cent of Labour's top elite declared that they currently hold positions in LO or in individual unions at the *national* level. The decrease – compared with the results from the 1990s as shown by Sundberg's project (Sundberg 2003) – reflects that DnA's tradition of electing the LO chair to the executive committee was abandoned in 2001. But interestingly, despite the time limit of study, the routine was reinstated in 2005 (Arbeiderpartiet 2005a). If we take account of elite members who were, or had been, *union staff*, the total share of elite members with current or former trade union positions is almost 40 per cent, which means 8 out of 21 elite members.[122]

Those officials and staff in the party elite who do not belong to the trade union movement come primarily from community-centred organisations within the field of culture, sports, the elderly, etc.: 20 per cent of Labour's top elite has experience in the decision-making bodies or headquarters of such associations, which means that the link is almost into the 'strong' classification. Yet, it should be noted that this category is a relatively broad one. Medium strong links also exist to internationally-oriented organisations and organisations aiming at Norwegian EU membership. No overlaps exist with the smallholders' and fishermen's unions.[123]

However, although there are some well-known members of DnA who work for the Confederation of Norwegian Enterprise (NHO) and its associations (*Aftenposten* 14.04.03), (former) officials from the business and trade organisations do not populate DnA's central organisation. Moreover, positions in religious and temperance organisations, internationally-oriented organisations, and humanitarian organisations might include experience from groups associated with the labour movement, like the Norwegian People's Aid (*Norsk Folkehjelp*). Due to the already large number of organisational categories, respondents were not asked

122. It should also be noted that the *remaining* 62 per cent respond that they are members of LO. Furthermore, although the focus here is on the party node, the party leader and the party secretary still attend the meetings of LO's General Council (*Representantskap*). By common practice, the party representatives attend without the right to speak but it happens that they are asked to contribute to the discussion (Kolberg [2003]).

123. For the record, this kind of link to the primary industry organisations has never been strong: the leaders of smallholders' and fishermen's unions used to be members of Labour, but not part of the executive, and in the 1950s, non-socialist party members gained ground as top officials in these organisations (Bergh 1987: 175, 179).

about these sub-groups of organisations separately. To conclude, Norway's Labour Party is linked with some organisations by personal overlaps and transfers, but extensively with the trade union movement only.

Contact between individuals may also link a party with an interest group. By studying the actual contact of elite members, we may both reveal the actual intensity of contact in organised, official settings, and the strength of informal contact between individuals. Well-organised links for contact do not necessarily result in the most intensive informal contact: lack of fixed meeting places perhaps increases the need for such interaction. To find the extent of *formal* and *informal elite contact* with interest groups of relevance for work in the central party organisation, I asked those party elites who had contact with interest groups about the general frequency of their various *forms* of contact. The results are shown in Table 7.3.

Table 7.3: Labour Party top elite. frequency of formal and informal contact with interest groups in 2003. Per cent[1]

		Daily/ Weekly	Monthly	A few times	Never	No resp.	Total	N
Formal contact	Formal meetings or teleconferences	10	29	42	14	5	100	21
	Speakers at each other's seminars/conferences	0	29	33	33	5	100	21
	Formal written hearings or letters (incl. electronic)	5	19	47	24	5	100	21
Informal contact	Informal meetings, conversations, telephone conversations	29	42	24	0	5	100	21
	Informal written communication via SMS and e-mail	34	37	24	0	5	100	21
	Informal written communication like personal letters and memos	19	29	33	14	5	100	21

1 *Question:* 'Next, we would like you to state how often you had contact with interest groups *in different ways during the past year*. We distinguish between *formal* and *informal* contact:

- About how often did you have formal contact – of relevance for your work in the party's central organisation – with representatives of different interest groups in the following ways the past year? (tick off one alternative per line)
- About how often did you have informal contact – of relevance for your work in the party's central organisation – with representatives of different interest groups in the following ways the past year? (tick off one alternative per line)'

Above all, the data show that informal contact was the most common type of elite contact with interest groups in 2003 and 2004. More than 70 per cent of DnA's top elite had contact with interest groups through informal meetings and telephone conversations monthly or more often, and an equal share made use of SMS messages and e-mail at least on a monthly basis. About 30 per cent used these types of contact weekly or more often. In addition, on average 70 per cent of Labour's top elite had formal contact at least a few times with interest groups. The weak inter-organisational links do not seem to indicate limited contact with interest groups in practice.

To what extent does this activity include contact with interest groups other than the trade unions? A summarising analysis shows that 90 per cent of Labour's top elite had at least monthly contact, formal or informal, of relevance for their work in the party's central organisation with one or several interest groups. The sociogram (Figure 7.2) reveals how often and to what extent DnA's elite had formal and informal contact with various kinds of interest groups (see Chapter 14 for table of frequencies).

We observe that at the individual level, too, DnA definitely has more extensive contact with the trade unions than with others. Indeed, party headquarters includes two positions responsible for links with LO and the Norwegian Union of Municipal and General Employees in particular. In addition, a small number of party executives take part in joint committees. But these persons are apparently not the only top-elite members to have regular contact with the trade unions. More than 70 per cent of the respondents – 16 out of 21 – had contact with LO and LO unions monthly or more often about matters relevant for their work in the party's central organisation. A more detailed analysis shows that almost 30 per cent had contact with LO or LO unions at least on a weekly basis, and there is no organisation category which is more repeatedly mentioned as one of the *three most frequent contacts* than the trade union movement.[124] Exact assessment of how strong a link the frequencies represent requires comparison with other parties (cf. Chapter 1). However, the fact that we cannot expect all elite members to have regular contact with all kinds of organisations suggests that the frequent contact with LO and unions is in any case very extensive. Equally interesting, it indicates that Labour's executive members and national political advisers also had contact with union representatives *independently* of official meetings.

The frequency of contact with organisations outside the LO family was generally lower. But DnA has a *strong degree of contact* with humanitarian and social aid organisations and community-centred organisations related to sports, youth elderly etc. (about 60 per cent with monthly contact). Then again, this contact may include organisations associated with the labour movement. About 30 per cent had contact with employees' and professional organisations outside LO and internationally-oriented organisations at least once a month. The contact with many other kinds of organisations is of *medium strength*: about 25 per cent had regular

124. *Question:* 'First, we would like you to write down the names of those (maximum three) organisations you had most frequent contact with last year. (….). Use the blank below (….).'

contact with environmental organisations or immigrant and refugee organisations. More than 75 per cent had had contact with employers' federations, business and trade associations a few times the past year. Thus we see that individual behaviour confirms that the existence of few standing inter-organisational arrangements does not necessarily mean that contact is equally limited at the individual level.

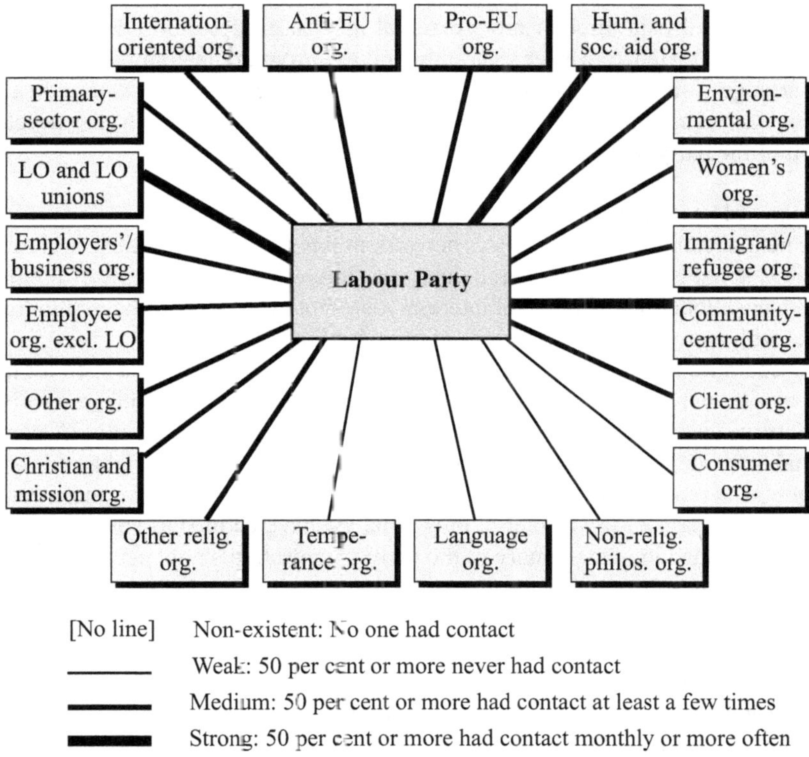

Figure 7.2: Labour Party links through the top elite's frequency of contact with various interest groups in 2003.[1] *N = 21*

1 *Question:* 'Could you please state how often you had contact – of relevance for your work in the party's central organisation – with one or more organisations within the following categories during the past year? The question includes both formal and informal, more random contact, written as well as oral communication.'

If exactly 50 per cent reported having contact 'seldom', the link is categorised as either 'medium' or 'strong'.

What about contact with interest groups during to the manifesto-making process in particular? The analysis of inter-organisational links revealed that no general hearing is arranged with external organisations, but that some organisations are invited to seminars and have organised meetings with party representatives. What about other members of the programme committee, executives and headquarters staff assisting them? In order to get a certain indication, those survey respondents who were officials or staff members in the central organisation prior to the 2002 congress were asked about their experiences.[125] More than 60 per cent answered that they had been in touch with at least one or two organisations during each phase of the manifesto-making.[126] External contact seems particularly extensive during the late stages of this process, when most of the platform is already determined. Throughout the debate about the final manifesto proposal, 40 per cent communicated with three or more external interest groups before the party congress of 2000. Hence, we see that, although the programme committee itself did not arrange systematic hearings, a significant part of the party's top elite at the time did in fact communicate with interest groups when contributing to the development of the party manifesto.

Range of Relationships

The next question is whether DnA's network of links with organisations is broad or narrow. What characterises its relations with interest groups in terms of numbers of organisations and the range of interests represented? Does DnA have significant links with many and different kinds of organisations?

According to internal strategy discussions, DnA acknowledges a need for having a wide network of links with interest groups. It aims to be linked into civil society in general and not be embedded in particular segments only. A party's actual network of links is assessed on the basis of the survey material as this is the only type of data that systematically cover all organisation categories in particular. However, as argued in Chapter 4, only what we have defined as significant links will be included in our summary of the party organisation's total network of links, i.e. cases where 50 per cent or more of the elite at least had contact a few times the past year.

Figure 7.3 thus shows that out of the total number of twenty organisation categories, the proportion of actual interest group categories with which DnA is linked – at least through its elite's contact – is 0.80. We see that most major organisation categories in Norway are included in DnA's network of links in the early 2000s. Most importantly, the party is linked with interest groups *across* old cleavages.

Despite the existence of few organised links for contact with employers' organisations and business/trade associations, a majority of the top elite nevertheless report having formal or informal contact with the major opponent of the trade unions. The DnA elite also connect the party with employees'/professional organisations outside the old trade union movement, client organisations and with humanitarian/social

125. *Question:* 'How many interest organisations did you have contact with – about one or several subsections – during the different phases of the manifesto-making before the party congress in 2000?

- Before the first draft was presented.
- During the debate over the manifesto draft.
- During the debate over the manifesto proposal.'

126. Contacts seem to be more extensive among the top elite than the congress delegates in this process: 32 per cent of the delegates in 2000 answered that they had been contacted by 'people outside the party' about the party manifesto (Heidar and Saglie 2002: 213). However, it should be noted that the question in our survey includes *all* contacts, independent of who initiated them.

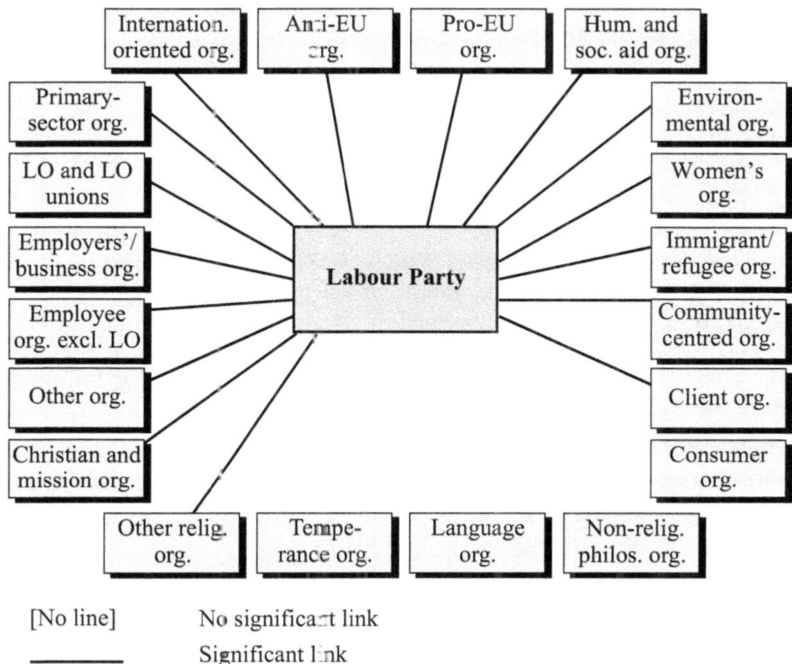

Figure 7.3: The Labour Party's total network of significant links with interest groups. N = 21

1 Significant links are cases where 50 per cent or more at least had contact a few times the past year (see Chapter 4).

aid organisations and community-centred organisations, like groups for the elderly, youth and sports associations. The relative importance of the old socio-cultural cleavage in the early 2000s makes the weak links with the old counter-cultural organisations not very surprising.

Equally interesting, Labour has links at the individual level with organisations associated with post-industrial – 'new' – politics, like environmental groups and women's organisations, and with internationally-oriented organisations, which might include the peace movement or the more recent anti-globalisation movement.[127] The party has significant links both with groups working for and against Norwegian membership in the European Union. In brief, DnA's network of significant links includes a wide-range of interest group categories.

However, the closeness of relationships varies significantly between the different categories of organisations. DnA has strong inter-organisational links with the

127. However, this organisation category may as well include an important organisation affiliated with the labour movement called 'Norwegian People's Aid' (*Norsk Folkehjelp*) and organisations promoting Norwegian membership in EU.

trade union movement only. Outside the LO system, it seems to be closest to humanitarian and internationally-oriented organisations, women's organisations and community-centred organisations.[128] The central organisation has not established collective routines for regular organised contact with major employees' and professional organisations outside LO (Kolberg 2003, 2004 [interview]; Jota 2003, 2004 [interview]). Few elite members have organisational experience from white-collar employees' and professional organisations.

The fact that LO's largest union – the Norwegian Union of Municipal and General Employees (*Fagforbundet*) – includes both civil servants and auxiliary nurses, and that other white-collar unions are also organised in LO, does not outweigh this result. As will be elaborated in Chapter 16, large groups of salaried employees are affiliated with other organisations. Nor is organised contact with employers' organisations, business and trade organisations a 'standard procedure' outside Parliament in DnA, and very few individual elite members report that they have frequent contact with this segment. Furthermore, only about 20 per cent report monthly contact with the kind of organisation associated primarily with 'new politics' issues: environmental groups. To conclude, the range of links seems broad, but DnA *at large* has well-organised links with a few kinds of organisations only.

SUMMARY AND CONCLUSIONS

Taken together, the closeness and range of relations depict a party's general pattern of relationships with interest groups. The mapping leaves no doubt as to whether links with interest groups are regarded as superfluous. The party's strategy discussions show that the party leadership considers links with various organisations as an adequate response to societal challenges. 'Openness' and 'dialogue' are key words. Interestingly, however, this approach is not systematically reflected in DnA's actual relationship with interest groups.

Regarding *the closeness of relationships*, previous studies have indicated that links with the trade union movement have declined. Above all, the Labour Party became structurally autonomous from LO and its unions when it abolished collective membership in the late 1990s (Allern and Heidar 2001; Sundberg 2003). Nevertheless, this study has revealed that the relationship with LO and its unions is still relatively close. Aylott (2003) argues that despite abolition of collective membership in the Swedish case, the development towards weak links is patchy at the local level. We observe that strong inter-organisational links characterise the Norwegian Labour Party-union relationship at the national level in the early 2000s. In recent years, the organised links for contact with LO have in fact been consolidated, perhaps even intensified, after a period of decline. Confirming Sundberg's study from the late 1990s (2003), my survey further shows that LO officials are indeed represented in the Norwegian Labour elite. Additionally, it reveals that DnA is strongly linked with the trade union movement through extensive actual

128. As will become clear, Norwegian parties' contacts with women's organisations are generally weak. In Chapter 14, I discuss the possibility that DnA's link reflect contact with groups within the labour movement, not feminist groups outside.

contact at the individual level, seemingly also outside organised settings. In terms of the typology developed in Chapter 4, there is little doubt that the Norway's social democrats are incorporated in a full-blown *alliance* with LO and its unions.

Relations with other interest groups are, in contrast, more distant. DnA does have organised links for contact, but the practice of consulting external organisations seems to have limitations at the organisational level. There seem to be relatively few specific organisations with which DnA as a whole attempts have well-organised contact links. During the manifesto-making process, contact with external interest groups does take place, but no *systematic* hearing had been arranged before the 2001–2005 Manifesto was developed. On the other hand, a great majority of DnA's top elite are, or have been, officials or staff in one or more organisations, and relatively weak organised links do not prevent extensive ad hoc contact at the individual level with some kinds of organisations. Contact with humanitarian and community-centred organisations even approaches the archetype of *informal partnerships,* as most of the elite have regular (monthly) contact with such organisations.

With regard to the *range of the relationships* with interest groups, the survey shows that DnA has relationships with a variety of interest groups. Links have been identified with groups related to opposite flanks of both old and new cleavages. In the early 2000s, Labour's political decisions are made by a heterogeneous elite group, with a rather complex web of links within civil society. However, the party's close relationship with LO and the relative distance from other labour market organisations and organisations associated with 'new politics' issues weakens the impression of wide-ranging relations. The strategy of seeking access to diverse interest groups, and salaried employees in general, is not systematically followed up in practice.

Neither the relative closeness nor range of relationships with various interest groups can be fully assessed before the cross-party comparison in Chapter 14. However, in preliminary overall conclusion, there is no doubt DnA aims to have *both* a fairly close relationship with the trade unions *and* wide-ranging organised ad hoc relationships with others. The question is whether this strategy of backing two horses acts to constrain the development of organised links with organisations outside the labour movement.

chapter eight | the conservatives: network of weak links with business profile?

This chapter focuses on the traditional antagonists of social democracy in Norway, the Conservatives. Unlike the case in many other countries, the Norwegian Conservatives did not emerge from the rural aristocracy, but came from traditional elites and higher civil servants who opposed the introduction of parliamentary government in the late nineteenth century (Svåsand 1998b: 173). In the wake of the industrialisation of the Norwegian economy, it grew to be a secular, urban party for self-employed citizens with significant links to the business community. The party promoted classical conservative core values such as private property, individual freedom and limited state interference (cf. von Beyme 1985: 46). As in the case of the Labour Party, the backdrop is a long history of relationships with interest groups, and eventually mainly in terms of links with business, trade and employers' organisations.

BACKDROP: TOWARDS A NEO-LIBERAL PEOPLE'S PARTY?

Ideologically, the Conservatives have seen significant changes since the early decades of the twentieth century. The party aimed for abolition of economic controls as quickly as possible after the Second World War, but has not been a radical conservative party in the second half of the twentieth century. According to Widfeldt (2005: 113–14), the Norwegian Conservatives have kept more emphasis on gradual change and traditions than have their Swedish counterpart, but the policies supported in practice have not been characterised by limited state interference. Although DnA was the major force behind the development of the welfare state, the right wing followed suit by eventually supporting policies that contributed to this development (Kuhnle *et al.* 1986: 465; Sejersted 2003: 329). In practice, the Norwegian Labour Party and the Conservatives approached each other on important issues such as nationalisation, regulations, finance policies, agricultural policy and social legislation during the 1950s and 1960s (Sejersted 2003: 264, 329; 175).

In line with typical conservative pragmatism, the party manifesto was initially very narrow, but later adapted to the mass party model of extensive party programmes (Sejersted 2003: 388–91). Gradually, the Norwegian Conservatives began to see themselves as a centre-oriented conservative party with a pronounced belief in progress, but did not change the name 'Høyre' ('Right') to a less defining concept, like the conservative parties elsewhere in Scandinavia (von Beyme 1985: 49). Along similar lines it has been argued that Norway's conservative party has been less influenced by neo-liberalism than has, for example, its Swedish equivalent since the late 1970s (Widfeldt 2005: 114).

Nevertheless, when environmental issues – representing post-industrialist 'new politics' – emerged on the public agenda in the 1970s, the growth ideology dominated the Conservative Party's response. The party had sympathy for classical nature conservation (Bjørklund and Hellevik 1988: 418), but did not adapt to the new, more radical environmental movement. The party leadership emphasised economic liberalism, not value-based conservatism (Knutsen 1997: 244). Moreover, Norway's increasingly successful Progress Party may have contributed to significant changes in the political profile of the Conservatives in recent years. Harmel and Svåsand (1997: 323, 336) show that on issues relevant to the Progress Party's identity, the Norwegian Conservative Party has moved to the right, to a certain extent re-orienting itself towards liberalism. Conservative Party members are less ideologically heterogeneous than the case within DnA (Heidar and Saglie 2002: 120), but the tensions between the social conservative and liberal faction have certainly not vanished (see *Verdens Gang* 06.01.06).

In terms of its electorate, the Conservatives are also more diffuse than before. The socio-economic changes of the twentieth century have primarily enhanced the Conservatives' potential for electoral success (cf. Berglund 2003: 117). The heterogeneous nature of the rising middle class challenged the traditional class-voting in favour of centre-right parties. During the 1950s and 1960s, the Conservative Party identified as its major priority the increasing number of civil servants, administrators, clerks and the like (*funksjonærer*), at the expense of large-scale, self-employed farmers. As the future prime minister Kåre Willoch then argued, according to Sejersted (2003: 184–5): if the non-socialist parties took stand for the farmers, and left the role as employees' party to DnA, Norway would be assured socialist government everlastingly. In order to restrain their prime adversary, the Conservatives had to become more of a 'people's party'.

From the late 1970s, the cross-class strategy did pay off in elections (Selle 1997: 155), and the Norwegian Conservatives experienced an unprecedented electoral growth. The party improved its standing in rural areas and in the north (Kuhnle *et al.* 1986: 448). Due to the reduced importance of socio-cultural cleavages, the party has also, at times, gained voter groups traditionally representing the Norwegian counter-cultures (Bjørklund and Hagtvet 1981: 42). Since the 1990s, however, support has declined, with the 2001 election as a notable exception (see Appendix E). Even if there has been a general swing towards the right among workers, the conservative electorate is in the early 2000s still dominated by the self-employed and administrators, clerks and the like (*funksjonærer*) in the private sector with higher education (Svåsand 1998b: 175–6; Berglund 2003: 129). But employers are no longer so distinctly inclined to vote Conservative – their support decreased from around 40 per cent in the 1970s to about 20 per cent in the 1990s. The employer vote is spread across all the non-socialist parties, with the Conservatives more strongly supported by the 'higher level service class' (Knutsen 2004b: 66–9). Thus, Norway's Conservatives are to a greater extent a liberal cross-class party today, but with conditional electoral success. In recent years, the party does not appear to have been particularly concerned with the socio-demography of voters, according to available material. Instead, the focus has been on correlations between different policy views and party preferences (Wickstrøm 2005 [e-mail correspondence], Høyre 2005a).

The approach to the interest-group community seems also to have changed over time, but not radically. In the post-war years, the organisational strength of the labour movement was considered a major challenge but the Conservative identity as an 'anti-party party' remained clear. In the 1950s and 1960s, the party was still primarily a campaign organisation (Sejersted 2003: 53–63). Moreover, business organisations hesitated to be closely associated with the Conservatives and concentrated on public administration and the government in the 1950s (*ibid*: 167). Contact with interest groups took place primarily in the parliamentary arena (*ibid*: 157–8), and the relationship between the Conservative Party and Norwegian business organisations was not always friendly (*ibid*: 169).

The establishment of the business association *Libertas*, previously mentioned in Chapter 6, showed that business and industry working for neo-liberalism felt the need for contact outside the corporate channel (Sejersted 2003: 169). The umbrella organisation supported non-socialist parties financially and established various 'information institutes' itself; it combined '(...) the function of channeling funds with that of engaging in a variety of parallel action and long-term opinion-influencing activities' (Heidenheimer and Langdon 1968: 111). The party leadership feared that association with Libertas would harm the Conservatives' public image (Sejersted 2003: 70–1), and in 1948, the Libertas organisation was publicly exposed. The financial donations to the Conservative Party ended (*ibid:* 76), but instead the party received more direct, regular support from business and industry, while individual politicians continued to have contact with Libertas (*ibid*: 79, 218, for details see Heidenheimer and Langdon 1968: 111).[129]

In general, however, Norwegian business and industry circles were discontent with the Conservative Party leadership, criticising the party manifesto, and electoral and parliamentary strategies. In 1959, Libertas launched its own action programme and carefully supervised the candidate selection of non-socialist parties. Later an alternative government budget was developed (Sejersted 2003: 213; Heidenheimer and Langdon 1968: 127). Some argued that *Libertas* should establish a new party, whereas the Conservatives claimed that the umbrella organisation would have to be abolished (*ibid*: 215, 217). The result of this conflict was allegedly that the Conservative Party became consolidated whilst Libertas decided to not launch political issues on its own (*ibid*: 218–9). In fact, relations with business and industry were more cordial in the 1970s than in the 1960s.[130]

Hence, there have been no formal co-operation agreements between the Conservatives and employers', business or trade organisations after the Second World War. The contact has instead materialised through more or less organised contact with individual organisations and personal overlaps or transfers (Sejersted 2003: 171). From 1945 to 1960, about 60 per cent of the members of the party executive also held positions in trade, business or primary-sector organisations

129. Sejersted (2003: 205–6) argues that the head of Libertas was first asked to raise money, but when he required the right to formally participate in the manifesto-making process the idea was abandoned.

130. In 1988, Libertas was abolished as an organisation (Source: CAPLEX, http://www.caplex.no/Web/ArticleView.aspx?id=9320914).

(Haaversen-Westhassel 1984: 98).[131] As far as other organisations are concerned, Haaversen-Westhassel (1984: 102) has shown that from 1945 to 1981 no executive member in the Conservative Party reported experience as an official in the trade union movement, and few were holding or had held positions in other kinds of organisations (*ibid*: 114–5, 119–20).

Gradually, however, the organisational development in the Conservative Party gave better conditions for extra-parliamentary links into civil society. About 1970, organisational restructuring strengthened the party organisation *vis-à-vis* the parliamentary party and the central office *vis-à-vis* the province and local associations (Kuhnle *et al.* 1986: 457–9; Svåsand 1998b: 178). Numerous policy committees were established by the executive committee. Throughout the 1960s and 1970s the party leadership increasingly envisioned the party as a well-organised mass movement. By the 1980s there had been a significant rise in membership and grassroots activities (Svåsand 1998b: 178; Sejersted 2003: 398).

More importantly, the Conservatives worked to give white-collar organisations the right to negotiate with the state on the same terms as the trade unions (LO). Yet the development was not reflected in a significant rapprochement with interest groups outside the Storting. The parliamentary group remained more independent of the party organisation than in the case of Labour (Heidar and Saglie 1994: 133). Over time, the Conservatives changed from a strategy of merely supporting independent professional organisations to working for a politically neutral LO. They did not promote well-organised co-operation between the party and these interest groups (Sejersted 2003: 171–2; 185–6). Concurrently, the share of personal overlaps with business and industry organisations declined during the 1970s (Haaversen-Westhassel 1984: 98–9).

In the late 1970s, the party officially invited the trade unions (LO) to co-operate (Sejersted 2003: 171–4), but was rebuffed. Nevertheless, the Conservatives have continued to focus on the relationship with employees' organisations. In the early 1980s, the Conservatives established a working group elaborating political issues concerning labour and trade (Conservative Party Annual Report 1981: 100, 1986: 12). Moreover, Selle (1997: 161) indicates that the party increasingly opened up the manifesto-making process to various external organisations in the 1990s. Hence, the development depicts a party whose links with its traditional core organisations have weakened, and that to a certain extent has attempted to expand its organised network. What characterises the party's relations with interest groups in the early 2000s?

---

131. A well-known example from the individual level is the aforementioned Kåre Willoch, who was consultant for the Norwegian Shipowners' Association (*Norges Rederiforbund*) from 1951–52, MP from 1958 to 1989, the party's secretary-general from 1963 to 1965, and who was employed as staff in the headquarters of the Norwegian Confederation of Industry (*Norges Industriforbund*) from 1954, and continued to work for this organisation also after he was elected MP for Oslo in the 1960s (Source: Aschehough og Gyldendals Store Norske Leksikon, 4th edition 2005–07, http://www.snl.no/article.html?id=805790; see also http://epos.stortinget.no/Biografi.aspx?initialer=K%c3%85WI).

RELATIONSHIPS WITH INTEREST GROUPS TODAY

Unlike the Labour Party, today's Conservatives do not seem to put much emphasis on organised contact with external interest groups. Neither available party documents such as annual reports and organisational evaluations nor key informants indicate that establishing links with range of interest groups is a major strategy for the party at large outside the Storting (see Conservative Party Annual Reports 1992–2004). But in day-to-day politics, the presupposition is that the party staffs rely on their personal acquaintances (Hole 2003 [interview]). Is this articulated strategy of distance from interest groups followed up in practice?

Closeness of Relationships

Inter-organisational Links for Contact with Interest Groups

The Conservatives do not have very fixed routines for organised contact with any kind of interest group (see Table 8.1). Given the above-mentioned strategy, it does not come as a surprise that written co-operation agreements, liaison committees, and joint conferences are non-existent, or that external interest groups are not invited as guests or speakers to the party convention (Hole 2003 [interview]). But, according to the party's secretary-general, it is not usual either to invite interest groups to dialogue seminars, or to internal party meetings, seminars and conferences. According to the party's annual reports, independent experts are occasionally asked to contribute to the work of policy-making committees, but little is said about interest groups (see Conservative Party Annual Report 1993: 26).

However, the fact that a research report was commissioned by the Conservatives *together with* the Shipowners' Association in 2001 indicates the existence of some organised links for contact with interest groups (Conservative Party Annual Report 2001: 17). Furthermore, the committee responsible for raising financial support for the party (*Økonomistyret*) invites business owners and leaders of major Norwegian companies to 'breakfast meetings' at party headquarters about every second month. Here questions related to business and industry are discussed, and the meetings sometimes involve MPs (and prospective ministers and state secretaries) informing those invited about political issues currently being discussed in the Storting. The meetings with the business community are informal in the sense that they are not recorded, and have until recently not been widely known. Although people are invited as individuals, it is worth noting that the present committee leader is himself a former chair of the Confederation of Norwegian Enterprise (*Næringslivets Hovedorganisasjon*, NHO)[132] (Høyre 2005b; *Verdens Gang* 08.05.05).

As shown in Table 8.1, a certain exception has also to be made for the Business Channel (*Bedriftskanalen*), a dialogue forum for small and medium-sized business. And after this study was finished, the Conservatives invited selected interest organisations to address their party congress, including the leader of the LO union

132. Formerly the Employers' Association of Norway (*Norsk Arbeidsgiverforening*, NAF), which merged with the Norwegian Confederation of the Craft Industry and (*Norges Håndverkerforbund*) and Norwegian Confederation of Industry (*Norges Industriforbund*) in 1989.

United Federation of Trade Unions (*Fellesforbundet*) (*Dagsavisen* 14.05.06). It is furthermore assumed that the party staff members take advantage of their personal acquaintances in the interest-group community when performing their functions (Hole 2003 [interview]). In general, however, the practice of consulting interest groups seems limited in the Conservative Party at the organisational level.

Table 8.1: Conservative Party inter-organisational links with interest groups 2000–04

	Existence	If yes, what kind
Permanent joint committee	No	
Temporary joint policy committees	No	
Joint conferences	No	
Written or tacit agreements about regular meetings	No	
Invitation to the party congress	No	But in 2005, the Conservatives invited selected interest organisation leaders to address their party congress.
Invitations to party meetings, seminars and conferences	No/ unsettled	Not usual to invite interest groups to party arrangements.
Specific dialogue seminars and hearings	No/ unsettled	Not usual outside the Storting. However, the party arranges closed 'breakfast meetings' with business owners and leaders of major companies. Furthermore, a forum for communication between the party leadership, the parliamentary group and small- and medium-sized business about policies for business and industry has existed since 1994.
Meetings outside party bodies	Yes	Yes, individual officials, committee members and staff are assumed to meet with representatives of interest groups, but having organised meetings is not 'standing operating procedure' in party headquarters.

Sources: Various party documents (see Appendix A), Hole (2003 [interview]), Hole (2005 [e-mail correspondence]), and Lunde (2003 [interview]).

This notwithstanding, the impression of a party organisation emphasising organised contact with interest groups is to a certain extent strengthened when we examine the manifesto-making process in particular. The party leadership has tried to compensate for the power centralisation implied by the organisational reforms in the late 1960s by inviting the grassroots to greater involvement in the manifesto debate (Sejersted 2003: 392–6). Organised contact during the manifesto-making process also includes external contributors. According to Selle (1997: 161), by the 1990s the Conservatives had opened up for interest groups in general through the use of 'hearings'.

In connection with the 2001–2005 Manifesto, no workshops were arranged and the committee primarily invited only experts who sympathised with the party as external contributors. But the basic material for debate is presented to a wider audience on the party's website homepage (Lunde 2003 [interview]; see also Conservative Party Annual Report 1996: 31). Most importantly, the committee received and reviewed written comments from numerous interest groups. On the initiative of various organisations – including the Norwegian Confederation of Enterprise and trade unions – meetings were arranged when the first draft was worked out. To meet with those organisations that request appointments themselves is defined as an important part of the committee's tasks. Finally, it should be mentioned that the Business Channel was formally asked to comment during the initial phase (Lunde 2003 [interview]).[133] Still, as in the case of Labour, a practice of formally inviting various interest groups to a 'manifesto hearing' had not been established before the process of drafting the 2001–2005 Manifesto.

Unorganised Links for Contact with Interest Groups and Frequency of Actual Contact

Certainly, the Conservatives' relationship with interest groups is much less organised than that of the Labour Party, although the inter-organisational links with the trade, business, industry and employers' segment seem somewhat stronger. What do individual-level data tell us about the relationships? Many Norwegians will remember the co-operation between former party leader Kaci Kullmann Five and the environmental group *Bellona* in the early 1990s (*Dagbladet* 17.06.98). But little is known about the extent of the Conservatives' less organised contact. Let us start by looking at the links created by transfer or overlap of leadership and staff between the party organisation and interest groups (see Figure 8.1; see Appendix D for complete frequencies).

First, it should be noted that due to the low number (N), the figure must be interpreted carefully. In theory, replies from only a few more respondents could, at worst, have had a significant impact on the total result, although the characteristics of the non-response do not make that seem very likely (see Appendix B). In sum, the survey reveals that more than half of the Conservative Party's top elite – four out of seven – have experience from work in interest groups (see Appendix D). As noted in Appendix B, because of the 'under-representation' of executive members the total extent of such experience is perhaps significantly greater in the population as a whole. Nonetheless, some major tendencies can be identified.

133. The secretary also worked closely with the political advisers of the parliamentary group. In this way, contact with interest groups in relation to parliamentary deliberations may indirectly have played a role in the process (Lunde 2003 [interview]).

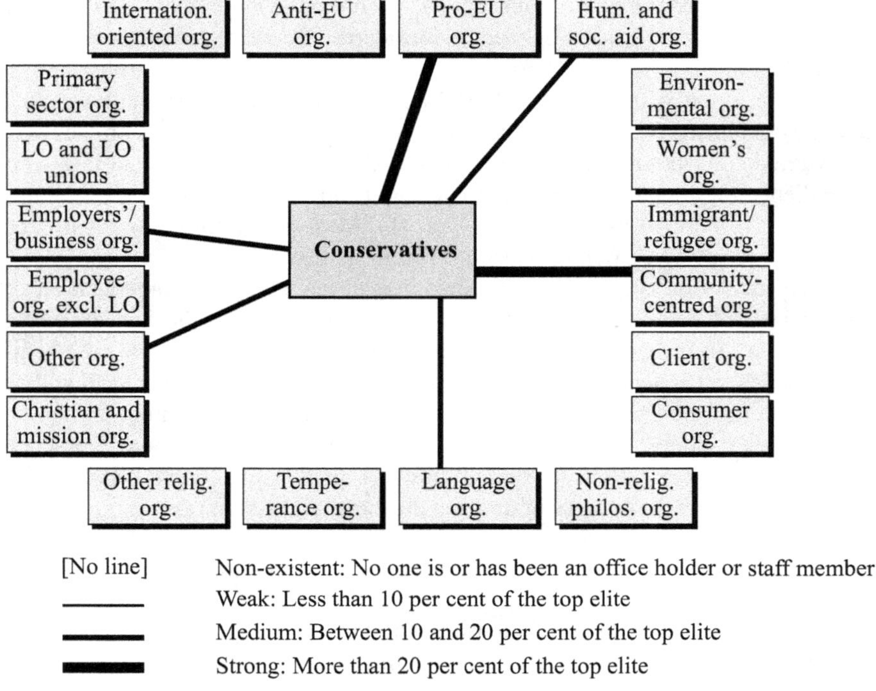

Figure 8.1: Conservative Party links, by top elite members who hold or have held office/who are or have been staff members at the national or local levels in various interest groups 2003/2004.[1] *N = 7*

1 If a respondent is/has been an official and also is/has been a staff member, the answer is registered only in the 'official category'.

The figure shows that *strong* links exist only with organisations working for EU membership and community-centred organisations (related to culture, sports, youth, elderly, hobbies and so forth). More than 40 per cent – three out of seven – have worked as officials or staff members in pro-EU membership organisations. In the case of the community-centred organisations, however, one should not read too much into the difference since this category is fairly broad. More importantly, the link in terms of personal overlap and flows is of medium strength in the case of employers', business and trade organisations, language associations, human and social aid organisations, and others. This only implies *one* person due to the low N, but in any case we may conclude that the Conservatives do not mainly seem to recruit their top elite from the business community and employers' groups.[134]

134. This is also reflected at the membership level. According to Heidar and Saglie (2002), only 11 per cent are members of business, trade or employers' organisations. Thus, the pool of potential leaders with this kind of organisation experience is rather limited.

Table 8.2: Conservative Party top elite: frequency of formal and informal contact with interest groups and their representatives in general in 2003. Per cent[1]

		Daily/ Weekly	Monthly	A few times	Never	No resp.	Total	N
Formal contact	Formal meetings or teleconferences	0	29	29	29	14	101	7
	Speakers at each other's seminars/conferences	0	0	43	43	14	100	7
	Formal written hearings or letters (incl. electronic)	43	0	29	14	14	100	7
Informal contact	Informal meetings, conversations, telephone conversations	14	29	57	0	0	100	7
	Informal written communication via SMS and e-mail	29	29	42	0	0	100	7
	Informal written communication like personal letters and memos	29	0	57	14	0	100	7

1 *Question:* 'Next, we would like you to state how often you had contact with interest groups *in different ways during the past year*. We distinguish between *formal* and *informal* contact:

- About how often did you have *formal contact* – of relevance for your work in the party's central organisation – with representatives from different interest groups in the following ways the past year? (tick off one alternative per line)
- About how often did you have *informal contact* – of relevance for your work in the party's central organisation – with representatives from different interest groups in the following ways the past year? (tick off one alternative per line)'

Weak inter-organisational links for contact and limited overlapping leadership notwithstanding, parties and interest groups may interact at the individual level through contact between official representatives or more informal contact. Table 8.2 reports how often the top elite in the Conservative Party had contact with interest groups in 2003, and distinguishes between formal and informal contact. First, we note that members of the Conservative top elite are more or less regularly in contact with interest groups. Informal meetings, telephone calls and written communication via SMS and e-mail seem the most widespread type of contact. In 2003, from about 45 per cent to 60 per cent – i.e. three to four persons out of seven – had contact with interest groups monthly or more often in this way. More than 40 per cent had contact through formal written letters, including electronic correspondence, at least weekly. Hence, the impression of a Conservative Party which does not have well-organised links with interest groups outside Parliament is partly confirmed. For the most part, the central party organisation relies on informal contact, through individual elite members.

However, Table 8.2 reveals that the Conservative Party – by means of individuals' contact – has regular access to numerous interest groups. More detailed analyses show that about 70 per cent of the party executive and staff members were at least monthly in touch with one or more organisations in 2003. To consider how strong the links are that the frequencies represent in a wider context requires systematic comparison with other parties. The question now is how extensive and frequent contact the Conservatives had with various organisations: did the greater part have contact at least monthly, a few times or never during the past year? Figure 8.2 sums up the major results in a sociogram.

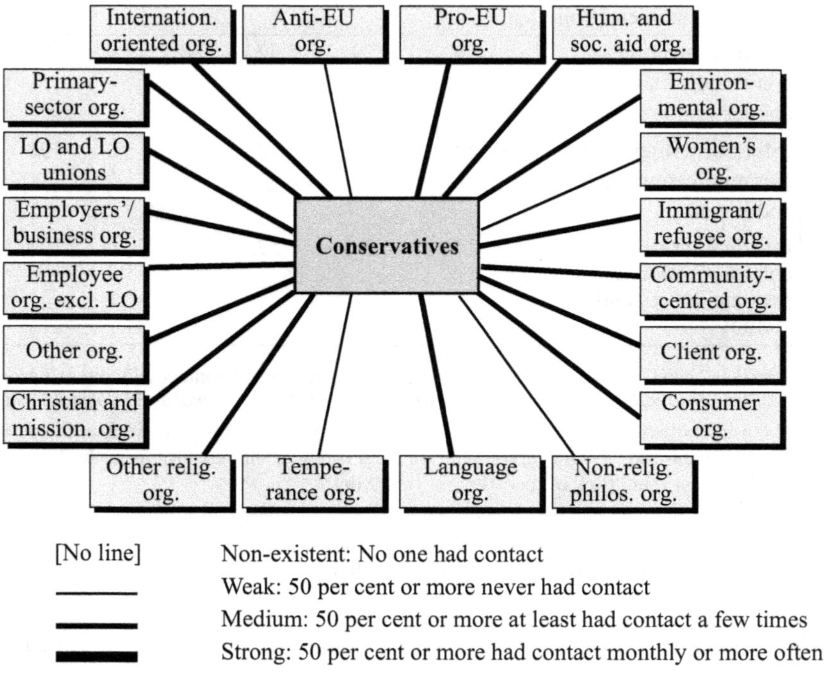

Figure 8.2: Conservative Party links through the top elite's frequency of contact with various interest groups in 2003.[1] *N =7*

1 *Question:* 'Could you please state how often you had contact – of relevance for your work in the party's central organisation – with one or more organisations within the following categories during the past year? The question includes both formal and informal, more random contact, written as well as oral communication.'

If exactly 50 per cent reported having contact 'seldom', the link is categorised as either 'medium' or 'strong'.

We observe that the top elite did not have *strong* contact with any kind of organisations in 2003. This could perhaps partly be due to 'under-representation' of elected officials with positions in the Storting and government, but the results nonetheless indicate that the extra-parliamentary contact with organised interest groups is somewhat limited. 30 per cent of the elite (two out of seven) report at least monthly contact with business and industry organisations.

Furthermore, nearly the majority (three out of seven) had been in touch with employees' and professional organisations outside LO, various community-centred organisations related to culture, sport, youth and so forth, and organisations working for Norwegian EU membership once a month or more often. A great number of organisations are linked through contact at least a few times a year with a majority of the top elite, representing contact of medium strength. In several cases, and for example in the case of employers', business and trade organisations, almost the entire top elite seem to have been in touch with one or more organisations within this category more than once. In fact, more detailed analyses show that there is no organisation category which is more repeatedly mentioned as one of the *three most frequent contacts* than the employers' and business organisations.[135] Thus, in terms of *individual* organisations, not whole categories, the employers' and business segment is more closely linked with the Conservative Party than the figure suggests. To conclude, the Conservatives still seem to have particularly strong contact with at least some employers' and business organisations.

In connection with the making of the party manifesto, the party had no collective strategy of contacting interest groups, but still the committee secretary reports extensive communication. Was this also the case among executive members and staff? The survey includes a question about contact during the manifesto-making process before the 2000 party congress,[136] but unfortunately only half of the respondents were also part of the national top elite at that time. Thus, the analysis has to be content with stating that among the respondents who did have positions in the central organisation of the Conservatives at the time, two out of three report having been in touch with between two to more than five different interest groups during the initial debate, with respect to the first draft, and in relation to the formal manifesto proposal. If these answers are typical, consulting interest groups might be more widespread in the Conservative Party when working out party platforms in practice than the organisational routines suggest.

Range of Relationships

How wide-ranging is the Conservative network of links with interest groups altogether? The party organisation attempts to reach out to voters across old class distinctions, but the leadership does not seem to put particular emphasis on developing extra-parliamentary relations. Nevertheless, the party is linked with diverse interest groups through formal and informal contact at the individual level. Figure 8.3 summarises the significant links – not the weak ones – based on the survey material.

---

135. *Question:* 'First, we would like you to write down the names of those (maximum three) organisations you had most frequent contact with last year. (….). Use the blank below (….)'.

136. *Question:* 'How many interest organisations did you have contact with – about one or several subsections – during the different phases of the manifesto-making before the party congress in 2000?

- Before the first draft was presented
- During the debate on the manifesto draft.
- During the debate on the manifesto proposal.'

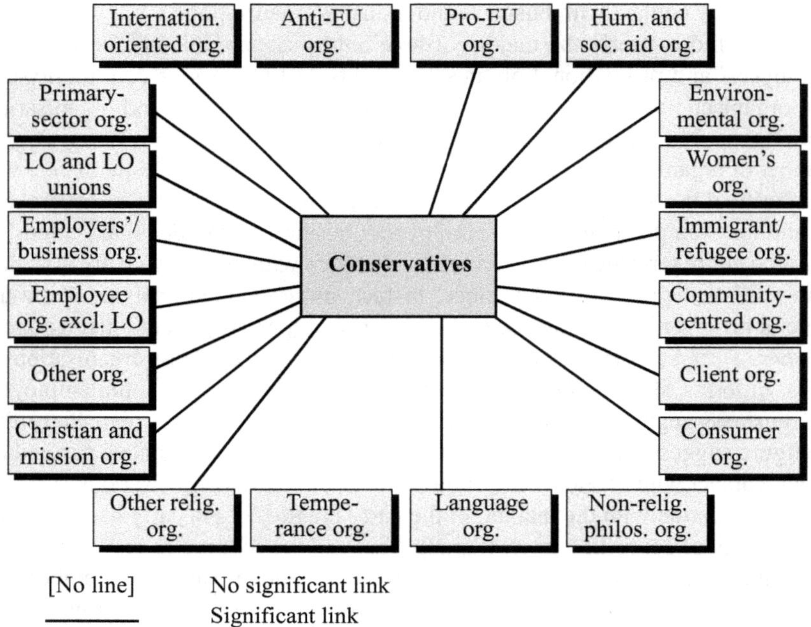

Figure 8.3: The Conservatives' total network of significant links with interest groups.[1] *N = 7*

1 Significant links are cases where 50 per cent or more at least had contact a few times in the past year (see Chapter 4)

According to the sociogram, the proportion of potential kinds of organisations with which the Conservatives have links is 0.80. The party is linked with more than a majority of the major alternatives. Furthermore, we observe that the Conservatives have links with various interest groups, *across* old cleavages: the figure shows that relationships exist with most of those organisation categories initially defined as included in a wide-ranging network. Despite the lack of well-organised links through the national elite, the party organisation has contact with employees' and professional organisations inside and outside the LO system. The network also includes humanitarian organisations, community-centred organisations and client organisations. The figure also shows that the Conservatives are linked with at least *some* interest groups representing 'new politics' issues – environmental groups, women's organisations, internationally-oriented organisations yet not organisations advocating non-religious philosophies of life. It should also be noted that the Conservative Party – unlike Labour – has more links that provide contact with groups related to the old socio-cultural cleavages through contact with language organisations. However, this 'pro EU-membership party' is not linked with anti-EU organisations.

Furthermore, while the degree of closeness does not vary *strongly* between organisation categories, certain differences exist. The party seems to concentrate its limited organised effort on employers', business and trade associations. If we take into account the intensity of various individual links, three kinds of organisations additionally stand out: professional and employees' organisations outside LO, community-centred organisations, and organisations working for Norwegian membership in the European Union. There are few signs of a veritable rapprochement between the Conservatives and LO trade unions. Relations with 'new politics' organisations, such as environmental and later anti-globalisation organisations, appear equally distant in the early 2000s. To conclude, the range of the relationships altogether is rather wide, but the network of links at the organisational level appears narrow.

SUMMARY AND CONCLUSIONS

What characterises the Conservatives' overall relations with interest groups today? This is the question that has been explored in this chapter. The party's contemporary strategic discussions do not seem to put emphasis on particular socio-demographic voter groups, nor organised contact with external interest groups outside the Storting. Also, we have identified few inter-organisational links for contact. The Conservatives seem linked mainly with the business and employer segments, albeit far less so than Labour is linked with the trade unions. The extent of actual contact indicates that the relationship does not resemble a true *alliance*.

During the manifesto-making process, organised meetings take place with various organisations, but no organised hearing among various organisation were arranged before the 2001–2005 Election Manifesto was prepared. On the other hand, about half of the elite interviewed through the survey are, or have been, officials or staff in one or more interest groups. Moreover, contact with interest groups does exist at the individual level. But the majority of the elite do not have frequent contact (monthly or more often) with any organisation category; individual contacts are often informal, and few contacts are results of official initiatives by the party as such. Thus, in general, the Conservative Party's relationship with interest groups appears fairly distant, also characterised by relationships that resemble the *virtual separation type* more than informal partnerships or organised ad hoc relationships. However, systematic comparison with other parties is needed if one is to draw definite conclusions on the degree of closeness.

With regard to the range of the relationships, the survey shows that the Conservatives' network of links is not so narrow, despite the lack of well-organised links with most organisations. The network includes numerous organisation categories and represents various and traditionally conflicting interest groups, cutting across old cleavages. The party does have organised links with some organisations and the elite only has a more or less 'strong' degree of contact with business, trade and employers' organisations, employees'/professional organisations outside LO, community-centred organisations, and organisations working for Norwegian EU membership.

Hence, as in the case of DnA, the well-organised and the inner part of the Conservative network seems to consist of a limited range of interest groups. In sum, the question arises as to what extent Norway's Conservative Party approaches the alternative of having generally weak links into interest-group community.

chapter nine | the liberals: towards general separation from interest groups?

So far we have seen that two of Norway's oldest political parties are linked with interest groups in quite different ways. The Norwegian Liberals (*Venstre*) have traditionally been classified, comparatively speaking, as a conservative social liberal party. Since the rise of a separate agrarian party and religious party in the 1920s and 1930s, it has been marked by an orientation towards the nation as a whole in terms of ideology. On the relationship between the state, society and economy, they have remained a 'centre' party. Liberals '(...) have stressed the rights of individuals, but on the other hand the party has also emphasised the rights of the state to intervene in society to prevent the more unwanted consequences of free-market liberalism' (Leiphart and Svåsand 1988: 321). The party emerged from social movements in the late nineteenth century, but distanced itself to a large extent from interest groups before the Second World War.

BACKDROP: PARTY IN SEARCH OF A DISTINCT LIBERAL PROFILE

Throughout the twentieth century, the Liberals repeatedly presented themselves as a mediator between the left and right by adapting to the political agenda of the major antagonists in the Norwegian party system. According to Malmström (2005: 148), the Norwegian Liberals made no mention of the term 'liberal' in their party manifestos before 1949. After the Second World War, the political platforms became gradually extended. The party has leaned towards both Labour and the Conservatives, which has often led to shifting positions on specific political issues. Unlike their Swedish counterpart, for example, the Liberals have been largely negative to membership in the European Union (Malmstrøm 2005: 158).

After the EC controversy in the early 1970s, the party split and was halved in strength (Leiphart and Svåsand 1988: 322). Thereafter, the majority (which retained the party name), and the young radicalised liberals in particular, transformed *Venstre*'s traditional ideology into a green platform whose manifestos were dominated by environmental policies. Policy documents now de-emphasised the radical liberal perspective (Grepstad and Rattsø 1986: 45–6), but 'became system critics within the new politics cleavage'. At elections, they competed with the Socialist Left Party along this axis (Knutsen 1997: 246).

However, this political transformation was not an immediate success. An overly narrow focus on environmental issues was singled out as one of the major explanations for the fatal election results of 1985. Traditional fields like regional and housing policy had been 'pushed into the background' (Leiphart and Svåsand 1988: 322–3). In the 1990s, the party re-oriented itself towards a broader, liberal political agenda (cf. Liberal Party Annual Report 1993: 43). It still sees itself as an alternative to both new left socialist and non-socialist voters. But as coalition partner in a centrist cabinet and in a government dominated by the Conservatives (*Høyre*), the Liberal Party has clearly distanced itself from the left wing. Today, the Liberal Party seems torn between emphasising its character as a general social liberal alternative, and their admitted need for making the party's policy profile more apparent (Annual Report 1997: 45; 2002: 8).

The voter profile is also characterised by heterogeneity, or lack of distinguishing features. Historically, the cross-class profile was considered an advantage when the Norwegian Liberal Party competed for the votes of the underprivileged, as well as for those of farmers and the urban middle class (Rokkan 1967; Kristinsson 1991: 43). Then, in the pre-war and post-war era, this lack of group identification became a liability. Norwegian society had become widely organised by interest groups, many of whom supported a particular party. In contrast, the Liberals were left without any social organisations to rely upon, and the party was not able to clearly identify alternative potential core voters (Leiphart and Svåsand 1988: 317–19). Ever since the 1960s, the social profile of *Venstre*'s voters has been relatively vague (Berglund 2003: 130, but see Bjørklund 1984: 194).

It could be argued that this is in line with a primarily cross-class profile, but the party has not managed to recruit many voters from new groups as the old voters vanished. During the 1950s and 1960s, urban voters began to outnumber rural ones (Bjørklund 1984: 189). As the number increased, so did the share of civil servants, administrators, clerks and the like (*funksjonærer*) among *Venstre*'s voters. Civil servants emerged as the occupational group with the most support for the Liberals (Leiphart and Svåsand 1988: 318–9). In the late 1990s, women and youth were in fact suggested as particular target groups (Liberal Party Annual Report 1999: 38). However, in terms of number of votes, the history of the Liberal Party is one of more or less continuous electoral decline (Leiphart and Svåsand 1988: 304, 311). Since 1945, the share of the popular vote has not exceeded 14 per cent. In the words of Leiphart and Svåsand (1988), the Liberals have – after numerous splits – developed from being a 'political pioneer to a political footnote'. True, the party has enjoyed political influence through non-socialist coalition governments in recent years, and increased support in the 2005 election, but the Liberals are today without doubt a small party.

The question is whether the party's relationship with interest groups has also changed during the same period. Although little is known about the development of this aspect of the party's organisation, there are some indications that the Liberals have attempted to form new alliances with major interest groups since the Second World War. In the 1960s, the Liberal Party successfully developed its extra-parliamentary organisation (Moe 1984: 257–8), and its annual reports indicate considerable efforts to approach various industrial organisations in the 1970s (Annual Report 1981: 13, 1982: 11). The ideological reorientation after the party's electoral collapse in 1973 led to an advance towards the new and emerging social movements (Liberal Party Annual Reports 1983–97). However, the party failed to gain a dominant position within the increasingly important environmental movement (Selle 1997: 157; Knutsen 1997: 247).

In contrast, the party worked rather closely with the Norwegian Confederation of the Craft Industry (*Norges Håndverkerforbund*) from the late 1970s. In 1981, this collaboration resulted in an action programme for small- and medium-sized businesses (Liberal Party Annual Report 1981: 13). The Confederation was later invited to the party congress, together with the Fishermen's Association (*Norges Fiskarlag*), the Farmers' Union (*Norges Bondelag*), the Farmers' and Smallholders' Union and the Norwegian Union of Food and Allied Workers (*Norsk Nærings- og nytelsesmiddelarbeiderforbund*, NNN) (Annual Report 1982:11).[137] Moreover, in the late 1980s, drafts of the party election manifesto were distributed to numerous organisations, which were invited to express their opinions (Annual Report 1988). By the late 1990s, however, these relations seemed to have soured (Selle 1997: 157). Thus we can say that efforts were made to establish more links with interest groups after the Second World War, but with limited success. Have the Norwegian Liberals made new attempts since then?

RELATIONSHIPS WITH INTEREST GROUPS TODAY

In the mid-1990s, the Liberals launched a concept called *Borgerforum* ('Citizens' Forum'), which encouraged local party branches to arrange open policy conferences (Liberal Party Annual Report 1995: 33). However, party documents do not describe these efforts as a part of a well-defined national strategy (see Venstre 2000a; Venstre 2000b). According to the secretary-general of the party, links with interest groups are generally not a major priority for the Liberals (Nyhus 2003 [interview]). In the public debate, the Liberals' leaders are among those who level most severe criticism at close relations between economic interest groups, specific political parties, and the state (see Liberal Party Annual Report 2003: 17, 31, *Dagens Næringsliv* 08.07.06). The decline in party members, and the size of the party organisation, is considered a problem, but links with interest groups are not identified as the way to compensate. In fact, party documents and informants suggest that keeping some distance from social organisations in general, and from special interests in particular, is the 'Liberal Way'. What then is the party's actual practice at the organisational and individual level?

Closeness of Relationships

Inter-organisational Links for Contact with Interest Groups

Table 9.1 summarises the Liberals' inter-organisational links with interest groups. We note that the party has no well-organised links with any organisation in the early 2000s. The Liberals do not try to ally with any interest group in particular, and existing inter-organisational links seem even weaker than in the case of the Conservatives. There are no written agreements, joint committees or mutual conferences. Interest groups are usually not invited to the party congress any longer.

On the other hand, some ad hoc policy committees open to non-members were established in the early 2000s, but it is less clear whether this implies communication with a range of interest groups. Party headquarters and the parliamentary

137. NNN is a trade union affiliated to LO; it did not attend the congress.

group do arrange policy seminars at which representatives of various organisations have been asked to participate. Party headquarters occasionally meet with interest groups on an ad hoc basis, but usually not at the specific request of the party (Nyhus 2003 [interview]). Thus, maintaining contact with interest groups appears not to be a standard operating procedure in the party's central organisation. By and large, the Liberals do not emphasise organised contact with external organisations outside the Storting. The strategy of distance is not only rhetorical at the organisational level: the focus is on the internal life of the party organisation.

Table 9.1: Liberal Party inter-organisational links with interest groups 2000–04

	Existence	If yes, what kind
Permanent joint committee	No	
Temporary joint policy committees	No	
Joint conferences	No	
Written or tacit agreements about regular meetings	No	
Invitation to the party congress	No	
Invitations to party meetings, seminars and conferences	Yes	In particular, seminars are co-arranged with the parliamentary group to which representatives of interest groups have been invited. Besides, open ad hoc policy committees are established, but organisations have not been invited as such.
Specific dialogue seminars and hearings	No	Not common outside the Storting. No systematic hearing is arranged during the manifesto-making process.
Meetings outside party bodies	Yes	Primarily the secretary-general sometimes meets with interest groups at their request.

Sources: Various party documents (see Appendix A), Nyhus 2003 [interview]), and Bjørlo and Molandsveen (2003 [interview]).

For the committee drafting the 2001–2005 Manifesto, contact with interest groups was not a priority. The party's central organisation did not systematically ask interest groups to comment on the party manifesto and there are few indications of radical changes in the near future. Thus, the practice initiated in the 1980s has not become a routine. Drafts are published on the Internet, but external organisations are not formally consulted. The committee drafting the 2001–2005 Manifesto did not initiate any dialogue meetings with selected groups, nor were organisation representatives invited to seminars and conferences (Bjørlo and Molandsveen 2003 [interview]). On the other hand, party activists with experience from interest groups – like organisations within the environmental movement – were asked to contribute. More importantly, numerous and varied interest groups sent reports, comments and viewpoints on the manifesto drafts, and a few consultative meetings were arranged on request. This limited extent of contact was in fact a deliberate choice. All external requests and written contributions were first dealt with by the committee's secretaries: their role was to function as a 'filter', or gatekeeper, against unwarranted influence from what were defined as 'special interests' (Bjørlo and Molandsveen 2003 [interview]).

Unorganised Links for Contact with Interest Groups and the Frequency of Actual Contact

The Liberals' inter-organisational links with interest groups are clearly weak, especially compared to the Labour Party's relationship with the trade unions. What do individual-level data tell us about the relationships? Unfortunately, the response rate to the survey conducted among the party top elite in 2003/2004 was low, with only 29 per cent – 4 out of 14 – replying. Of these, three are executive members and one is employed by the party headquarters. Consequently, as noted in Chapter 1, the results from the questionnaire will not be included in tables and figures in the case of the Liberals and have to be interpreted particularly carefully.

As far as personal overlaps and transfers are concerned, only one respondent holds or has held office/is or has been a staff member at the national or local level in an interest group out of the four who replied. This person has experience from internationally-oriented organisations and community-oriented organisations. Hence, it seems unlikely that Liberals recruit their top elite mainly from old social movement organisations, and the findings point in the direction of limited overlap with newer movement organisations.[138] The overall experience of the four respondents is in line with the information provided by the party's secretary-general as key informant: having positions in organised interest groups is not a criterion for selection of Liberal Party leaders. In fact, the converse holds, especially with regard to economic-functional interests: it is seen as a problem if executive members also hold central offices in interest groups such as business and trade organisations (Nyhus 2003 [interview]).

Despite the weak emphasis on organised contact with interest groups, it is furthermore suggested that contact does take place due to external requests – but to what extent? The existing material does not allow any definite conclusions. On the whole, formal, or official, contact appears less common than informal contact.[139]

138. For the record, Heidar and Saglie (2002) find that Liberal Party members are primarily affiliated to employees' organisations outside LO, to environmental organisations as well as charitable, humanitarian and community-centred organisations.

139. *Question:* 'Next, we would like you to state how often you had contact with interest organisations in *different ways during the last year*. We distinguish between formal and informal contacts:

- About how often did you have formal contact – of relevance for your work in the party's central organisation – with representatives from different interest organisations in the following ways the past year? (tick off one alternative per line).
- About how often did you have informal contact – of relevance for your work in the party's central organisation – with representatives from different interest organisations in the following ways the past year? (tick off one alternative per line)'.

Thus, the *collective* strategy of distance seems reflected at the individual level. On the other hand, the behaviour of the interviewed party elite members may indicate that in practice the Liberals do interact with certain interest groups. Although the survey data are not robust with regard to the party elite as whole, we should note that informants report having had contact with external organisations. Two out of four had formal meetings or telephone conversations monthly in 2003. Three out of four respondents were in contact with interest groups informally through e-mail and SMS at least once a month in 2003. Altogether, three out of four report having – formally *or* informally – had at least monthly contact with one or more organisation. Hence, the lack of a collective strategy does not exclude individual initiatives and even formal contact.

Certain groups seem to be more intensively linked to the Liberals in this way than others. Three out of four elite members reported having been in touch with employers, business and trade organisations and environmental organisations at least once a month the past year. These kinds of organisations also are dominant among the individual organisations that are reported as being the most frequent contacts.[140] The same number – 3 – had contact at least a few times with employees' and professional organisations outside LO, organisations representing non-religious philosophies of life, language associations, pro-EU membership organisations, women's organisations, immigrant and refugee organisations, client organisations and others. The findings thus suggest that environmental organisations and business and trade organisations are among those most strongly linked to the Liberal Party through contact at the individual level.

Is this also the case in regard to the manifesto-making process at the individual level? The party as a whole did not formally invite external organisations to participate in the development of the party's political platform in the early 2000s. However, three of the liberal respondents were also part of the party's top elite during the process resulting in the 2001–2005 Manifesto, and two of them report having been in touch with a few interest groups during this process.[141] Again, lack of organised initiatives does not preclude actual contact, although the extent of such contact seems limited.

Range of Relationships

Unfortunately, due to the low survey response rate, it is not possible to accurately describe the range of party relationships with interest groups based on the individual data in the case of the Liberals. Informal contact may well exist to

140. *Question:* 'First, we would like you to write down the names of those (maximum three) organisations you had most frequent contact with last year. (....). Use the blank below (....)'.

141. *Question:* 'How many interest organisations did you have contact with – about one or several subsections – during the different phases of the manifesto-making before the party congress in 2000?

- Before the first draft was presented.
- During the debate over the manifesto draft.
- During the debate over the manifesto proposal.'

organisations not mentioned by the elite members who did reply to the questionnaire about positions and contacts.

However, in line with Selle's (1997:157) earlier research, the Liberal network of links into the associational life seems narrow in the qualitative sense at least. The party places generally weak emphasis on organised contact with interest groups. The degree of closeness does not vary greatly among groups, but it seems as if the party concentrates on contact with the employers and industrial segment and the environmental movement. In conclusion, the range of relationships does not appear to be particularly broad.

SUMMARY AND CONCLUSIONS

In the early 2000s, the Liberals' strategy is mainly to keep some distance from all kinds of interest groups. Previous attempts to establish links with the business community and new social movements such as environmental groups belong to the past. Very few inter-organisational links for contact have been identified. In this sense, the Liberals appear to have more distant relationships with interest groups than either Labour or the Conservatives. During the manifesto-making process drafting the 2001–2005 programme, some organised contact did occur, but mostly on the initiative of the organisations themselves.

Nor do the less well-organised or informal links seem strong. Leaders of interest groups are seldom recruited to the party leadership – holding office in a major interest organisation is regarded a problem, not an advantage. Individual representatives do meet with spokesmen of other organisations, but relationships with interest groups appear distant. Unlike the Conservatives, the Liberal elite do not even seem to be involved in contact as a result of numerous external requests and initiatives. In relation to many organisation categories, the Liberals seem characterised by *issue-based contact* and approach the state of *virtual* – or actual – *separation.*

It is not possible to accurately assess the *range* of the existing network of links but the informants indicate that the Liberals are only significantly linked with business, trade and employers' organisations and the environmental movement. Hence, findings suggest that Liberals are more weakly and narrowly linked into civil society than the rest of the first 'generation' of Norwegian political parties. The Norwegian Liberals seem to come fairly close to the pattern of *general* separation from the interest-group community.

chapter ten | the centre party: approaching a wide network of organised links

The Centre Party – the former Farmers' Party – (Sp)[142] belongs to the small and rather heterogeneous family of European agrarian parties, and traditionally to the 'centre' of Norwegian politics on issues related to state inference and economy. Here we have a prime historical example of how an interest group may establish a political party – but hardly survive as one. Unlike the Norwegian labour movement, the farmers' movement did not choose to be involved in a close relationship once the division of labour between the political and corporate wing was established. A special relation remained, but not an integrated or well-organised one.

BACKDROP: TOWARDS A CENTRIST PEOPLE'S PARTY?

During the war, some leading personalities had sympathised with the Nazis and the Norwegian National Socialists (*Nasjonal Samling*), yet Sp was re-established as an agrarian party after 1945 (Christensen 2001: 38–9). It is a quite different Centre Party that faces the Norwegian interest-group community today than the one that struggled to restore its reputation among core voters after the Second World War (Christensen 2001: 38–9), but policy changes remained modest during the first decades. The party name was not changed until 1959, after its Swedish counterpart had successfully renamed itself the Centre Party (Christensen 2001: 39–41; Madsen 2001: 13–14). Leaving the large-scale farmers' profile behind appeared risky, in view of the competition from other parties. Smallholders mostly supported Labour, whereas farmers also voted for the Liberals, the Christian People's Party and the Labour Party (Christensen 2001: 50). Only in 1965 were numerous policy-developing committees established and the party manifesto radically changed. A broad range of issues was incorporated, including concerns of small industry, defence policies, cultural issues, health care and family policies. Regional policies, decentralisation and environmental policies became new core elements. According to Christensen (2001: 47), the Sp manifesto of 1965 was more or less 'lifted from' he Swedish Party's 1959 programme.

Thereafter, the party's attitude towards the state has been modified considerably. The relative importance of state subsidies for net farm income increased from the 1950s, and Sp increasingly promoted public intervention in the agricultural sector (Christensen 2001: 45–7; Gjerdåker 1995: 73–4). In line with the general acceptance of Keynesian principles, the party changed from promoting modest public expenditures to defending extensive public subventions. Throughout the 1970s, Sp's traditional profile as a non-socialist, conservative alternative weakened (Madsen 2001: 25). In 1973, the party concluded that 'environmental poli-

142. Although the Farmers' Party did not rename itself until 1959, I only use the 'Centre Party' label, for the sake of simplicity.

cies' and 'resource economy' were 'superior to the contemporary market economy' (quoted in Madsen 2001: 26, my translation). Indeed, it could be argued that the Norwegian Centre Party – like its Finnish and Swedish counterparts – became more heavily politicised and ideological during this period. The conflict between rural and urban interests became its prime political orientation (Widfeldt 1999: 2).

However, the amount of policy change was more modest in the Norwegian Centre Party than in for instance the Swedish case (Christensen 2005: 170). The traditional aim of income equality between agriculture and industry remained (Madsen 2001: 207–8). Competition from other parties has been greater in Norway with regard to agrarian, rural, and regional concerns, as well as environmental interests (Kristinsson 1991: 174, 181; Christensen 1992: 103; Madsen 2001: 306). Not until 1977 did Sp develop an action programme for the cities: and '(...) even in 1985 agriculture, fisheries and forestry received three times the space devoted to industry in the Centre Party's Manifestos' (Christensen 2001: 46). The question of European integration has temporarily reinforced the image of the Centre Party as primarily representing regional and farm interests. In other Nordic countries the former agrarian parties have become advocates of European integration, whereas Norway's Centre Party has remained firmly opposed to EU membership (Christensen 2005: 159).

But in the 1990s, after a certain re-orientation towards conservative economic policies following the decline of Keynesianism, the party distinguished itself as a protector of welfare services. During the public debate preceding the EU membership referendum of 1994, Sp presented a massive critique of modern capitalism (Christensen 2001: 48). Hence, Sp has in fact gone against the general flow, moving from the economic right towards the left in recent years (Madsen 2001: 313), a development which is visible at the voter level as well (Aardal 1999: 86; 2003b: 86). In 2004, the programme committee proposed that Centre Party policies should more strongly emphasise economic growth and stimulation of business and industry (Senterpartiet 2004a) – but in 2005 Sp formed a coalition government with both the Labour *and* the Socialist Left Party.

The party's constituencies also gradually changed throughout the twentieth century. The first decades after the Second World War, the Centre Party concentrated on rural communities in general, but in the mid-1960s it concluded that support from urban areas was needed for future survival (Madsen 2001: 15–6). The share of voters employed in the primary sector was in decline (Christensen 2001: 32). New 'target groups' in elections were defined: workers, civil servants, administrators, clerks and the like (*funksjonærer*), and in particular teachers and working women (Madsen 2001: 15–16). While more than 70 per cent of Sp's voters were farmers or fishermen in 1957, about one third belonged to this segment by 1981. It also seems that the remaining traditional core voters are less likely to vote Sp than before. The share of salaried employees has increased (Christensen 2001: 49), but the party does not have a firm grip on other occupational groups (Berglund 2003: 127–8). From 1957 to 1989, between 70 per cent and 80 per cent of Sp's voters lived in sparsely populated areas (Christensen 1992: 80–1). The party's relative success in urban areas in the 1993 election before the EU referendum in 1994 did not mark a lasting turning point. Today, the Centre Party voters are marked by a more rural profile in Norway than in Sweden (Christensen 1992: 93; Christensen 2005: 179). In short, Sp is no longer a pure agrarian party, but has kept a non-urban voter profile, and it is currently leaning more towards the left in terms of policies.

Although limited research has been conducted on this topic, the Centre Party's approach to the Norwegian interest-group community seems also to have changed since the 1950s. In the first post-war decades, emphasis was on expansion of the party organisation and 'the centre movement' – an ancillary youth association and women's organisation among others (Madsen 2001: 16–21). Externally, Sp was primarily oriented towards the Farmers' Union and the economic, agricultural organisations which were united in the Agricultural Central Federation (*Landbrukets Sentralforbund*) from 1946, which became the Federation of Norwegian Agricultural Co-operatives (*Norsk Landbrukssamvirke*) from the 1980s.[143]

The co-operation agreement implying that the party programme should reflect the programme of the Farmers' Union was abolished immediately after the war (Rovde 1995: 227; Ohman Nielsen 2001: 351), but historians nevertheless describe the links with the Farmers' Union as fairly strong in the first decades after the formal divorce in the 1930s (Madsen 2001: 30–3; Steen 1988: 225). Some of Sp's major politicians in the 1960s, 1970s and 1980s belonged to the top leadership of the Farmers' Union (Madsen 2001). Sundberg (2003: 110–1) has shown that in the 1950s and early 1960s slightly less than one fifth of the executive members in the Centre Party also held positions in the Farmers' Party (see also Allern and Heidar 2001). Madsen (2001: 214) notes that as late as the 1980s the party's agricultural policy was primarily based on consultations with the Farmers' Union and the Federation of Norwegian Agricultural Co-operatives.

The Norwegian Farmers' and Smallholders' Union (NBS) did not immediately approach the Centre Party after the link with DnA started to weaken (see Chapter 7). The Farmers' Union several times attempted to merge the two organisations, but the Smallholders' Union refused (Steen 1988: 243). The debate over EU membership made the smallholders reconsider their traditional preference for Labour, and the distance between NBS and the Centre Party has diminished. One of the most profiled national politicians in the Centre party during the last years, Per Olaf Lundteigen, is a former leader of NBS (Allern and Heidar 2001: 121). However, Sp's link with the Farmers' Union declined concurrently. In the 1990s, there were no personal overlaps between the party and the union in the respective executive bodies (Christensen 1992: 53; Allern and Heidar 2001: 127), and greater attention was paid to the party's relationships with other kinds of interest groups.

In 1996, a project called *Let's open the party doors* (*Vi åpner partiets dører*) identified links as a possible way to make Sp more attractive to core circles. Party members were encouraged to have dialogue meetings with various

143. In 1980, the confederation was abolished and incorporated in the Farmers' Union. After being renamed the Federation of Norwegian Agricultural Co-operatives, the professional organisation for agricultural co-operatives was later re-established as an autonomous unit. Its board, however, assembles leaders of not only the largest co-operative but also representatives of the farmers' organisations (Source: www.landbruk.no).

kinds of organisations at the local level, and the party elite and local activists were asked to make use of their circle of personal acquaintances (Senterpartiet 1996; Centre Party Annual Report 1996: 8; see also Senterpartiet 2001: 11).

Hence, in sum, the Centre Party's relationship with the farmers' organisations had weakened by the late 1990s, and the party started to aim for openness towards a wide variety of interest groups. What characterises its relationships today in terms of closeness and range?

RELATIONSHIPS WITH INTEREST GROUPS TODAY

By the early 2000s, the emphasis on links with various interest groups seems to have grown stronger. Forming what is called 'alliances' with various kinds of interest groups is highlighted as a key task for the national party organisation. Norway's main anti-EU membership organisation is defined as a major ally (Senterpartiet 2003: 5). According to its strategic plans, the Centre Party attempts systematically to build alliances with organisations concerned with regional and industrial policies, welfare and EU-related issues. The current party strategy stresses the need for links with economic organisations in general. Primary-sector organisations, business organisations for craft industries and for small and medium-sized companies, municipal industrial and travel business organisations, trade unions and professional organisations are seen as relevant groups for contact. Also mentioned as important are voluntary social and health-oriented organisations, welfare action groups, cultural organisations, student organisations, consumer organisations, and environmental groups (Senterpartiet 2003:7; Senterpartiet 2004b: 6; Sundsbø 2003 [interview]). To what extent is the ambition of organised and wide-ranging network of links with interest groups translated into practice? Let us start by looking at the organisational aspect.

Closeness of Relationships

Inter-organisational Links for Contact with Interest Groups

As shown in Chapter 6, the Centre Party did not establish a liaison committee or a formal co-operation agreement with the Farmers' Union after the integrated relationship had been untied. Table 10.1 demonstrates that today it has no such inter-organisational links with other interest groups. The Centre Party does not usually invite interest groups as guests to its party congress, not even the Farmers' Union. According to the party's secretary-general, the organised link with the primary sector has been replaced by less formal connections (Sundsbø 2003 [interview].

However, inter-organisational links with interest groups do exist, both with agricultural organisations and others. A party-union internal committee has been founded, charged with establishing stable contact with trade unions and professional organisations (Annual Report 1996; 2001: 11). The committee consists of party members who also are trade union activists (Allern 2001). In 2005, the party certainly broke a barrier when it organised a joint conference on public sector reforms with the Norwegian Union of Municipal and General Employees (*Fagforbundet*), which is the LO union that organises public-sector employees at the local level (Senterpartiet 2005).[144]

Table 10.1: Centre Party inter-organisational links with interest groups 2000–04

	Existence	If yes, what kind
Permanent joint committee	No	But the party has established an internal party-union committee that is assumed to provide contact with employees' organisations in particular.
Temporary joint policy committees	No	
Joint conferences	No	But in 2005, a joint conference with the Norwegian Union of Municipal and General Employees (Fagforbundet) was arranged for the first time.
Written or tacit agreements about regular meetings	No	
Invitation to the party congress	No	
Invitations to party meetings, seminars and conferences	Yes	Common to invite interest groups to seminars, conferences and even to arrangements in connection with meetings in the party's executive bodies.
Specific dialogue seminars and hearings	Yes	The central organisation has arranged specific dialogue seminars with interest groups. Contact with interest groups is common during the manifesto-making process. The manifesto committee has invited organisations to workshops, and meetings have been arranged by the committee as a whole and by individual members.
Meetings outside party bodies	Yes	Headquarters staff and the party leadership meet with various kinds of interest groups.

Sources: Various party documents (see Appendix A), Sundsbø (2003 [interview]) and Igland (2003 [interview]).

144. It might be added that the Centre Party also interacts with external organisations through joint actions. In relation to the long-drawn debate over gas-fired power plants, the party has collaborated with environmental organisations (and other parties) through temporary ad hoc groups like *Gasskraftaksjonen* and *Klimaalliansen*.

Furthermore, the Centre Party invites spokespersons of interest groups to party seminars, to conferences and in connection with party meetings at the national level. Although some of these arrangements have concerned the primary sector in particular, issues and organisations related to other policy fields have also been included (Annual Reports 1977–2003). Dialogue seminars have been arranged with certain circles, such as those represented by immigrant organisations in recent years (Annual Report 1999: 7). Both the party headquarters and the party's top leaders occasionally have ad hoc meetings with interest groups. Above all, the party leadership officially meets with primary-sector organisations, business and trade organisations and environmental organisations (Sundsbø 2003 [interview]). Hence, the Centre Party seems to have *generally* stronger links to interest groups at the organisational level than the case with either the Conservatives or the Liberals.

A closer look at the manifesto-making process prior to Sp's 2001 party congress corroborates the impression of emphasis on links with interest groups. With regard to environmental policy – which was pinpointed as a particularly important section to develop in the late 1990s – the committee completing the programme for 2001–2005 officially invited major environmental organisations[145] to workshops (Igland 2003 [interview]). Later, the manifesto committee received specific comments on drafts (Allern 2001). In addition, the committee, the secretaries and individual members responsible for separate manifesto sections met with various organisations. Interestingly, formally consulting primary-sector organisations *in particular* does not seem to be a tacit norm, but these organisations are more intensively involved than others through the informal presence of organisation 'representatives' in the manifesto committee and other policy-making committees.[146] Finally, the manifesto committee received numerous requests for contact from interest groups, which were asked to send written comments (Igland 2003 [interview]).

Unorganised Links for Contact with Interest Groups and Frequency of Actual Contact

Certainly, the Centre Party has inter-organisational links with interest groups. In the early 2000s Sp seems generally to have more well-organised contact than any other party examined so far, although it has no organised link as strong as the DnA-LO link to any organisation. What do the data from the individual level tell?

First, the survey reveals that about 60 per cent of the top elite in the Centre Party are current or former officials or staff members in one or several interest groups. Figure 10.1 shows the share of top elite members who hold or have held office, or who are/have been staff members, at the national or local levels in vari-

145. Primarily Friends of the Earth Norway (*Naturvernforbundet*), Nature and Youth (*Natur og Ungdom*), and Bellona.

146. For example, the leader of the Norwegian Farmers' and Smallholders' Union (NBS) from 1986 to 1992, and Sp secretary-general from 1997 to 2000, was a member of the committee preparing the 2001–2005 Manifesto. The parliamentary group's contact with interest organisations is also indirectly relevant by means on parliamentary policy documents used in the manifesto-making process (Igland (2003 [interview]).

ous interest groups (for complete frequencies, see Appendix D).

Obviously, there is no longer a norm 'dictating' extensive top-level representation of Farmers' Union. Less than 10 per cent – one person – report being or having been officials or staff members of an organisation within agriculture or fisheries at the time of the research, although the grass roots in Sp are still affiliated to primary-sector organisations to a significant extent (Heidar and Saglie 2002: 274).

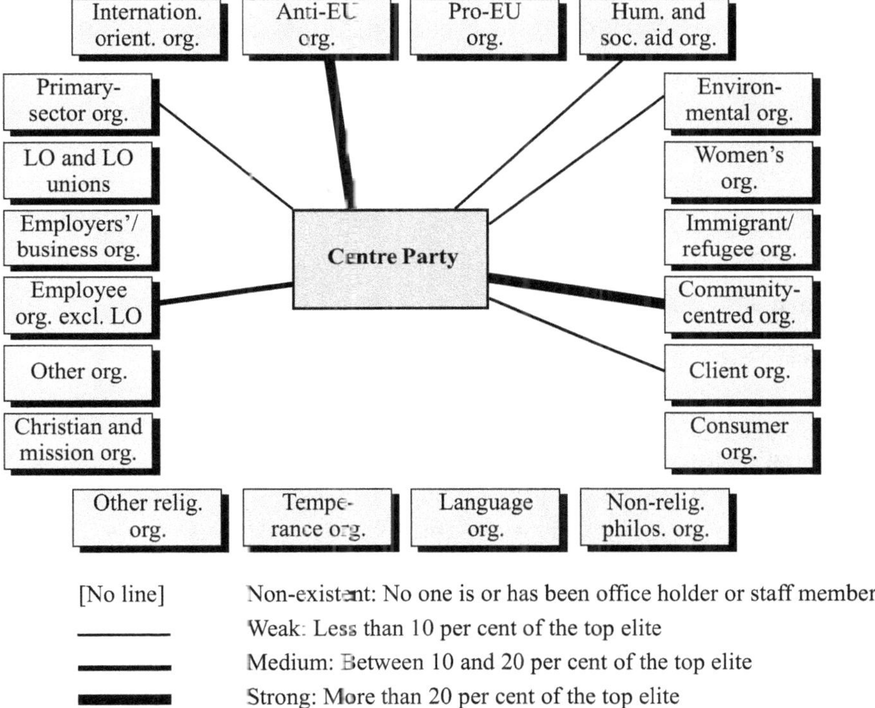

[No line] Non-existent: No one is or has been office holder or staff member

Weak: Less than 10 per cent of the top elite

Medium: Between 10 and 20 per cent of the top elite

Strong: More than 20 per cent of the top elite

Figure 10.1: Centre Party links, by top elite members who hold or have held office/who are or have been staff members at the national or local levels in various interest groups 2003/2004.[1] *N = 13*

1 If a respondent is/has been an official and also is/has been a staff member, the answer is registered only in the 'official category'.

Strong links only exist with organisations working against EU membership and community-centred organisations at the top elite level. True, the former category is very wide, but the frequencies show that almost 40 per cent of the Centre Party elite – 5 out of 13 – have experience as officials or staff members in anti-EU organisations. The link with employees' and professional organisations outside LO is of medium strength, and thus stronger than the link with primary-sector organisations. There are also former and current officials and staff members from other kinds of organisations among the Centre Party's top elite, but their share is not large.

Table 10.2: Centre Party top elite: frequency of formal and informal contact with interest groups in 2003. Per cent [1]

		Daily/ Weekly	Mon- thly	A few times	Never	No resp.	Total	N
Formal contact	Formal meetings or teleconferences	23	15	15	39	8	100	13
	Speakers at each other's seminars/conferences	0	31	46	23	0	100	13
	Formal written hearings or letters (electronic ones included)	0	23	38	31	8	100	13
Informal contact	Informal meetings, conversations, telephone conversations	23	31	38	8	0	100	13
	Informal written communication via SMS and e-mail	46	8	31	15	0	100	13
	Informal written communication like personal letters and memos	23	32	15	15	15	100	13

1 *Question:* 'Next, we would like you to state how often you had contact with interest groups *in different ways during the past year*. We distinguish between *formal* and *informal* contact:

- About how often did you have *formal contact* – of relevance for your work in the party's central organisation – with representatives from different interest groups in the following ways the past year? (tick off one alternative per line)
- About how often did you have *informal contact* – of relevance for your work in the party's central organisation – with representatives from different interest groups in the following ways the past year? (tick off one alternative per line).'

The impression of a party linked into the interest-group community is strengthened by the survey on actual contact at the individual level. Table 10.2 shows that the Centre Party elite have regular contact with interest groups in one way or another. Again we note that informal meetings, telephone calls, SMS, e-mails, letters and memos are the most widespread form of contact – more than half of the top elite had contact with interest groups in these ways at least once a month in 2003. Almost 50 per cent – 6 out of 13 – report to have had contact with interest groups through e-mail and SMS on a weekly basis or more often. Almost 40 per cent had formal meetings or telephone conferences of relevance for their work in the central party organisation at least once a month. Thus, we can conclude initially that the Centre Party seems involved in extensive contact at the individual level as a result of both organised links and informal contact between individual elite members.

To what extent did this activity include organisations other than the primary-sector segment? A summary analysis of contact with various organisations shows that more than 70 per cent of the Centre Party elite had – formally or informally – at least monthly contact with one or more interest groups about issues of relevance for work in the party's central organisation in 2003. The sociogram of Figure 10.2 shows how often and extensively the top party elite had formal and informal contact with various kinds of interest groups. We note *strong* contact only with anti-EU organisations: More than 50 per cent – 7 out of 13 – of the Centre Party elite had monthly contact with this kind of organisation in 2003. More detailed analyses show that almost a quarter has such contact on a weekly or daily basis.

Further, almost 50 per cent have been in touch with community-centred organisations related to culture, sports, elderly and so forth every month or week. Furthermore, the Sp elite had medium strong contact with a range of organisations, including various employees'/professional organisations, LO unions, business and industry organisations and environmental groups. A majority of the elite – and up

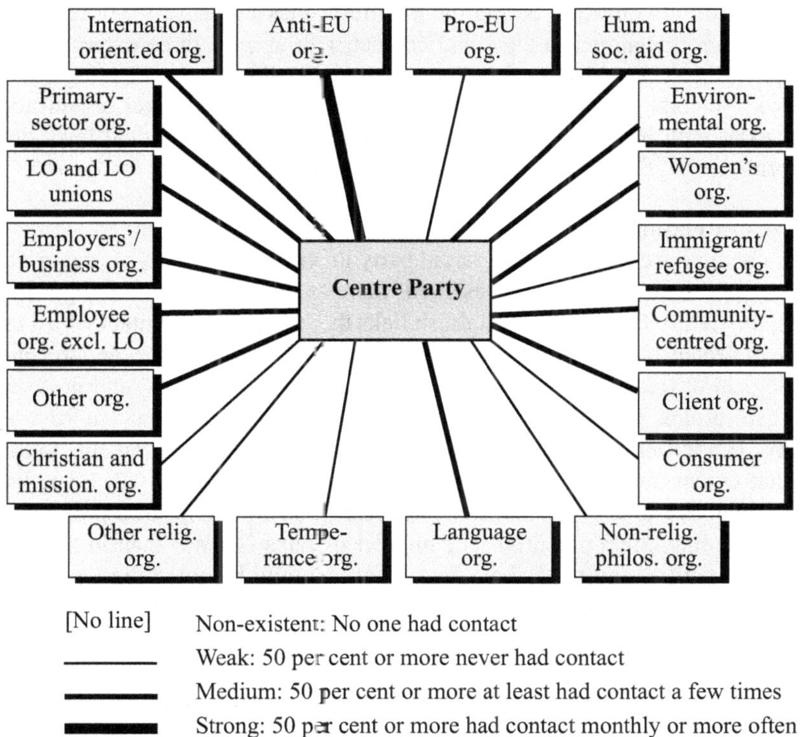

Figure 10.2: Centre Party links through the top elite's frequency of contact with various interest groups in 2003.[1] N = 13

1 *Question:* 'Could you please state how often you had contact – of relevance for your work in the party's central organisation – with one or more organisations within the following categories during the past year? The question includes both formal and informal, more random contact, written as well as oral communication.'

If exactly 50 per cent reported having contact 'seldom', the link is categorised as either medium or strong.

to 90 per cent (12 out of 13) in the case of business and industry – had contact with these kinds of organisations at least a few times. Interestingly, only 30 per cent – 4 out of 13 – were involved in contact at least monthly with organisations representing the primary sector.

However, to the question of the three individual organisations with which the elite had been most frequently in touch during the past year, primary-sector organisations rank second after anti-EU organisations.[147] To conclude, the Centre Party elite has extensive contact with organisations working against EU membership, but has also frequent contact with all kinds of labour market, business, trade and primary sector organisations, in addition to environmental groups.

Correspondence between the organisational initiatives and individually reported contact also exists in relation to the manifesto-making process, according to survey responses. Some of those in the Sp elite who were also officials or staff in the central organisation during the manifesto-making process before the 2002 Party Congress claimed to have had contact with at least three external interest groups.[148] However, the majority (five out of eight) did not recall having had contact with interest groups of any kind. To conclude, although inter-organisational links exist with many interest groups, the data from the individual level do not uniformly strengthen the impression of fairly close relationships in all cases.

Range of Relationships

What characterises the former agrarian party in terms of numbers of organisations and the political variety of represented interests? According to strategy discussions, the Centre Party aims to establish links that can provide contact with a broad range of organisations. The pinpointed target groups among voters and the party's ideological development suggest a specific focus on employees' and professional organisations, business, trade and industry organisations, and environmental groups, in addition to the primary sector. The survey among the top elite indicates to what extent the party has succeeded. According to Figure 10.3, Sp is linked with a majority of the organisation categories, corresponding to a proportion of 0.65 of the maximum potential. The number of links is lower than in the case of the Conservatives and the Labour Party, but it should be noted that only *one* respondent differentiates a 'significant' from a 'non-significant' link in the case of pro-EU organisations, immigrant and refugee groups and consumer organisations.

Moreover, Sp is certainly involved in contact with interest groups *across* the old cleavage lines. The party is not only linked with primary-sector organisations, but also for example has links to business and trade organisations, employers'

147. *Question:* 'First, we would like you to write down the names of those (maximum three) organisations you had most frequent contact with last year. (….). Use the blank below (….).'

148. *Question:* 'How many interest organisations did you have contact with – about one or several subsections – during the different phases of the manifesto-making before the party congress in 2000?

- Before the first draft was presented.
- During the debate over the manifesto draft.
- During the debate over the manifesto proposal.'

organisations, LO and LO unions, other employees'/professional organisations. However, few links exist to the organisations representing the old counter-cultures, but the relatively limited political significance of the associated conflict of interests suggest that we should not put strong emphasis on this limitation. Moreover, the most prominent 'no-party' in Norway lacks links with pro-EU groups. Then again, significant links exist to client organisations, humanitarian and other voluntary organisations, but only certain organisations associated with post-industrial – 'new' – politics are included in the network of the Centre Party, among them environmental organisations. The link to woman organisations possible includes contact with farmer women's organisations. Hence, the party network does not include links with all kinds of groups that can be argued to characterise wide-ranging relationships.

On the other hand, the strength of links does not vary very much among organisations. Although links with some organisation categories seem to be weak or missing, the number of organisations with which Sp has inter-organisational links seems fairly wide-ranging. Its elite primarily has extensive and organised contact with organisations working against Norwegian EU membership, but seems also rather extensively involved in frequent and formal contact with all kinds of labour

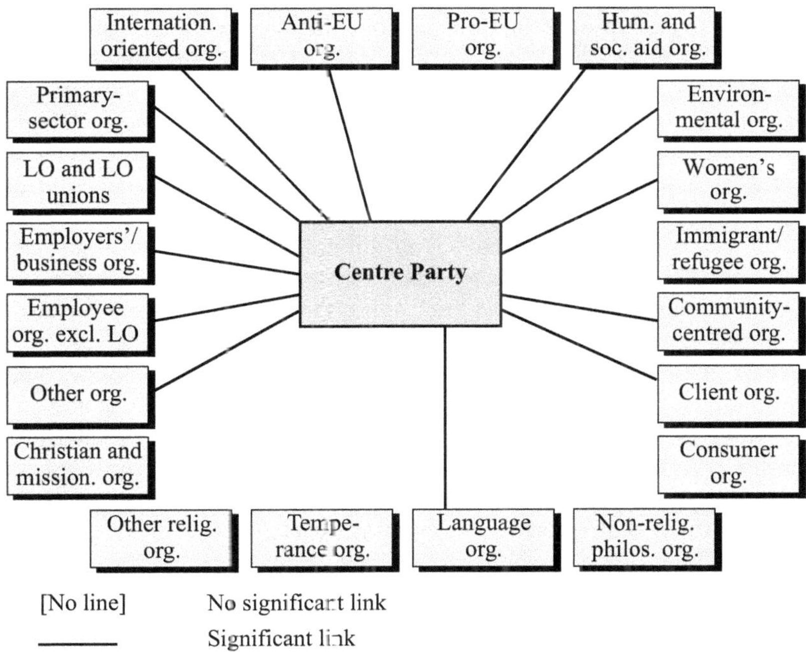

Figure 10.3: The Centre Party's total network of significant links with interest groups.[1] N = 13

1 Significant links are cases where 50 per cent or more at least had contact a few times the past year (see Chapter 4).

market organisations, business, trade and the primary sector, as well with environmental groups. Interestingly, there has recently been official co-operation between the Centre Party and one of the major LO unions. Centre Party is today linked with organisations across both old and new cleavages.

SUMMARY AND CONCLUSIONS

As regards interest organisations, the Centre Party's (Sp) formal affiliation with the Farmers' Union ended already in the late 1930s, and Sp put the Smallholders' Union and the Farmers' Union on an equal footing after the war. Today it defines a large part of the Norwegian interest-group community as potential allies. In general, the Centre Party seems to seek access to interest groups more systematically than the Norwegian Labour Party, and differs in this sense from the other centre-right parties examined so far. Several inter-organisation links have been identified, including a joint conference and dialogue seminars. Although no formal hearing was arranged with the interest-group community during the manifesto-making process preparing the 2001–2005 Manifesto, the drafting committee had extensive contact with various organisations.

The data from the individual level strengthen the impression of a party seeking to establish alliances with a range of interest groups. A majority of the top party elite are current or former officials or staff members in one or several interest groups. There is no doubt that much of the Centre Party elite have formal contact with interest groups on a regular basis. In addition, informal contact with interest groups is also common. Its well-organised attempts to establish 'alliances' with interest groups seem to have resulted – in terms of the typology presented in Chapter 4 – in numerous *organised ad hoc relationships*. Furthermore, the party seems to be involved in a genuine alliance with the anti-EU organisations. In fact, the Centre Party comes close to having *an alliance* or at least *informal partnership* with various kinds of labour market, business, trade and primary sector organisations, in addition to environmental groups. In all these cases, a significant share of the elite had regular (monthly) contact with organisation representatives.

As far as the range of relationships is concerned, the survey shows that the Centre Party is linked with a majority of the organisation categories and groups representing interests across old cleavages. Interestingly, the long-established relationship with the primary sector is no closer than the relationships with many other organisations – in fact, the link with anti-EU organisations seems stronger. Less than 10 per cent report having been an official or staff member of an organisation within agriculture or fisheries. But the primary-sector organisations are among those with which the party elite have contact most frequently.

Equally importantly, the network of organised links does not seem much narrower than the range represented by the informal links. In other words, it seems that the party's strategy discussions are followed up in practice. More than the other parties examined so far, the Centre Party seems to be involved in a range of organised ad hoc relationships with interest groups. However, a definite conclusion requires systematic comparison with all parties along both the dimensions of closeness and of range.

chapter eleven | the christian people's party: organised network with religious profile

This chapter deals with Norway's religious party, the Christian People's Party (KrF), and its relationships with interest groups. The setting of this portrait of the third Norwegian 'centre party' can be traced back to the 1930s, when KrF was established in opposition to the profile of the established political parties in moral issues. KrF's original core voters were organised Christians (Bjørklund 1983b: 84), and the party organisation had significant links to religious organisations and parts of the state church (Bjørklund 1983a; Opdahl 1976).

BACKDROP: THE RISE OF NORWEGIAN CHRISTIAN DEMOCRACY?

In the first post-war years, the defence of Christian values and institutions remained at the core of KrF's political platforms (Berg 2003: 34). The main emphasis was on moral-cultural topics such as alcohol (temperance) policy and Christian education in public schools (Korsvold 1974: 169–71; Opdahl 1976: 65, 77), and later abortion (Sæter *et al.* 1985: 108). Over time, however, the manifesto has been extended to numerous policy fields.

During the 1960s and 1970s, KrF developed policies for industry and economy, international aid, welfare and families in particular (Annual Report 1979–81: 9; Ringdal and Sæter 1985: 138ff; Høybråten 1985: 190ff). In the 1980s, the party evaluated the role of Christianity in the party political platform, and a clearer distinction between basic values and policies was introduced (Richard and Demker 2005: 198). Analyses of party manifestos from recent decades show that KrF, like other parties, covers a considerable range of issues in its electoral platforms (Bilstad 1994). Increasingly, it has attempted to compete with other parties along the left-right axis, as its continental counterparts do (Heidar and Saglie 2004: 45–6). Although KrF is a centre party, it has been leaning more and more towards the left in economic issues. In 1993, three alternative Christian parties were established, and contested elections, in opposition to this development (Richard and Demker 2005: 215).

Concurrently, KrF's character as a cultural *anti-establishment party* has become less prominent. Today, the party presents itself as a 'Christian Democratic third way', complementing both liberal and socialist alternatives (Aardal 2000: 132; Heidar and Saglie 2004: 45ff, Kristelig Folkeparti 2004, see also Kristelig Folkeparti 2005; Bondevik 2006). In English, KrF in fact applies the label 'Christian Democratic Party' in stead of Christian Peoples' Party.[149] However, KrF has remained less liberal than significant parts of the (Evangelical Lutheran)

149. Source: Venås (2006 [telephone conversation]), see also http://www.stortinget.no/english/alphabetic.html).

Church of Norway in important moral questions – such as abortion and homosexuality (Heidar and Saglie 2004). KrF still explicitly bases its policies upon 'the fundamental values of Christianity' (KrF Election Manifesto 2001–2005) and has not tried to weaken its Christian profile as much as has its Swedish sister party (Richard and Demker 2005: 215). Manifesto analyses show that in general, KrF's political platform is mainly distinctive in moral-religious issues compared with the policies of other parties. This conflict is still dominant, also at the voter level (Aardal 2000: 132; Heidar and Saglie 2004: 49–50). Furthermore, KrF has not adapted to the rise of 'new politics' issues on the political agenda as extensively as have Norway's other 'centre parties'. During the 1970s, it integrated environmental issues into the party manifesto by arguing that nature conservation represents 'protection of God's creation'. Otherwise, though, KrF is the Norwegian centrist party with the least distinct profile along the new politics dimension (Knutsen 1997: 247).

The party's constituency has also to a certain extent become more heterogeneous in recent years. After the war, the competition for KrF's core voters was fierce (Valen 1992: 184). It was only in the 1970s and 1980s that the Norwegian Christian People's Party consolidated its position as the counter-cultures' own party (Valen 1992: 186–7; Bjørklund 1983b: 81). Active Christians and teetotallers also voted more frequently for the Centre Party and the Liberals than for other parties. The split in the Liberals in 1972 and their long-term decline have contributed to KrF's increasing dominance in these voter segments. Yet its electoral performance has been increasingly challenged by the process of secularisation. In the 1970s, the decline in actively religious voters and teetotallers spread to the southwest of Norway, the traditional home of the old laymen's movement (Bjørklund 2001: 41). In response, as indicated above, KrF has attempted to modify its image as a *pietistic* party, arguing that it represents widely-held Norwegian values across social and territorial dividing lines. Immigrant adherents of non-Christian religions are also seen as potential constituencies (*Aftenposten* 08.04.95). Although new Christian parties have been established and recently developed into one theologically conservative Christian party,[150] the party leaders have indicated that it is not necessary to believe in God to vote for KrF (Heidar and Saglie 2004: 45, my translation). KrF's first female party leader was elected in 1995, and she soon publicly claimed that 'we don't ask people what they believe in' (*Aftenposten* 08.04.95). It has also been underscored that the party's restrictive alcohol policies do not necessarily mean teetotalism: 'You may well enjoy a glass of red wine even though you vote for KrF' (Heidar and Saglie 2004: 46).

The attempt to attract new groups was partly successful in the 1990s, and the density of members of religious organisations and teetotallers among KrF's voters has declined in the last elections (Bjørklund 2001: 48–9). Naturally, in a secularised society, electoral success means a decline in the religious profile of voters

150. The three afore-mentioned Christian parties merged in 1998 under the name 'Kristent Samlingsparti' (http://www.ksnettavis.no/cgi-bin/npublish/viewnews.cgi?id=987153540), which is more conservative than KrF in economic as well as religious issues (Richard and Demker 2005: 215).

(Aardal 2000: 137). In 1997, KrF obtained more votes than ever before, and it led a centre-based coalition government until 2000. In 2001, the party nearly managed to repeat its election success, and formed a coalition with the Conservatives instead of the Centre Party. However, this success can obscure the fact that KrF is characterised by a fairly distinct voter profile. Some 70 per cent of teetotallers and religious affiliates in south-western Norway have steadfastly supported KrF from 1965 to 2001. In fact, support is greater today than in the early 1960s, even though the significance of religion has weakened (Berglund 2003: 126–7).[151] As van Kersbergen (1994: 35) argues, '(...) religion as an electoral magnet is very much like a real magnet: it has the disposition to both attract and repel'.

Furthermore, the party's election success in 1997 was '(...) not a result of an increased appeal among liberal-conservative voters. Christian voters are left-leaning with respect to economic issues; this is in particular true regarding redistribution of wealth (…)' (Aardal 2000: 136). For KrF's voters, religion is more important in determining their vote than it is for Christian voters who support other parties (*ibid*: 138; Richard and Demker 2005: 196). Thus, even though it has weakened its anti-establishment profile in recent decades, KrF is clearly not a full-blown Christian Democratic party of the continental ilk. Norway's Christian People's Party is a distinctly religious party that mobilises voters from well-defined religious segments.

Nonetheless, important changes have been made in KrF's approach to the interest-group community in the second half of the twentieth century. After the war, KrF concentrated on recruiting members and officials from more diverse religious circles, and on developing a national party organisation (Høybråten 1985: 189; Ringdal and Sæter 1985: 146). In 1945, 94 per cent of its executive members were concurrently or formerly active members in Christian organisations or the Church. Party leaders also had experience from the temperance movement (Valen and Katz 1964: 320; Opdahl 1976: 44). In the 1970s, also non-Lutheran churches drew closer to the party and the anti-abortion movement became an informal partner in the work against a more liberal abortion law in Norway (Selle 1997: 156). Equally importantly, an intra-party committee responsible for deliberating questions concerning business, trade, industry and the labour market arranged several meetings with all kinds of organisations within the labour market, and with LO in particular in the 1970s and 1980s (Christian People Party Annual Report 1977–79: 6; 1987–88: 9; 1989–90: 8).

In the 1990s, the party leadership initiated a debate about the need for further widening the range of organisations with which KrF was linked. An internal memo identified several potential target groups, including parents of young children, senior citizens, youth, handicapped citizens, professionals within health care and education, in addition to state church Christians, and charismatic/sectarian Christians (Kristelig Folkeparti 1992: 30–1). It concluded that for many of them the party culture might seem unaccustomed: '(…) the chapel might be too peculiar a place to visit for many people' (*ibid:* 20–1, my translation). The then party leader added

151. This can partly be related to the fact that the Liberals have declined as a 'counter-cultural' party.

in a speech to the national committee that KrF's recruitment to party positions had been too narrow, and concluded that the party's organisations would have to open up and search for supporters outside the religious organisations, as in the environmental movement and sports associations (Bondevik 1991: 8–9). According to Repstad (2002: 121), the party elite's informal contact with Christian leaders had declined by the late 1990s and the party's top leadership to a lesser extent populated by people from the Free Churches. The new generation of KrF leaders have other kinds of acquaintances, he concludes (*ibid:* 122).

Thus, the development indicates a party that has at least started to replace a traditionally close relationship with religious organisations, with more distant but rather wide-ranging relationships with various interest groups. Have these attempts succeeded?

RELATIONSHIPS WITH INTEREST GROUPS TODAY

Ten years later, the aim of opening the party remains on the KrF agenda (Heidar and Saglie 2002: 64). In 2001, the national leadership asked the local party branches to arrange open meetings before the general elections – openness was in fact mandatory if national politicians were to pay them a visit (Heidar and Saglie 2002: 64). However, links with interest groups are not a key issue in recent available organisational documents. Focus seems to be on how the central organisation can stimulate increased involvement by the party's own grass roots (Annual Reports 1997–2004; Venås 2005 [e-mail correspondence]). The question is, however, whether the general strategy of opening the party organisation to external and more varied circles implies some sort of relationships with a range of interest groups in practice. But let us start by examining the closeness – or distance – of KrF's relations with Norway's interest-group community.

Closeness of Relationships

Inter-organisational Links for Contact with Interest Groups

Despite the impression of a modestly developed strategy for such relationships – compared to for example the Centre Party – the Christian People's Party certainly has organised links with interest groups in the early 2000s. Table 11.1 summarises the existing ones.

True, KrF does not have a permanent joint committee or co-operation agreement with religious organisations or any other organisation, and recently decided to continue the tradition of *not* inviting interest groups to the annual congress (Venås 2003 [interview]) – but external organisations are invited to policy-oriented seminars and conferences within the party (see Christian People's Party Annual Report 1999–2000: 15; 2001–2002: 17). Topics debated here include issues concerning the labour market, business and industry, and environmental policy. Internal policy committees draw on external resources in their work (Venås 2003 [interview]), and organised contact with interest groups also takes place through dialogue seminars with various kinds of organisations. Dialogue meetings and seminars with Christian leaders and organisations are arranged every year (Annual

Reports 1993–97). During these seminars, the party has informed about how the organisations successfully might influence parliamentary decision-making, and the organisations have expressed their grievances and opinions on current political issues (see Annual Reports 1993–97). By the early 2000s, such a routine has been developed for contact with the environmental organisations as well (Venås 2003 [interview]). An internal party-union committee no longer exists (Annual Report 2003–04), but various voluntary organisations and employee and employers' organisations have occasionally been invited to similar arrangements in recent years (Annual Report 1993–94: 9; 2001–02: 17). The party leaders also come together occasionally with leaders of major interest groups, like representatives of the Confederation of Norwegian Business and Industry, in separate meetings (Venås 2003 [interview]).

Table 11.1: Christian People's Party inter-organisational links with interest groups 2000–04

	Existence	If yes, what kind
Permanent joint committee	No	
Temporary joint policy committees	No	
Joint conferences	No	
Written or tacit agreements about regular meetings	No	
Invitation to the party congress	No	
Invitations to party meetings, seminars and conferences	Yes	Usual to invite interest groups to party seminars and conferences.
Specific dialogue seminars and hearings	Yes	The central organisation has arranged specific dialogue seminars with various interest groups. Such meetings take place on an annual basis with Christian organisations and environmental organisations. Written hearing among interest groups in general has been arranged during the manifesto-making process.
Meetings outside party bodies	Yes	The party leadership occasionally meets with interest groups in separate meetings

Sources: Various party documents (see Appendix A), Venås (2003 [interview]) and (Holhjem 2003 [interview]).

The impression that inter-organisational links actually exist is strengthened by looking at KrF's manifesto-making process in particular. The committee that prepared the 2001–2005 Manifesto started the process by officially inviting members, voters *and* numerous external organisations to contribute. The home page on the Internet was an important communication channel. A special official invitation to a 'manifesto hearing' was sent to more than 100 Norwegian interest groups (Holhjem 2003 [interview]). This type of arrangement materialised for the first time in the second half of the 1990s (Venås 2003 [interview]). Many kinds of organisations were asked to participate, either by sending KrF written comments to the manifesto or by requesting a special meeting. The invitation letter also – in general terms – encouraged organisations to contact the party between elections (Holhjem 2003 [interview]). Thus, KrF seems to have some routines for organised contact with interest groups, but not as well-developed practices as has the Centre Party.

The committee received written responses from almost half of the invited organisations. Some sent their action programmes, others specific comments. Almost every policy field in the manifesto was covered by the hearing, and the responses were distributed to those responsible for relevant sections. Later, both the draft and the proposal were made public through the Internet. Organisations also contacted the party in the final stages of the process, just prior to the party congress (Venås 2003 [interview]). However, the number of meetings between the committee leadership, secretariat and organisations was limited (Holhjem 2003 [interview]).[152]

Unorganised Links for Contact with Interest Groups and Frequency of Actual Contact

Certainly, the Christian People's Party has established organised links with organisations other than purely religious ones. But what do individual-level data tell us about the relationships?

First, as regards unorganised links, the question is if KrF's top elite members hold or have held office, or are or have been staff members, at the national or local levels in other organisations (see Figure 11.1). In general, the survey shows that less than a majority, but more than 40 per cent, were present or former officials or representatives in one or several interest groups in 2003/2004 (see Appendix D). However, the 'under-representation' of executive members – with positions in Parliament and government – which is discussed in Appendix B may have resulted in a generally lower level of overlaps and transfers. Moreover, it should be borne in mind that the relatively low N means that the addition of only a few more responses could in theory cause significant changes in the distribution.

Nevertheless, some major tendencies can be identified. A formal rule still dictates that all KrF's officials and representatives should profess Christianity and share the party's fundamental values (§2 in KrF's party statutes). As the sociogram shows, there are also in practice strong links to Christian organisations and other

152. The party manifesto was written mostly by staff or officials in KrF's parliamentary group and in government. In this way, exchange with interest organisations in relation to public decision-making may indirectly have played a role in the process (Holhjem 2003 [interview]).

religious organisations or organised religious communities in terms of personal transfers and overlaps. In fact, the frequencies (Appendix D) show that more than 40 per cent of the KrF top elite – 4 out of 9 – hold or have held office, or are or have been staff members at the national or local levels in Christian organisations.[153] Hence, despite the decline of leaders from Free Churches as Repstad points to, the personal overlaps with Christian circles are still fairly extensive. Additionally, more than 20 per cent – 2 out of 9 – are, or have been officials or staff other religious organisations. Altogether, more than half of the KrF top elite report to have experience from either Christian or other religious-based groups.

However, no respondent reported being *currently* an office holder in Christian or missionary organisations. Furthermore, this kind of link to temperance organisations seems weak if not non-existent. The fact that only 7 per cent of the party

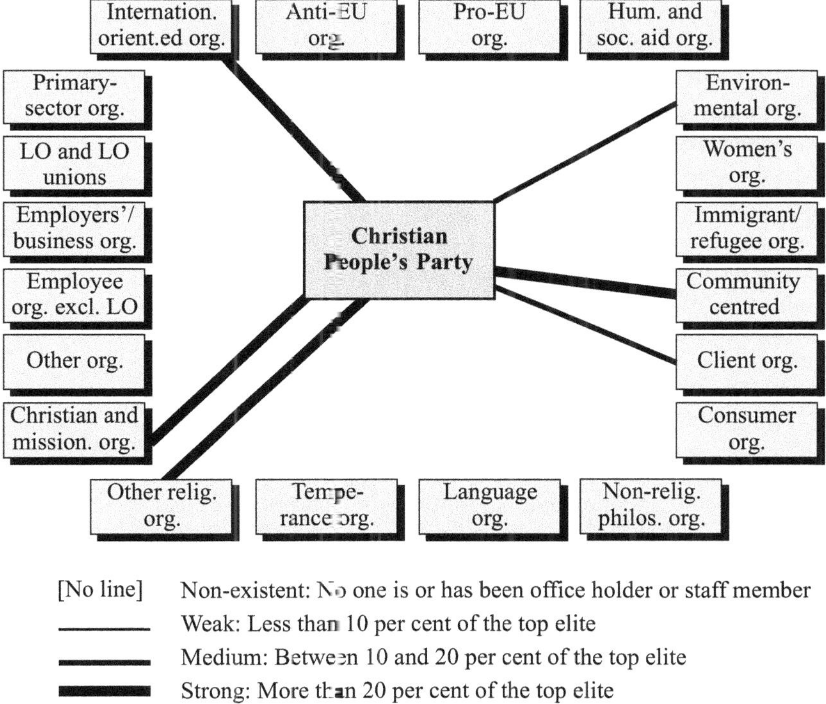

Figure 11.1: Christian People's Party links, by top elite members who hold or have held office/who are or have been staff members at the national or local levels in various interest groups 2003/2004.[1] *N = 9*

1 If a respondent is/has been an official and also is/has been a staff member, the answer is registered only in the 'official category'.

153. The large proportion is in accordance with the fact that a majority of the members and the congress delegates of KrF were holding or had held positions in religious organisations in 2000–01 (Heidar and Saglie 2004: 59).

Table 11.2: Christian People's Party top elite: frequency of formal and informal contact with interest groups in 2003. Per cent[1]

		Daily/ Weekly	Monthly	A few times	Never	No resp.	Total	N
Formal contact	Formal meetings or teleconferences	0	0	56	33	11	100	9
	Speakers at each other's seminars/conferences	0	11	67	11	11	100	9
	Formal written hearings or letters (incl. electronic correspondence)	11	11	45	22	11	100	9
Informal contact	Informal meetings, conversations, telephone conversations	0	22	78	0	0	100	9
	Informal written communication via SMS and e-mail	0	56	33	0	11	100	9
	Informal written communication like personal letters and memos	0	22	33	33	11	99	9

1 *Question:* 'Next, we would like you to state how often you had contact with interest groups *in different ways during the past year*. We distinguish between *formal* and *informal* contact:

- About how often did you have *formal contact* – of relevance for your work in the party's central organisation – with representatives from different interest groups in the following ways the past year? (tick off one alternative per line).
- About how often did you have *informal contact* – of relevance for your work in the party's central organisation – with representatives from different interest groups in the following ways the past year? (tick off one alternative per line).'

congress delegates in 2000–01 were holding, or had held positions, in temperance organisations makes the result seem plausible. Equally interesting, the extent of personal transfer from the Christian segment does not *preclude* experience from other interest groups. There also seem to be strong links of this kind to internationally-oriented organisations and various voluntary associations related to sports, youth, the elderly and so forth. KrF has a medium strong link to environmental organisations and client organisations, although it should be noted that the low N means that only one elite member had such a background in this case. On the whole, the KrF elite seem significantly linked with more than Christian organisations in this way.

Contact between individuals can also link a party with an interest group, formally or informally. As mentioned before, well-organised links do not necessarily mean the most frequent contact between decision-makers. To reveal the extent of formal and informal contact at the individual elite level, the survey mapped the general frequency of various *forms* of contact. Table 11.2 shows the results in the case of the Christian People's Party.

First, we observe that the top KrF elite have regular contact with interest groups in one way or another although very few are in weekly contact with interest groups. Second, Table 11.2 shows that informal contact is the most widespread method for contact with other organisations, and supplements the organised arrangements. More than 50 per cent of the top party elite – 5 out of 9 – had contact with interest groups informally through e-mail and SMS at least once a month in 2003. But no respondents reported at least monthly formal meetings or telephone conferences of relevance for their work in the central party organisation. It seems as if only a limited share of KrF's top elite has frequent formal contact with interest groups.

Determining the exact strength of the links represented by the frequencies would require comparison with results from other parties. The question in the meantime is whether the links include more contact with religious organisations. A summary analysis shows that altogether slightly less than half of the KrF top elite are in touch at least once a month with one or more interest groups about issues of relevance for the work in the extra-parliamentary organisation. But how extensive and frequent are the contacts with different kinds of organisations? Did most elites have contact at least monthly, a few times or never with the various organisations the past year? Figure 11.2 presents the major results of the analysis.

We note that the KrF elite do not really have a *strong* degree of contact with any kind of interest group. There is no organisation category with which a majority of the elite have monthly contact. On the other hand, there are many who were in touch a few times a year. The Christian and other religious organisations or organised religious communities stand out only to a very limited extent: No more than 22 per cent of the elite – 2 out of 9 – are in contact with either one of these kinds of organisations at least monthly. The same applies for the temperance organisations. This impression is confirmed by the more detailed analysis of the most frequent contact. Religious and temperance organisations are not mentioned as one of the *three most frequent contacts* much more repeatedly than others.[154]

Furthermore, contact with environmental organisations is at least equally strong. Although only a minority of the elite respondents were in touch with environmental groups at least once a month, almost 90 per cent – 8 out of 9 – reported having such contact at least a few times a year. Moreover, we observe that the KrF elite have medium strong contact with numerous kinds of organisation despite the lack of shared former or present elites in many cases. In some instances, at least a few elite members had monthly or more frequent contact with primary-sector organisations, employers' organisations, humanitarian and social aid organisations, internationally-oriented groups, and various community-centred organisations. With regard to EU-related organisations, the difference is small: 56 and 44 per cent in favour of the pro-membership organisations.

154. *Question:* First, we would like you to write down the names of those (maximum three) organisations you had most frequent contact with last year. (….). Use the blank below (….).

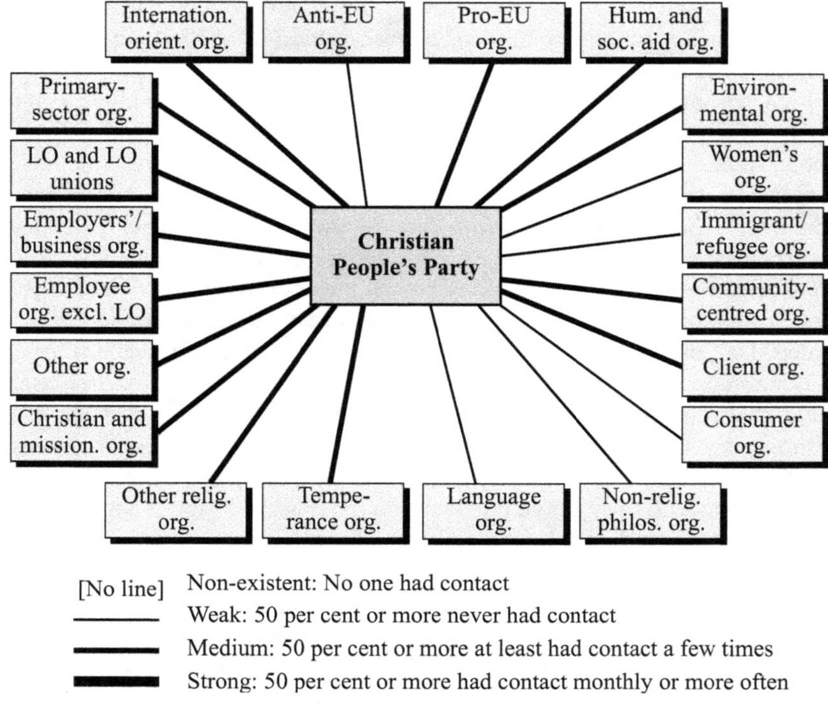

Figure 11.2: Christian People's Party links through the top elite's frequency of contact with various interest groups in 2003.[1] *N = 9*

1 Question: 'Could you please state how often you had contact – of relevance for your work in the party's central organisation – with one or more organisations within the following categories during the past year? The question includes both formal and informal, more random contact, written as well as oral communication.'

If exactly 50 per cent reported having contact 'seldom', the link is categorised as either 'medium' or 'strong'.

The existence of inter-organisational links with interest groups is connected first and foremost with the manifesto-making process. As mentioned above, however, much of the actual preparation is performed by individual officials, representatives, advisers and secretaries, and we do not have data describing their activities. But by asking those members of the current top elite who were also official and staff in the central organisation in the early 2000s about their experiences, we get at least an indication.[155] A minority of the five respondents reported

155. *Question:* 'How many interest organisations did you have contact with – about one or several subsections – during the different phases of the manifesto-making before the party congress in 2000?

- Before the first draft was presented.
- During the debate over the manifesto draft.
- During the debate over the manifesto proposal.'

having been in touch with interest groups during the preparation of the 2001–2005 Manifesto. Before the first draft was presented, and at some stage in the debate over the manifesto draft, two out of the five report having communicated with one or several organisations. During the deliberations over the final proposal, only one of the respondents reported having been in touch with interest groups. Hence, there seems to be a certain involvement of external circles on the individual elite level in the course of manifesto-making.

Range of Relationships

How wide-ranging is the Christian People's Party's network of links with interest groups? KrF aims to reach more than (organised) Christian voters, and the party leadership has to a certain extent developed a strategy of establishing links with *various* organisations and external circles. To what extent have the party's central organisation followed up this aspect in practice? The analysis above indicates that the range of the relationships is fairly wide. Figure 11.3 summarises the Christian People's Party's *significant* links – not the weak ones – based on the survey material.

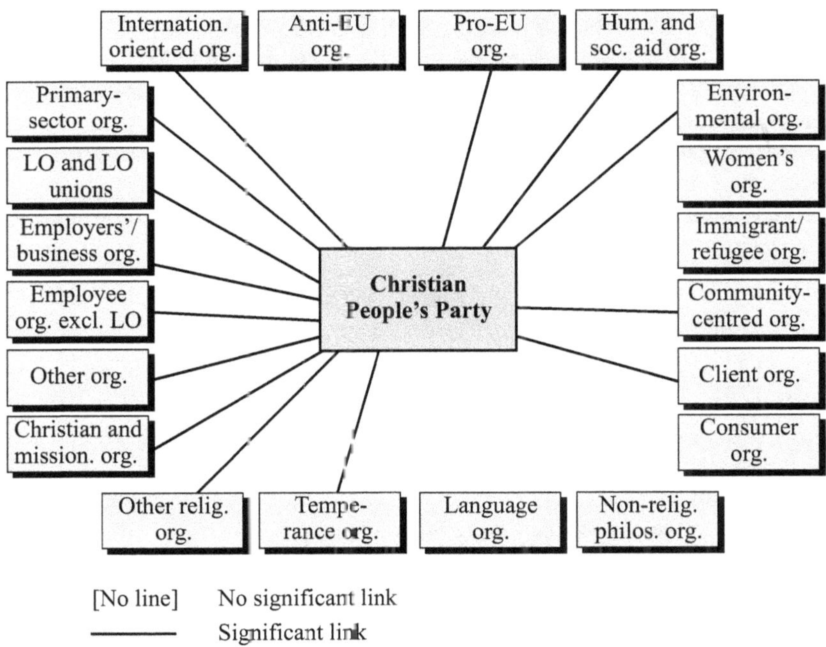

Figure 11.3: The Christian People's Party's total network of significant links with interest groups.[1] *N = 9*

1 Significant links are cases where 50 per cent or more at least had contact a few times the past year (see Chapter 4).

From the sociogram we see that the proportion of organisation categories with which KrF is linked is 0.70 (14 out of 20 organisations). In other words, the number of links is lower than in a couple of the other parties, but it should be noted that only *one* respondent differentiates a 'significant' from a 'non-significant' link in the case of anti-EU organisations and immigrant and refugee groups. Furthermore, we see that the party network does not include links with interest groups reflecting different flanks of the old socio-cultural axis. KrF has significant contact with the old counter-cultural organisations, but is not linked with organisations that promote non-religious philosophies of life, and has links only to some organisations representing 'new politics' values – internationally-oriented organisations and environmental groups. On the other hand, the network does involve primary-sector organisations, LO and its unions, other employees'/professional organisations and business, trade and employers' organisations. KrF also has significant links with client organisations and voluntary humanitarian, social aid, and community-centred organisations. Thus we may conclude that KrF is not linked with many more organisation categories than those traditionally associated with a strictly Christian party.

Still, it is worth noting that the degree of closeness does not vary *considerably* between organisation categories. KrF does not recruit elite members with experience or positions from labour market organisations and seems to have most actual contact with old and new value-based organisations. It could also be argued that the party focuses its organised effort on such groupings, but the inter-organisational links do include organisations within the labour market – employers', business and trade organisations in particular. In connection with the manifesto-making process the central party organisation invites a wide range of interest groups. The links measured at both the individual and organised level appear to be somewhat wide-ranging, but not extremely so.

SUMMARY AND CONCLUSIONS

Norway's Christian People's Party – KrF – approached the twenty first century by presenting itself as a general Christian Democratic alternative appealing to voters across the old moral-religious cleavage, and has seen organised contact with interest groups as a way to pursuit this goal. The party's organised attempts to establish links with interest groups are more systematic than with the case of either the Conservatives or the Liberals, but less systematic than those general efforts documented in the case of the Centre Party.

Some inter-organisational links do exist. Dialogue seminars are arranged with several kinds of organisations, and holding a formal hearing among interest groups in general is common practice during the manifesto-making process. On the other hand, the impression of organised contact is not uniformly strengthened by the data from the individual level. The KrF elite do not have frequent well-organised contact with organisations. Outside the Storting, formal contact seems limited. Less than a majority of the respondents reported holding or having held a position in one or more interest groups, and the majority of the elite have not more than occasional contact with interest groups. Hence, relationships generally approach the *organised ad hoc-type* or *issue-based contact*. However, KrF comes very close to being involved in an *organised alliance* or *informal partnership* with Christian and religious organisations. Indeed, the link in terms of transfer or overlap of leaders and staff is very strong – and strongest – to these organisations, but not to temperance organisations.

With regard to the range of relationships, the survey shows that the Christian People's Party is linked with a majority of the organisation categories and to a certain extent with groups representing interests and values across cleavages, especially in connection with the preparation of the party manifesto. Hence, the preliminary conclusion is that the network is rather wide at the organisational level, but no significant links have been identified with organisations promoting a non-religious philosophy of life. Interestingly, the range of relationships is wider within the labour market than in connection with value-based and cultural organisations.

Furthermore, the extent of actual contact seems generally limited. Thus, the limitations in Norway's main religious party's attempt at widening its political profile party appear mirrored by its organisational network. On the whole, KrF is not generally separated from the interest-group community, but it corresponds only partly to the pattern associated with parties aiming to 'catch' voters across social and cultural segments. A final conclusion has to await systematic comparative analysis with the other parties.

chapter twelve | the socialist left party: towards wide-ranging, organised links

In this chapter, we move from the Norwegian parties that were established before the Second World War to one of those that have later challenged the political establishment. Norway's Socialist Left Party (originally SF; from 1975 Socialist Left Party, SV) is one of the few significant European New Left parties that emerged in economically advanced, small and corporatist welfare states in the 1960s (Kitschelt 1988).[156] During its first years, SV cultivated links with both the old trade union movement and new anti-establishment groups, but not well-organised ones.

BACKDROP: CONSOLIDATION OF A 'NEW POLITICS PARTY'

After the electoral success in the early 1970s, SV found itself pushed to the sidelines of Norwegian politics, until a new election breakthrough in the late 1980s. Meanwhile, the party's ideological profile had changed significantly. According to Ersson's analysis (2005: 67–8) of the Manifesto Data (see Volkens and Klingemann 2002), the leftist orientation of SV's party programmes was definitely less pronounced in the 1980s and 1990s. SV has continued to promote itself as a radical left-wing alternative concerning domestic policies, but less so in terms of nationalisation of industry, state management, and a controlled economy. Marxist ideas have partly been replaced by less radical economic policies and new politics values such as participation and individual autonomy (Knutsen 1997: 247–8; see also SV's Election Manifesto 2001–2005).

Changes have also occurred along the other axis on which the Socialist Left was originally based. In 1989, the revolutionary events in Eastern Europe transformed the left socialists' 'bridge-building neutralism' in foreign policy into 'a blind alley' (Christensen and Midtbø 1998: 4). Although the war in Iraq – and especially the trans-Atlantic relationship with the United States – has made foreign policy more salient in recent years, this policy field is usually no longer SV's primary focus in elections. Attention has been increasingly paid to environmental policy. Anti-capitalist arguments have declined in SV's environmental policies, and more modest concepts like 'justifiable ecological development' were introduced during the 1980s and 1990s (Aardal 1993: 147–8, 164). Particular attention has also been paid to children's living conditions and public education (Socialist Left Party Annual Reports 1997–2001).

In other words, the Socialist Left has consolidated itself as Norway's left-libertarian party, linking green and libertarian values with the Old Left's emphasis on equality (Kitschelt 1988; Knutsen 1997; Knutsen 1998b: 25). But it should be noted that de-emphasis of traditional Marxist ideas has not been replaced by a

156. Although SV and SF were formally two different parties, I will use only the label Socialist Left (SV) for the sake of simplicity.

strongly *ideological* 'new politics' profile. In the early 2000s, the Socialist Left presents itself – in the public sphere – as a rather pragmatic left-wing party. The political platform is today extensive, covering a wide range of policy fields. After decades of permanent opposition in the Storting, it even decided to form a coalition government with the Labour Party and the Centre Party in 2005.[157] Although the party organisation certainly has had a hard time adapting to SV's new role as a part of the government, there is no doubt that SV's policies have become less radical and the anti-establishment profile has decreased.

SV's electorate has also approached the pattern predicted by 'new politics theory'. At the voter level, in its early years SV did not primarily appeal to the new middle class, more highly educated, and post-war generations: it was supported more strongly by workers than other groups of employees (Knutsen 1990: 522; Knutsen 1998b: 52).[158] Originally, it termed itself a 'people's party' (SF), inspired by the Danish equivalent. The purpose was to highlight what the party founders saw as the *common interests* of employees, farmers, fishermen, benefit recipients, homemakers, and youth in putting capitalism to an end (Alldén 1980: 58). Party members were blue-collar workers and white-collar workers as well as students (*ibid:* 256). From the late 1970s the voter profile changed. Economic growth and the advanced character of the welfare state brought a relatively heavy emphasis on post-materialist values in the Nordic countries (Knutsen 1989), and in elections SV increasingly focused on civil servants, administrators, clerks (*funksjonærer*) and voters with higher education.

Election studies show that SV has become a party for the new middle class. According to Berglund (2003: 130) highly educated voters have been gradually more attracted to the Socialist Left Party, but that in general the party's social profile is diffuse. However, Knutsen (1998: 52, 59) demonstrates there is an increasing tendency for the Socialist Left to gain especially from the new middle class since the late 1970s, and from public-sector employees since the late 1980s. In fact, sector is more closely correlated with SV support than is social class (Knutsen 1998b: 52, 59). Moreover, in the 1990s 'the proportion of women supporting the left socialist parties is nearly twice as high as the proportion of men' (*ibid*: 68, 86).[159] SV has clearly attracted the most post-materialist electorate in Norway in terms of anti-authoritarian and green values (Knutsen 1990). SV's voters are also characterised by a particularly secular orientation (Aardal 2003b: 87–8), as the counterpart of KrF in moral issues (Heidar and Saglie 2004: 60). Thus, today's Socialist Left seems to be an indication of a post-industrial cross-cutting cleavage in Norwegian politics (Knutsen 1990, 2004b). Equally important, the party itself aims to hold on to this broader range of core voters among the middle class (Melve

157. Already in 1993, the party leader introduced the idea of formal collaboration with DnA for the first time.

158. The underlying figure includes both the Socialist People's Party (SF) and Norway's miniscule Communist Party.

159. The figure includes both the Socialist Left Party and the very small Red Electoral Alliance (RV).

1999: 140).[160] Beyond doubt, SV has consolidated its profile as a new politics protest party since the 1970s.

What characterised SV's approach to the interest-group community during the 1980s and 1990s? No systematic research exists, but there is little doubt that SV continued to cultivate relationships with both the old trade union movement and new anti-establishment groups. Like green parties and socialist left parties elsewhere, SV established a participatory party organisation, in opposition to the traditional socialist centralism. Over time, the emphasis on alternative modes of organisation has weakened (Svåsand *et al.* 1997: 118), but interaction between the parliamentary group, the party organisation with its numerous policy-making committees, and external movement organisations and citizens' initiatives was a part of its *modus operandi* in both the 1970s and 1980s (see Socialist left Party Annual Report 1979–81, 1983–85: 2). The peace movement, international solidarity organisations, and the women's movement continued to attract the party's attention. Party activists and officials were encouraged to keep in touch with numerous protest groups (see Annual Reports 1977–85). The proportion of local office holders from the trade unions in the party's executive committee remained relatively large throughout the 1970s (Haaversen-Westhassel 1984: 102–3, 114–5).

As electoral support and number of parliamentary seats increased towards the end of the 1980s, SV gave less priority to both internal and external extra-parliamentary work (Heidar and Saglie 1994: 139), but consideration for social movements did not disappear. The idea of mass participation and interaction with social movements remained a core value in party accounts (Heidar and Saglie 1994: 139; Socialist Left Party Annual Report 1985–87: 1). True, the peace and women's movement have declined over time in Norway, but environmental groups are still significant actors and new protest organisations, like Attac, have emerged. Accordingly, the party leadership has increasingly emphasised contact with the environmental movement.[161] Furthermore, in the early 1990s, the general concept of the 'Open Party' (*Åpent parti*) was launched. The idea was to incorporate external circles in traditionally internal decision-making processes like manifesto-making and candidate selection (Allern 2001: 32).

However, the *dual* anchorage in old and new politics did not vanish despite increased emphasis on the new middle class and libertarian values throughout the 1980s. An important long-term goal has been to make the trade unions more independent of the Labour Party. In the 1980s, the internal party-union committee – consisting of members and officials from various LO unions – suggested that the special links between DnA and LO should be replaced by a contact committee for

160. The party leader from 1987 to 1997, Erik Solheim, explained the disappointing 1997 elections by arguing that the members '(...) had forced the party to adopt policy stances that scared away the voters' (Christensen and Midtbø 1998: 23). He further held that the party organisation would have to be more inclusive, in order to reach beyond the subculture of the traditional SV supporter, the one who usually 'drinks red wine, listens to jazz music, has pinewood furniture and drives a Lada' (Solheim 1999: 113, my translation).

161. Yet, it has also been argued that the environmental groups grew to be sceptical to party politics and ideology after a period of politisation in the 1970s (Gundersen 1991).

the labour movement as a whole, including SV. Tensions between the unions and DnA over wage settlements paved the way for more, but not sufficient, support for this attempt, according to SV's Annual Reports (Socialist Left Party Annual Report 1983–85: 10–11). The internal party-union committee managed to meet officially with the leadership of LO once, but the attempt of making such contact routine failed (Annual Report 1989–91: 13).

To conclude, links with social movement organisations have remained a distinguishing feature of SV, but the party organisation has since the very beginning had a better-organised approach to trade unions than that often associated with 'new politics' parties. What then characterises SV's relationships with interest groups today?

RELATIONSHIPS WITH INTEREST GROUPS TODAY

Recent organisational documents from the Socialist Left underscore the need for openness towards the party environment. Cultivating links with various interest groups seems in general to be a priority (Sosialistisk Venstreparti 1999; 2000a). SV's central organisation and headquarters have continued to work for more binding co-operation with both individual trade unions and LO (Annual Reports 1991–97). Since the struggle over Norwegian EU membership prior to the 1994 referendum, party strategies have increasingly emphasised organised co-operation with various organisations and ad hoc groups (Socialist Left Party Annual Report 1993–95: 3; 1995–97: 20). Involvement in ad hoc campaigns has remained 'standing operating procedure' in party headquarters, and contacts with the more established *No to the EU* (*Nei til EU*) are also a major priority for the central organisation. In addition, the anti-globalisation organisations like Attac and citizen initiatives against the war in Iraq have received considerable attention in recent years, besides the traditionally organisations associated with SV (Solhjell 2003 [interview]).

Yet, SV still seems to consider the trade unions in LO and the environmental movement to be more important than others (Socialist Left Party Annual Report 1995–97: 20). The party-union committee does not seem to emphasise any particular need for more focus on employees' organisations outside the traditional labour movement (Annual Report 1995–97; 2001–03). To what extent does this ambivalence characterise existing links with interest groups as well? Before we turn to this question, however, we need to assess the closeness of the party's various relationships.

Closeness of Relationships

Inter-organisational Links for Contact with Interest Groups

Table 12.1 shows that in the early 2000s, no joint committees or conferences exist and agreements about regular meetings with certain organisations have not materialised in the case of the Socialist Left. Co-operation agreements have been discussed with the Norwegian Graphical Union (*Norsk Grafisk Forbund*) and the Union of School Employees (*Skolenes Landsforbund*) in LO, but contact continues to take place ad hoc. There may have been some ambivalence in the party leadership regarding the formalisation of relationships (Annual Report 1993–95: 6; Kiran 2005 [interview]).[162] According to the internal party-union committee, relations with the trade union movement stagnated towards the late 1990s (Annual Report 1995–97: 46). In the early 2000s, the party leaders and LO chairmen have met officially to discuss the potential for more co-operation, but no formal agreement has yet been established (Solhjell 2003 [interview]).

Table 12.1: Socialist Left Party inter-organisational links with interest groups 2000–04

	Existence	If yes, what kind
Permanent joint committee	No	
Temporary joint policy committees	No	
Joint conferences	No	
Written or tacit agreements about regular meetings	No	
Invitation to the party congress	Yes	Various organisations are normally invited as guests. Several also generally give speeches, and consultative meetings are arranged with between party and organisation leaders during the congress.
Invitations to party meetings, seminars and conferences	Yes	Common to invite interest groups to party arrangements like conferences and occasionally to committee meetings.
Specific dialogue seminars and hearings	Unsettled	No routine for such particular arrangements, but open conferences fill a similar function. Formal hearing among interest groups is arranged during the manifesto-making process.
Meetings outside party bodies	Yes	Meetings with representatives of interest groups are a part of the top leaders and headquarters regular working methods.

Sources: Various party documents (see appendix A) and (Solhjell 2003 [interview])

162. Interestingly, the 1993–95 Annual Report (p. 6) presents the co-operation agreement as already established, which was in fact not the case. However, the Union of School Employees (*Skolenes Landsforbund*) mentions both co-operation with DnA and co-operation with SV in its self-presentation on its official website (www.skoleneslandsforbund.no/informasjon/utdanning.htm).

However, numerous other kinds of inter-organisational links exist. In contrast to many other parties in Norway, SV usually invites various interest groups to its party congress – among them, major employees' confederations and unions, youth organisations, environmental groups, and internationally-oriented organisations, including *No to the EU* and Attac (Thomassen 2005 [e-mail correspondence]). A significant number usually turn up, and one person from party headquarters is responsible for taking care of each representative. Some even get their expenses covered by party (Solhjell 2003 [interview]). The organisation representatives are guests and observers, but they also have the opportunity to address the delegates in plenum. In the early 2000s, representatives of trade unions, the environmental movement and some international organisations have made speeches to the party congress (Party Congress Books of Minutes 2001–03). During the sessions, meetings are also arranged with party leaders (Solhjell 2003 [interview]). In 2003, the LO leadership attended – and the LO deputy chairman addressed – the SV congress for the first time in history (Party Congress 2003 Books of Minutes; see also *Aftenposten* 05.02.04)). In 2001 SV had been – also for the first time – invited to the LO Congress. In 2005, the SV party leader gave a speech at the LO Congress, on equal footing with the Labour Party (Strand 2005).

Equally important, SV still has numerous permanent policy-making committees and temporary working groups which have contact with relevant organisations between congresses. According to the current party secretary, it is common to invite representatives of external organisations to party arrangements like committee meetings and the numerous internal and open conferences. Interest groups contribute by giving talks or participating in discussion panels. The internal party-union committee and the committee for international affairs are among the organisational bodies that frequently invite external contributors. In recent years, external organisations have even been invited to speak at some meetings of the party's executive committee (Solhjell 2003 [interview]).

Whereas specific dialogue seminars are not routine, ad hoc meetings apparently take place quite frequently, for example with employees' organisations, parts of the environmental movement, anti-EC organisations, peace groups, cultural organisations and so forth, according to the party secretary (Solhjell 2003 [interview]). After the rapprochement with the LO leadership in 2002, some ad hoc consultations have been arranged between LO and the SV leadership. Annual reports from the late 1990s conclude that the interaction with the environmental movement is significant, but ad hoc based (see Socialist Left Party Annual Report 1995–97: 20, 1997–99: 18).[163] With regard to the trade unions, the relationship has become closer in recent years, through more official interaction between elites. Thus we see that SV has more inter-organisational links with interest groups than many long-established Norwegian parties, and relations appear better organised – institutionalised – than what is usually expected of a new left party.

163. SV has itself supported various ad hoc groups, like the Climate Alliance (*Klimaalliansen*), an environmental umbrella organisation working against the establishment of (polluting) Norwegian gasworks.

The impression of a party with fairly organised relationships with interest groups in general is strengthened by an in-depth look at the manifesto-making process. As a part of the general project known as 'Open Party' in the early 1990s, SV intended to invite external individual and organisations to contribute in the discussion at all levels (Socialist Left Party Annual Report 1991–93: 20). Over time, the idea of greater openness has also been translated into practice. Inclusion of external interest groups in the manifesto-making process has become routine both in local parties and at the national level (Solhjell 2003 [interview]); Brostigen 2003 [interview]). When developing the 2001–2005 Manifesto, the preparing committee invited numerous organisations to have a say through a hearing of memos to organisations covering various policy fields. The party received written comments from various organisations, albeit only from a limited proportion of those who had been contacted (Socialist Left Annual Report 2000: 9; Brostigen 2003 [interview]).[164] Later, the final proposal was published on the Internet, but the response from organisations at this point was low (Brostigen 2003 [interview]). Some organisation leaders were invited to give talks to the committee (Allern 2001: 31), although written comments were the preferred form of communication (Brostigen 2003 [interview]). One committee member, and the committee secretary himself, had previously worked in the headquarters of Friends of the Earth Norway (*FoEN – Norges Naturvernforbund*). A former leader of this organisation was engaged to draft the section on energy policy. Two other committee members served as national secretaries of an LO union at that time. In this way, the environmental movement and the trade union movement were particularly involved in the SV manifesto-making process.

Unorganised Links for Contact with Interest Groups and Frequency of Actual Contact

Do fairly strong inter-organisational links indicate that there is not that much unorganised contact, or are the organised links supplemented by informal ones in SV? We start by looking at elite's personal experience from associational life in Norway. The survey reveals that, at the time of the research, as much as 75 per cent of the Socialist Left's top elite had experience as office holders or staff members in interest groups (see Appendix D for complete frequencies). Figure 12.1 shows there are strong links at the national level in SV to three organisation categories: LO and LO unions, organisations working against Norwegian membership in EU, and community-centred organisations.

In fact, more than 40 per cent – 5 out of 12 – are/or have been officials and staff in anti-EU organisations. About 25 per cent of the elite were currently holding national positions in the category of 'no'-organisations at the time they were asked. Hence, SV is, like the Centre Party, deeply involved in the non-partisan work against Norway's joining the European Union. Furthermore, we observe that despite the dominance of Labour in the central leadership of the Trade Union Federation (LO), 25 per cent SV's top elite (3 out of 12) have local or national

164. Others sent their action programmes, but probably by routine and not as a direct result of the invitation (Sosialistisk Venstreparti 2002b-e; Brostigen 2003 [interview]).

background from executive bodies or the administration of LO and LO unions.[165] More than 30 per cent have such experience from community-centred organisations, but we should not put much emphasis on the difference since this category is much broader. Otherwise, the link in terms of personal overlaps and transfers is of medium strength to organisations related to non-religious philosophies of life. However, the SV elite do not seem to be a bastion for leaders of international solidarity groups or peace organisations. Neither are officials and staff from feminist organisations and environmental organisations well-represented in the top elite. Significant links of this kind might well exist in the population as a whole, at least with the environmental movement. However, it should be noted that only 8 per cent of the 2001 congress delegates in SV had present or former positions in environmental organisations (Heidar and Saglie 2002: 279).

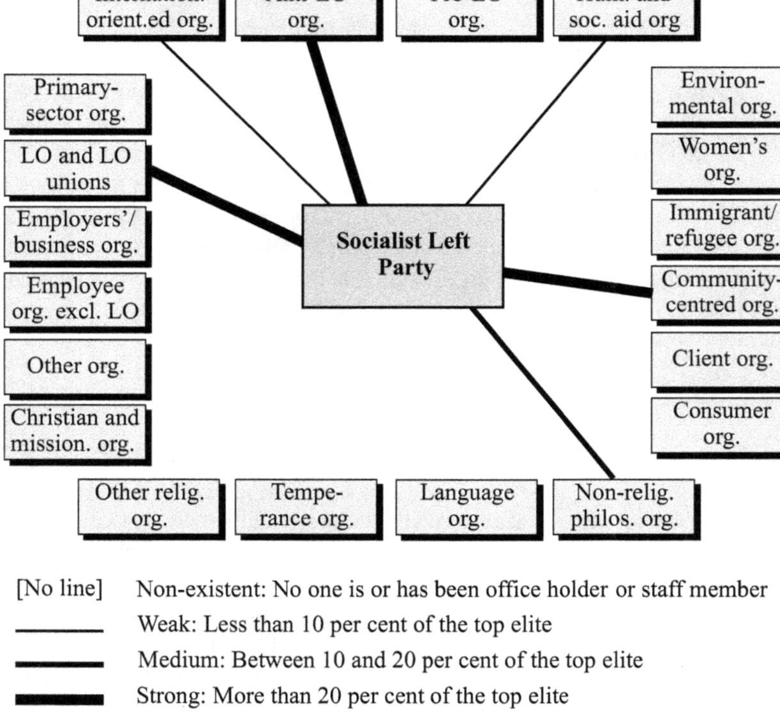

Figure 12.1: Socialist Left Party links, by top elite members who hold or have held office/who are or have been staff members at the national or local levels in various interest groups 2003/2004.[1] N =12

1 If a respondent is/has been an official and also is/has been a staff member, the answer is registered only in the 'official category'.

165. Hence, the embeddedness in LO seems not to have weakened so much over time. Haaversen-Westhassel (1984: 102–5) reports that about half of the national executive committee held positions in the trade union movement at the local level. For the record, at the 2005 Congress, two out of the nine elected onto the party executive held national positions in LO unions.

Limited personal transfers and overlaps do not necessarily mean correspondingly limited contact. Rather, this may increase the need for formal contact between organisations and party representatives. Table 12.2 shows how often the top elite of SV had contact with interest groups in 2003 in various ways.

First, we observe that a large part of the SV elite is often involved in contact with external interest groups. Informal meetings and conversations or SMS and e-mail seem the most common mode of contact. In 2003, about 45 per cent were in contact with interest groups weekly or more often in this way. About 90 per cent had contact in both ways at least once a monthly. More than half had contact with interest groups through formal letters or by attending each others' seminars each month or more frequently. There can be little doubt that the Socialist Left's emphasis on well-organised links is reflected in the significant number of elite members who had official contact with interest groups. In addition, the SV elite maintain extensive contacts with social organisations outside the party in less formal ways.

Table 12.2: Socialist Left Party top elite: frequency of formal and informal contact with interest groups in 2003. Per cent[1]

		Daily/ Weekly	Monthly	A few times	Never	No resp.	Total	N
Formal contact	Formal meetings or teleconferences	0	27	55	9	9	100	11
	Speakers at each other's seminars/conferences	0	55	36	0	9	100	11
	Formal written hearings or letters (incl. electronic communications)	9	46	36	0	9	100	11
Informal contact	Informal meetings, conversations, telephone conversations	45	46	0	0	9	100	11
	Informal written communication via SMS and e-mail	45	46	0	0	9	100	11
	Informal written communication like personal letters and memos	36	27	27	0	9	99	11

1 *Question:* 'Next, we would like you to state how often you had contact with interest groups *in different ways during the past year*. We distinguish between *formal* and *informal* contact:

- About how often did you have *formal contact* – of relevance for your work in the party's central organisation – with representatives from different interest groups in the following ways the past year? (tick off one alternative per line).
- About how often did you have *informal contact* – of relevance for your work in the party's central organisation – with representatives from different interest groups in the following ways the past year? (tick off one alternative per line).'

Is the contact equally intense with all kinds of interest groups? A summary analysis shows that, independent of form of contact, more than 80 per cent of SV's top elite were in touch with one or more organisations at least once a month in 2003. Only one elite member reported no contact with external organisations at all. Figure 12.2 shows how often the party elite had contact with various categories of organisations (for table of frequencies, see Chapter 14).

We observe that the SV elite had *a strong degree* of contact with three kinds of organisations in 2003: LO and LO unions, internationally-oriented organisations and anti-EU groups. In fact, more than 80 per cent – had contact with an organisation within all these categories – and various community-centred organisations related to culture, sports etc. – at least a few times. Almost 60 per cent had been in touch with LO and LO unions at least once a month. In addition, 50 per cent

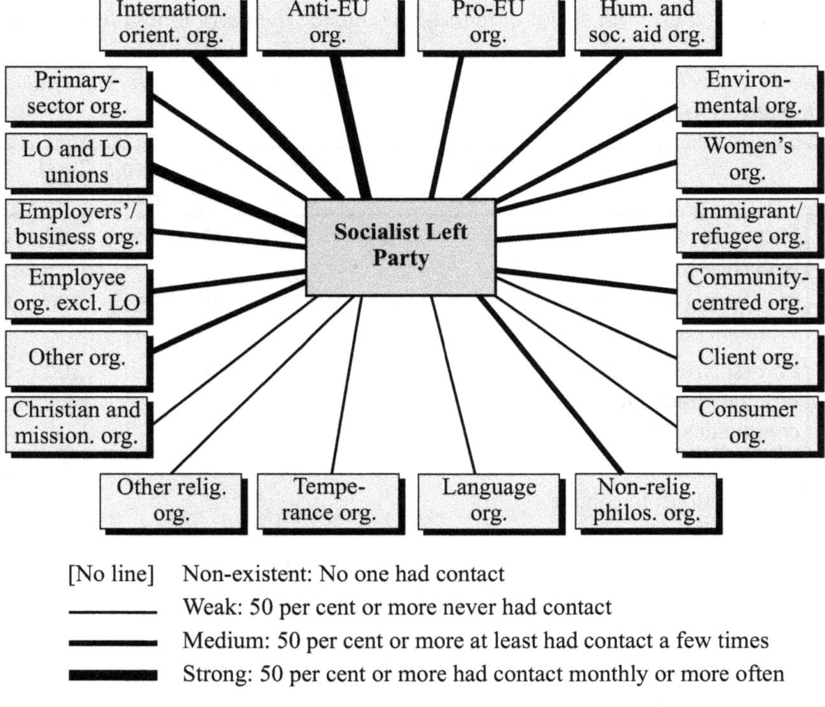

Figure 12.2: Socialist Left Party links through the top elite's frequency of contact with various interest groups in 2003.[1] *N = 12*

1 *Question:* 'Could you please state how often you had contact – of relevance for your work in the party's central organisation – with one or more organisations within the following categories during the past year? The question includes both formal and informal, more random contact, written as well as oral communication.'

If exactly 50 per cent reported having had contact 'seldom', the link is categorised as either 'medium' or 'strong' (includes organisations related to organisations for non-religious philosophies of life, organisations pro-EU membership and women's organisations).

or more had contact at least a few times with eleven different kinds of organisations, representing links of *medium strength.* Non-LO employees' organisations, environmental groups and women's organisations are among these. Hence, despite the party strategy of emphasis on social movements in general, SV has not maintained extensive contact with all kinds, not even the environmental groups. Internationally-oriented organisations seem more important. Among the employees' organisations, the party elite still concentrates on LO: in terms of actual contact, the link with white-collar organisations outside the traditional trade union movement is significantly weaker, as only half as many reported having monthly contact with such organisations.

More detailed analyses strengthen the impression of particularly intense contact with LO and its unions. No organisation category was mentioned more repeatedly when respondents were asked to indicate the organisations they 'most frequently had contact with'.[166] About one third reported the trade union movement in each case. To conclude, today's Socialist Left elite seem to have extensive actual contact with numerous external organisations, both formally and informally, and with the trade union movement in particular.

Is the organised consultation of interest groups during the manifesto-making process also mirrored at the individual level? Unfortunately, less than half of 2003 top elite had held similar positions during the manifesto-making process from 1999 to 2001. Therefore, we cannot put much emphasis on the indications given by the survey responses to the question of extensiveness of external contact during this process. That said, among the respondents who did have positions in the central organisation at the time, one out of five reports contact with one or two different interest groups during the initial debate, three out five with respect to the first draft, and two out five in relation to the formal manifesto proposal.[167] Thus we note that consultation with interest groups in working out party platforms takes place also at the individual level. If the respondents are typical of the elite as whole, however, the number of groups included in the manifesto-making process through elite contact is rather limited.

Range of Relationships

What, then, do the data suggest as regard the range of SV's relationships with interest groups? Figure 12.3 shows the actual range of the network of links as measured by the survey data. SV is linked with a clear majority of the organisation categories, and more specifically to a proportion of 0.70 – indicating that it is linked with organisations within fewer categories than a couple of the long-

166. *Question:* 'First, we would like you to write down the names of those (maximum three) organisations you had most frequent contact with last year. (....). Use the blank below (....).'

167. *Question:* 'How many interest organisations did you have contact with – about one or several subsections – during the different phases of the manifesto-making before the party congress in 2000?

- Before the first draft was presented.
- During the debate over the manifesto draft.
- During the debate over the manifesto proposal.'

established parties, but it should be added that only *one* respondent differentiates a 'significant' from a 'non-significant' link in the case of client organisations.

What about the qualitative aspect of this relational dimension? Certainly, SV has retained its links with the new social movements it was associated with in the early years: the anti-EU organisations and internationally-oriented organisations, which might include what remains of the peace organisations and new citizen initiatives such as the new anti-globalisation movement – Attac. Significant links also exist to the environmental movement, women's organisations and organisations advocating non-religious philosophies of life. Furthermore, SV's network includes other groups that are less politically powerful in the Norwegian context, such as immigrant and refugee organisations.

We observe that SV's other origin in the *old left* is reflected by the significant link with LO and LO unions, but also the employees' organisations and professional organisations outside LO which more uniformly represent the new middle class associated with new politics than LO does.

Moreover, the figures show that SV is in addition well linked with pro-EU groups, primary-sector organisations, business, trade and employers' organisations,

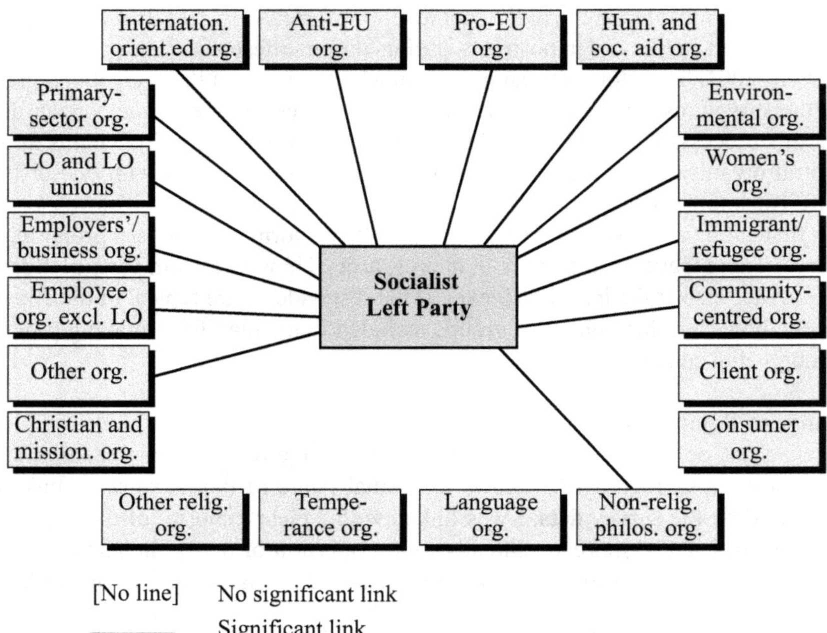

Figure 12.3: The Socialist Left Party's total network of significant links with interest groups.[1] *N = 12*

1 Significant links are cases where 50 per cent or more at least had contact a few times the past year (see Chapter 4).

humanitarian organisations and community-centred organisations through significant formal and informal contact. Do these findings – which include a significant link to the traditional antagonist of both employees and the environmental movement – mean that the Socialist Left has, in fact, a fairly wide network?

First, the degree of closeness indeed varies between organisation categories. As shown above, SV is generally much closer to LO and its unions, internationally-oriented organisations, anti-EU groups and the environmental movement than it is to business and industry or humanitarian organisations. The link with environmental organisations appears weaker than expected, but here we should recall that SV was never a specifically 'green' party founded by environmental activists. The party strategies for the organisation as a whole emphasise contact with the environmental movement. Second, we observe that the party organisation has no significant link to the old counter-culture in Norwegian politics, such as language organisations, religious organisations or organised religious communities and the like. In this, SV's network corresponds to its electoral status as the libertarian counterpart of the Christian People's Party in moral and religious issues.

At the same time, there is no doubt that SV puts LO and other employees' organisations on a different footing. SV is definitely closer to the LO system than to other employees' organisations despite its emphasis on occupational groups – like teachers and nurses – who to a significant extent are organised outside LO. In other words, SV seems still to be struggling to establish a balance between its link with the more industrially-oriented trade union movement and its relationship with the environmental movement. To conclude, the Socialist Left has a relatively wide network of links, but is still marked by its historical roots in internationally-oriented protest movements and the trade unions of the labour movement.

SUMMARY AND CONCLUSIONS

As far as the *closeness* to interest groups is concerned, we have seen that SV is not linked to any group by means of overlapping organisational structures, but there are numerous inter-organisational links. For example, SV invites various organisations to attend its party congress, and to address the congress delegates in plenum. Meetings with the party leadership and the headquarters are a norm, and during the manifesto-making process a formal hearing is arranged with various organisations. Hence, SV seems to have links that are better organised than what is traditionally seen as typical of new politics or left-libertarian parties (see Kitschelt 1989: 226, 232). SV has even attempted to establish some sort of binding co-operation with LO and its unions. Data from the individual level strengthen the impression of fairly close relationships with interest groups. More than 70 per cent of the top party elite are or have been officials or staff in external interest groups. In addition, the extent of actual contact is reported to be great at the individual level, although a definite conclusion requires systematic comparison with the other parties. The organised links are supplemented by regular informal contact. In sum, SV seems to have something similar to an *alliance* with the old trade union movement, internationally-oriented organisations and anti-EU groups, and *organised ad hoc relationships* with several others.

Regarding *the range of SV's relationships*, the survey shows that the party elite are linked with various interest groups. The network of significant links includes organisations representing both old and new politics, across cleavages. SV is, for example, to a certain extent involved in significant contact with business, trade and employers' organisations. On the other hand, the profile of those organisations with which SV is most closely linked is more in line with new politics theory. The Socialist Left has a closer relationship with LO and its unions, internationally-oriented organisations and anti-EU groups, and the environmental movement, than with others. The link with organisations for non-religious philosophies of life corresponds to its status as the libertarian counterpart to the Christian People's Party. Yet SV seems to have a closer relationship with LO and its unions than with other employees' organisations that organise a large proportion of the new middle class groups in the labour market.

To conclude, SV has a fairly close relationship with interest groups, and the overall network of links is rather wide. Today SV's relationship to interest groups approaches the pattern of relationships found among Norway's more established parties, at least in terms of the range of relations.

chapter thirteen | the progress party: the rise of a networking populist right

For the final stop on our journey across the universe of Norwegian parties and interest groups, we need to look back to the early 1970s. The Progress Party (FrP, known as Anders Lange's Party until 1977) belongs to the heterogeneous European group of new right-wing parties. According to Mudde (2007), FrP is not a *populist radical right party* but *a neo-liberal populist party*. As we shall see below, this conclusion is disputable but not crucial in our context. More importantly, like many other – radical and non-radical – populist right parties, FrP was originally an anti-establishment party marked by a fairly loose organisational structure, charismatic leadership and no links with interest groups.

BACKDROP: REINFORCEMENT OF A POPULIST ENTREPRENEURIAL PARTY?

There is little doubt that FrP has undergone significant changes as an organisation and as a political alternative since the 1970s. In protest at the party's lack of organisational structure and political platform, Carl I. Hagen, who went on to become party leader from 1978 until 2006, had temporarily resigned his membership in what was then 'Anders Lange's Party'. After the death of Anders Lange, under the leadership of Carl I. Hagen, the party organisation started to search for a degree of organisational normalcy, and the party manifesto was soon expanded to encompass all major political issues (Harmel and Svåsand 1993: 79). Whilst tax policy and bureaucracy had been the original core issues, immigration became the most important policy field in the second half of the 1980s (Svåsand 1998a: 84; Andersen and Bjørklund 2000: 204; Widfeldt 2000: 491).

Today, no other Norwegian party devotes as much of its manifesto to immigration-related issues as the Progress Party (Svåsand and Wörlund 2005: 267). At the outset, its position in this field was related to neo-liberal arguments. In principle, the party would prefer free immigration, but laws providing equal social rights to immigrants made such a policy difficult in practice. But in the 1990s, more emphasis was put on the cultural and what were defined as the problematic aspects of immigration. The party concluded that active integration and restricted immigration was needed in order to promote a society without ethnic minorities, although the Norwegian FrP did not appear as hostile as its Danish counterpart (Bjørklund and Andersen 2002: 113–4; Svåsand and Wörlund 2005: 267). Hence, the Progress Party is not an *extreme* anti-immigration party, but FrP is an example of a fairly successful case of mobilisation of opposition to immigration in Western Europe (Ivarsflaten 2008).

FrP has also increasingly paid attention to welfare issues. Despite its belief in market forces, it has always argued for higher expenditure on public health and state pensions (Andersen and Bjørklund 2000: 203). In recent years, FrP has made the case for a general increase in public expenditure based on funds generated from the Norwegian oil industry. However, although some of its more radical proposals for reforms of political institutions have been abandoned, the party remains marked by a critical outlook on the state. It also promotes more extensive use of referendums (Svåsand and Wörlund 2005: 266). Hence, Norway's Progress Party does not exhibit the features of either a classic neo-liberal nor an archetypal radical-right party. Mudde excludes it from the family of radical right parties, while others include Frp in this category (e.g. Kitschelt 1995; de Lange 2008).[168] It could be argued that FrP is instead a largely neo-liberal populist right party (Mudde 2007), but more important here, FrP has certainly retained substantial elements of populism in terms of opposition to the political establishment even if it is no longer a narrow protest party.

At the voter level, the development of support for FrP fitted with the pattern associated with other populist right parties, but its support has moved away from this pattern in recent years. After its electoral breakthrough, the party experienced a significant growth in voters from the working class in the following years. It has changed from appealing mainly to businessmen, to identifying salaried employees as its main target group. From the late 1970s and throughout the 1980s, the party became the first non-socialist party not being under-represented among workers as the proportion of workers among its supporters then started to deviate positively from the proportion of workers in the entire electorate according to survey data (Andersen and Bjørklund 2000: 216).

However, it is not evident that the support of manual workers can be interpreted as representing the counterpart to the New Left along a new value-based cleavage. According to Bjørklund and Andersen (2002: 120), the social equality so characteristic of Scandinavian countries contradicts Kitschelt's (1995) hypothesis of a marginalised working class resulting from the globalisation of national economies. On the other hand, the decline of class identity and collective solidarity seems to have opened up some sort of a 'new politics' dimension in Norway as well. The electorate of the Norwegian right wing tends to hold negative attitudes toward immigration and foreign aid, authoritarian opinions with regard to law and order, and to a certain degree, articulate scepticism towards environmentalism. Thus, the success of FrP might indicate what Ignazi (1992) called a 'silent counter-revolution' – a reaction to the libertarian post-materialist attitudes that emerged in the 1970s (Bjørklund and Andersen 2002: 121–2).

This notwithstanding, the constituencies of today's Progress Party are not clearly defined. In recent elections, the party has attempted to recruit more than working-class voters. In strategic documents, FrP defines itself as a 'liberal people's party' for 'ordinary people' against the political establishment. Interestingly, FrP moved its headquarters to the building next door to Labour in the mid-1990s,

168. FrP itself argues that it has more in common with the British Liberal Party and the German FD (*Freie Demokratische Partei*), than with the *Front National, Vlaamse Blok* or the Austrian FPØ (*Freiheitliche Partei Österreich*) (Svåsand and Wörlund 2005: 263).

overlooking the old square where the Norwegian labour movement holds its big rallies on May 1. In recent years, the party leadership has just as symbolically argued that FrP is in fact 'the new labour party' in Norway (see Salvesen 2003). But FrP also attempts to construct an image as a full-blown political alternative seeking public office (Progress Party Annual Report 1999–2000: 28). Like its Danish counterpart, FrP has tried to make itself more trustworthy and accountable towards other parties in recent years (Svåsand 1998a: 78). Furthermore, by appealing to '*Joe Public*', FrP addresses more than the traditional protest voters of new far right parties. As noted, welfare for the elderly has long been a core FrP issue. Christian circles outside the Church of Norway have also been in focus in recent years, for example by emphasis on FrP's firm support of the state of Israel in the conflicts in the Middle East. Later, urban and young voters have been identified as specific target groups (Fremskrittspartiet 2001: 6; Progress Party Annual Report 2000–01: 28, 2004–05: 69).

Equally important, the change in direction of a 'catch-all' strategy has had at least partial success in recent elections. By 2001, the number of FrP voters supporting religious values had increased significantly (Aardal 2003b: 88). The party was primarily supported by workers, trade union members and voters with lower education, but its current social profile is not very distinct (Berglund 2003: 131–1). Originally, younger people and men also dominated the FrP electorate, but also this composition has seen some change. From 1995, the age distribution approached that of the population at large (Bjørklund and Andersen 2002: 118). In other words, today's FrP captures traditional core voters of the Conservatives as well as of Labour, the Liberals and the Christian People's Party. FrP's profile as a distinct protest party has weakened in the sense that its electorate comprises a variety of voter groups, across the distinction between wage workers and self-employed (Svåsand and Wörlund 2005: 275). In 2000, the party leadership even decided to seek access to office, alone or by means of a coalition (Fremskrittspartiet 2001: 1).[169] In 2005, the Progress Party received 22 per cent of the vote, becoming Norway's largest non-socialist party (see Appendix E). Thus, FrP has in some respects taken a significant step away from its anti-establishment profile.

The 'normalisation' of the party is also visible in terms of its organisational features. The change of leadership in 1978 not only resulted in extended party manifestos, it also initiated radical organisational changes. The establishment of a strong party organisation has ever since been seen as a precondition for success at the polls. In 1983, a national extra-parliamentary organisation was established, and the party leadership encouraged local units to structure their activities equally (Harmel and Svåsand 1993: 80). Along with election success and increased public subventions, the party headquarters has been extended. In 1990, after its unprecedented success in general elections, FrP subordinated its parliamentary group to the party organisation (Svåsand and Wörlund 2005: 257). Despite numerous internal conflicts, the membership organisation is now nationwide, with member-

169. For the record, FrP moved its headquarters again in 2006, to a building in a position facing the Norwegian Parliament

ship figures increasing after a decline in the early 1990s (Heidar and Saglie 2002: 35; Progress Party Annual Reports 2002–04). In the early 1990s, FrP also aimed at developing an organised network in addition to the membership organisation – a *progress movement* modelled on the old labour movement (Heidar and Saglie 2002: 59). However, emphasis was on communication with individual citizens, not organised interests, and the Progress Party remains, without question, still organisationally distinctive in line with the model associated with more organised populist right parties (Taggart 1995): the party organisation is relatively centralised, and the national level is compared to a 'firm', within which the party executive serves as the 'board of directors' (Progress Party Annual Report 2000–01).[170]

RELATIONSHIPS WITH INTEREST GROUPS TODAY

An examination of key organisational documents from the early 2000s suggests that today's FrP is not unfamiliar with the idea of having links with the interest-group community. In fact, the numerous policy-making committees in the central organisation are – in their mandates – encouraged to be involved in contact with various external circles, such as experts and organised interest groups (Progress Party Annual Reports 1999–04). There is also the possibility of inviting external contributors to address committee meetings (Annual Report 2002–03: 45). Thus, having contact with various interest groups seems to be regarded as a norm for those involved in national policy-making. Moreover, party members affiliated to a union within LO have been encouraged to take active part in trade union work (*LO-Aktuelt* 24.6.04).[171] However, according to its secretary-general, the Progress Party does not aim at establishing more binding links, such as co-operation agreements, with anyone (Mo 2003 [Interview]). What kinds of links actually exists?

Closeness of Relationships

Inter-organisational Links for Contact with Interest Groups

Table 13.1 shows that the Progress Party has succeeded in establishing some inter-organisational links with interest groups. We observe that joint committees and conferences are non-existent, and FrP has not invited any organisation to formalised long-term co-operation (Mo 2003 [Interview]). But, as indicated above, the central organisation invites spokesmen of interest groups to party arrangements. The policy-making committees request external experts and organisation representatives to contribute both in relation to committee meetings and at conferences. It is emphasised that the party also invites organisations that disagree with the Progress Party's basic policy views (Mo 2003 [interview]). As the number

170. The extra-parliamentary party is superior to elected representatives at all levels (Heidar and Saglie 1994: 141–2), and FrP is the most centralised Norwegian party (Svåsand and Wörlund 2005). At headquarters there are formal 'divisions' for organisational matters, education, policy-making etc. By 2005, a unitary leadership for the central organisation and the parliamentary group was established (Annual Report 2004–05: 11).

171. According to Flote (2008) the strategy of seeking contact with LO and its unions in particular dates back to the late 1990s and represents a break with FrP's traditionally hostile attitude towards the trade union movement.

of such committees has increased since the 1970s, numerous opportunities for contact with interest groups are thus provided (see Progress Party Annual Report 1990–91: 39; 1991–92: 27; 2002–03: 36; 2004: 21).

Furthermore, FrP has also opened up its party congress to active participation by experts and spokesmen of organised interest groups. Organisations are asked to give speeches, talks and participate in the debates. External guests, from interest groups, consultancy firms, and research institutions, give talks about the issues to be discussed both in plenum and group sessions. The choice of who is invited each time depends on the topics on the agenda. Since 1997, various kinds of interest groups have attended FrP congresses, the range of which includes employees' organisations, business and employers' organisations, an interest group for taxpayers, a women's organisation for housewives, and two major environmental groups. The list of speakers has included the Chair of NHO and also the Chair of LO (Party Congress Agendas 1997–2003). In this sense, the Progress Party seems to have as strong organised contact with interest groups as the Socialist Left Party.

Specific dialogue seminars appear not to be routine, but some party conferences and committee meetings seem to fulfil a similar function. Furthermore, ad hoc

Table 13.1: Progress Party inter-organisational links with interest groups 2000–04

	Existence	If yes, what kind
Permanent joint committee	No	
Temporary joint policy committees	No	
Joint conferences	No	
Written or tacit agreements about regular meetings	No	
Invitation to the party congress	Yes	The party invites various organisations to each congress, dependent on the agenda.
Invitations to party meetings, seminars and conferences	Yes	By routine, especially in relation to the arrangements of policy-making committees.
Specific dialogue seminars and hearings	Yes	Not routine, but some of the conferences arranged by the internal committees have a similar function.
Meetings outside party bodies	Yes	Meetings are arranged, but mostly on the request of organisations. Such contact is not routine for party staff.

Sources: Various party documents (see Appendix A) and (Mo 2003 [interview]).

meetings with interest groups are arranged, although the party does not often initiate such contact itself on the subject of current issues, according to the secretary-general. Staff meetings with external groups are unusual, but they mediate ad hoc requests from representatives of interest groups to party officials (Mo 2003 [interview]). In sum, FrP seems to be among the Norwegian parties with the more organised links for contact with interest groups, at least in regard to long-term policy-making.

A closer look at the party manifesto-making process strengthens this picture. Since the mid-1990s, FrP has started deliberations by sending the old manifesto and asking for comments from numerous and various organisations. More than 300 addressees received a formal invitation in connection with the preparation of the 2001–2005 Manifesto.[172] It is emphasised that the committee did not make any selection when sending out the invitations (Mo 2003 [interview]; Røste 2005 [interview]). No workshops and few formal meetings with organisation representatives took place, as the organisations were asked to give their feedback in writing, which was also the required response from those who contacted the party themselves at a later stage. The response rate was, however, rather low. But the comments of those who did reply were distributed to the committee as a whole and discussed in plenum. According to the manifesto committee's secretary, the hearing among the interest groups functioned as a parallel to the internal deliberations (Røste 2005 [interview]). Finally, it should be noted that the leader of one specific environmental organisation – Green Warriors of Norway (*Norges Miljøvernforbund*) – was separately asked to suggest environmental policies that could be compatible with the basic values and policy views of the party (Røste 2005 [interview]).[173] Also here we observe that FrP does not discriminate according to organisation category at the organisational level.

Unorganised Links for Contact with Interest Groups and Frequency of Actual Contact

The Progress Party has certainly established inter-organisational links for contact with interest groups. Do the data from the individual level strengthen or weaken this quite surprising conclusion, and do informal links exist as well?

One way a party can be linked informally with interest groups is through currently or formerly shared leaders and personnel. Altogether, less than a majority but more than 40 per cent of the FrP top elite have experience as officeholders or staff members in one or more interest groups.[174] Figure 13.1 shows FrP's linkages to various kinds of organisations by top elite members who hold or have held office/who are or have been staff members at the national or local levels in

172. Some private firms were included here.

173. Moreover, several MPs were members of the manifesto committee. These are assumed to have made use of the network of contacts they have in connection with their parliamentary work (Røste 2005 [interview]).

174. The finding is validated by the fact that FrP party members are affiliated to other organisations generally to a lesser extent than members of other parties, according to Heidar and Saglie (2002: 274–7).

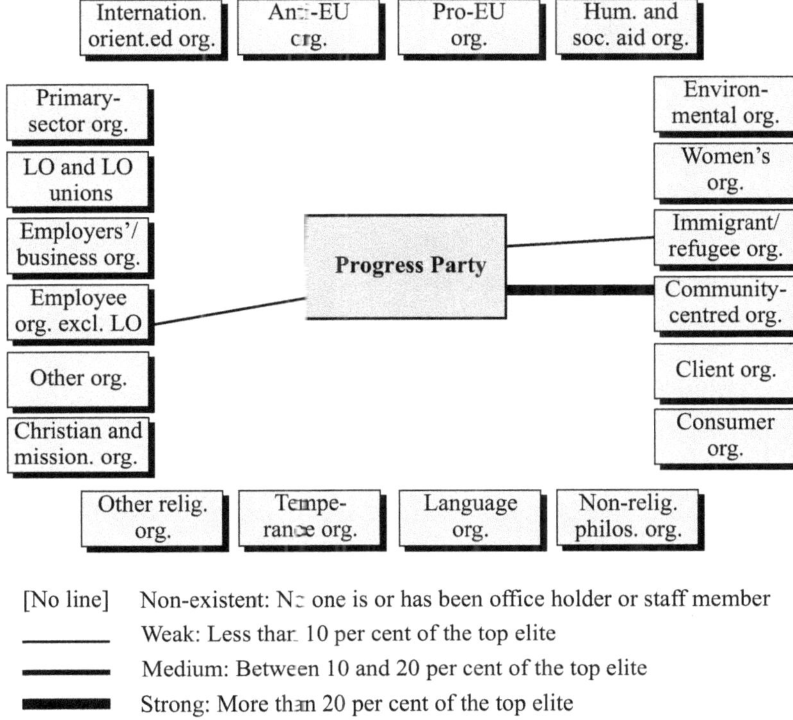

Figure 13.1: Progress Party links, by top elite members who hold or have held office/who are or have been staff members at the national or local levels in various interest groups 2003/2004.[1] *N = 12*

1 If a respondent is/has been an official and also is/has been a staff member, the answer is registered only in the 'official category'.

various interest groups in 2003/2004 (for complete frequencies, see Appendix D).

A *strong link* exists to only one kind of organisation – but more than 40 per cent – four out of twelve – are or have been staff or officials in community-centred organisations related to culture, sports, the elderly etc. Moreover, 8 per cent – one out of twelve – holds or has held positions in employees' organisations or professional organisations outside LO or in immigrant/refugee organisations.[175] In any case, the Progress Party is generally weakly linked with few interest groups in this way. The party elite do not take an active part in other organisations, with the notable exception of community-centred organisations – something which seems to characterise Norwegian party elites in general.

175. The latter may seem somewhat implausible, but as will be discussed below, when interpreting the result one should remember that this category includes a large number of different organisations (cf. Allern *et al.* 2001; Predelli 2003: 13).

Table 13.2: Progress Party top elite: frequency of formal and informal contact with interest groups in 2003. Per cent[1]

		Daily/ Weekly	Mon-thly	A few times	Never	No resp.	Total	N
Formal contact	Formal meetings or teleconferences	16	0	51	33	0	100	12
	Speakers at each other's seminars/conferences	0	8	59	33	0	100	12
	Formal written hearings or letters (incl. electronic communications)	17	17	41	25	0	100	12
Informal contact	Informal meetings, conversations, telephone conversations	16	25	51	8	0	100	12
	Informal written communication via SMS and e-mail	25	17	41	17	0	100	12
	Informal written communication like personal letters and memos	17	17	41	25	0	100	12

1 *Question:* 'Next, we would like you to state how often you had contact with interest groups *in different ways during the past year*. We distinguish between *formal* and *informal* contact:

- About how often did you have *formal contact* – of relevance for your work in the party's central organisation – with representatives from different interest groups in the following ways the past year? (tick off one alternative per line).
- About how often did you have *informal contact* – of relevance for your work in the party's central organisation – with representatives from different interest groups in the following ways the past year? (tick off one alternative per line).'

However, lack of this kind of links does not necessarily mean weak contact among party and organisation elites. In fact, it might increase the need for contact. Table 13.2 shows how often the top FrP elite had contact with interest groups in 2003, whether formally or informally. Above all, we observe that only a minority of the FrP elite had frequently – once a month or more often – contact with external interest groups. Informal meetings and conversations or SMS and informal e-mails are the most common modes of contact, with about 40 per cent – 5 out of 12 – in contact with interest groups in this way at least once a month in 2003. Some 30 per cent – 4 out 12 – had contact through formal letters and meetings, and a few had formal meetings of relevance for the extra-parliamentary organisation on a weekly basis. The great majority had such contact only a few times or not at all.

A precise conclusion must await a systematic cross-party comparison, but in sum it seems as if the relatively weak emphasis on ad hoc meetings is confirmed, but to a certain degree balanced by more informal contact. A separate analysis shows that independent of type of contact, about 75 per cent of the top FrP elite were in touch with external organisations at least once a month, while 25 per cent had no organisation contact at all.

To what extent does the frequency of the reported contact vary between organisation categories? From Figure 13.2 we see how often the party elite had contact with various kinds of organisations in 2003 (for table of frequency distributions, see Chapter 14).

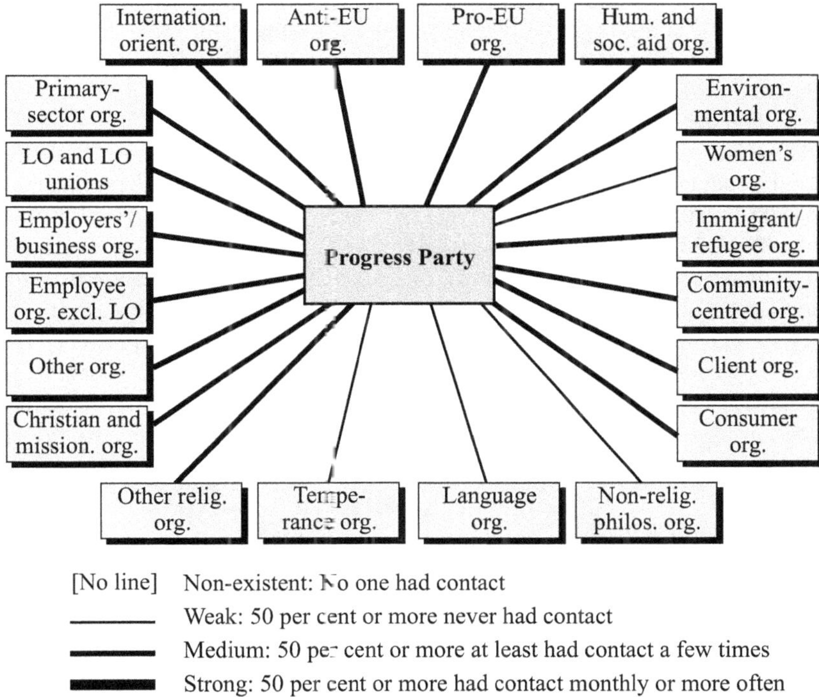

Figure 13.2: Progress Party links through the top elite's frequency of contact with various interest groups in 2003.[1] *N = 12*

1 *Question:* 'Could you please state how often you had contact – of relevance for your work in the party's central organisation – with one or more organisations within the following categories during the past year? The question includes both formal and informal, more random contact, written as well as oral communication.'

If exactly 50 per cent reported having contact 'seldom', the link is categorised as either medium or strong (includes primary-sector organisations and immigrant and refugee organisations).

We observe that the FrP top elite did not have *strong* – extensive and frequent – contact with any kind of organisation, but contact of *medium strength* with numerous organisations, and not only those associated with the party's old core issues. Half or more had contact at least a few times with *all kinds* of organisations, with the exception of some of the old counter-cultural ones (language and temperance) and women's organisations. However, more than 30 per cent – 4 out of 12 – had contact monthly or more often with employers', business and trade organisations, employees' organisations outside LO and community-centred organisations. About 25 per cent had regular contact with immigrant/refugee organisations and humanitarian and social aid organisations. Interestingly, about 17 per cent – 2 out of 12 – reported contact with trade unions in LO at least once a month. More detailed analyses show that employers', business and trade organisations and employees' organisations (within and outside LO) were those most repeatedly mentioned as one of the three organisations with which the respondents had most frequent contact in 2003.[176]

However, we find greater correspondence between the inter-organisational links for contact and the activity reported by individual elite members in connection with manifesto making in survey responses.[177] Most of the party elite members of 2003/2004 had held positions in FrP's central organisation also before the party congress of 2001. The majority of them report having contact with one or more interest groups during *all* the major phases of the manifesto process. It seems as if there are most extensive contacts at an early stage, as some 40 per cent – 4 out of 10 – had been in touch with at least three organisations before the first draft was presented, 30 per cent with five or more organisations. Hence, consulting external interest groups about the party manifesto seems a fairly widespread activity in the Progress Party.

Range of Relationships

There is no doubt that the Norwegian Progress Party has established links with interest groups, although no enduring ones with particular organisations. Now the question arises: how wide-ranging is the existing network of *significant links*? From sociogram depicted in Figure 13.3, we see that the Progress Party has one or more link to sixteen out of twenty categories of interest groups, so the proportion of the potentially interlinked organisations is high: 0.80. As will become clear in the next comparative chapter, FrP has what we define as significant links with more numerous organisation categories than many other parties in Norway today.

The network corresponds to the cross-class and FrP's materialist profile: em-

176. *Question:* 'First, we would like you to write down the names of those (maximum three) organisations you had most frequent contact with last year. (....). Use the blank below (....).'

177. *Question:* 'How many interest organisations did you have contact with – about one or several subsections – during the different phases of the manifesto-making before the party congress in 2000?

- Before the first draft was presented.
- During the debate over the manifesto draft.
- During the debate over the manifesto proposal.'

ployers', business and trade organisations, employees' organisations, consumer organisations and humanitarian organisations and community-centred organisations are all included in the network. Whether the party has links with anti-immigration groups – in line with the authoritarian profile – is difficult to say on the basis of the data. Such organisations could be included in the category of 'other organisations', but it should be noted the party has officially dissociated itself from racist and nationalist organisations. Association with these groups is seen as harmful for the party's public image, and argued to be in conflict with the FrP's '(...) statutes, programme and basic attitudes' (Progress Party Annual Report 1995–96: 11, my translation).[178] In contrast, it is beyond doubt that the network of FrP includes links with religious organisations, and that the Progress Party is not linked with old counter-cultural organisations such as temperance organisations.

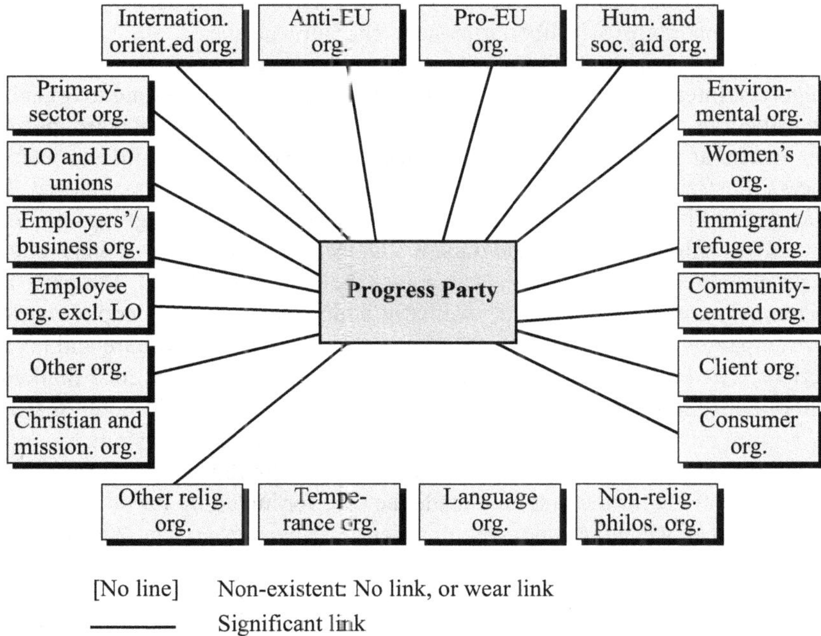

Figure 13.3: The Progress Party's total network of significant links with interest groups.[1] N = 12

1 Significant links are cases where 50 per cent or more at least had contact a few times the past year (see Chapter 4).

---

178. When an FrP MP attended a meeting which was arranged by the 'Norwegian Association' (*Den Norske Forening*) – and included various nationalist organisations and neo-Nazis – to speak on FrP immigration policy prior to the 1995 general elections, he was soon after asked to withdraw from the election campaign (Progress Party Annual Report 1995–96: 11). Moreover, the party leader Carl I. Hagen decided that he would thereafter be the sole party spokesman on issues related to immigration (Ekeberg and Snoen 2001: 269–70, 302).

On the other hand, the analysis has revealed that FrP has significant ad hoc contact with some organisations which represent a *counterpart* to the value-based new politics axis: environmental organisations, internationally-oriented organisations and immigrant and refugee organisations. The link with immigrant organisations is perhaps particularly unexpected. However, it is not evident that one can interpret this finding as indicative of truly wide-ranging relations. There is little doubt that this part of the Norwegian interest-group community is quite heterogeneous (Allern *et al.* 2001; Predelli 2003: 13), and may also include contact with fairly 'friendly organisations' as seen from FrP's point of view. For example, it is well-known that the Progress Party's parliamentary group in recent years has had contact with an organisation called 'Human Rights Service', which focuses on problems related to issues like forced marriages and female circumcision.[179] Thus we see that the relationships of today's FrP with interest groups cut across the post-materialist-materialist – or libertarian-authoritarian – cleavage.

Moreover, the degree of closeness does not vary greatly between organisation categories. Interestingly, FrP does not seem to discriminate according to organisation categories at the organisational level. The fact that environmental groups have been guests at the party congress and indeed involved in the manifesto-making process illustrates this aspect of FrP's approach. However, in terms of *actual* elite contact, two kinds of organisations stand out: business and trade groups and employees' organisations within and outside LO. Hence, the network of links reflects the party's attempt to appeal to voters across the old left-right axis. The party has a liberalist economic policy, but explicitly addresses 'ordinary people' in election campaigns through a combination of emphasis on public welfare and tax reductions. The presence of the LO leader at the party congress in 2002 marked a symbolic milestone in the party history of FrP. Yet, there is little doubt that FrP has a more friendly relationship with the business segment. Illustratively, prior to the 2005 elections, the head ('president') of the Confederation of Norwegian Enterprise (NHO) for the first time made the case for including FrP in the binding co-operation between the centre-right parties in Norway (Øverland 2005).

SUMMARY AND CONCLUSIONS

On the whole, the stepwise analysis presented in this chapter shows that by the early 2000s, FrP has established fairly organised links with interest groups. Interest groups from various sectors are regularly consulted in relation to extra-parliamentary policy-making and debate, they are invited to take part in political discussions at the party congress, and the previous election manifesto is sent out for comments to a large number of various interest groups even before the committee has started work on a new proposal. In fact, the strength of FrP's inter-organisational links with interest groups in general approaches the strength of the relationships of the Labour Party, the Centre Party and of the Socialist Left Party.

However, the links at the individual level appear more limited than in many other parties. There are only significant links in terms of personal overlap and

179. Human Rights Service is a cross between a voluntary organisation and a think-tank.

transfers to community-centred organisations. Ad hoc contact seems mainly to take place at the request of interest groups, and elite contact tends to take the form of informal meetings. The majority of the FrP elite is not frequently (at least once a month) in touch with any kind of interest group. Although a final conclusion has to wait until the cross-party analysis, it is clear that no relationship approaches an *alliance* or an *informal partnership*. However, more or less *organised ad hoc relationships* do seem widespread.

As far as the range of relationships is concerned, the survey shows that FrP is linked with more numerous and varied interest groups. In line with its materialist, cross-class approach, Frp is linked with LO and its unions, as well as with other employees' organisations and employers' business and industry organisations and primary sector. Links with anti-immigration groups have not been found, but the network does include contacts with other organisations associated with non-libertarian values, namely religious organisations. However, FrP has also relationships with organisations that represent a counterpart to the new politics axis: environmental organisations, internationally-oriented organisations and immigrant/refugee organisations. Interestingly, the party does not seem to discriminate according to group category at the organisational level. On the other hand, in terms of actual contact, employers', business, trade organisations, employees' organisations and professional organisations are prominent.

To conclude, the Progress Party is not characterised by tenuous links into civil society. The party organisation has to some extent become 'normalised' in terms of its relations with Norwegian associational life, along *both* the dimension of closeness and range. In Chapters 14 and 16, this relative lack of difference between FrP and the established parties will, indirectly, be further explored.

chapter fourteen | patterns of contemporary relationships: a comparative analysis

To what extent are contemporary political parties linked with interest groups in Norway – how are parties linked and with what organisations? Does a predominant pattern of relations exist among, at least, the established parties? Or do the party relationships with interest groups vary to a significant extent? The preceding chapters have provided detailed insight into Norwegian party-interest group relationships. The degree of closeness of each party to various kinds of organisation has been discussed and the total range of network of links measured. We have observed that all party organisations have significant links with interest groups, but that differences exist in each party's degree of closeness to different segments of the universe of interest groups. It has also been suggested that parties vary in terms of their overall pattern of relationships. However, systematic cross-party comparison is necessary to characterise precisely the relationships along both the dimension of closeness and range. So in what follows, we will move from a party-based to a comparative analysis of the available data. But first, it will be useful to briefly recapitulate the specific research questions to be examined based on the data material as a whole.

RESEARCH QUESTIONS REVISITED

As demonstrated in Chapter 3, existing empirical studies indicate that parties historically closely linked with certain organisations have declined over time, but that this trend may not be uniform (cf. e.g. Padgett and Paterson 1991: 216; Thomas 2001c; Allern *et al.* 2007). The degree to which established parties are today characterised by weaker relations with a broad range of interest groups is open to debate. Still, numerous scholars have forcefully argued that we are about to witness such a general development. It is widely agreed that structural changes like de-industrialisation, changed patterns of employment, and the erosion of old collective identities have weakened the rationale for close relationships with the interest groups traditionally associated with specific political parties. Instead, today's party environment calls for relatively distant relationships with a wide range of interest groups (Kirchheimer 1966). Some scholars have even argued that we now experience an era in which parties have tenuous links into civil society in general, due to for example generous public subventions to parties and what is argued to be a weak degree of party competition in contemporary politics (Katz and Mair 1995).

Following the terminology developed in this book, the literature emphasising system-level characteristics has thus led us to expect that *political parties tend to have organised but not very strong links – organised ad hoc relationships – with a wide range of interest groups today*. Alternatively, it was suggested that *parties tend to mostly have distant relations – informal issue-based contact – or to be nearly separated from the interest-group community in general.* Both expectations imply that the old pattern of close relations with particular interest groups belongs to the past, and that a predominant pattern in terms of closeness and range of party relationships exists today. Moreover, existing party networks of links are assumed to be largely overlapping not polarised within a given system: party links cut across cleavages. Also to be examined is the implicit assumption of correlation between the closeness and range of party relationships with interest groups.

However, it is important to recall that parties are seen as autonomous actors that are even capable of acting upon their context themselves. Hence, the described patterns are not expected to be uniform. But system-level differences and organisational factors will allegedly not prevent a 'period effect' from materalising in established democracies. The most common exceptions to the general rule are usually argued to be parties founded after the Second World War – new right, new left, and green parties – as these have been established as a *reaction* to 'old politics' (Katz and Mair 1996: 531). This, then, led us to expect that *the new parties are distinctively different from old parties as regards the pattern of relationships with interest groups*. Moreover, it is often suggested that *new left, green and right parties are distinctively different from each other*: while *new left-wing and green parties tend to have informal but significant links – informal partnerships – with social movement organisations, populist radical right and right populist parties are hypothesised to be usually characterised by lack of significant links with interest groups in general.*

As far as Norway is concerned, the relevant parties to study against this background are on the one (old) hand the Labour Party (DnA), the Conservatives (H), the Liberals (V), the Centre Party (Sp) and the Christian People's Party (KrF), and on the other (new) hand the Socialist Left (SV) and the Progress Party (FrP). The historical backdrops presented in Chapters 7 to 13 showed that all Norway's major long-established parties have survived the twentieth century, but that individual political parties have changed in numerous respects. The limited research undertaken as regards relationships with interest groups indicates that party links with the traditionally associated organisations have declined in most cases. Furthermore, most established parties have, at some point, acknowledged the need to establish a wide network of links with interest groups as a part of their general debate over organisational matters. But to what extent has such a development actually taken place?

I start by comparing the parties' closeness to interest groups in general and to various organisation categories in particular. Instead of individually analysing the range of relationships for every major kind of link, a brief analysis of the overall network of links is presented in the last part of the analysis. Thereafter the major findings are summarised and the expectations of the party literature are examined. In conclusion, I briefly consider to what extent internal variation in the Norwegian social structure and economy, particularly in the vote-mobilising potential among traditional core voters, may shed light on the revealed differences between established parties.

TOWARDS DISTANT PARTY-INTEREST GROUP RELATIONSHIPS?

In this section, we will first look at the organisational level, and thereafter the issue of links reported by individual data. In both contexts, the general picture is discussed, before comparing the links of individual parties to traditional associates in particular and to organisations in general.

Overlapping Organisational Structures

As argued in Chapter 4, we can distinguish three major classes of links, reflecting varying degrees of closeness in general: *overlapping organisational structures*, *inter-organisational links* and *unorganised links*. The former class includes statutory links like collective affiliation to the party as a whole, guaranteed representation in party executive and local collective membership (see Chapter 4). Today, however, there are in Norway no links of this kind between political parties and external (not internal, party-created) interest groups. Mutual and formal representation of DnA and LO in their respective executive bodies ended in the 1920s; the Centre Party's organisational structure became fully independent of the Farmers' Union in 1931, and Labour's collective affiliation of union members was gradually abolished in the 1990s (Allern and Heidar 2001). The question is whether this disintegration of organisational structures represents one step towards the general erosion of inter-organisational links between parties and interest groups.

Inter-organisational Links for Contact with Interest Groups

Potential and existing *inter-organisational links* are summarised in Table 14.1, where it can be seen that Norwegian parties do have organised links for contact with interest groups. Joint committees and formal co-operation agreements exist. All party headquarters report that meetings are occasionally set up between representatives of the party's central organisation and organised interest groups. Most parties also occasionally invite interest groups to attend party events like seminars and conferences, and quite a few arrange specific dialogue seminars fairly regularly.

However, the strength, i.e. number and kind, of inter-organisational links varies significantly among parties. Labour has more such links than any other party, and only Labour has entered into co-operation agreements with any organisation. DnA is also the only party with a liaison committee with an external interest group. A few years ago, DnA's relationship with the Confederation of Trade Unions (LO) was internally evaluated, but both the party congress and LO congress of 2002 agreed that this well-organised relationship should continue. Top leaders from LO and the party still meet regularly in the Joint 'Co-operation Committee' to discuss a broad range of political and organisational matters. Since 1997, the Committee has met at least once a month. A permanent liaison committee also exists with national unions within organising civil and military personnel in the armed forces. Furthermore, a formal co-operation agreement was established with a few individual unions as late as the 1970s, today including a separate liaison committee with the public-sector dominated Norwegian Union of Municipal and General Employees (*Fagforbundet*). Collective membership was abolished in the 1990s,

Table 14.1: Parties' central organisations: inter-organisational links with interest groups 2000–04

	DnA	H	V	Sp	KrF	SV	FrP
Permanent joint committee	X						
Temporary joint policy committees	X						
Joint conferences	X			[1]			
Written or tacit agreements about regular meetings	X						
Invitations to the party congress	X	[2]				X	X
Invitations to party meetings, seminars and conferences	X		X	X	X	X	X
Specific dialogue seminars and hearings	X	(X)[3]		X	X	(X)[4]	(X)[5]
Meetings outside party bodies	X	X	X	X	X	X	X

1 But one 'dialogue conference' was arranged together with the Norwegian Union of Municipal and General Employees (*Fagforbundet*) in 2005.

2 But the Conservatives invited some interest organisation leaders to address the party congress in 2005.

3 A permanent arrangement exists for seminars/meetings with small and medium-sized businesses (*Bedriftskanalen*), and 'breakfast meetings' are arranged with large-scale firms and businesspeople four to six times a year.

4 Some open conferences fulfil a similar function.

5 Some conferences arranged by internal committees fulfil a similar function.

Source: Various party documents and interviews with key informants (see Appendix A). See also discussions in Chapters 7–13.

but further thematically organised branches at workplaces ('trade branches') have to some extent been established instead (see Chapter 7).

Sp abolished its co-operation agreement with the Farmers' Union much earlier right after the Second World War. SV has attempted to establish a similar kind of link with individual trade unions and the Confederation of Trade Unions, but has not succeeded. Only three out of the seven parties studied here invite external organisations to visit and speak to the party congress: the Labour Party, the Socialist Left Party and the Progress Party.[180] Together with the Centre Party, these are the parties that seem to have most inter-organisational links for contact with interest groups. In the case of SV, its links with the trade union movement have in fact grown stronger during the early 2000s. In 2003, the LO leadership attended, and

180. The latter even invite organisation representatives to active debate (see Chapter. 13). In contrast, KrF recently considered inviting external organisations to the congress, but decided against such a routine (see Chapter. 11). On the other hand, the Conservatives invited some interest organisation to address their party congress in 2005, including the leader of the LO union United Federation of Trade Unions (*Fellesforbundet*) (*Dagsavisen* 14.05.06).

LO's vice-chairman addressed, SV's national congress for the first time in history. And in 2005, SV's party leader gave a speech to the LO congress on an equal footing with the Labour Party.

With invitations to party meetings, seminars and conferences, numerous dialogue seminars and some ad hoc meetings, KrF represents an intermediate case. A formal rule (§ 2) still specifies that all KrF officials and representatives are to profess Christianity, and an annual dialogue seminar is arranged with Christian leaders and organisations and with the environmental movement. However, there exists no formal co-operation agreement with any religious organisation or organised religious community.

The Conservatives and the Liberals seem to have generally relatively weak or few inter-organisational links. In the first decades after the Second World War, the Conservatives' interaction with trade and business organisations led to frequent tension but was a rather close relationship (cf. Chapter 6). Today, the party organisation's links with interest groups seem fairly loosely organised outside the Storting, in comparison with other parties' links. The relationship with the Confederation of Norwegian Enterprise (NHO) is, above all, less evident than the Labour Party's relationship with LO. However, a joint research report presented in 2001 with the Shipowners' Association indicates that more organised co-operation also exists. Furthermore, collective routines are certainly established for communication with small and large-scale firms and *individual* businesspeople. For example, the committee responsible for raising financial support to the party (*Økonomistyret*), invites business owners and leaders to regular meetings about current political issues (see Table 14.1).[181]

As to the Liberals, they were from early on '(...) left without any mass organization to rely upon', due to party splits and new competitors that had well-defined voters' groups (Leiphart and Svåsand 1988: 317). In the 1970s and 1980s, the party turned to various industrial organisations and attempted to establish links with environmental groups (Selle 1997: 157). However, these initiatives never resulted in routines, and the Liberal strategy and practice has remained for the party organisation to keep distance from interest groups.

Dialogue about the election manifesto is a particularly important way for parties to open the passage of legislation up for civil society. Inter-party differences seem in fact to be somewhat less in this context: by the early 2000s, as all parties except the Liberals had deliberately opened up the internal debate to external groups in one way or another. Prior to the 2001 elections, individual organisations requested contact or sent comments on their own initiative to all parties. FrP, SV, Sp and KrF arranged formal hearings, or something very similar, when drafting their 2001–2005 Manifestos: by distributing the old manifesto and asking for comments (FrP), by sending organisations memos within various policy fields (SV), by means of a general invitation to contribute by mail or meetings (KrF) or

181. In 2004, a liberal think-tank – Civita – was also founded; main shareholders are the Confederation of Norwegian Business and Industry and the Norwegian Shipowners' Association (Civita 2005). However, it has no formal links to the Conservative Party, nor to other parties for that matter.

through special invitations to workshops within specific policy fields (Sp). Some ad hoc meetings were also arranged with individual organisations.

In the case of Labour and the Conservatives, interest groups have also been included in the process, but in a less systematic way. In DnA, LO is normally represented unofficially in the manifesto committee and thoroughly consulted in relevant issues, whereas other organisations may be invited to seminars or may request meetings themselves. In the Conservative Party, meetings were arranged with various organisations, but the committee did not initiate them itself in connection with the 2001 elections. In both these parties, the emphasis has been on experts when it comes to use of external sources. The Liberals arranged a formal hearing with interest groups in the 1980s, but have not made this a routine.[182] Altogether, Norway's political parties seem to have rather extensive contact with interest groups when working on the party manifesto, but not all parties consult organisations systematically.

Unorganised Links for Contact and Frequency of Actual Contact

Even if inter-organisational links are weak or generally non-existent, this does not necessarily mean separation or limited contact between decision-makers. For one thing, parties and interest groups can be informally linked by means of *overlaps or transfers of officials and staff*. Moreover, we need to assess *the frequency of actual – formal and informal – contact*.

To what extent have party elites held positions in other organisations, previously or at present? The survey[183] reveals that altogether, almost 70 per cent of the extra-parliamentary top elite members report that they hold or have held office/ that they are or have been staff members at the national or local levels in various interest groups in 2003/2004. Thus, Norwegian parties and interest groups are indeed not without links in terms of shared staff and leaders, at least not when examined over time. Detailed analyses show that the Progress Party has the lowest proportion of elite members with experience from one or more organisations (about 40 per cent) whereas SV, KrF and DnA have the highest (from about 75 per cent to 88 per cent) (see Appendix D).

The sociogram in Figure 14.1 shows the share of office holders and staff members of the party elites from various organisations. Here we should recall that the small size of the elite population makes it generally crucial to be aware of those incidents where only a few differing answers could have influenced the conclusions: thus we should emphasise only the major observed differences in the material. As in the party-based analysis, the figure distinguishes between *strong*, *medium* and *weak links* according to the percentage share of former or current office holders or staff.

182. Also, committee members may have drawn upon their individual acquaintances. For example, the environmental movement was linked with SV's process by a former leader and staff member serving as committee members. In the case of the Conservatives, the secretary's experience from parliamentary work meant numerous potential contacts (see Chapters 7-13).

183. Due to the low response rate among the Liberals, answers from these persons are treated as information from individual informants, not as robust data regarding the top elite as a whole (cf. Chapter 1).

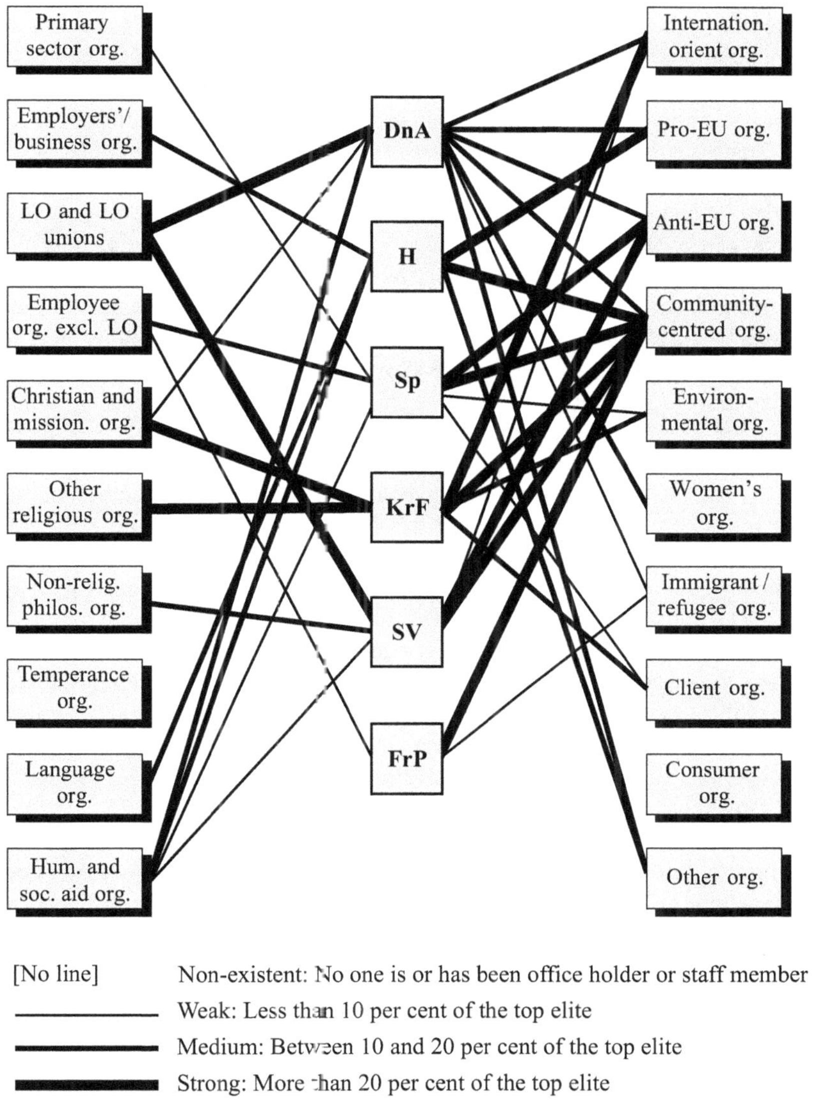

Figure 14.1: Party to organisation links by top elite members who hold or have held office/who are or have been staff members at the national or local levels in various interest groups 2003/2004[1]

1 For the N of each party, see Appendix D.

The motivation for presenting the data as relative figures is, as argued in Chapter 1, to facilitate systematic comparison among parties. Since the size of elite populations varies considerably, it is not reasonable to equate one person's organisational experience across all parties. An individual elite member's experience from or contact with interest groups is likely to be more significant for small elites than for large ones. But for the same reason, it should be noted that *medium strong* links include only *one* elite member in the case of the Conservatives and the Christian People's Party due to the particularly small size of these elites, whereas the same category may include up to *four* persons in the case of the Labour Party.

We observe that the personal overlaps and transfers represent *strong* or *medium strong* links in numerous cases. All parties have a strong link, i.e. more than 20 per cent of the elite either hold or have held office or staff positions, to at least one kind of organisations. The figure shows that all party elites have extensive experience from community-centred organisations. This means that the political elite are not so different from the general population in this regard, since the level of involvement in local voluntary work is fairly high in Norway (see Chapter 2).

Some parties have more and stronger links than others. DnA has most links (about ten) of this kind, whereas FrP has fewest (about three), and KrF has the greatest number of *strong* links. Moreover, most parties have a strong link to their traditionally-associated interest group, but note that these proportions vary among them.[184] Detailed analyses show that less than 10 per cent of the Centre Party elite hold or have held positions in primary-sector organisations in general, whereas less than 15 per cent of the Conservative elite have experience from business and trade organisations (see Appendix D). As the response rate among the Liberals was low, they are excluded from the frequencies. But the existing information suggests that few links exist, and that the Liberal Party is not populated by people from old social movement organisations (see Chapter 9).

Hence, DnA and KrF are those of the old parties who recruit most elite members from traditional circles: about 40 per cent of the top DnA elite have or come from positions in LO and individual trade unions, whereas more than 40 per cent of the KrF elite have backgrounds from the leadership or administration of Christian organisations at the national and local levels (see Appendix D).[185]

SV's background in new social movements is less visible: the SV elite are not a bastion for leaders of the women's movement, environmental organisations and peace groups, although a weak link of this kind to the environmental movement may well exist. On the other hand, more than 40 per cent of the SV elite report that they are or have been officials and staff in anti-EU organisations, and about 25

184. The proportions may have decreased over time, but comparable data do not exist. See Chapters 7–13 for post-war links.

185. Only 10 per cent of Labour's top elite declared that they *presently* hold positions in the National Federation or in individual unions at the national level. The decrease – compared with the 20 per cent reported in Sundberg's (2003) project from the 1990s – reflects that DnA's tradition of including the LO chair in the executive committee was terminated in 2001. The routine was reinstated in 2005, and about 15 per cent of the party executive (three persons) currently hold seats in the LO Executive.

per cent have local or national experience from LO and LO unions (see Appendix D).[186] In contrast, in FrP, fewer links exist, and only one strong link.

Next, we need to find out how often the party elite actually are in touch with interest groups. Even if inter-organisational links are few, this may not necessarily mean that there are hardly any *organised meetings* or limited *informal contact* between party and interest group representatives. In practice, it is difficult for respondents to distinguish official meetings clearly from unorganised contact in relation to each organisation category (individually), but the respondents were asked to report about the general frequency of formal and informal contact separately. Table 14.2 shows how often the various top elites had contact with interest groups in 2003 in both ways, on issues relevant to their work in the party's central organisation.

Table 14.2: The party top elites' formal or informal contact with interest groups in 2003. Shares with contact at least once a month. Per cent[1]

		DnA	H	Sp	KrF	SV	FrP	All[2]
Formal contact	Formal meetings or teleconferences	39	29	38	0	27	16	25
	Speakers at each others seminars/conferences	29	0	31	11	55	8	22
	Formal written hearings or letters (incl. electronic)	24	43	23	22	55	34	34
Informal contact	Informal meetings, conversations, telephone conversations	71	43	54	22	91	41	54
	Informal written communication via SMS and e-mail	71	58	54	56	91	42	62
	Informal written communication like personal letters and memos	48	29	55	22	63	34	42
N		21	7	13	9	11	12	73

1 *Question:* 'Next, we would like you to state how often you had contact with interest groups *in different ways during the past year*. We distinguish between *formal* and *informal* contact:

- About how often did you have *formal contact* – of relevance for your work in the party's central organisation – with representatives from different interest groups in the following ways the past year (tick off one alternative per line)?
- About how often did you have *informal contact* – of relevance for your work in the party's central organisation – with representatives from different interest groups in the following ways the past year (tick off one alternative per line)?'

2 Average numbers across parties, Liberals excluded. N = 73 because one respondent reported not having had this kind of contact at all in 2003.

186. At the 2005 congress, two out the nine persons elected onto the party executive currently held national positions in LO unions.

Table 14.3: The party top elites' formal and informal contact with various interest groups in 2003. Shares with contact at least once a month. Per cent[1]

	DnA	H	Sp	KrF	SV	FrP	All[2]
Primary-sector organisations	10	0	31	11	8	0	10
Employers' organisations, business and trade organisations (incl. NHO)	5	29	8	11	16	33	17
LO and LO Unions	76	14	23	0	58	17	31
Employees' organisations outside LO	29	43	16	0	25	33	24
Christian and missionary organisations	0	14	8	22	8	0	9
Other religious organisations and organised religious communities	5	0	8	11	8	0	5
Organisations related to non-religious philosophies of life	0	0	8	0	8	0	3
Temperance organisations	0	0	15	22	17	0	9
Language organisations	0	0	15	0	8	0	4
Community-centred organisations related to culture, sport, youth, elderly, hobbies etc.	66	43	46	22	34	33	41
Humanitarian and social aid organisations	52	14	23	11	25	25	25
Internationally-oriented organisations	34	14	23	11	50	0	22
Organisations in favour of EU membership	10	43	15	0	8	16	15
Organisations against EU membership	5	0	53	0	50	16	21
Environmental and conservationist organisations	24	29	23	11	33	0	20
Women's organisations (feminist groups, housewives' and farm women's unions)	20	14	23	0	25	0	14
Immigrant and refugee organisations	24	14	15	0	17	25	16
Client organisations	10	14	23	0	25	8	13
Consumer organisations	0	14	15	0	0	8	6
Other organisations	29	14	23	11	33	17	21
N	21	7	13	9	12	12	74

1 *Question:* 'Could you please state how often you had contact – of relevance for your work in the party's central organisation – with one or more organisations within the following categories during the past year? The question includes both formal and informal, more random contact, written as well as oral communication.'

2 Average numbers across parties, Liberals excluded.

As indicated by the individual party chapters, informal contact is the most common mode of communication. On average, about 60 per cent said that they had contact with interest groups by e-mail and SMS at least once a month in 2003, a little less through informal meetings or conversations. Between 25 per cent and 30 per cent had contact as often with organisation representatives in formal contexts. Hence, formal meetings, representing inter-organisational links for contact, are supplemented by less informal ones. Interestingly, also the elite of those parties that have *least inter-organisational links* with interest groups outside the Storting – the Conservatives and the Liberals – are engaged in this kind of contact. Hence, lack of organised links does not at the general level equal separation.

There are, however, distinct differences among parties. It is the SV elite that, in almost every way, had most regular contact with interest groups in 2003. About 90 per cent had informal contact monthly by e-mail, SMS or through more personal meetings and conversations. A great majority of the DnA elite also reported regular informal contact with interest groups. Relatively strong inter-organisational links (DnA, Sp, SV and FrP) correspond to a generally higher level of both formal and informal contact, but not necessarily. Both FrP and KrF seem to have a generally lower level of contact, whereas the Conservatives do not have least contact, despite their comparatively weak inter-organisational links. As to general contact, regardless of form, the survey shows that on average about 74 per cent of the different party elites had at least monthly contact with one or more interest groups in 2003. More detailed analyses reveal that KrF had the least contact: only about half its elite communicated with external interest groups on a monthly basis, as against about 80 per cent and 90 per cent for SV and DnA, respectively. As we can hardly consider all organisations to be a potential acquaintance to every elite member, it is also worth noting that all parties had some contact with all the organisation categories examined here.

Moreover, we see from Table 14.3 that the extent of frequent contact varies among parties and individual kinds of organisations. The party analyses distinguished between *weak*, *medium* and *strong* links if 50 per cent or more had contact never, at least a few times or at least once a month, respectively. The Labour Party and the Socialist Left seem to have the *strongest* links in general. Furthermore, also in this way, the DnA elite report a stronger link with the trade union movement than do the Conservative elite as regards their traditional associate within the labour market. More than 70 per cent of the DnA elite – 16 out of 21 – reported contact with the trade union movement on a monthly basis, whereas only about 30 per cent of the Conservative elite – 2 out of 7 – was involved that often in contact with the organised business community. Likewise, only about 30 per cent of the Centre Party elite – 4 out of 13 – had monthly contact with primary-sector organisations in 2003, and slightly more than 20 percent of the KrF elite – 2 out of 9 – were involved that often with religious organisations. All parties, with the exception of KrF, have also extensive, frequent contact – strong links – with other organisations, primarily EU-related and other international organisations, humanitarian organisations and social aid organisations.

The SV elite is most involved in contact with LO and unions, as well as EU-related and other internationally-oriented organisations. In the Progress Party, contact with labour market organisations dominates. In fact, and quite surprisingly, FrP's contact with employers', business and industry organisations *and* employees'/professional organisations is more or less as extensive as the Conservatives' contact with such organisations. Although the survey data are not robust with regard to the Liberal Party elite, it is worth noting that those who responded had contact with external organisations, but mostly in an informal way.

The findings suggest that environmental groups and business and trade organisations are among those most closely connected with the Liberal Party through ad hoc contact. To conclude, the contact frequencies make clear that there is no simple correspondence between the general strength of inter-organisational links for contact and the frequency of actual contact.

However, if the contact reported at the individual level is to be interpreted as an indication of the party's attempt to establish links with interest groups, we have, for the record, to examine whether the party elite members actually do initiate some of the meetings themselves. The contact reported might, in theory, be primarily the result of interest group initiatives, and the meetings thus not an indicator of the party elite's attempts to establish an inter-organisational or informal links in terms of regular ad hoc meetings. Interestingly, most secretaries-general and party secretaries report receiving numerous invitations to interest-group arrangements each year. Table 14.4 summarises the frequency of contact for all parties in the case of those organisations they had most frequent contact with, that is to say, the shares of party elites that initiated the contact at least sometimes. As the question concerned only those three individual interest groups with which the elite had most frequently been in touch the past year, exactly which organisation categories we are talking about will vary across respondents.

The table reveals a certain correspondence between the extent of party-initiated contact and strength of inter-organisational links. On average, the parties with the

Table 14.4: Frequency of contact initiated by party representatives in 2003. Shares that initiated the contact at least sometimes. Per cent[1]

	DnA	H	Sp	KrF	SV	FrP	All[2]
Organisation no. 1	100	43	73	74	90	55	73
Organisation no. 2	90	43	50	83	80	36	64
Organisation no. 3	64	20	80	66	60	25	53
Average across organisations	85	35	68	74	77	39	63
N	17–20	5–7	10–11	6–8	10	8–11	56–66

1 *Question:* 'When contacts with these organisations were not the result of random meetings the past year, to what extent did you/the party initiate them?'

2 Average numbers across parties, Liberals excluded.

most organised links for contact in terms of dialogue seminars and the like – DnA, Sp, SV – also tend to initiate more of the contact reported by the elite. The exception is the FrP: and here the finding confirms the secretary-general's specification that the party staff meetings with external groups are not routine, but that they mediate ad hoc requests from representatives of interest groups to party officials (Mo 2003 [interview]). Furthermore, the KrF elite also initiate a lot of their contacts themselves, but the frequencies, of course, also reflect the demand for contact with different parties among interest groups. Hence, inter-organisational links may be weak, but this need not preclude attempts by the party's top elite to be linked with interest groups at least on an informal ad hoc basis. On the whole, the differences among parties have to be interpreted carefully.

Finally, the question is to what extent there is correspondence between the degree to which the party systematically consults interest groups during the manifesto-making process and the individually reported contact in connection with the internal debate. Was sporadic contact also the case among executive members and staff in those parties without well-developed organised routines? In order to get an answer, a question dealing specifically with elite contact during the last manifesto-making process was included in the survey.[187] Unfortunately, but not surprisingly, not all respondents were part of the national top elite during the manifesto-making prior to the general elections in 2001. Therefore, we cannot place much emphasis on this part of the responses. A systematic cross-party comparison is ruled out. I content myself with concluding that in all parties, those elite members who could respond to this question report having been in touch with interest groups at some point during the manifesto-making process (see Chapters 7–13). In this way, the manifesto-making process confirms the general finding that inter-organisational links are echoed by individual elite members' behaviour, but that weak links at the organisational level do not necessarily mean lack of actual contact. Norwegian parties are, to varying degrees, linked with interest groups.

TOWARDS WIDE-RANGING RELATIONSHIPS OF PARTIES?

Even though a party has generally closer relationships with interest organisations than other parties have, this party is not necessarily linked into the greatest part of the interest-group community. Rather, as suggested in Chapter 4, there would be a *trade-off* between closeness and range of links, i.e. that closeness to a certain extent would entail exclusiveness. As mentioned initially, it is widely assumed that today's established parties have a wide-ranging network of links with interest groups, instead of having close relationships with a few. Thus, the question to be discussed in the following sections is what characterises Norway's political par-

187. *Question:* 'How many interest organisations did you have contact with – about one or several subsections – during the different phases of the manifesto-making before the party congress in 2000?

- Before the first draft was presented.
- During the debate over the manifesto draft.
- During the debate over the manifesto proposal.'

ties in the early 2000s in terms of *numbers of organisation categories (quantitative aspect)* and the *variety of represented interests (qualitative aspect).* Do the existing networks generally cut across old and new cleavages, or are there significant differences? As the survey material is the only type of data that covers all group categories systematically, and includes contact both within formal and informal settings, the range of links is primarily assessed on basis of these data.

The preceding analyses have shown that Norwegian parties generally have a fairly wide-ranging network of links. Since the 1970s, in all well-established parties the leadership has identified a need for a wide network of links to circles outside the party organisation, but to varying degrees. Additionally, both the newer Socialist Left and the Progress Party define some sort of links with external interest groups as a goal according to party documents and key informants. From Table 14.3 we saw that *all* party elites keep in touch with a variety of organisations. In one way or another, all parties seem to have numerous links, and also some links cutting *across* old cleavages.

However, to exclude what one may consider to be links of limited significance, only the links where 50 per cent or more had contact at least a few times the past year were included in the party assessments. The results as regards the total range of links in the numeric sense are summarised in Table 14.5. Here the links are measured as a proportion: the actual number of organisation types to which the party is linked, divided by the maximum number of organisation types to which a party could have been linked according to the categorisation applied here.

Table 14.5: Norwegian parties' total network of significant links with interest groups: proportion of 20 organisation categories

	DnA	H	Sp	KrF	SV	FrP	Average
Proportion of organisations	0.80	0.80	0.65	0.70	0.70	0.80	0.74

We see that all parties have fairly high proportions, but there are important differences among the old parties as far as the total network of links is concerned. We see that the Labour Party (0.80) and the Conservatives (0.80) have links with most organisations, whereas the Christian People's Party (0.70), the Centre Party (0.65), and have the fewest. However, these differences must not be exaggerated: the strength of contact is also dependent upon the demand of interest groups. In this perspective, it should come as no surprise that the traditionally largest parties (in terms of votes) have links with most interest groups in terms of actual contact. Moreover, as shown in previous chapters the Christian People's Party, the Centre Party, as well as the Socialist Left Party, came very close to qualify for having significant links with a couple more interest group categories. Indeed, it is also worth noting that both the new parties have wide-ranging networks in the numerical sense: the Progress Party is marked by a proportion of 0.80 whereas Socialist Left's score is 0.70.

The qualitative aspect of the parties' range of links was measured and presented by separate figures in the previous chapters (see Chapter 3 and Chapters 7–13). These sociograms showed that all parties have networks including numerous groups within various organisation categories and links across old and new cleavages. As far as the left-right axis is concerned, the centre-of-left parties, Labour Party and the Socialist Left, have significant links with employers', business and industry organisations, whereas all the centrist or right parties are involved with contact with various kinds of employees' organisations, including LO. Furthermore, all established parties are linked with client organisations, humanitarian and social aid organisations and community-centred organisations.

Few parties have significant links to the groups representing the primary sector and the old counter-cultures associated with the moral-religious axis. But, as most of these organisations represent less significant voter groups in the early 2000s, one should perhaps not put strong emphasis on this particular result. In contrast, all parties have links with *at least some* interest groups associated with 'new politics' issues like environmental organisations and internationally-oriented organisations.

However, if we concentrate on data from *the organisational level,* the network of links seems narrower in the case of Labour and the Conservatives than the range depicted by the sociograms. The party-based analyses showed that these parties do not seem to be among those that most systematically cultivate links with a broad range of organisations. Their 'inner circles' consists of groups belonging to a more limited number of organisation categories.

Put differently, the old major parties have considerably closer relationships with some kinds of organisations than others. The Conservatives' official invitation in the 1970s to LO and unions has not been further developed, whereas Labour is linked at the organisational level with other employees' organisations and employers,' business and trade associations in a rather more sporadic way. The Conservatives are more closely connected with the business community by means of some inter-organisational links, and Labour is particularly closely connected with the traditional trade union movement, through liaison committees, co-operation agreements, shared leadership, and extensive contact at the individual level. The Christian People's Party has closer relationships with religious groups than others, and we note that it has no significant link to organisations for non-religious philosophies of life.

Furthermore, the old parties have not uniformly established links with organisations that represent newer social movements. The Conservative Party, the Labour Party, and the Centre Party are rather close to internationally-oriented organisations. But the old parties' links are weaker with those organisations that can be argued to represent 'new politics' – like women's organisations, environmental groups, and immigrant/refugee organisations. In fact, only the Labour Party and the Centre Party have a significant link to external women's organisations. However, as the category includes more than feminist groups (like for example farmers' women's organisations), the links revealed are not necessarily an indication of contacts with newer social movements. It can also be noted that the relationship with EU-oriented organisations reflects the party's stand in this issue:

the Centre Party has not a significant link with pro-EU organisations, nor do the Conservatives have significant links to pro-EU organisations. Labour's internal division on this issue is mirrored by almost equally strong links with both categories.

As regards this particular aspect of the new parties' network, there is little doubt that the Socialist Left is marked by its historical roots in internationally-oriented protest movements and in the trade unions of the labour movement. SV's relationship with white-collar employees' organisations outside LO is significantly more distant than its relations with LO and unions. Internationally-oriented organisations and anti-EU organisations are those groups that SV has the closest relations with in practice, in addition to the trade unions.

Interestingly, as indicated above, the Progress Party is linked with all major kinds of interest groups within the labour market. FrP's contact with both employers' business and industry organisations and employees' organisations is almost as extensive as the Conservatives' contact with such organisations. Significant links with anti-immigration groups have not been found, but the FrP network includes links with religious organisations. On the other hand, the party has also relationships with organisations representing the counterpart of the new politics axis: environmental organisations, internationally-oriented organisations and immigrant/refugee organisations. In fact, the party does not seem to discriminate much according to category at the organisational level, although in terms of actual contact two kinds of organisations stand out: on the one hand, employers', business, trade organisations; and employees'/professional organisations on the other hand.

OVERALL PATTERNS OF RELATIONSHIPS

With regard to the *closeness of relationships* with interest groups, we observe that Norwegian parties in general do not have very strong links with interest groups in the early 2000s. But, despite the lack of overlapping organisational structures, links for contact do exist. Only the Labour Party has enduring inter-organisational links like joint committees and formal co-operation agreements with any organisation, but several parties have routines for inviting external groups to party arrangements, including meetings of policy-making committees and the party congress. During the manifesto-making process, some sort of active consultation of interest groups is fairly common.

At the individual level, a significant proportion of the national elite in all parties is, or has been, officials or staff in one or more interest group, although the extent of *leadership overlaps* is limited. Activism (or career) in political parties and in interest groups are not mutually exclusive, which indicates that experience from the associational life still matters in the recruitment of party activists and leaders in Norway. Furthermore, party elites seem to regularly be in touch with interest groups in all parties. Although such links cannot replace organised links in terms of closeness, this indicates that lack of the latter does not necessarily imply a separation of parties and interest groups in practice.

However, there are not many organisation categories with which the parties are linked through *extensive* regular contact. The most common type of relationship is, in other words, not a very close one. In terms of the typology of relationships developed in Chapter 4, we find numerous *organised ad hoc relationships* and if such relations do not exist, *issue-based contact* at the individual level provide a relationship with many other organisations. In all parties, informal contact is a common way to communicate with interest groups.

Nevertheless, there are important differences. Political parties in Norway are also included in what can be seen as *organised alliances* or *informal partnerships* with certain interest groups. Some parties have extensive regular contact with specific organisations provided by either links at the organisational or individual level – major examples being the Labour Party and the trade unions, the Centre Party and the anti-EU groups, and the Socialist Left and internationally-oriented organisations. In other words, the general summary buries important differences *among* parties.

First and foremost, we note the variation in the strength of party links with interest groups representing old core voters. Above all, the Centre Party and the Liberals have far more distant relationships as compared to the Labour Party with the social movement organisations from which they emerged. In these cases, we find few well-organised links to the organisations traditionally associated with the party. The Conservatives are a less clear-cut case. Their inter-organisational links with employers', business and trade organisations appear not particularly strong, but the organised, regular contacts with individual business people and companies suggest that the relationship is closer than it might seem. Contact frequencies partly confirm this idea: one third of the Conservative elite report having contact with employers', business and trade organisations on a monthly basis.

More importantly, the Christian People's Party and, above all, the Labour Party do not appear to be in the midst of an inter-organisational 'divorce' from religious organisations or old trade unions, respectively. The proportion of the KrF elite who has regular contact with religious organisations and organised religious communities is not that extensive, but KrF still recruits leaders from Christian circles and has fairly well-organised routines for contact with them. Despite the recent abolition of collective membership, DnA relations with trade unions and LO include numerous and permanent kinds of links at the organisational level and extensive contact reported at the individual level. In fact, the organised links have recently been consolidated, and key informants suggest that the relationship is more intense than it has been in years. With regard to new parties, the Socialist Left still maintains rather close relationships with the organisational circles in which the party was involved in the 1960s and 1970s.

There is also variation in *the general closeness* of party relationships. Although DnA has particularly close relations with the trade unions organised in LO, and together with SV is the party with most strong links at the individual level, it is not among those parties that have the strongest inter-organisational links with interest groups in general. The party at large, i.e. the leadership and headquarters, seeks generally less systematic contact with external interest groups than hypothesised.

Of the other political parties established before Second World War, the Centre Party, Christian People's Party and the Conservatives represent intermediate cases. When emphasising inter-organisational links for contact, Sp stands out, but the

Conservatives dominate in terms of actual contact at the individual level, which corroborates the need to look beyond the organisational charts and statutes, at various forms of contact. In general, the KrF elite are not involved in frequent contact with interest groups to a great extent.

Even if we cannot draw any definite conclusions concerning the Liberals due to lack of robust data, there seems to be an organisational norm for the Liberal Party to keep its distance from interest groups in general. At the national level, this party has generally tenuous links into, or it could even be said is *virtually separated* from, the associational life.

Finally, both the new parties are among those with closer relationships with interest groups in a comparative perspective. SV has relatively strong inter-organisational links with interest groups in general compared with the DnA, and is also characterised by relatively strong links according to the data from individual level. FrP has generally weaker links, but also in this case, the manifesto-making routines stand out.

The displayed *range of the relationships* with interest groups indicates that the networks of Norwegian parties are rather wide. Numerous links, with more than half of the organisation categories, and links related to opposite sides of both old and new cleavages have been identified. However, significant differences exist with regard to the parties' strongest links. When we limit the analysis to the probably most politically significant ones, a more traditional pattern of relationships materialises. Parties have closer relationships with particular and different groups. The Labour Party does not put the old trade unions and other employees' organisations on an equal footing and the links to business and trade organisations are weak compared to the parallel links of other parties.

Hence, the preliminary conclusion of Chapter 7 is strengthened: DnA's strategy of both maintaining a special relationship with LO *and* establishing relationships with a wide range of interest groups is not that easy to translate into in practice. As assumed, a high maximum degree of closeness to a certain extent entails exclusiveness. Likewise, the Conservative Party leadership and headquarters do not seem to cultivate links *systematically* with employees' organisations outside the Storting. Moreover, no other party is as strongly linked with the trade unions in LO and to the employers', business and trade organisations as these two parties. Thus, the established parties' networks of links are to a certain extent polarised and not overlapping.

Although Labour and the Conservatives have the most wide-ranging links as measured by frequencies of both formal and informal contact, they have to a lesser extent attempted to actively include various interest groups in the party network than have many other parties at the organisational level. In other words, the pattern of interest conflicts, on which the system of Norwegian parties was originally based, is fairly visible among the old parties as far as the most significant party-interest group links are concerned. In this sense, some of the long-established parties have a more narrow range of relations.

So do political parties, as suggested by numerous scholars emphasising system-level circumstances, tend to have organised but not very strong links – organised ad hoc relationships – with a wide range of interest groups today? Or are they characterised by distant relations – informal issue-based contact – or do they appear to be nearly separated from the interest-group community in general? To conclude, a general contemporary tendency is revealed in established parties' relationships with interest groups, but general distance or separation from civil society, as the cartel party thesis would suggest, is to a very limited extent an accurate description of Norwegian parties' relationships with interest groups at the national level. As alternatively proposed, political parties in Norway are on the whole rather characterised by semi-organised and fairly wide-ranging relationships with interest groups. However, this is not to say that the expectation associated with the catch-all party thesis and similar analyses has received unambiguous support. Indeed, marked differences in closeness to external organisations exist, among organisation categories as well as parties, and the range of the total network of links is in some cases somewhat limited.

Equally interesting, the new parties have somewhat more wide-ranging relationships than expected on the basis of the 'new politics' literature. The number of interlinked organisation categories in the case of the Socialist Left and the Progress Party does not differ markedly from that of the older parties. Hence, the hypothesis that such a new right populist party would be virtually separated from the established interest-group community does not receive much support. FrP has, for example, almost as extensive frequent contact with the organised business community as has the Conservative Party and significant contact with environmental organisations at the organisational level. At the same time, we see that the Socialist Left's network does not clearly reflect its status as the party for the new middle class, as suggested by 'new politics' theory. SV does not put the trade unions of LO and other employees' organisations on an equal footing. Moreover, it seems to be struggling somewhat with the balance between its link with the industrially-oriented trade union movement and its relationship with 'new politics' organisations like the environmental groups.

CONCLUSIONS

In the twentieth century Norway underwent rapid economic and social change. As measured by international standards (see Chapter 6), Norway is today characterised by a small class of manual, industrial workers and farmers, a large share of employees in the service sector, and a fairly heterogeneous new middle class. Old cleavages have decayed and voter volatility has increased significantly.

Earlier research shows that some of the relationships with old associates, for example DnA's links with the trade unions, had declined by the late 1990s (Allern and Heidar 2001; Sundberg 2003), but this study reveals that the Labour Party has thereafter not chosen to further distance the LO and its unions. In the early 2000s, DnA prefers to have a quite close relationship with the trade unions, and more distant relations with alternative employees' organisations outside the Storting. Only one party, the Liberals, can be said to seek and to have a very distant, almost separated, relationship in general. In other words, the general societal circumstances that are often argued to call for a specific pattern of relationships, have not lead to considerable homogeneity in party links with the interest-group community in Norway.

But does the variation revealed correspond systematically to party-related differences *within* the Norwegian social structure and economy? Do the major differences in the parties' relationships reflect the fact that some parties in general have had stronger reasons not to have narrow-ranging and close relationships than others? Even though no statistical analysis can be conducted here, there seems to be limited evidence pointing in that direction. The Centre Party (Sp) has been challenged the most by the employment pattern that has emerged in recent decades, but the party had loosened its links with the Farmers' Union *before* the Second World War. The Labour Party has also experienced a relatively dramatic decrease in core voters, but nevertheless keeps a rather close relationship with the trade union movement. The Christian People's Party and Liberals find themselves faced with a society in which the counter-cultures are no longer predominant forces. Whereas the former have quite close links with religious organisations, the latter maintains a general distance. A possible explanation is that the process of secularisation confirms KrF's very *raison d'être,* but there is little doubt that the party will need to attract broader voter groups if it is to survive as an influential force over time. Finally, the new parties that could be expected to diverge significantly from the general tendency, according to 'new politics' party literature – the Socialist Left and the Progress Party – prove to be not that different.

Hence, there is indeed reason to discuss what other factors than those related to the general social structure and other system-level circumstances shape party relations with the interest-group community. To what extent the major differences are in line with the expectations of the theory perspectives elaborated in Chapter 5 requires a comparative analysis including numerous exogenous and endogenous factors at the organisational level. First, however, it remains to be seen to which degree the party links with interest groups have substantial value. It is one thing to establish links; it is quite another to adopt the input from external interest groups when making political decisions. To what extent links with interest groups do in fact matter for the decision-making of political parties is the question to be discussed in Chapter 15.

part four
patterns of party relationships: political significance and shaping factors

chapter fifteen | political significance of relationships with interest groups

The preceding chapters have shown that Norwegian parties certainly are linked into the interest-group community. Not very close and quite wide-ranging relationships are common, but significant differences also exist among parties.

A general supposition underpinning this analysis is that party relationships with interest groups have political consequences. A major reason for studying such links is the assumption that links with externally organised interests, or lack thereof, are an important characteristic of political parties as intermediary institutions. On the other hand, it should not be taken for granted that the existing relations actually matter. Parties may choose to involve themselves in relationships with interest groups in order to map grievances, opinions and policy views, but they may also consult interest groups primarily as symbolic acts, for example, to signal openness towards the society (see Chapter 5).

In this chapter, we return to party relationships with interest groups by *exploring the general political significance of existing links*. What is presented is not a full-scale impact assessment, but assessing the political impact provides a test of whether the identified relationships with interest groups have substantial value. It is important to recall that the analysis is confined to a few indicators based on interviews with key informants and survey data (see Chapters 1 and 4). The more specific research questions explored are recapitulated below.

RESEARCH QUESTIONS REVISITED

As elaborated in Chapter 4, the discussion begins by querying to what extent links with interest groups *generally* matter for political decisions made by parties: *do the interest groups, with which the parties are interlinked, influence the parties to formulate different policies than they would have developed without such links?*

Next, the significance of the relationships' specific characteristics is explored. Here, the question is, first, *to what extent does the degree of closeness of the parties' relationships with interest groups matter?* Close relationships, in terms of well-organised links and intensive contact, are generally assumed to involve more influence than more distant ones. In contrast to informal contact, organised links may connect an interest group directly with ruling bodies. Strong inter-organisational links, in terms of, for example, formal co-operation agreements, may involve almost binding contact in practice. But how strong is the correlation between the degree of closeness and political significance? As argued in Chapter 4, the impact of interest groups can be truly significant also in informal settings at the individual level of the central party organisation, stronger links can be established as a means to temper conflict, and intense contact might be a result of increased tensions between a party and an interest group. Moreover, although the focus here is on the party side of the relationship, we should also bear in mind that strong links make it more likely that parties will exert influence *on* interest groups. For example, it is widely agreed that social democratic parties have historically enjoyed industrial appeasement and assistance in policy implementation in return for favourable (short-term) policies (Howell 2001: 13).

As a part of the analysis of closeness and significance, Labour's relationship with the trade union movement is studied in depth in a separate section. There are two reasons for this: first, Labour is the only Norwegian party and interest group to be linked through truly strong inter-organisational links. Hence, if the degree of closeness does matter considerably, we can indeed expect DnA's links with the trade unions to be significant. Second, the very nature of this relationship makes it easier to explore political impact of interest groups on party policies. For example, the existence of a joint committee has made it possible to study formal reports on what has been discussed between the party and the interest group. Thus, the case of DnA and LO provides us with a valuable opportunity to learn more about how the contact between parties and interest groups may materialise as a power relationship.

Finally, to fully explore the significance of relationships' specific characteristics, we need to examine *whether individual parties are influenced by other organisations in accordance with the range of their relationships*. If the main intention is to indicate openness towards society, wide networks might be more symbolic than substantial. Moreover, it could be argued that parties more readily make use of information within policy fields and on social segments with which the party elite and organisation are already familiar. However, the data cannot be broken down to display the impact of interest groups for each party. Therefore, I content myself to report what kinds of organisations are considered to have been influential in general.

GENERAL SIGNIFICANCE OF RELATIONSHIPS WITH INTEREST GROUPS

A first indication of the actual political significance of party links with interest groups can be found from a closer look at the *content* of the parties' forms of contact. Second, we turn to the elites' view on the general political significance of various relationships.

Elite Views on the Content of Party Relationships with Interest Groups

According to the management of Norwegian party headquarters (the party secretaries or secretaries-general), organised contact with interest groups generally involves providing the party with more know-how, new perspectives and policy views. Links are seen as a way to map the viewpoints and grievances of the various external organisations (e.g. Mo 2003 [interview]; Solhjell 2003 [interview]; Sundsbø 2003 [interview]), although it should be noted that the representatives of the Conservatives and the Liberals primarily highlight the party's emphasis on 'comprehensive thinking' in relation to interest groups when asked about their links' political significance (Hole 2003; Nyhus 2003 [interview]),

The secretaries (see list of informants) for the internal committees working on the 2001–2005 Manifestos report that the comments, notes and proposals they received from interest groups during the process, orally or in writing, varied significantly in content. In addition to know-how and facts provided on request, the suggestions ranged from sending the organisation's general action programme, via lobbying for specified policy views, to submitting written proposals of entire paragraphs for insertion in the party manifesto. In other words, in the early 2000s, the organised contact during the manifesto-making process dealt with attempts at influencing both the political agenda and the specific policy views of parties, as well as detached facts or trivialities.

Do the survey data about the organised and informal contact in day-to-day politics confirm this general impression of politically relevant links? Table 15.1 shows the party top elite's view on the character of the meetings, conversations and correspondence they had with various interest groups between 2003 and 2004. Instead of asking for summaries including all contacts, I chose to search for less amorphous, and more accurate, information about the most important ones: the respondents were asked only about the contact with those *three* organisations with which they had been in touch most frequently during the past year. On this basis, averages have been developed across organisations.

Although respondents were not asked to rank the types of contents according to importance, we observe that party requests for facts and know-how seem to be the most common type of content. On average, more than 80 per cent of the party top elites responded that *at least some of the cases* involved this type of information. In comparison, about 50 per cent reported that the contact concerned know-how and facts *in most cases*. Of course, it is possible to argue that this hints at dominance of fairly apolitical links. In practice, however, so-called 'plain facts' may also play a political role. For example, facts can be used to make the case for a particular policy view, for example, by documenting how an undesirable policy would work out in practice. This means that the existence of much contact with such content is not necessarily an indication of many trivial meetings: it may reflect the technocratic norm that characterises public policy making in Western societies in general (Fischer 1990). Through expertise provided by interest groups, politicians seek to enhance their capacity to solve various societal problems, and through fact-based arguments, rather than moral reasoning, interest groups can influence policy-making (Uhrwing 2001: 259–60). Besides, the various types of arguments are not necessarily mutually exclusive means of persuasion (see Chapter 4).

The remaining indicators of the content of contacts presented in Table 15.1 support this interpretation. On average, a little less than 70 per cent of the party elites answered that the contact involved mapping the organisation's policy views in at least *some of the cases*, and approximately 30 per cent said that this happened in *most cases*. On nearly half of the occasions, the party elites in general experienced that the organisation actively attempted to exert political influence. Thus, despite reports on a lot of fact-oriented contact, the links identified by the survey data are not mainly apolitical. Interest groups are generally given the opportunity to influence the party organisation's policy-making. Mobilisation of support for the party's existing political viewpoints seems to be the least common type of content.

Table 15.1: The party top elites' view on how often their contact with interest groups in 2003 dealt with various types of content. Averages across the three organisations with which the elites reported most frequent contact. Per cent[1]

	DnA	H	Sp	KrF	SV	FrP	All[2]
Facts/know-how							
- Most cases	50	31	45	57	54	60	50
- Some cases	36	16	35	38	42	26	32
Party's request for arguments							
- Most cases	13	11	7	0	39	3	15
- Some cases	34	26	48	50	29	46	39
Mobilisation of support for party's viewpoints							
- Most cases	3	11	3	0	20	15	10
- Some cases	32	21	34	14	32	25	26
Practical co-operation							
- Most cases	47	10	12	20	30	31	25
- Some cases	28	22	40	32	31	24	30
Mapping the organisation's viewpoints							
- Most cases	28	12	16	50	50	38	32
- Some cases	48	25	55	29	25	34	36
Attempt of organisation to influence party							
- Most cases	13	7	0	0	22	29	12
- Some cases	44	16	32	50	45	20	35
N	16–20	5–7	9–11	4–8	8–10	7–11	(6)

1 Only those answering 'most cases' and 'some cases' are reported.
Question: 'About how often do you think that the contact – of relevance for your work in the party's central organisation – with organisation no. 1, 2 and 3 involved the following issues the last year?

- My need for facts/more know-how concerning problems and policies within a certain field.
- My need for arguments in a political debate.
- Attempt to mobilise support for the party's opinions in specific issues.
- My attempt to be informed about an organisation's viewpoints on a particular issue.
- Practical co-operation with respect to a certain issue.
- The organisation's attempt of influencing the party's agenda or my attitude in a particular case.'

2 Average numbers across parties, Liberals excluded.

However, differences among parties can be noted. The elite of the Conservative Party stand out as being significantly less concerned than others with mapping the policy views of interest groups: only about 40 per cent of its top elite describe the meetings, conversations and correspondence with external organisations as such attempts in at least some of the cases. DnA's contact involved more practical co-operation, whereas the SV elite report more extensive contact dealing with requests for arguments, mobilisation of support and the attempts of organisations to influence the party organisation than others. In other words, links with interest groups may have differing functions in different parties. What this can tell us about why parties differ in their relationships with interest groups will, however, wait until the analysis below.

Elite Views on Impact of Interest Groups on Party Decisions

The survey analysis concerning the content of contacts indicates that the links with interest groups do matter politically. In this section, we look into the perceived actual political significance. Here I rely on two types of material: interviews with key informants and the elite survey. Of course, responses to such questions must be interpreted carefully. Party relationships with interest groups are partly a normative, ideological issue for politicians, so party representatives may be tempted to give outsiders answers framed to maintain the 'appropriate' public image of their party. Moreover, it is not easy to remember the details about how various decision-making processes progressed in terms of external influences.

Nevertheless, the key informants proved able to give several examples of party decisions that had, in their view, clearly been affected by contact with interest groups in recent years. Most secretaries-general and party secretaries emphasise that their party critically reviews proposals from interest groups in order to avoid 'undue influence'. The secretaries-general of the Conservative and Liberal Party highlight the role of parties as responsible for the 'people' or 'society as a whole' in particular. But many key informants also underline that interest groups do colour party policies through organised and informal contact (Kolberg 2003 [interview]; Mo 2003 [interview]; Solhjell 2003 [interview]; Sundsbø 2003 [interview]; Venås 2003 [interview]). 'Sometimes we even adopt entire proposals of new policy formulations, as long as they are not in conflict with our fundamental ideological view' (Mo 2003[interview]).

Along the same lines, secretaries for the internal committees drafting the 2001–2005 Manifestos report that interest groups influenced the *agenda* by making the party aware of new political issues and alternative views on old topics. But some also argue that the contact affected the *policies* presented by the manifesto. For example: 'I certainly consider them *[the comments from interest groups]* to be important. And then I do not only have the specific *[policy]* suggestions in mind. It is also important to get new perspectives and outlooks. Such comments are, of course, important when they represent something new, something different from what you have perceived yourself' (Bråten 2003[interview]).

Some of the manifesto secretaries present the contact with certain interest groups as more important than others. For example, in the Labour Party, it is emphasised that the Confederation of Trade Unions (LO) was *de facto* represented in the manifesto committee, and that trade unions were consulted throughout the process on relevant issues, as they usually are in this context. It is also pointed out that since the LO chair holds a seat in DnA's national executive, he/she should be able to, by and large, defend the final document (Bråten 2003 [interview]). In other words, the trade union movement normally plays a role in all phases of the manifesto-making process in the Norwegian Labour Party.

The committee drafting the Socialist Left Party's 2001–2005 Manifesto included several members with top-level experience from environmental organisations. According to the committee's secretary, the party platform mirrored this link in terms of specific viewpoints drawn from the platform of the major Norwegian environmental organisation, Friends of the Earth Norway (*Norges Naturvernforbund*). The Progress Party, for its part, asked a leader of one environmental organisation (*Norges Miljøvernforbund*) to suggest (new) environmental policies that were in line with the party's overall ideology. According to the secretary of FrP's manifesto committee, these suggestions proved influential (Røste 2005 [interview]).

However, it is also remarked that several interest groups become actively involved fairly late in the process. Apparently, numerous groups contact the party just before the party congress, and hence, after many of the most important decisions are made (Bjerke 2003 [interview]; Venås 2003 [interview], for examples see *Dagsavisen* 29.03.05 and 31.03.05). In contrast, several informants point out the peak organisations within the labour market as the most professional and possibly influential ones (Sundsbø 2003 [interview]; Bjerke 2003 [interview]), which reminds us that the degree of influence depends on more than the strength of links, and probably also on the resources available to the interest group.

Next, a more representative indication of political influence exerted by interest groups is provided by survey data. Table 15.2 shows how the party top elites evaluate the significance of the meetings, conversations and correspondence they had with various interest groups for the political decisions made in the party's central organisation 2003–04. Again, respondents were asked only about the three organisations they had been in contact with most frequently. Altogether, on average, almost 40 per cent of the party elites considered the contact with interest groups to have been *rather or very important*. If we include those who answered that the contact was *truly important in some cases, but not in others*, the figure increases to more than 50 per cent. Hence, according to the top elite, organised and informal contact with external interest groups in 2003 was not only politically relevant but also significant for policy decisions.

Also here we note considerable differences among parties. More than half of the Progress Party elite characterise the organisation contact as rather or very important, whereas only about 17 per cent of the Conservative elite think the same. Although the survey data are not robust with regard to the Liberal Party elite, those who did answer indicated that the existing contacts were not particularly significant – none of the four describe their contact with interest groups as very important, and only one describes 'some' of the contact as rather important.

Table 15.2: The party top elites' view on the political significance of contact with interest groups in 2003. Averages across the three organisations with which the elites reported most frequent contact. Per cent[1]

	DnA	H	Sp	KrF	SV	FrP	All[2]
Very important	9	12	14	8	3	16	10
Rather important	31	5	29	35	30	38	28
Both important and unimportant	15	5	22	4	18	18	14
Limited importance	25	12	22	11	32	7	18
Unimportant	11	66	3	24	3	21	21
Don't know	6	0	0	13	14	0	6
No response	2	0	11	4	0	0	3
Total	100	100	100	100	100	100	100
N	16–19	5–7	9–10	5–8	9–10	7–10	(6)

1 Question: 'How significant do you feel that contacts – yours and others – with organisations no. 1–3 generally were for the political decisions made in the party's central decision-making bodies the last year (the Party Congress not included)?
Respondents who did not list any organisation names are excluded from the analysis, as are those who answered that 'such decisions were not made' to the question above.

2 Average numbers across parties, Liberals excluded.

Do the survey data describing the manifesto-making process in the early 2000s strengthen or weaken the general finding of political significance? As argued in the preceding chapters, we should not place too much emphasis on these responses as only some of the respondents were also a part of the top elite before the 2000/2001 party congress. However, to varying degrees, proportions of all elites reported having had contact with interest groups at some point during the process preparing the 2001–2005 Manifesto.[188] More detailed analyses show that on average, more than half of the party elite members felt that interest groups affected the policy formulation of this election manifesto. Only about 27 per cent of the elites, on average, did not experience such influence, while the remainder had no opinion or did not respond.[189]

To conclude, the survey data reflect the tendency suggested by key informants: links with interest groups have political consequences both in terms of agenda-setting and policy-formulation, but some parties appear to listen to interest groups more than others do. What might this tell us about the significance of the closeness and range of such relationships?

188. *Question:* 'According to your experience, did one or more interest organisations have influence– direct or indirect – on the formulation of the party manifesto for the period 2001–2005?'

189. Average numbers across parties, Liberals excluded.

SIGNIFICANCE OF THE DEGREE OF CLOSENESS AND ACTUAL RANGE OF RELATIONSHIPS

The next question is to what extent the specific degree of closeness and range of Norwegian parties' relationships with interest groups actually matters. First we need to see whether the degree of closeness makes a difference: are the closest relationships reported to involve more influential interest groups than the more distant relationships are? Here I do not aim to reveal any causality, only to check whether there seems to be some co-variation between relative distance and reported significance. As the degree of closeness to various categories of organisations is not assessed by a standardised measure, no statistical correlations are presented, but major tendencies will be indicated.

As we have seen, the dominance of relatively distant relationships with interest groups among Norwegian parties does not preclude external influence on the policy-making of party organisations. However, the degree of closeness of such relations does seem to matter. The post-war parties – the Progress Party and the Socialist Left – are among those with stronger inter-organisational links with interest groups according to contemporary standards. The data of elite perceptions presented above suggest that their relationships also are more significant than the links of many other parties. The content of the elite contact is certainly of political relevance in these cases, and both parties' key informants and elite as a whole consider such contact to be relatively influential. As noted earlier, the Liberals are only weakly linked with interest groups, and the impact of interest groups on the political decisions made by this party seems to be weaker than in many other cases. The Centre Party (Sp), in contrast, emphasises organised contact with external interest groups, and data from the elite survey indicate that these links have significant political consequences.

On the other hand, there are also findings that break with this pattern. The Conservative Party represents an intermediate case with regard to closeness to/distance from interest groups. It has organised links with the employers', business and trade organisations, and several significant links at the individual level with others, but responses from key informants and the elite survey suggest that they are not accordingly influential, in political terms. For example, as mentioned above, the Conservative elite report that its contact with interest groups is rarely about mapping organisations' policy views, although this could also be a case of some respondents adapting their answers to normative expectations. As will become clear in Chapter 16, the Norwegian Conservative Party does support the liberal view that parties and interest groups should play different roles in democracy, and its party elite might therefore want to appear as a party that maintains a distance from special interests. But they are not the only ones to emphasise this party role in democracy, so it seems striking that so many Conservative respondents characterise the contact as generally unimportant for the central party organisation's political decisions.[190] In contrast, the Christian People's Party has generally

190. A possible alternative explanation is that the position of the parliamentary group is (still) particularly strong in the Conservatives (see Chapter 16), but note that the question asks only about decisions actually taken by the extra-parliamentary party.

somewhat weaker links than the Conservatives, but existing ones are considered to be more important politically.

The Labour Party is also an ambiguous case, with weaker inter-organisational links with interest groups in general than some others, but a particularly close relationship with LO. The data presented in this chapter indicate that DnA collaborates with interest groups on practical issues more frequently than others, which perhaps reflects the particularly well-organised link within the old labour movement. But DnA does not generally stand out in other ways. Contacts are not described as especially relevant or politically significant. Hence, the significance of the link with LO is perhaps balanced by the limited importance of weaker links with others. Unfortunately, the survey material does not allow for an analysis of the significance of links with various kinds of organisations for each party. But we will return to the political impact of LO on DnA's decision-making below.

Next, we need to see whether parties with a wide range of relationships also report being influenced by various interests, or whether parties establish links to numerous groups but actually adapt to the preferences of only a few. As the data cannot be broken down to display the impact of interest groups for each party, we can only find out something about what kinds of organisations are considered to have been influential in general.

Table 15.3 shows to what extent those interest groups with which the elites had most frequent contact were seen as *rather* or *very important* for the political decisions made in the party's central organisation in 2003–2004, grouped according to organisation category. Here it is important to note that the percentage basis is the total number of *individual organisations,* within each category, listed by the party elites, and that the number of organisations varies among categories. Some organisation categories are better represented among the frequent contacts of Norwegian party elites than others. In sum, about 150 individual, but partly overlapping, interest groups were listed by the party elites. In order to assess the importance of each organisation category, we should therefore both look at the relative number of individual organisations within each category *and* the extent to which the contact was considered as important.

We observe that a wide range of organisations are considered to have had an impact. 16 out of 20 organisation categories are represented among the party elites most frequent contacts, and they are all regarded influential by some elite members. However, some kinds of interest groups seem more significant than others, largely corresponding to variation in frequencies reported in Chapter 14.

On the whole, contacts with labour market organisations, and in particular primary-sector groups, employers', business and trade organisations, and LO and LO Unions, seem most important for Norwegian party elites. Such interest groups were listed by numerous respondents: close to 50 per cent (74 out of 151) of the individual organisations mentioned belonged to one of these categories, and at least 39 per cent of those who had most frequent contact with such groups describe the contact as 'rather important' or 'very important'.

The significance of LO seems particularly strong. Out of 151 listed individual interest groups, 25 per cent were either LO itself or an individual LO union and a

Table 15.3: The party top elites' view on the political significance of contact with various interest groups in 2003. Percentages of individual organisations, with which the elites reported most frequent contact, considered to be 'rather important' or 'very important', by organisation category.[1] Weighted figures (except N)[2]

	Number of organisations	% Very important	% Rather important
Primary-sector organisations	7	14	57
Employers' organisations, business and trade associations (incl. NHO)	18	22	17
LO and LO Unions	37	8	46
Employees' organisations and professional organisations outside LO	12	8	8
Christian and missionary organisations	3	0	33
Temperance organisations	5	20	40
Community-centred organisations related to culture, sport, youth, elderly, hobbies etc.	11	9	18
Humanitarian and social aid organisations	9	11	0
Internationally-oriented organisations	10	10	30
Organisations in favour of EU membership	4	0	0
Organisations against EU membership	9	22	22
Environmental and conservationist organisations	9	0	44
Women's organisations (incl. organisations of housewives and farm women's unions)	1	0	100
Immigrant and refugee organisations	6	0	0
Consumer organisations	2	0	0
Other organisations	8	25	0
Total number organisations	151		
Average across organisation categories	(16)	9	26

1 First: *Question:* Please list the names of the (maximum) three organisations with which you had most frequent contact during the last year, numbered from 1 to 3. Second: *Question:* 'How significant do you think the contacts – yours and others – with organisations no. 1–3 generally were for the political decisions which were made in the party's central decision-making bodies the last year (the Party Congress not included)? The alternatives were: 'Very important', 'rather important', 'both important and unimportant', 'a little important', 'not at all important'.

2 Since not all party elites mentioned organisations within the all/the same categories, I have not first calculated percentage shares within each party and then averages across parties. Instead, and because response rates vary among parties, all figures are weighted according to the individual party elite's share of the total elite population. In this way, the elite members are made representative of the party elite at large with regard to party affiliation. It is thus important to remember that when there is great variation among parties, the percentages are dominated by the largest parties. Due to their low response rate, respondents from the Liberals are excluded. For further explanation, see main text.

majority of these respondents described the union contact as being 'rather important' or 'very important'. Here, however, we should keep in mind that when there is great variation among parties, the percentages are dominated by the largest parties, and hence the Labour Party, due to weighted numbers.

Finally, it is worth noting that humanitarian and social aid organisations, internationally-oriented organisations, EU-related groups and environmental organisations are mentioned quite few times. Organisations working against Norwegian EU-membership and environmental groups are considered to be rather or very important by more than 40 per cent.

To conclude, we see that the total range of party relations cannot be taken as a clear indicator of the extent to which various interests actually influence party policies. Although parties have a wide range of politically significant links, some categories of interest groups seem more important than others.

A SPECIAL CASE: THE LABOUR PARTY AND THE TRADE UNIONS

If the degree of closeness matters greatly for the political influence of interest groups on party decisions, we can at least expect DnA's links with the trade unions to be significant. No other interest groups are tied to any party through such links as co-operation agreements and joint committees in Norway. But, in practice, is the relationship as politically important as it seems?

In recent years, Norwegian newspapers have been brimming with articles indicating that DnA's political decisions are heavily influenced by the trade union movement. For example, it has been argued that Labour's attempt of modifying the sickness benefit system in 2000 was blocked by LO. The present LO chair claimed in public debate that LO would not campaign for DnA if the Labour cabinet in office introduced modifications of the sickness benefit system (Takvam 2002: 29, 155). It is also widely suggested by political journalists and others that the election manifesto for 2005–2009 represents a rapprochement to the trade unions' policy views in welfare and economic issues (see the newspapers *Aftenposten* 16.08.03, 07.04.05, *Dagsavisen* 04.02.05, *Dagens Næringsliv* 30.03.05; *Klassekampen* 09.04.05). During the 2005 election campaign, non-socialist politicians frequently said of DnA that the party leadership is 'in the pocket of LO (see *Dagens Næringsliv* 03.07.06).

As argued above, however, informal links are not necessarily less significant than formal ones. Equally important, a close party-group relationship also opens up more party influence on the interest group. Although parties serve as gatekeepers to public office, they may also try to influence the policy views of the interest groups themselves. A brief look at the historical debate on how the links between the Norwegian Labour Party and the trade unions have functioned as power relationship may illustrate this point, and point out the need to study links between LO and DnA today from this more balanced perspective.

As shown in Chapter 6, the historically close relationship uniting the political and corporate wing of the labour movement has been based on several shared core issues and policy views. Historical observers emphasise that the contacts between DnA and the unions have not only been a matter of political actors trying to make each other change political opinions, but have also involved extensive co-operation and co-ordination of political activities (cf. Halvorsen 2000: 214). In 1957, DnA vice-president Trygve Bratteli addressed the LO Convention with the following words:

> We often hear that the LO is directed by the government. But just as often it is said that it is this organization [LO] which in reality decides all that is done by the Party and the government. The actual situation is that that these two organizations, through tradition, and mature consideration, have divided the labor tasks between themselves. This our opposition clearly cannot understand (quoted in Millen 1963: 124–5).

Along similar lines, Galenson (1968:170) concluded that '(...) It is only on the borderline of trade union-party interest that conflict arises' in the late 1960s. 'The cement which binds is compounded out of ideology and practicality', wrote Millen (1963: 128).

Also emphasised is the mutuality in terms of two-way influence: both sides have been compelled to compromise in certain issues (Millen 1963: 128). LO's representation in the party's national executive and 'Co-operation Committee' has historically secured the trade unions direct impact on, for instance, DnA's price policies (Heidar 1981: 8–9). Labour could simply not follow 'a course of action destructive of the worker's position in society or his living standards' (Millen 1963: 135). The system of local collective membership has furthermore opened up for influence, through local party branches, the selection of party leaders, candidates for public office, and the party's manifesto-making in general (Valen and Katz 1964: 316; Haraldseth 1989: 123).[191] However, the trade unions have also made significant policy concessions to the party. From a comparative perspective, Norway's trade union movement has been characterised as disciplined organisations contributing to industrial appeasement and nation-building (Halvorsen 2000: 124; Millen 1963: 138). On several occasions, LO has adapted its policies to the party's emphasis on moderate wage growth, despite opposition from individual unions (Bjørgum 1999: 51). With this historical backdrop in mind, let us turn to the links of today.

Contemporary Party-union Links and the Issue of Power

In the early 2000s, a fairly close relationship still tied the Labour Party to the trade unions, but the core values traditionally unifying the Norwegian labour movement has been significantly challenged in recent decades (see Chapter 7). Therefore, there is reason to believe that the level of political tension between the parties is today relatively high, despite strong inter-organisational links. To fully disentangle the pattern of influence between the party and the unions organised in LO is a task beyond the scope of this study. But in the following section, an attempt is

191. In a Scandinavian context, however, Elvander (1980: 174) argues that traditionally, Norway's LO has not been as important a supplier of general political ideas as have the Swedish trade unions. The union policy-making unit of experts in Sweden (the brain trust in LO's *Utredningsavdelning*) did not have a Norwegian counterpart.

made to illuminate the issue systematically by 1) further clarifying the procedural status of the organised link with the trade union movement, 2) taking a closer look at the activities of the Joint 'Co-operation Committee', and 3) critically examining how the key informants and, to a certain extent, the Labour Party elite describe the significance of DnA's relationship with LO in particular.

Procedural Status of the Organised Contact with LO and Unions

Various kinds of party links with interest groups imply differing degrees of closeness to the party's decision-making process. Some links give organisations direct access to the party's executive bodies, whereas others are limited to contact with individual elite members. The abolition of the collective membership in DnA meant that the trade unions got weaker bottom-up access to party decision-making. However, when this arrangement ended in the 1990s, only about one fifth (19,000 in 1995) of Labour's members were affiliated in this way (as against about one third (52,000) in 1979 (Svåsand 1992: 744). Furthermore, the representation of members with experience from LO unions has remained fairly stable (Heidar and Saglie 2002: 279). Branches at workplaces and joint party-union committees have been established at the local level. Hence, as in the Swedish case (Aylott 2003), the end of collective membership was perhaps more important symbolically than in terms of trade union influence on the party organisation from below.

Equally important, the relatively persistent *de facto* representation of the LO chairperson, and some union leaders, in the national executive indicates that the unions as a whole, through the elite, still have direct access to national party decisions. As the LO chair (from 2001 to 2007) allegedly once phrased it: 'I am a member of DnA's executive for one reason, which is to protect the interests of, our *[LO's]* members' (quoted in *Aftenposten* 01.10.05, my translation). In addition, the two largest *individual* unions in LO are in practice 'represented': the industrial Norwegian United Federation of Trade Unions (*Fellesforbundet*) and the public-sector dominated Norwegian Union of Municipal and General Employees (*Fagforbundet*). The latter is also linked with Labour through a separate joint committee (see Chapter 7).

In addition, the 'Co-operation Committee' connects the party's national executive with LO as a whole. As described in Chapter 7, top leaders from both sides meet in this forum to discuss behind closed doors. As a liaison committee for different organisations, the committee does not take formal decisions on behalf of the party or the unions. The consultations provide an informal starting point for later proceedings in the respective decision-making bodies (Arbeiderpartiet 2003a: 2). Accordingly, the committee is barely mentioned on the party and LO's web pages. As made clear in Chapter 7, it is an *inter-organisational* arrangement that enable the party and LO to meet, to deliberate and to co-ordinate activities on a regular basis (cf. Jota 2003 [interview]).

But the 'Co-operation Committee' undoubtedly provides the mechanism for stable and potentially influential elite contact. Sometimes, the deliberations result in joint documents. Prior to the local elections of 2003, as before the general elections in 1993, a joint election manifesto was developed (Labour Party Biannual

Report 1992–94; DnA-LO 1993; Hågensen 2004: 238; DnA-LO 2003). Even in periods of acute conflict and political tensions, there are fixed routines for dialogue. When DnA is in government, the committee includes the prime minister, and other cabinet members as requested. As mentioned, meetings take place behind closed doors, and the minutes are not made public. As will be further discussed below, this probably makes the discussions less formal and thus promotes efficient communication (cf. Skjeie 1999). Moreover, although our focus here is on extra-parliamentary relations, it is also worth noting that the existence of the Committee gives the trade union movement privileged access to a Labour Party in power, independent of regular corporate arrangements and public hearings. The question thus is how important this link with LO is in practice. To what extent does it seem that LO in this way actually influences party decisions (outside the Storting)?

The 'Co-operation Committee': Books of Minutes

An examination of the books of minutes (*møteprotokoller*) of the 'Co-operation Committee's permits more, systematic insight into the general significance of these meetings.[192] It enables us to take a closer look at the type of participants, frequency of meetings, the content of the agenda, as well as the forms of consultation.

First, the *extended list of participants* may give an indication of the Committee's *de facto* status as a forum for political consultation. From time to time, individual union leaders attend, to put forward their case in relevant issues.[193] Likewise, key MPs are invited when their fields of policy are on the agenda, to inform, discuss and mediate. When in government, ministers and state secretaries are also (or instead) asked to discuss cases currently debated in their ministries.[194] This practice has not changed after Labour formed a coalition government with the Centre Party and the Socialist Left Party (Jota 2006 [e-mail correspondence]). Occasionally, guests are also invited who are not union or party officials in relation to specific projects, like researchers from FAFO, the trade union movement's research centre. No doubt the 'Co-operation Committee' is much more than a regular dialogue forum. In sum, the Committee appears as a genuinely intermediary institution at the elite level. It serves to connect LO, individual unions, other parts of the traditional labour movement, the party organisation and headquarters, the parliamentary group and the prospective party in government.

Second, a more detailed examination of the *frequency of meetings* is needed to assess the intensity of contact that takes place through the Joint Committee. In

192. The minutes are not transferred to the Norwegian Labour Movement Archives and Library due to their confidential status, but I was granted access by DnA and LO.

193. However, it should be noted than only two individual unions are regular members. From time to time, this relation causes tension within LO (see *Klassekampen* 02.10.02; *LO-Aktuelt* 06.03.03).

194. According to Jota (2003 [interview]) it is routine to invite cabinet members when 'their' cases are discussed. However, during the Jagland Cabinet in 1996–1997 and Stoltenberg I from 2000–2001, ministers did not attend to the same extent as in the 1970s (Skjeie 1999). Most likely, the character of meetings to some extent changes when the party is in government, but its beyond the scope of this project to explore such distinctions.

Table 15.4 we see that between one and two meetings have been arranged every month since 2002, which is relatively high also seen from an historical perspective (see Skjeie 1999: 108). Hence, the Committee enables the LO and DnA leaderships to consult with each other not only on long-term policies, but also in connection with day-to-day politics.

Table 15.4: Number of meetings in the 'Co-operation Committee' 1997–2004. Nominal figures[1]

	1997	1998	1999	2000	2001	2002	2003
Number of meetings	27	25	35	30	28	21	13
Frequency per month[1]	2–3	2–3	3–4	3	2–3	2–3	1–2

1 The frequency is based on 10 active months per year.

Since DnA spent very little time in government between 1997 and 2001 it is hard to say whether the meeting frequency depends on whether DnA is the party in power or not. On the other hand, the frequency clearly decreased after peaking in 1999 with more than three meetings a month, i.e. meetings almost every week (cf. Labour Party Biannual Report 2000–02). This development can, of course, be seen as a general indication of decline in actual importance. Yet peaks in terms of particularly frequent meetings may also hint at a temporarily high level of conflict.

As Skjeie (1999: 108–11) has shown, the frequency of committee meetings has since the 1950s varied significantly due to political conflicts and personal matters like divided party leadership. For example, meetings in the 1970s developed in a way that indicates that the government was close to being directed by LO: 'It does not seem very probable that it was the Prime Minister himself who found it necessary to meet as much as almost forty times a year in LO's headquarters' (*ibid*: 115, my translation). In the 1980s, meetings became less frequent. Prime Minister Gro Harlem Brundtland managed, according to Skjeie (1999: 115), better than her predecessors did, '(…) the art of balancing in states of "controlled disagreement"' (my translation).

The recent decision of limiting the number of meetings was also taken after a period of severe political tension in DnA. In 2000, the extra-parliamentary and parliamentary leadership had become separated. The party organisation experienced a serious crisis when a faction later started to promote the unitary leadership of parliamentary leader Jens Stoltenberg, and the former parliamentary leader Thorbjørn Jagland refused to relinquish the party leadership without a fight before the forthcoming party congress (see Takvam 2002; Hågensen 2004). Thus, it is likely that the peak of meetings primarily reflects co-ordination problems in times of intra-party conflicts, not party-union conflicts. According to the key informants, almost weekly attendance is difficult to handle for busy top leaders. Less frequent but sometimes more comprehensive meetings are therefore preferred by members of the Committee in the early 2000s (Jota 2003 [interview]). Furthermore, the present party leader and LO chair (until 2007) have publicly explained that they also meet privately to discuss current political issues (*Dagsavisen* 21.09.05; *Aftenposten* 01.10.05). Hence, the decline in number of committee meetings since 1999 can hardly be interpreted as indicating a decrease in the significance of DnA's links with LO.

Third, a closer look at the *content* of the Committee agenda may tell us something essential about the substantial relevance of the organised contact with the trade union movement. To avoid capturing what is only a temporary tendency, and reveal possible short-term changes, *the total number of items* was counted for the period from 1997 to 2003. The general principle for constructing the record has not changed significantly during this period. Table 15.5 shows that the number of items has decreased significantly in recent years. The average number of items debated per meeting was higher in 2003 than in 1997, but the total number of items declined significantly during this period. Since the way of reporting issues has not changed much during the same period, we may conclude the agenda was less extensive in 2003 than it was in the late 1990s.

Table 15.5: Number of items discussed in the 'Co-operation Committee' 1997–2004[1]

	1997	1998	1999	2000	2001	2002	2003
Number items on the agenda per year	84	61	110	87	86	61	47
Average number of items per meeting	3	2	3	3	3	3	4

1 The formal approval of the minutes from the last meeting is not included, as this item is not mentioned every time. What are counted are not issues or cases, but *items* (formal numbers) on the agenda. Thus, one item might cover only a single issue or case, or a single issue or case might be represented by several items (as some issues and cases are discussed repeatedly).

The strength of this decline indicates that it is not due solely to 'natural fluctuation'. The fact that meetings are arranged less frequently does limit the content of the organised contact. It seems as if the Joint Committee is not used for consultation as much as it once was, but whether this means reduced significance is far from evident. As argued above, fewer organised meetings do not necessarily mean less contact. It seems more likely that the trade union and party leadership in the early 2000s have decided to adjust their way of working together, as key informants suggest, than that the party-union link has been significantly 'devalued' in practice.

Fourth, a closer look at the *thematic content of the agenda* supports this interpretation. By the end of the twentieth century, LO had developed into a broadly-oriented interest organisation (Nyhamar 1990: 561).[195] According to the menu of

195. The development can be traced back to the late 1960s when LO launched its first action programme. According to Nyhamar (1990: 71), the preceding internal debate among union members represented an attempt to further develop a mutual political frame of reference within the labour movement and link the party and the unions even more closely.

policy issues presented on the official website, LO's major fields of interest are in 2005: equal opportunities, wages/collective agreements, working life, industrial policies, health and environment, welfare, education, employment and international issues (LO 09.10.05 [online]). Hence, the Norwegian trade union movement today is concerned with much more than wages and working environments. LO and its unions are not on the verge of developing into what Poguntke (1998: 158) has described as 'insurance companies' whose survival depends on the supply of selective incentives to individual members. Does the agenda of the 'Co-operation Committee' reflect this relatively broad political profile?

According to DnA's web page, the 'Co-operation Committee' deliberates 'all important matters of common interest' (DnA 17.01.03). According to Skjeie (1999: 108) the Committee has debated increasingly diverse political issues since the 1970s. Although price and wage policies are no longer so dominant, the books of minutes from 1997 to 2003 reveal that the range of debated topics is still wide. There are deliberations on bills, public reports, as well as cases debated in the Storting or Government, or in the trade union movement. Since 1997 the Committee has discussed wage policies and bills affecting working environments, but also, for example, government budgets, monetary policy, the level of Norwegian executive salaries, public ownership and privatisation of the public sector, tax policy, oil and energy policy (including the establishment of gasworks), a major hospital reform, boycott of Israel, the pension reform, sickness benefits, a new 'Solidarity Alternative'[196], and more general topics like 'the current political situation'. Through temporary sub-committees the Committee has dealt with contentious issues like 'the modernisation of the public sector' and 'reorganisation of public companies'. In addition, major organisational events, like electoral campaigns, party congresses and international labour conferences, are usually discussed.[197]

Thus the Committee debates politically significant issues of various extent, and both short-term and long-term policies. Due to rather frequent meetings it is able to mediate in internal and public decision-making processes at short notice. In major controversial cases, like the pension reform, the contact has been intense in recent years. Interestingly, the party manifesto and LO's action programme are *not* deliberated by the Joint Committee. But as described in Chapter 7, consult-

---

196. The original 'Solidarity Alternative' (*Solidaritetsalternative*) was a five-year agreement dating back to 1992 and a public committee for employment issues including the two sides of the labour market and representatives of political parties. The agreement involved union moderation in wage policies and active policies regarding monetary relations, finance and the labour market (Caplex 17/10/2005 [online]). It was a cross-party and organisation agreement which ended in about 1998 (Bergh 1999).

197. Underlining the formal autonomy of LO and DnA, the committee does not formally deliberate on the party manifesto and LO's action programme (Jota (2003 [interview]). However, as mentioned in Chapter 7, topics relevant for the party programme are indeed discussed and the trade unions and LO are consulted in other ways. Moreover, as long as the LO chair holds a seat in the DnA national executive committee, she/he takes part in the final decision about the proposal to be presented to the party congress.

ing LO about the party manifesto is still standard procedure in DnA. Hence, LO seems to be informed or consulted about most major DnA decisions of relevance for salaried employees and the industrial sector.

A final, major indicator of the general significance of the 'Co-operation Committee' is the *form of consultation*, which can also tell us something about the extent to which there is mutual influence. According to Skjeie (1999), the Committee concluded fairly often in terms of genuine decisions in the 1970s. During the 1980s, however, the committee to a large extent ended their discussion by 'passing issues on' to other forums. This is also very much the case today. In some issues the two sides meet simply to inform each other, and the autonomy of organisational structures is emphasised by conclusions like 'the party has to consider how to respond to the *[debated]* request itself'. A typical formulation is that a case is 'sent back to LO', or that 'the case is further debated in party and LO bodies', or that the 'debate continues at the next meeting'.

Nevertheless, the Committee also reaches decisions in many cases, according to the minutes. Not all debates are only 'taken into consideration'. In valence issues, future efforts in the public decision-making process are in focus of committee meetings. In situations of conflict, the Committee aims to explore the possibilities for reaching a unified conclusion (cf. Skjeie 1999). The semi-formal discussions without long-lasting general introductions and public records facilitate efficient exploration of possible compromises. Sometimes this takes time. Alternatively, and more finally, the party leader and the LO chair are 'empowered to complete the document'.

There are also numerous examples where the Committee itself reaches agreement, such as that 'the Co-operation Committee supports' a certain conclusion or policy. Labour MPs and ministers are often asked to 'follow up' the cases in the Storting and Government. The conclusions are not instructions, but weighty premises for further proceedings, otherwise, top leaders would probably not convene so many meetings. As Skjeie (1999: 95f) observed in the 1990s, the consensus orientation implies that options are gradually limited throughout the process. Hence, the suggestions made by the Committee are thoroughly prepared and, accordingly, difficult to ignore. Therefore, the actual significance of the Co-operation Committee appears to be stronger than its formal status might indicate.

Elite Views on the Impact of LO and Unions on Party Decisions

What can the elite's own views on this particular relationship tell us? Historically, the labour movement elite have usually characterised the 'Co-operation Committee' as a powerful arrangement. Internally, the name is said to be pronounced with a capital C (Haraldseth 1989: 120). As a former LO chairperson once phrased it: 'There is only one such committee. No one ever bothers using its entire name (…). What the committee thinks one ought to do is normally done' (Haraldseth 1989: 121, my translation). In other words, even if its conclusions are modest in form, they have served as influential statements, according to former elite members. Interestingly, the joint 'Co-operation Committee' between LO and DnA has often been described as a *unitary* power base.

However, the very nature of the Committee means that DnA and LO have had to adapt mutually to each other's views in contentious issues *over time*. The party secretary from 2002 to 2009, who also has lengthy experience from the secretariat of the parliamentary group, considers the 'Co-operation Committee' still to be powerful, but indicates that it is probably less significant as *an entirety* than in the post-war era:

> I will characterise the committee as very important. What we agree upon weighs heavily. But its – and this is only my personal view – authority has weakened over time. This is related to the general organisational culture in our society. The culture of 'some people has been talking together' has practically vanished. One does not deal with conflicts 'in private' any more. Some decades ago that was a stronger tendency and there was more room for such behaviour. Thus, it is also clear that the committee was more significant before (Kolberg 2003 [interview]).

So even if the relationship has been re-intensified as a whole after a period of decline, the Committee's role as a communication channel has apparently declined from a long-term perspective because, apparently, both sides have to approach their respective ruling bodies more carefully than before. The party secretary also emphasises cases when compromises cannot be reached:

> It is important to be aware of the fact – which is often ignored in public debate – that the committee never passes any proposals (…). Only the party's national executive and LO's secretariat are allowed to make decisions on behalf of their respective organisations. To argue that the conversations are not important would be like 'cheating'. If they were not influential, the communication would be without any meaning, obviously. However, there are examples of opinions developed in the 'Co-operation Committee' which are not possible to develop further because of opposition from the LO secretariat, the party's executive and so forth. Thus, it *[the committee]* is an important forum for exchange of viewpoints, for keeping contact and good relations – and there is political strength in such communication, of course. But it is not an executive body as often presented (Kolberg 2003 [interview]).

More importantly, the party secretary argues that the consensus orientation generally makes it difficult to identify 'who loses and who wins' in cases of conflict:

> It is not a give-and-take situation – we discuss (…). And then, we deliberate on specific, important issues in different contexts. That's what makes it [*the relationship*] binding, of course. Sometimes we think that ideally we would have done things differently, but because we respect each other, we don't. But that's not being under each other's thumb. It's only sensible political behaviour.
>
> I would not call the relationship an exchange relationship, you see. I hear this is frequently mentioned by others (….). But it's wrong; it *[the relationship]* is more like a process during which one reasons things out and discusses topics about which co-operation is relevant. Sometimes the result is shared opinions, but not always (…). (Kolberg 2003 [interview])

The party secretary thus echoes the former LO chair who opposed the traditional metaphor of 'Siamese twins' by arguing that the relationship more resembled a piece of paper: '(…) if you use a piece of paper for the purpose for which it is originally produced – to jot down thoughts and ideas – you will never write the same words on both sides' (Haraldseth 1989: 122–3, my translation). In some cases, the party is compelled to make political concessions, but sometimes no agreement is reached. This aspect of the party-union co-operation is also emphasised by the other key informant, who is formally and specifically responsible for DnA's contact with LO at party headquarters:

> To claim that the committee is insignificant would be like lying. The composition of members is in itself an indication of the importance of the committee's conclusions. But on the other hand, it does not make formal decisions. Let's say that you debate a specific issue, and viewpoints from both sides are presented. OK, in this way one knows each other's positions, and one returns to each other's respective decision-making bodies to further discuss the case. No one can say that 'this is decided by the "Co-operation Committee"' and put one's foot down. The importance is connected to the fact that leaders have discussed thing in advance. No one uses the 'Co-operation Committee' to press various parts of the [labour] movement. (Jota 2003 [interview])

Hence, the Committee is certainly perceived as important, but there seem to be subtle organisational norms regulating how much power is, in fact, located in the Committee. As one of the secretaries for the committee drafting the 2001–2005 Manifesto phrases it: 'A *[Labour]* manifesto may have some sections diverging from the policy views of the trade union movement. But there cannot be a lot of such cases. I think. To have numerous 'wars' of this kind going on *[with LO]* is hard to imagine' (Bråten 2003 [interview]).

Despite the general agreement among key informants, their statements about the political significance are, after all, personal viewpoints. In order to obtain a more general indication, I mapped the views of the DnA elite on the significance of the relationship with LO through the survey, examining to what extent those, who felt that their most frequent contacts (the three organisations) were important, made reference to trade unions. Among those who report these contacts to have been *very important*, the referred communication includes LO or LO unions *in all cases* as far as the first organisation is concerned. Moreover, 75 per cent of those who think they were *rather important* also refer to trade unions. In any of the cases, alternative kinds of organisations are regarded as more influential for decisions made by the party's central organisation than LO and its unions.

Hence, we can conclude that the links with LO are strong not only in organisational terms. Within the mechanism of the Committee, formal decisions are not taken, but comprehensive debates take place. DnA's organised and informal contact links with LO and its unions cover a broad spectrum of political issues, and are regarded by the national elite as highly significant for party decisions. Yet, the closeness does not eliminate the fact that the party and the trade unions are autonomous actors, collectives which in turn may be internally divided. How influential the trade unions are *relative* to the party in this relationship is less clear-cut.

Although conflicts today seem to arise not only on the borderline of trade union-party interest, the very existence of a joint committee presupposes consensus on at least some fundamental values and policy views. Furthermore, the numerous and lengthy deliberations hint at a generally complex type of correspondence. There is still mutuality in terms of two-way influence: both sides are still being compelled to compromise in certain issues. To find out which side has, from a short-term perspective, yielded the most in recent years would require separate policy studies. In this sense, little has changed since the post-war era as Millen (1963: 128) described it: 'The process of informal bargaining takes place with each passing day on matters big and small, in order to harmonize differences within the structure. Tempers are lost; power plays are made'. The well-organised links between DnA and the trade unions make up a dynamic relationship, through which not only unions exert political influence.

CONCLUSIONS

The empirical analysis presented in Chapters 7 to 14 showed that political parties in Norway have links with interest groups but that the closeness and range of such relationships vary significantly among parties. The general aim of this chapter has been to assess the political significance of the links for the parties' political decisions, in order to examine critically whether the relationships identified with interest groups actually have substantial, and not only symbolic, value. The analysis has been limited to some fairly crude indicators. Nevertheless, some conclusions can be drawn.

First, we see that despite extensive fact-oriented contact, the links that Norway's political parties have established with interest groups are clearly not trivial. Through organised arrangements, and in more informal ways, organisations are given the chance to affect the party organisation's policy-making in day-to-day politics and, from a long-term perspective through contact about the party manifesto. Both the key informants and the top elites report that such contact to a significant extent deals with attempts at mapping policy views, and that it includes efforts to influence party decisions. Thus, in a significant number of cases, the mapped links with interest groups are relevant to the parties' political decision-making.

Second, the existing relationships also seem to influence the outcome of party decision-making processes about party policy. Again, both key informants and the survey data suggest that interest groups lead parties to formulate policies different from what would have developed without such links. Organisations do not need to be involved in standing arrangements in order to have a say; the established weaker links also represent more than legitimising exercises. However, we find significant differences among parties. Key informants from the Liberal Party and the Conservative Party in particular emphasise a critical attitude towards the attempts of interest groups to affect party policies. Accordingly, they also indicate that the actual impact on their policy-making is more limited.

The discussion has also examined whether the degree of closeness and range of party relationships with interest groups matters. Closer relationships, as in the case of the Socialist Left Party and the Progress Party, may seem more politically significant than more distant ones, but surprisingly we have found no strong tendency. For example, the political impact on decisions reported by the Conservative elite does not reflect any relative strength of links of this party as a whole. The Labour Party does not stand out with regard to reported general political significance, despite its close relations with LO and significant links with organisations.

This discrepancy might reflect normatively-biased responses. The informants of the Conservatives emphasise that interest-group influence is a potentially negative phenomenon, and DnA's relations with the trade union movement have been much disputed in the public debate. Thus, it is not unreasonable to assume that the threshold for reporting about influential interest groups is relatively high. Moreover, the in-depth analysis of the well-organised links between the Labour party and the trade unions show that they are much more than symbols for internal use. The relationship makes LO deeply involved in the party's decision-making processes in practice. In fact, a reasonable question to ask is if there is much room left for influential contact with other organisations about the issues that DnA and LO debate. Hence, this in-depth analysis supports the preliminary conclusion from Chapter 7 that the links with the trade unions serves to moderate the extent to which Labour opens up its decision-making for other interest groups.

It has not been possible to document the significance of links with different kinds of organisations for each party. Hence, the possibility that some parties are linked with various interest groups, but are nevertheless selective when it comes to actual accommodation to when making political decisions, is not ruled out. Nor have I been able to examine whether parties more readily make use of information within policy fields and on social segments that the party elite and organisation are already familiar with. This notwithstanding, we have seen that some organisations in general seem more influential than others. Those labour market and industry organisations with which the elite generally had most frequent contact are considered to be most important. Despite a wide range of politically significant links, some are closer and in practice more influential than others. Hence, the range of party relationships is not necessarily an indication of the extent to which various interests actually influence party policies.

To conclude, variations in the relationships with interest groups seem relevant. Fairly weak links are not merely symbolic exercises: they affect party decisions, and make a wide range of interest groups politically significant. But the degree of closeness of relations does matter for the degree of influence exerted by interest groups. In most cases, closeness seems to strengthen the impact of external organisations on party decisions. In other words, the contemporary dominance of relatively weak links with interest groups indicates the generally limited significance of links with *individual* organisations. DnA's link with LO is still a major case, but it is not typical.

chapter sixteen | variations in relationships: an explanatory analysis

The aim of this chapter is to throw light on the question of what specific conditions affect whether parties opt for different patterns of relationships with interest groups. Despite a social and cultural structure calling for links with a wide range of interest groups, and institutional and political developments hinting at separation, there is certainly variation in how political parties in Norway are linked into the interest-group community. Chapter 14 showed that there is a general tendency towards fairly distant – not very strong links – and wide-ranging relationships with interest groups, but that significant differences in these relationships exist beneath the surface. The variation does not seem to correspond systematically to party-related differences in general external circumstances such as the relative size of traditional core voter groups. Can more actor-oriented theory help us to understand better the *major* differences between Norwegian parties?

VARIATION TO BE EXAMINED – AND HOW

The analysis revolves around the explanatory issues identified in Chapter 5. First, the question is which factors explain that a party chooses to have a close relationship with a specific kind of organisations, while others prefer a more distant relationship. Here, the most relevant divergence to analyse is the fact that *the Labour Party (DnA) has a much closer relationship with the trade union movement than other parties have*. Indeed, Labour has links with the Confederation of Trade Unions (LO) that may serve as a genuine 'institutional framework' to decrease the transaction costs of exchange. However, as truly close relations most likely presupposes consensus on some basic policy issues (cf. Chapter 5), basic ideological differences may call for different preferences as regards potential 'partners' for the closest types of relationships. Therefore, we shall also have a closer look at the differing degrees of closeness to the parties' traditional associates. In this regard, we noted that *the Christian People's Party (KrF) and in particular the Labour Party have closer relationships with their traditional associates than the other parties have.* Third, to give a crude indication of what might explain variation in the *overall* degree of closeness to/distance from parties to the interest group universe, we may, above all, examine the following findings: *The Liberals (V) prefer to maintain some distance from the interest-group community as whole, whereas the Socialist Left Party (SV) is marked by fairly close relationships with numerous interest groups within different categories*. Finally, I will briefly explore variation in the overall range of party relationships: if we concentrate on deliberate attempts to establish organised links, *the Centre Party (Sp), the Christian People's Party (KrF), the Socialist Left Party (SV) and the Progress Party (FrP) have a wider range of relationships than have the Conservatives (H) or the Labour Party*

(DnA). Why? Indirectly, the analysis will thus also throw light on the fact that the newest parties do not differ so markedly from the old parties, as suggested by the literature on new right and left parties.

I start by examining the explanatory utility of the cost-benefit model developed based on general rational-choice theory on political parties: do party-interest groups, by and large, vary in line with the expectations of rational choice institutionalism? I first explore the issue of relations with individual group categories, and second the patterns of general party relationships with interest groups. Hence, the analysis does not take account of the possibility that closeness to an individual group may exist and be useful even if the relationship with the organisation category as a whole is fairly distant and not very advantageous. Thereafter, I turn to the hypotheses informed by historical and normative institutionalism and deviations from the rational course to explore the relative significance of other factors. To the extent that the cost-benefit model is not able to explain variation in party-interest group relationships, what does? Specific contextual or political events? Historical constraints? Or mainly accommodation to party identity and norms?

How can we go about analysing these questions? Party documents, income accounts, election studies, the elite survey and in-depth interviews are primary sources of evidence. Before presenting and exploring the various specific hypotheses, parties' internal debates on party-interest group relationships are briefly discussed. But as argued in the introductory chapter, neither party goals nor cultural norms can be observed directly. Exchange of resources between parties and interest groups can, however, be readily measured, even though it has not been possible to map accurately the extent of the benefits of organisational support. Furthermore, time series, i.e. describing the supply of votes and finances over time, are included as the relative usefulness of a relationship may fluctuate naturally from one year to another. Also, previous records of benefits represent a basis for evaluating the current advantages of links with interest groups for individual parties themselves. The party leadership may not necessarily be familiar with the exact figures to be presented, but it is reasonable to presuppose that the top elite keep themselves informed about such major trends in one way or another. The shares of interest group members' votes are, obviously, distorted by party size, the parties' overall vote share each election, but this problem will be discussed throughout. As relevant time series are not available for all kinds of interest groups, the empirical analysis concentrates on the relationship with economic interest groups, and is based upon secondary literature in most other cases.

VARIATIONS IN RELATIONSHIPS: A QUESTION OF COSTS AND BENEFITS?

Based on the cost-benefit model we expect intra-party debates to be characterised by calculations as to the usefulness for the party's pursuit of party goals (office and policy by means of votes). A cost-benefit model looks at party relationships with interest groups as results of deliberate reasoning and choices. Limited active and utility-oriented decision-making, based on conforming to the party's original *raison d'être* and democratic expectations, would weaken the empirical support for the cost-benefit model in general.

The Intra-party Debate on Party-interest Group Relationships

There is little doubt that Norwegian parties look at links with interest groups as tools or mechanisms with which they can instrumentally pursue various goals more efficiently. As shown in Chapters 7 to 13, many parties describe their relationship with interest groups in fairly 'instrumental terms' in party documents and the like: openness towards various interest groups is seen as one of the preconditions for the party's ability to survive as significant political party over time.

The party secretary of DnA states that as regards contemporary relationships: '(…) By having a well-developed co-operation with major organizations, the party gets numerous "opinion surveyors". In this way, you get a lot of valuable viewpoints suggesting what people really think. And you can communicate back (…)' (Kolberg 2003 [interviews]). Alternatively inputs from interest groups are seen as what can be called 'competent opinions' (cf. Hole 2003; Solhjell 2003 [interviews]). In general, getting access to know-how or policy expertise is more frequently emphasised as a motivating force by party strategists. Such groups help parties to make their policies more accurate and their arguments more persuasive (see Hole 2003; Mo 2003; Sundsbø 2003 [interviews]). Others reported that they also look at links as a way to promote party policy (Mo 2003; Sundsbø 2003 [interviews], and to communicate with people independent of the mass media (Kolberg 2003 [interview]).

However, few parties, and not even Labour, spontaneously describe links with interest groups as a way to provide a more reliable exchange of more tangible resources than 'information' like votes, money and policy rewards. Indeed, the party informants also refer to their party's relationships as influenced by values and shaped by normative deliberation as well. Statements like 'contact is important for the role of political parties in democracy', 'without interest groups, party democracy would be weakened' or 'special interests should be filtered through political parties' were also mentioned in reply to the question of why the party seek to have contact with other organisations outside the Storting. In one way or another, most party secretaries and secretaries-general emphasised that parties need to keep in touch with organised interest groups in order to be able to reflect public opinion and create some sort of linkage to public policy (e.g. Kolberg 2003; Nyhus 2003; Sundsbø 2003 [interviews]).

In any case, we cannot take leaders' statements about why a party chooses to be linked in a specific way at face value (cf. Chapter 1 and Chapter 5). As previously argued, party leaders will probably hesitate to present links with interest groups as a way to increase the party's competitiveness at the polls through exchange of resources, even if major decisions are based on such cost-benefit considerations. So we now need to explore the specific hypotheses developed in Chapter 5 by looking at the variation in party-interest group relationships mentioned above. In general, we expect differences to primarily follow variation in the actual balance of costs and benefits. I start by looking at the benefits of links for parties general goal-seeking (office and policy by means of votes), concentrating on the provision of votes on the one hand, and financial donations and organisational resources on the other.

Party Benefits of Closeness to Individual Kinds of Interest Groups

We hypothesised *that a party with a relatively close relationship with one kind of interest group tends to be provided with significantly more benefits (votes, financial resources, organisational support) for the pursuit of goals (office and policy) by the given organisation(s) than other parties receive.* Does this pattern match the Labour Party's relatively close relationship with the trade union movement?

Degree of Closeness of Relationships with the Confederation of Trade Unions (LO)

Even before the Second World War, Labour (and the trade unions) had chosen to separate the party's organisational structures from the unions at the national level so that DnA would not be seen as a 'trade union party', according to Valen and Katz (1964: 316). By the turn of the Millenium, local collective membership had also been abandoned. But, in the early 2000s, DnA still has a fairly close relationship with LO. Due to the survival of some basic ideological differences, it is hardly unexpected that there exists some discrepancy between the relations of the centre-right and the centre-left with the trade unions. The question is if whether DnA's relative closeness to the trade unions corresponds to the supply of resources from LO. According to the party secretary, DnA's links with trade unions are a valuable method to get informed and to persuade voters directly, independent of mass media:

> I look at the party-union co-operation as the tool I have as a party secretary to communicate with people independent of the media (....). If you have well-organized links with major interest groups you are provided with 'surveyors of opinions'. You get a lot of valuable views on what are people's real opinions, and you are able to communicate both ways. Hence, the co-operation is based on ideology, but also on organizational strength (…) (Kolberg 2003 [interview]).

However, one thing is to communicate regularly as organisations, another is to, for example, keep a permanent joint committee and provide LO's leadership with access to the party executive. Is the relative vote-catching potential towards the more weakly linked parties accordingly strong?

Until recently, LO has officially endorsed DnA prior to elections, not least through occasional joint party-union campaigns and manifestos. This is valuable assistance when it comes to getting out Labour's traditional core voters. Table 16.1 – displaying the distribution of votes among LO members – shows that the endorsement is followed up at the membership level. There is still no party in Norway that is as strongly supported in the LO segment as the Labour Party. In the late 1990s and early 2000s, between 33 and 54 per cent of LO's members voted for DnA. The Socialist Left Party – which has the strongest link with LO and unions after Labour – received only between 7 and 17 per cent of the LO members' votes in 1997 and 2001. There can thus be no doubt that Labour has a stronger electoral incentive for having a close relationship with LO than other parties.

Table 16.1: Distribution of votes among LO members, 1957–2001

	1957	1965	1969	1973	1977	1981	1985	1989	1993	1997	2001
DnA	84.4	70.4	75.1	55.6	64.2	57.3	63.2	56.2	60.9	53.8	32.8
H	3.9	7.0	6.7	3.5	11.4	18.0	14.1	9.7	6.0	5.8	18.1
V	2.8	7.0	6.4	3.5	4.0	4.0	2.9	2.5	1.4	3.0	2.7
Sp	0.7	3.1	2.3	4.3	5.2	3.0	1.7	1.5	12.6	4.8	3.5
KrF	4.3	1.7	4.4	7.4	6.7	4.5	5.1	3.7	4.3	12.0	10.7
SV	–	9.5	4.1	20.2	4.9	7.5	9.8	14.7	8.0	6.8	16.5
FrP	–	–	–	2.3	0.7	3.8	1.2	9.0	3.7	12.0	10.4
Others	3.9	1.4	0.9	3.1	3.0	2.0	2.0	2.7	3.2	2.1	5.4
N	282	358	342	257	405	400	410	402	350	400	375

Source: The Norwegian Election Studies and Aardal (2003: 267).

However, Table 16.1 also shows that it is no longer the case that most LO members vote for DnA. In 1957, 84 per cent of LO's members voted for the Labour Party; by 1993, this figure had fallen to about 60 per cent. Since then, the decline has been steep: in 2001, it plummeted to 33 per cent. This reflects, to some extent, a poor election result (see below), but no doubt a significant proportion of LO's members today prefer several other parties, including both the Socialist Left and the Progress Party. The effect of appealing specifically to LO members is in the early 2000s far weaker than it was in the 1950s and 1960s. The 'LO electorate' fluctuates and spreads its votes, just as the Norwegian electorate as a whole does. Having strong links with LO is certainly no guarantee of success on Election Day.

This said, a closer look at the most recent general elections, gives nuances to this conclusion. Prior to the 2001 election, the abolition of collective DnA membership of union branches had followed a long-term decline in electoral support. Between the 'earthquake election' of 1973 and the general elections in 2001, the average share of votes for Norwegian Labour fell by almost 10 percentage points when compared with the peak years between 1945–69 (Arter 2003: 95). In the early 1990s, the party leadership concluded that organisational reforms were needed to reverse the trend. The historically close relationship with the state apparatus and LO was no longer enough, it was argued (Myking 1997: 60). Nonetheless, the party did *not* choose the option of weakening the links further at the turn of the century.

In 2001, DnA experienced a veritable 'electoral shock' when it ended up with no more than 24 per cent of the total vote (see Figure 1, Appendix E). Certainly, it would not have come as a surprise if this experience had stimulated the party to further dilute its links with the trade unions. The former, and allegedly union-oriented, party leader Thorbjørn Jagland suggested that the 2001 electoral result pointed in this direction (Foss 2005). However, Labour chose instead to revitalise its relationship with the trade unions, apparently concluding that re-consolidation of its links with LO was a tool with which the party could more efficiently recover. The decline of support among LO members to about 33 per cent was identified as one the factors that could explain the historically poor electoral result in 2001.

Although this study embraces the period from 2000–2004, it is worth noting that DnA's party secretary described the electoral strategy in the following way at the Labour Congress in 2005: 'Then I say: the trade union movement, the trade union movement, the trade union movement. We have asked for the support of LO and have had the wish fulfilled. A new majority [*government*] requires broad popular support, but also the involvement and assistance of the trade union movement (…)' (Kolberg 2005, my translation).[198] So there is little doubt that the party leadership in 2002 concluded that links with LO might still be useful for electoral and office-seeking purposes. Interestingly, according to opinion polls, the share of DnA votes was restored to about 50 per cent before the 2005 elections (*LO-Aktuelt* 08.09.05 and 19.09.05). Forty-eight per cent of LO's members actually voted for the Labour Party in 2005 (Berglund 2007: 155), and Labour captured 33 per cent of the total vote. This indicates that the relative closeness to LO was not an obstacle, and probably contributed, to the restoration of a *certain* level of electoral support for the party. Hence, DnA does not receive as many voters from LO as the relative strength of the links might indicate, but the degree of closeness is connected with the electoral resources provided by LO.

Next, the question is whether other types of benefits, such as financial donations and organisational support, strengthen or weaken this impression that links with trade unions are fairly, if not very useful, for DnA. DnA has always received monetary and organisational support from the trade union movement. Table 16.2 shows that it still does. Between 1998 and 2004, the party received NOK 48.6m (about €6.1m) from LO and individual unions. True, the LO Congress decided in 2001 for the first time to fund the Socialist Left's general election campaigns, as individual unions had already been doing, but that support is limited in comparison. Altogether, SV received NOK 1.7m (about €0.2m) from 1998 to 2004.[199] Interestingly, the Progress Party has demonstrated its negative view of the close relationship between LO and DnA by applying for financial support from LO, but without success (see *Aftenposten* 03.08.97; *Dagsavisen* 29.01.06). A single LO union – the Seamen's Union – did in fact donate money to non-socialist parties probably for the first time in 2003, but this was a matter of only small amounts. But compared to what DnA receives from trade unions, the money supply to others is very modest.

DnA also receives significant organisational resources from LO, in the form of activists, labour and, above all, through the unions' independent campaign efforts.

198. The statement followed comments on the choice of forming a 'red-green' coalition with SV and Sp (Kolberg 2005).

199. SV received NOK 1.6m from LO and unions in the election year of 2005. However, the figure in the case of Labour was NOK 13.4m (Allern and Saglie 2008).

The party's annual reports conclude that DnA has enjoyed organisational support from trade unions during the election campaigns in the late 1990s and early 2000s (see Labour Party Annual Report 1981–82: 52; 1998–2000: 59; 2000–02: 38, see also *Aftenposten* 23.07.97). Other parts of the Norwegian labour movement – like the educational organisation AOF, represent an additional common pool of resources.[200] Also, as requested by the party secretary, trade unions carried on the tradition of campaigning for Labour in 2005. One year before the general elections, LO embarked on a project dubbed 'the Long Campaign'. The Confederation remained formally non-partisan during the election campaign, and the grass roots were first asked to rank the political issues and policy views they consider to be most important. But several union leaders explicitly endorsed the red-green coalition alternative and encouraged voters to support the Labour Party, Centre Party and Socialist Left Party (Fagforbundet 2005; Fellesforbundet 2005). Meanwhile, the LO chair all but directly asked LO members to vote for specific parties in her electoral appeal (Valla 2005b). So there can be no doubt that the aim

Table 16.2: Monetary support from interest groups to the various parties' central organisation 1998–2004. NOK 1000 and percentage of total revenues[1]

	DnA	H	V	Sp	KrF	SV	FrP
LO	34697	–	–	–	–	500	–
LO Unions	13876	–	–	25	–	1183	25
NHO	–	21200		–	3850	–	–
RF	–	2500	–	–	1290	–	1500
Oslo RF	–	–	–	–	–	–	225
Sum total	48573	23700	–	25	5140	1683	1750
% of total revenues[2]	10.7	10.0	–	0.02	2.2	1.5	1.0

LO = Norwegian Confederation of Trade Unions
NHO: the Confederation of Norwegian Enterprise
RF: Norwegian Shipowners' Association, Oslo RF: Oslo Shipowners' Association

1 It was not possible to identify the relevant figures from SV's accounts from 1998, 1999 and 2000, but the figures were provided by the present Finance Manager Hilde Longva (Longva 2005 [e-mail correspondence]).

2 The figures are not directly comparable as accounting conventions seem to differ somewhat between parties.

Source: Parties' income accounts.

200. For an overview of the various branches of the labour movement, see Helgesen (1995). Yet it should be mentioned that this book is published by the Conservative Party and ought to be read accordingly.

of the campaign was to get a new, red-green government elected.[201] In other words, the *prospect* of this type of support may have stimulated the party leadership to re-consolidate rather than weaken its links as they most likely would make the support of LO more reliable.

True, we may question the actual value of LO's monetary support. Mainly due to generous public subventions (see Chapter 6), LO support represents only about 11 per cent of DnA's total revenues in the early 2000s. Moreover, such donations are often criticised by other parties, and may well alienate voter groups in the same way as do the organised links for contact. The DnA party secretary clearly rejects the idea that the party's links with LO are motivated by monetary support (Kolberg 2003 [interview]). Nonetheless, there is little doubt that DnA, in contrast to other parties, has a fairly strong financial incentive for maintaining a close relationship with LO. Weakening the inter-organisational link might imply loss of significant privileges. Although the party has other and more important reasons to be linked with the trade unions, the financial support from LO and its unions does certainly strengthen the incentive for closeness. On the whole, the correspondence between closeness to trade unions and benefits seems stronger than the contemporary party literature often suggests it generally is, but it does not perfectly match a cost-benefit model.

Degree of Closeness of Relationships with Traditional Associates

The next question to explore is why parties relationships with their traditional associate varies: *a party with a relatively close relationship with its traditional associate(s) tends to be provided with significantly more benefits (votes, financial resources, organisational support) for the pursuit of goals (office and policy) by the given organisation(s) than parties with more distant relations receive.*

Does this pattern match the variation in the different parties' links with their traditional associate in Norway? DnA's relationship with LO and its unions is closer than any other party's relationship with its traditionally associated interest group(s). For example, the Conservatives have stronger links with employers', business, and trade organisations than with other groups, but these are definitely not as well-organised and intense as the relationship between the Labour Party and the trade unions. Hence, we may first ask: does LO provide DnA with a greater vote-catching potential than do other groups previously closely linked to a specific party?

Table 16.1 showed that in recent elections DnA has been supported by between 30 and 50 per cent of LO's members. A look at the voter profiles of other parties shows that their support among members in traditionally associated organisations is not systematically weaker. Since business and employers organisations are not based on individual memberships, the co-variation between such organisation memberships and support for the Conservatives has not been computed. However, as a typical Conservative voter is a self-employed or higher functionary in the

201. The campaign included ads in major newspapers from individual unions. For more details on this campaign, see Allern and Saglie (2008).

private sector (Berglund 2003: 123), there is reason to believe that the level of support among organised employers and business people is not much lower than is the proportion of DnA voters in the trade union movement.

Also, there are parties that have a firmer grip on their traditional core voters than Labour. Table 16.3 shows, albeit with certain reservations due to the low N, that in 2001, members of primary-sector organisations were more inclined to vote for Sp than LO members were to vote for DnA: 63 per cent as opposed to 33 per cent. If we look at members of the Farmers' Union *only* – and not those primary-sector organisations (included in Table 16.3) which used to be more closely associated with the Labour Party – the potential for stable support appears even stronger. In 2001, almost 80 per cent of such voters preferred Sp to other parties. Ever since the 1950s, this figure has never been much lower than 60 per cent.

Table 16.3: Distribution of votes among members of primary-sector organisations, 1957–2001[1]

	1957	1965	1969	1973	1977	1981	1985	1989	1993	1997	2001
DnA	17.3	14.3	10.4	6.3	11.9	7.8	8.9	9.8	8.0	13.9	6.7
H	5.8	6.5	13.4	6.3	11.9	19.6	10.7	5.9	4.0	0.0	3.3
V	13.5	7.8	7.5	4.8	4.8	5.9	1.8	5.9	2.0	2.8	0.0
Sp[2]	59.6	66.2	62.7	69.8	64.3	54.9	62.5	47.1	76.0	66.7	63.3
KrF	3.8	3.9	4.5	11.1	4.8	7.8	10.7	9.8	4.0	8.3	10.0
SV	–	1.3	1.5	1.6	0.0	0.0	1.8	5.9	4.0	5.6	10.0
FrP	–	–	–	0.0	0.0	2.0	1.8	11.8	2.0	0.0	3.3
Others	0.0	0.0	0.0	0.0	2.4	2.0	1.8	3.9	0.0	2.8	3.3
N	52	77	67	63	42	51	56	51	50	36	30

1 Includes the Norwegian Farmers' Union (*Norges Bondelag*), the Norwegian Farmers' and Smallholders' Union (*Norges bonde- og småbrukarlag*) and the Fishermen's Association (*Norsk Fiskarlag*). The Norwegian Forest Owners' Association (*Norges Skogeierforbund*) is not included, as it has not been applied as a separate alternative every year.

2 Includes members who voted for joint lists between the Centre Party (the Farmers' Party) and the Conservative Party in 1957.

Source: The Norwegian Election Studies

Likewise, it seems as if the organised core voters of KrF up to now have contributed significantly to the party's relatively stable share of votes in general (see Figure 1, Appendix E). Occasionally, religious organisations have endorsed the party before general elections (see Chapter 11), and about 70 per cent of teetotallers and religious affiliates in south-western Norway have steadily supported KrF (Bjørklund 2001: 45). The regional dimension has weakened, but the relationship between membership in religious organisations and support for KrF remains very strong. In fact, support among organised religious voters is today much stronger than is the correlation between LO membership and DnA voting (Berglund 2003: 123, 126–7). Since KrF has a closer relationship than other parties have with their traditional associates, this can be interpreted as supporting the general hypothesis of correspondence between closeness and benefits.

The Liberals' lack of significant links with the traditional counter-cultural organisations – the farmers', language and teetotallers' movement – matches their vote-mobilising potential among such groups. By the 1950s, party secessions had already led to the associated traditional core voters preferring other parties. Active users of *nynorsk* tend to support the Liberals (see Chapter 2), but the correlation is not significant according to Norwegian election studies. After the Second World War, the Liberals' voter profile has generally been vague (Berglund 2003: 130), and the incentive for reconsolidating historical links has similarly been weak – the party would more likely benefit from establishing links with new groups. Thus, we can note correspondence between vote-catching potential and closeness, but it is not very strong.

Thus far, however, our analysis has ignored one highly relevant factor: the size of organisation's membership. Obviously, a large share of votes in a particular segment need not mean a great number of votes. Just as the number of core voters has declined, the number of organised ones might be limited. Table 1 in Appendix E presents the development of membership figures in the economic organisations within the labour market and of the total number of individuals entitled to vote. There is little doubt that LO connects the Labour Party with a substantial part of the electorate in a comparative perspective. The total number of members in LO has increased, from about 540,000 in 1955 to about 830,000 in 2004. Hence, given that relatively few LO members are below the voting age, the trade union movement still represents a significant proportion of the 3.4 million people who constitute the Norwegian electorate. Despite the decline of blue-collar workers and the increase of white-collar employees, LO has survived as the largest individual federation in Norway.

In contrast, the employers', business and trade organisations do not connect the Conservatives directly with individual voters at all, as these are based on collective company membership. Moreover, there are, of course, more employees than there are employers. Hence, there can be no doubt that the Conservative Party reaches fewer voters in absolute terms through its traditional associate than does Labour. The Confederation of Norwegian Enterprise (NHO) is not able to mobilise large voter groups as LO can.

Membership figures also reveal that the vote-mobilising potential of the Centre Party in agricultural organisations is, in practice, significantly weaker than DnA's potential among LO members. Farmers are loyal voters, but this is a small occupational group (see Chapter 6), and organisational density was only around 50 per cent in the mid-1980s (Steen 1988: 254). In the late 1950s, the then party leader of Labour, Einar Gerhardsen, questioned the usefulness of links with small-scale farmers (Bergh 1987: 52). In 1965, only 3.7 per cent of farm workers were organised in the Farmers' Union compared to 2.7 per cent in 1998 (Allern and

Heidar 2001). Table 1 in Appendix E shows that even if we include the members of the Smallholders' Union, only about 66,900 people, out of 3.4 million voters in Norway, were organised farmers in 2004. Thus, there are more than twelve times as many LO members as there are members of farmers' unions. Sp does not reach a large number of voters through its traditionally associated organisations.

By contrast, KrF's relationships with religious organisations are somewhat closer than the size of the organised religious electorate might indicate. According to Andersen (1999: 46), the number of individuals affiliated to religious organisations has not decreased significantly in recent decades, but these membership figures are certainly also modest compared with the figures for LO membership: in 1983, 9 per cent of all Norwegians belonged to religious organisations; by 1997 the figure was only 7 per cent (Andersen 1999).[202] To sum up, the correspondence between the degree of closeness to traditional associates and vote-catching potential appears to be more systematic when we take account of actual membership figures.

Second, the question is whether the financial and organisational support provided by these other old interest groups makes the relative utility of DnA links with LO seem weaker or stronger. Historically, the non-socialist parties have, and in particular the Conservatives, been funded by business and trade organisations. After the Second World War, a secret donors' cartel – *Libertas* – was established (see Chapters 6 and 8). Today, income accounts show that the Conservatives receive significant financial donations from individual businesspeople, but from Table 16.2 we saw that they were provided with only half as much monetary support by business and industry organisations as was the Labour Party between 1998 and 2004 by LO and its unions (NOK 23.7m, about €3.0m).

Nor is there reason to believe that the Conservatives receive as much organisational support from these groups as does DnA from the trade unions: business and industry have maintained a less partisan profile in elections after the Second World War than the trade union movement (see Valen and Katz 1964: 309–10). The Farmers' Union has not funded Sp since 1938. It is true that co-operative agricultural organisations have funded Sp (Allern and Heidar 2001: 131–2), but not any longer. The Liberals receive nothing from the groups with which they were once fairly strongly linked. Neither does the Christian People's Party, which has relatively strong links with religious organisations, but is not as close to such groups as is the Labour Party to the trade unions.

Again, the general usefulness of financial benefits can be questioned, as all the major parties now receive considerable public support. Moreover, the Confederation of Norwegian Enterprise (NHO) was willing to donate significant amounts to non-socialist parties for a long time *without* having well-organised links for contact. However, no doubt DnA's links with the trade union movement are far more useful in terms of financial and organisational support than are other parties' links with their traditional associates. DnA get monetary and organisa-

---

202. In contrast, about 85 per cent of the population was affiliated to the State Church in 2004 (Statistics Norway 2005, see http://www.ssb.no/emner/07/02/10/trosamf/tab-2004-10-21-02.html).

tional support from, and gains access to, relatively large voter groups through LO, and the competition for these votes is certainly keener than the struggle for many other old core voters. Taken together, there is a significant degree of correspondence between the degrees of closeness to traditional associates and benefits. The steep fall in recent elections inspired DnA to place special emphasis on this voter group prior to the 2005 elections. However, it is also a fact that the trade unions are not a particularly reliable source of votes today, which raises the issue of whether the benefits actually exceed the costs of the relationship.

Costs of Closeness: Labour and the Confederation of Trade Unions

Parties will, according to a cost-benefit model, also react to what they have to 'pay' for the interest group support. I specifically hypothesised that *the costs of the relatively close relationships – integrated relationships or alliances – with interest groups, in terms of the risk of repelling other voter groups and/or coalition partners and policy sacrifices, tend to be fairly limited in general (compared to benefits).* Does DnA's relatively close relationship with the trade unions match this pattern?

Let us begin by looking at the risk of repelling voters. In the early 2000s, DnA strategy documents emphasise that the party must appeal to salaried employees in general: 'In order to remain a social democratic people's party our organisation has to be especially oriented towards the major groups of wage earners (…). At the same time, we have to reach the growing number of voters with higher education' (Arbeiderpartiet 2002a: 18, my translation). Thus, for DnA, it is of paramount importance that their organisational strategies do not push less traditional voter groups away. Already in the late 1960s, Martin (1974: 83–4) observed that the social democratic elite were dissatisfied with the political usefulness of collective union membership for several reasons. For example, party functionaries pointed to the membership's low popularity and legitimacy among various groups in the population, including white-collar employees. As noted, the rule that all party members 'shall' be members of an LO union was relaxed as early as 1969 (*ibid*: 81).

Later, as shown in previous chapters, the Confederation of Trade Unions has had some success in recruiting new groups, including white-collar employees (see also below). Consequently, the conflict between recruiting old core voters and the new middle class was probably reduced. However, there is little doubt that a close relationship with LO and unions risks alienating a significant number of potential voters in the 2000s who do not feel closely attached to the labour movement as a whole. Labour Party members are themselves affiliated to several other interest groups (Heidar and Saglie 2002: 274) and represents a coalition of numerous, conflicting political interests, values and attitudes (*ibid*: Chapter 5). The fairly close relationship with the trade unions, and the donations from this source, are still regularly criticised in public debate, and causes concern internally for signalling that the party is committed, and indebted, to LO, in particular after the election. But exactly *to what extent* many voters today find the existing links and monetary support hard to accept is not clear.

Whether Labour has faced a significant risk of repelling potential coalition partners is also a somewhat moot point. Until 2005, the Norwegian Labour Party had never previously entered any coalition; the party leadership had for a long time preferred minority one-party governments. So most likely, the concern for other parties' views has traditionally not been a significant part of Labour's utility calculation. However, throughout the 1980s and 1990s, Labour's minority governments had to make frequent ad hoc parliamentary deals with other parties. Therefore, by the end of the 1990s the party leader, Thorbjørn Jagland, advocated more binding co-operation with other parties (Takvam 2002: 128).[203] So when predicting that the links with unions would wither after the 2001 election he pointed to the need for coalition partners: 'We are prepared to form a coalition with other parties. Consequently, we cannot have meetings with LO where we discuss the cases the cabinet is dealing with on a weekly basis. As a movement, we have a lot to talk about. But we cannot deliberate cabinet cases with others in advance. That's not possible' (quoted in Foss 2005, my translation). The attempt in 2001 to recover alone as a party of government failed. In 2004, the party leadership made it officially clear that it was now willing to negotiate with others about office (Allern and Aylott 2009). So, even if the joint 'Co-operation Committee' survived, despite tensions, the subsequent coalition formation in 2005 (with the Socialist Left and the Centre Party), it is likely that Labour in the 2000s finds close relations with LO potentially costly in this particular sense.[204]

Finally, the question is what LO 'charges' for its resources in terms of policy rewards. Closeness to particular interest groups entails the risk of creating expectations which may later collide with other significant policies. As explained, it is beyond the scope of this study to assess the size by systematic comparison of the alleged 'policy rewards'. However, evidence exists at a general level suggesting that the relationship in terms of policy influence is not particularly unbalanced on the whole (cf. Chapter 15). On the one hand, the 'freedom debate' in the 1980s (see Chapter 7) revealed tensions between blue-collar and white-collar segments. Some unions and internal factions have accused DnA of scrapping its social-democratic core values (Heidar 1993: 70; Taylor 1993: 139; Takvam 2002; Hågensen 2004: 145–6). In recent years, the issue of the future financing of the Norwegian welfare state has intensified the potential for conflict within the social democratic movement as a whole. So the discrepancy between party interests and union demands might have increased. In public, we have witnessed individual unions 'threatening' to end their financial donations if the party does not adapt to its policy views on specific issues (see Takvam 2002; *LO Aktuelt* 20.11.05). Accordingly, DnA has been frequently 'accused' in the public debate for being

203. Labour even resigned from government in the elections in 1997, even though it won most votes, because the vote narrowly failed to meet a threshold set by the party leader before the election campaign (36.9 per cent of the vote – the same percentage as the preceding general elections). The backdrop to the party leader's message was a general concern about how functional minority governments were. By setting a specific threshold, a large party like Labour could reasonably hope to catch more of the floating voters (Allern and Aylott 2009).

204. Recently, the leader of the Liberals has publicly stated that a coalition with Labour is precluded partly due to the close DnA-LO relationship (*Aftenposten* 18.09.09).

heavily influenced by the trade union movement in recent years (e.g. *Aftenposten* 03.09.05).[205]

On the other hand, it has generally been argued that the trade unions have not been a strong hindrance for DnA's long-term ideological rejuvenation in Norway. As Taylor (1993) argues, LO has *itself* played an active part in DnA's ideological reform processes in the 1980s (see Chapter 7): 'the trade unions recognized that unless they participated, '(...) the initiative would be surrendered to unsympathetic elements (....). The LO co-operated with a wide range of social movements avoid being branded as a sectional interest (....).' (*ibid*: 139). Thus, to some extent, the unions have developed policy views which could be combined with ideological 'modernisation' of the party policies as a whole. A recent study of the Norwegian pension reform, illustrates that compromises are made between DnA and LO in important issues; unions have not one-sidedly influenced the party's new pension policy (Allern, Bay and Saglie 2009: 57).

Indeed, it has also been argued that the integration of trade unions in Norwegian party politics and government is associated with unions de-emphasising the strategy of protests and strikes. Norway's trade union movement has historically identified more than narrow union interests as 'legitimate objects of union concern' (Millen 1963: 137–8). The wage moderation accepted by the trade union movement during the economic reform period in the 1970s and the 1980s, a series of moderate wage settlements (the so-called 'Solidarity Alternative', see Chapter 15) during the 1990s, and the follow-up agreement between DnA and LO in 2003, might have all contributed to the survival of the close relationship between the two. When asked to describe the party's approach to LO, the party secretary replied:

> There are two main reasons for DnA's choice of keeping a close relationship with the trade unions. First, there is a purely political dimension. In Norway, we are so lucky as to have a trade union movement that accepts responsibility for society as a whole, a federation which is community-oriented, not a pure interest group for its own members. The difference is in fact important. LO's agencies analyse power structures, explain social development, and identify future challenges very much along the same lines as DnA does. These shared ideas constitute the basis for our co-operation (...). Without the support of the trade union movement we wouldn't be strong enough to mobilize sufficient democratic support *[to reach our political goals*]. Second, it provides us with

205. What happened after the formation of a red-green coalition in 2005 is beyond the scope of this study, but it is worth mentioning that the issue of political influence was again much discussed in public. The DnA-LO Co-operation Committee was accepted by the other parties, but the chair of LO, Gerd-Liv Valla, chose not to keep disagreements with the party leadership behind the committee's closed doors and confronted the red-green government on several contested issues in public. The issue of sick-leave regulations caused particularly severe tensions: A proposal to reduce this benefit, which seemed poorly prepared by the government, was interpreted as an 'ultimatum' by both Norwegian employees' and employers' organisations. For once, they joined forces to make the government back down. The party-union relationship appeared increasingly strained at elite level (Tranøy 2007; Valla 2007). In March 2007, Valla was compelled to resign as LO chair after a long-term conflict with an employee in LO's headquarters.

> parliamentary power. This view is not anti-democratic. The direction of social development is a result of various forces pulling in different directions. The combination of the number of LO members, LO's actual strength and Labour's electoral results may prevent social changes which are neither in the trade unions' interest, nor serve those we represent [in the Storting]. That's the basic foundation for the party-trade union movement co-operation (Kolberg 2003 [interview]).

Hence, the party secretary, as strategist, points to a basic ideological consensus underpinning close relations, but he also emphasises the trade unions' willingness to pursue more than sectional policy goals. No definite conclusions can be drawn, of course, but it is beyond doubt that the relationship involves two-way influence in the sense that both sides are still being compelled to compromise in certain issues (cf. Chapter 15). So even though conflicts today seem to arise not only on the borderline of trade union-party interest, the 'price' LO 'charges' for its support in terms of 'union-friendly policies' is not necessarily very high for Labour. The party leadership itself argues that a relatively close relationship with LO is a safer road to office and political influence than the more independent path.

This said, it is beyond doubt that the overall cost-benefit balance of Labour's relative closeness to the trade union movement is fragile. The various variable disadvantages seem to have increased over time and the links were critically evaluated at the turn of the Millennium. It is one thing to communicate more frequently with the trade union movement than with others, and something quite different to maintain organised links like a liaison committee with a particular interest group. At least, the exact relative degree of closeness does not seem to *perfectly* match a utility calculation for office- and pragmatic policy-seeking purposes.

The Possible Impact of Variation in Primary Goals

Finally, as regards closeness to particular interest groups, the question remains as to whether variation in primary goals might add pieces to the puzzle. Up to now, we have assumed that the parties discussed seek office intrinsically and/or to allow for policy implementation. Purely policy-seeking parties, in contrast, generally avoid office to cultivate their role as an ideologically 'pure' opposition to the political establishment or the political system as a whole. Accordingly, I hypothesised that *for office-seeking parties, the less useful the relationship with a given interest group for achieving executive office, the more likely they are to choose distance. Whereas a party involved in a relatively close relationship that in sum decreases the chances of accessing office on a regular basis, tends to be an 'ideologically purist' party.* Indications of general goal-orientations are provided by the parties' electoral strategies and ideological development

Can such variation explain why Labour keeps strong links with LO and its unions even if the utility of the degree of closeness can be questioned? Most likely not, as it is hard to define Labour as an 'ideologically purist' party. Despite its weaker parliamentary position from the 1960s, Labour has formed numerous minority governments by making frequent ad hoc parliamentary deals with other parties both to the left and right. The ideological long-term development of the

Norwegian Labour Party, as described in Chapter 7, strengthens the impression of a pragmatic party that gives priority to continued access to office above not diluting its ideological profile. On the other hand, the relationship with LO is not an example of links that clearly decrease the chances of accessing office on a regular basis. Hence, the extent to which the hypothesis related to variation in primary goals is weakened by this finding can be questioned as well.[206]

Degree of Closeness and Range in General: Variation According to Usefulness?
To give an indication of whether Norwegian parties' *overall* relationship with interest groups seem to vary according to relative usefulness, we shall now have a look at major characteristics of parties' closeness to/distance from the interest group universe as a whole, and variation in range of party relationships. The hypothesis was that *a party with relatively close relationships with interest groups in general tends to be provided with more benefits (votes, financial resources, organisational support) from different interest groups than are parties marked by general distance from the interest-group community,* and that *a party with a relatively narrow range of relationships with interest groups tends to be provided with significant benefits from comparatively few organisation categories, or particularly great benefits from one specific interest group.* Does the major variation in Norwegian parties' overall relationship with interest groups match this pattern? As noted above, the Liberals (V) prefer to maintain some distance from the interest-group community as whole, whereas the Socialist Left Party (SV) is marked by fairly close relationships with numerous interest groups within different categories. However, as such an analysis involves numerous weaker and not so costly links, most attention will be paid to the benefits which parties may derive from having fairly organised links with interest groups.

Degree of Closeness of Relationships with Interest Groups in General
As regards the supply of votes from interest groups, available data do not allow us to conclude on the level of voter support among organisation members in general, but a new look at Tables 16.1 and 16.3, and an examination of Tables 16.4 and 16.5, may give some indications.

Due to the low N, the figures in Table 16.4 must be interpreted with caution, and differences between individual years have to be ignored. Yet, there can be no doubt that the Liberals' vote-mobilising potential among labour market organisations is generally weaker than that of most other political parties in Norway. The party's share of votes has declined among members of LO (see Table 16.2); those affiliated to independent employees' organisations (see Table 16.4), and among voters organised in primary-sector organisations (see Table 16.3). About 6 per cent, or less, voted for the Liberals in these organisations in the late 1990s and the early 2000s. As the Liberals are marked by an indistinct voter profile (Berglund 2003:

206. The observation also indicates that it not easy to tell whether it matters that parties are in government or in opposition as, for example, Minkin (1991: 639–41) has suggested. Labour seems not to have weakened the link with LO and its unions in recent years depending on whether it has been in or out of government (see Chapter 7).

130, see Chapter 9), support among employers and business people is probably at a similarly low level. By contrast, the Socialist Left Party, which is characterised by closer relationship with numerous organisations than many other parties, is generally more strongly supported than the Liberals among organisation members.

However, the differences are not so large, and do correspond to the *general* level of voter support for the two parties. Hence, it could be argued that the Liberals' particularly limited share of votes primarily reflects the steep and long-lasting fall in the party's general electoral performance since 1969 (see Figure 1, Appendix E). In fact it seems reasonable to ask why the drop in votes has not instead *stimulated* the Liberals to systematically seek more contact with various kinds of interest groups. As argued in Chapter 5, links with interest groups might also be established to improve the party's vote-catching potential according to exchange models of politics. According to SV's party secretary, decreasing membership figures increase the need for such links: The membership organisation is not representative of the party's voters (Solhjell 2003 [interview]).

Table 16.4: Distribution of votes among members of employees' organisations/federations outside LO 1957–2001[1]

	1957	1965	1969	1973	1977	1981	1985	1989	1993	1997	2001
DnA	24.5	20.7	27.1	21.1	26.4	21.6	21.3	17.0	32.2	31.8	23.0
H	42.9	44.8	31.8	32.4	36.8	48.3	38.8	32.8	19.9	23.4	31.0
V[4]	14.2	16.1	20.0	4.2	5.7	7.8	10.1	8.9	6.3	5.7	5.3
Sp[3]	2.0	5.7	9.4	8.5	10.4	2.6	7.3	6.5	15.0	5.7	5.8
KrF	16.3	10.3	9.4	8.5	13.2	7.8	11.2	10.9	10.5	14.6	10.2
SV[2]	–	1.1	1.2	9.8	1.9	6.0	6.2	17.4	11.5	9.6	14.6
FrP	–	–	–	2.8	0.9	3.4	2.8	4.5	2.4	5.0	7.1
Others	0.1	1.1	1.2	12.7	4.7	2.6	2.3	2.0	2.1	4.2	3.1
N	49	87	85	71	106	116	178	247	286	261	226

1 There is a rupture in the time series in 1985. The table includes various independent employees' organisations until 1981. From 1985, the figures represent the Confederation of Vocational Unions (*Yrkesorganisasjonenes Sentralforbund*), the Confederation of Academic and Professional Unions in Norway (*Akademikernes Fellesorganisasjon* (until 2001) and the Federation of Norwegian Professional Associations (*Akademikerne* (from 2001)) and the Confederation of Higher Education Unions (*Utdanningsgruppenes Hovedorganisasjon* (from 2001), now the Confederation of Unions for Professionals *(Unio)*. Some independent organisations are probably excluded as it is not possible to distinguish memberships in independent employers' and employees' organisations.

2 Represents an alliance of SV, Communists and other left-wing groups in 1973.

3 Includes organisation members who voted for joint lists between the Centre Party (the Farmers' Party) and the Conservatives in 1957.

4 Includes organisation members who voted for joint lists between the Liberals and the Conservative Party in 1957.

Source: The Norwegian Election Studies

Moreover, the links discussed are not of the binding type, so the threshold for establishing them is fairly low: the benefits provided do not need to be very strong to exceed the costs. Finally, we observe that the two parties with the greatest electoral potential among labour market organisations, excluding primary-sector organisations, are the Conservatives and Labour, but these are not among those parties with the strongest organised links with interest groups in general. Of course, their support in the employee segment reflects the fact that these two are still among the largest Norwegian parties in terms of the total vote at elections. But this also suggests, as do the other findings, that Norwegian party organisations do not establish links particularly systematically according to the vote-catching potential among labour market organisations in general.

The party preferences of members of Norway's environmental organisations in the mid-1990s (see Table 16.5) strengthen the impression of not very strong correspondence between closeness to interest groups in general and the vote-mobilising potential of various parties in the interest-group community. Membership in several environmental groups has decreased in recent decades (Strømsnes 2001: 186), but such organisations represent important sources of information about the policy views associated with 'new politics'.

Table 16.5: Distribution of votes among members of environmental organisations, 1995[1]

	DnA	H	V	Sp	KrF	SV	FrP	Others	DK/NR[2]	N[4]
Old environmental organisations[3]	14.4	3.3	13.2	8.5	4.3	31.8	0.5	9.6	14.6	(3)
New environmental organisations[3]	16.7	9.1	12.6	7.4	1.5	24.4	4.8	10.8	12.7	(3)

1 The question asked was: 'Which party would you vote for if general elections were to be arranged tomorrow?' Please note that the fact that Labour Party was in power at the time the survey was conducted might have influenced the results (Strømsnes 2001: 294)

2 The Don't Know/No Response category includes respondents who refused to answer.

3 The category 'Old environmental organisations' includes the Norwegian Society for the Conservation of Nature/Friends of the Earth Norway (*Norges Naturvernforbund*), Nature and Youth (*Natur og Ungdom*, a member of Friends of the Earth), and the Future in Our Hands (*Framtiden i våre hender*). 'New environmental organisations' encompass the Bellona Foundation (*Miljøstiftelsen Bellona)*, Greenpeace and Green Warriors of Norway (*Norges Miljøvernforbund*)

4 The percentages show average support among members in the *three* individual organisations in each category (see note above).

Source: *Miljøvernundersøkelsen 1995*, in Strømsnes (2001: 292–5)

Table 16.5 shows that the Liberal Party is one of the political alternatives most widely supported by members of the environmental movement. In fact, according to Strømsnes' survey, support for the Liberals was ten times higher among members of environmental organisations than among the general Norwegian voting public in 1995 (Strømsnes 2001: 293–4). Nevertheless, the Liberals' organised attempts in the 1970s to establish links with environmental groups have not been followed up in the early 2000s. Thus, not even relatively *strong* vote-mobilising potential according to Liberal standards has resulted in significant organised links with interest groups. The Socialist Left was the party most extensively supported in the environmental movement in 1995, but it also emphasises contact with groups where the level of support is lower.

A closer look at the financial donations to parties from interest groups in recent years does not modify this general picture of a not very strong correspondence between the general degree of closeness to interest groups and the strength of benefits provided from the interest-group community (see Table 16.2). The Liberals' party organisation does not receive any monetary support, but this is due to a *deliberate* choice, as the party leadership has decided not to accept donations from organised interest groups. Nor does the generally closer relationship of the Socialist Left with interest groups seem to be driven by the prospect of financial and organisational support. The trade union movement has provided some support to SV in election years, but only to a limited extent. SV does not receive any benefit of this kind from other groups. Instead, the party has sponsored various ad hoc groups itself (Allern 2001). Of course, one cannot presuppose a perfect match, but based on a cost-benefit model one would expect a stronger correspondence than the one revealed as regards the general emphasis on organised links with interest groups.

Range of Relationships with Interest Groups

Finally, according to the rational choice model of costs and benefits, the actual range of more organised relationships with interest groups will also mirror variations in benefits (relative to costs) provided by interest groups outside the party's traditional subculture. If we concentrate on deliberate attempts at establishing organised links, the major finding to explore is the difference between the Centre Party, the Socialist Left Party and the Progress Party on the one hand, and the Conservatives and the Labour Party on the other.

As indicated above, this correspondence seems fairly limited. Tables 16.1 and 16.4 show us that SV and FrP, especially, have managed to recruit voters from LO and other employees' organisations in the early 2000s. But the tables also demonstrate that support for the two new parties is certainly weaker than are the Conservatives' and Labour's shares of votes outside old core segments. Hence, at least the range of relationships with labour market organisations does not appear to correspond to their inherent vote-catching potential. In fact, the Conservatives are the Norwegian party that attracts most support among voters affiliated to non-LO employees' organisations, albeit to a lessening degree. Furthermore, support for the Conservatives among LO members is generally higher after the 1980s than before that time. Yet, the Norwegian Conservative Party does not emphasise organised links with employees' organisations despite significant incentives for so doing. Meanwhile, support among new social movement organisations seems limited – fewer members of environmental organisations vote for the Conservatives than the Labour Party.

In the case of DnA, an additional question to ask is if the usual support among LO members compared to the share of votes among other organisations makes links with alternative groups seem almost superfluous. There is little doubt that the range of relationships is connected with the relative usefulness of Labour's traditional associate. Certainly, Table 16.1 shows that the share of votes for DnA in other employees' organisations has not increased along with the decrease of LO votes. The probability of trade union members voting for Labour is still significantly higher than in the case of other employees' organisations. Moreover, in the early 2000s, the largest union is the Norwegian Union of Municipal and General Employees (*Fagforbundet*), which organises municipal employees and auxiliary nurses. As in other European trade union movements (Koelble 1992), a shift towards public service employment and white-collar unions has taken place, weakening LO's cohesion. In other words, LO includes not only the traditional segment of blue-collar workers, but also clerks, members of the civil service, professionals and the like. Within local and state government, LO organised between 35 per cent and 50 per cent of the work force as of early 2004 (Løke and Pape 2004: 81).

Nonetheless, there is a strong argument that DnA, which defines itself as a welfare-oriented party for salaried employees in general, has experienced strong incentives to widen its network in the labour market. The organisational density of LO among salaried employees in general decreased from 50 per cent in 1955 to 29 per cent in 1998, whereas organisational density of alternative employees' organisations grew from about 10 per cent to 25 per cent during the same period (Stokke 2000: 17).[207] In comparison, the Swedish LO organised slightly over half, 53 per cent, of the work force in 1998 (Kjellberg 1998: 99).[208] LO is not as dominant as it used to be, or theoretically could have been: almost as many employees are organised elsewhere. Moreover, according to Berglund (2003: 123), the Labour Party's major challenge in elections over time has been to attract more voters with higher education. Interestingly, newer federations like Confederation of Vocational Unions (*Yrkesorganisasjonenes Sentralforbund*) and the Confederation of Unions for Professionals (*Unio*) also organise professions who are important to a social democratic welfare state, such as nurses and teachers. In 2001, the proportion of Labour voters among LO members approached that among those organised in alternative employees' organisations (see Tables 16.1 and 16.3). Hence, it seems unlikely that a successful Labour Party can primarily base its support on the more or less loyal voters organised in LO in the long run.

A brief look at benefits provided through financial and organisational support does not make the correspondence between range of relationships and variation in the potential utility seem stronger. Certainly, the Shipowners' Association has

207. These figures are based on lower membership figures than those presented in Table 1 in Appendix H, as members who are retired are excluded (Stokke 2000).

208. Norway's overall union density of 59 per cent is much lower than the case in Denmark and Sweden, where 80 per cent and 90 per cent of the workforce, respectively, belong to unions and professional organisations (ILO 2002b). The difference is probably mainly due to the different systems of unemployment insurance: In Sweden and Denmark the scheme is run by the unions, whereas in Norway it is managed directly by the state (Rothstein 1992).

started to finance the Progress Party and the trade union movement the Socialist Left Party (see Table 16.2). However, this new flow of benefits includes only a limited number of those organisations linked with FrP and SV and little money. In 1997, the Centre Party's national executive concluded, presumably on grounds of principle, that the party should generally reject future offers of financial support over a certain value. The decision has now been reversed – with limited economic result (Sundsbø 2003 [interview]). In other words, those parties that seem to have the most wide-ranging network of well-organised links are not supported financially by numerous interest groups.

The costs of relations are, as mentioned in Chapter 5, less relevant in such a summative analysis, but we suggested that *'office-seeking parties' are more likely to have a wide range of links than 'ideologically purist parties'*. However, it seems as if parties with the most distinct ideological profiles are in general among those with the widest range of (organised) links, not those parties who most closely approach the pragmatic 'catch-all model' in terms of voters – Labour and the Conservatives. Coalition formation and avoidance have usually been driven in Norway by pragmatic policy-seeking (Budge and Laver, 1993; Rommetvedt, 1991, 312, 1994, 246–7). The closest we get to an 'ideologically purist party' in Norway (until it finally decided to join a pre-electoral coalition in 2005) – the Socialist Left – places emphasis on establishing a wide-ranging organised network of links with interest groups. In any case, deviant goal-seeking does not explain why older parties seem less concerned with cultivating organised links to a wider range of interest groups.

Summary of Analysis

Political parties in Norway do assess their relationships with interest groups instrumentally in the light of party goals. Studying the major differences as regards closeness to particular interest groups, we have observed that relative closeness is positively correlated to the size of associated benefits and that the resources supplied are not clearly exceeded by the costs of closeness.

First, it is true that links with LO and its unions are much more useful for the Labour Party than for other parties, and the trade union movement certainly appears more valuable for DnA's office-seeking than is often assumed in the scholarly literature. To rephrase Minkin's (1991: 648) analysis of the British Labour Party: the abolition of links '(...) would not be an adjustment, it would be a metamorphosis involving the removal of contingents of mainly manual, service and clerical workers – groups who still make up a majority of the working population'. LO is by far the largest employees' confederation in Norway, and does also include white-collar workers. In addition, the electoral shock in 2001, and the decline of support of LO members in particular, stimulated the DnA leadership to appeal more specifically to the party's traditional core voters and re-emphasise the trade union connection. However, the voters affiliated to LO trade unions represent no guarantee of electoral success, numerous voters are organised elsewhere, and the value of monetary support does not constitute a significant share of total party revenues. The incentive for putting different employees' organisations on a more equal footing by weakening the links with LO seems fairly strong. Hence, the exact degree of closeness cannot fully be explained in terms of benefits for office-seeking purposes.

Second, we find support for the hypothesis that the strength of links with traditional associates will vary according to the extent of benefits, but again not unambiguously. The relative closeness of some parties does correspond to the electoral benefits, and the size of LO's membership figures renders links with the traditional associate more useful for DnA than for other parties. But there exist more loyal organised core voters, and other parties' links seem not to depend upon financial support.

Third, as regards the costs of the especially close DnA-LO relationship, we saw that closeness to trade unions do not necessarily imply radical policy rewards in the early 2000s. However, maintaining a relatively close relationship to LO has become more costly over time following the decrease of old voters, the need for coalition partners and increased tension in specific policy issues. The hypothesis related to variation in primary goals was not helpful as Labour is not an 'ideologically purist' party. Then again, the relationship with LO is not an example of links that clearly decrease the chances of accessing office on a regular basis.

Fourth, as regards the general degree of closeness, we have observed that the difference between the Socialist Left's overall strength of links with other organisations, and the Liberal Party's general distance from interest groups, do not systematically match the extent of provided or potential benefits. SV seems to have established links fairly independent of whether the specific interest groups can provide the party organisation with significant resources, whereas the Liberal Party's poor election results probably make all options seem worth trying.

Finally, we saw that the correlation between differences in the range of more organised relationships and the degree of utility for office-seeking purposes seems fairly weak. Those parties that appear to have the most wide-ranging networks of fairly organised links are not the ones most generously supported by interest groups in terms of votes and financial donations. Moreover, we noted that SV, which until the 2005 elections could be characterised as primarily a policy-seeking party, has developed organised links with various interest groups.

To conclude, the analysis of benefits and costs provides some support for the general expectation based on rational choice theory that variation in party relationships is largely about balances of costs and benefits. The hypotheses derived from the cost-benefit model certainly take us a fair step forward towards explaining the major variation revealed. This said, the analysed party-group relationships do not vary as systematically as expected if party-interest group relations were purely about utility maximisation. Limits do exist to the correspondence between benefits, costs and patterns of relationships. Some parties are more closely related to interest groups than a cost-benefit analysis would indicate, whereas others keep their distance even though it would seem that they could benefit from rapprochement with interest groups, or at least links with more organisations. So there is more to the relationship between parties and interest groups than cost-benefit calculations only. We see that it is somewhat difficult to calculate the rewards and disadvantages even in regard to links with single organisations like LO. Hence, the question arises as to what can explain the deviations from the assumed rational course.

VARIATIONS IN RELATIONSHIPS: ACCORDING TO HISTORICAL LEGACY?

Informed by the perspective based on historical institutionalism, the question is, above all, whether history might add more pieces to the puzzle. It was hypothesised that a *party that used to have a relatively close relationship – nearly an integrated relationship – with a specific kind of interest group is less likely to have a fairly distant relationship with its old associate(s), and a wide-ranging network of links with others, than are parties that used to have more distant relationships historically.* So the question first is whether historical structures might throw more light on the difference in closeness to traditional associates between the Labour Party and the other long-established parties.

Closeness to Individual Kinds of Interest Groups: Partly Following Historical Paths?

DnA, the Conservatives and KrF are among the parties which have been most strongly linked with specific interest organisations *over time,* but no party in Norway has enjoyed links as long-lasting and strong with any interest group as those of the Labour Party with the trade unions. So in this sense the variation in today's closeness to particular groups, the traditional associates, may reflect historical patterns: does Labour's experience of particularly strong connections at an early stage appear to have created a more binding relationship at a later one?

The Liberals' links with social movements had already eroded after the party splits in the 1920s and 1930s, and the Centre Party and the Farmers' Union had significantly distanced themselves from each other back in the 1940s. Accordingly, no other Norwegian party presents the significance of its original relationships in similar terms as does Labour, whether in party documents or through the descriptions given by key informants (see Solhjell 2003; Hole 2003; Mo 2003; Nyhus 2003; Sundsbø 2003 [interviews]). Hence, it seems as if the historical legacy is particularly 'heavy' in the case of Labour. The links themselves might well have given Labour a chain of benefits over time, which in turn makes the closeness hard to relinquish, and despite present circumstances calling for a close to the negative cost-benefit balance. For example, LO collective membership in DnA has probably contributed to the enduring electoral dominance Labour in Norway (cf. Poguntke 2002; Sundberg 2003: 94). Without this arrangement, it seems likely that the Social Democratic vote would have declined and the control over government weakened sooner. LO would, perhaps at an earlier point in time, have needed to invest significant resources in having more than one, prevailing relationship (cf. Allern *et al.* 2007: 629). As a consequence, the costs of reversal appear to be uncertain. In other words, a *historical* record of utility might, at least partly, explain why Labour did decide, around 2002, to give the fairly close relationship with LO the benefit of the doubt.

Moreover, even if this is hard to demonstrate, the continued existence of a close party-union relationship may reflect that the well-organised links have had a self-reinforcing effect over time (cf. Thelen 1999: 393). Historically, a division of labour developed within the labour movement and it could be argued that DnA and LO have adapted their general strategies to involvement in a close party-union relationship. For example, the relatively low level of actual contact with other employees' organisations at the elite level can be seen as an indication that the Labour elite do not emphasise efficient interaction with different, and non-partisan, groups of white-collar employees itself. When asked whether the party ought to have 'formal agreements with organisations sharing the party's overall goals for the development of society', only 30 per cent of the Labour elite answer that they fully agree with this statement. Thus, there is some scepticism of the closeness to the trade union movement among the top party elite. Party members, who argue that Labour needs to put other employees' organisations on at least an equal footing with LO, do exist, and they sometimes articulate this view internally and in public (see *Aftenposten* 18.01.02; 06.11.02; Gerhardsen 2002). Nonetheless, the active opposition to the leadership's choice of re-consolidation of the relationship with LO has been limited.[209] It seems as if the relative strength of links to the trade unions is to some extent taken for granted.

Meanwhile, we might also notice, even though a separate hypothesis on the party organisational origin was not formulated, that the Liberals and, in particular, the Conservatives have a legacy of relatively strong parliamentary groups compared to the externally created Labour Party, Centre Party and Christian People's Party. Norway's Conservative Party has a tradition of emphasising a civil society independent of the state, but not of well-organised links with interest groups. It has always been ambivalent towards its links with business and industry organisations. Despite the development of the extra-parliamentary organisation, the Conservatives never became a full-blown mass membership party of the classic, socialist type (see Chapter 8). Correspondingly, the secretary-general emphasises that party headquarters is only to a small extent involved in day-to-day politics (Hole 2003 [interview]). In this particular sense the cadre party structure has survived the twentieth century. Thus, the relevance of well-organised relations with interest groups outside the Storting is simply more limited at the national level for the Conservatives' – and perhaps also for the Liberals' – than for left-wing parties, the Progress Party or the Centre Party. All in all, historical legacies do seem to add a piece to the puzzle.

209. Even though collective membership was already being criticised in the 1960s, the arrangement was not abolished until 1992 (Allern and Heidar 2001). According to the party secretary, the major argument then was that collective members were few and not very active (Kolberg 2003 [interview]). Opponents to the decision were to be found in Oslo. A large share of the collectively affiliated members belonged to this particular branch of DnA. Abolishing the practice of collective membership would cause a loss of revenues as well as a reduced number of mandates to the party congress. In contrast, the youth organisation argued that the formal positions of these members did not correspond to their level of activity (Heidar and Saglie 1994; *Aktuelt Perspektiv* 12.09.92). When the party congress decided to reconsolidate the link with LO in 2002 after an internal evaluation, the opposition seemed weak (see Chapter 7).

Range of Relationships: Limited Impact of Organisational Legacy?

Second, it was suggested that the general variation in range of links with interest groups might be constrained by the strength of historical links to a particular interest group. The cost-benefit analysis revealed that several old parties – like the Conservatives, the Liberals and the Labour Party – have a narrower network of such links than one could expect. Can possible historical trajectories throw light on these deviations?

Historically, the Liberals, the Conservatives, as well as the Labour Party, had more or less close relations with particular interest groups. But so had the Centre Party and the Christian People's Party – and the new Socialist Left party – which are today all characterised by a fairly wide range of organised links with interest groups. Moreover, the Liberals soon weakened their links after the other centrist parties were established, and the Conservatives have not a particularly close relationships with their traditionally associate today. Neither does it seem relevant for the range of links whether a party emphasises extra-parliamentary activity or not. Hence, 'organisational legacies' is not able to explain much of the seemingly non-instrumental variation in today's range of relationships.

However, as DnA was involved in a particularly intimate historical relationship, and has kept many of the old links, it can be argued that DnA and LO have, to a certain extent, gradually come to *depend on* the contact that takes place, for example, in their Joint Committee. It is interesting to note that, confronted with the difference between the links with LO and other employees' organisations, the DnA party secretary replies:

> That is, indeed, a good question, and it is difficult to answer. Because, if we applied my theory as a whole we should have had fairly close relationships with the whole spectrum of employees' organisations. That's implicit. I don't think I get closer to an answer than that this is still unexplored terrain which we have to think more about. We are according to Norwegian standards a historical movement. We have existed as a party for 116 years. Then it is impossible to avoid tradition and inheritance; it is a part of the organization. In my view, our weakness is – because the wallpaper in this room has been too solid – that we have not managed to be sufficiently critical against the social development (….). Hence, you lose your grip on the spirit of the age. That is why young people think the Labour Party is grey and dull. Because we have been a party that has developed *[the society/welfare state]* (…). But in organizational terms, this means that we need time. One cannot move from the established – our heyday – into a new period without preserving the good elements of the old tradition. If we rush, we risk decimating ourselves as a party organization. And this point also applies to the relationship with interest groups (Kolberg 2003 [interview]).

Therefore, it could be argued that DnA and LO have not as systematically cultivated relations with other interest groups and parties and perhaps have become used to reliance on interaction with each other.

Summary of Analysis

In sum, some support was found for the secondary hypothesis that a party that was once involved in a close relationship with an interest group is less likely to be characterised by fairly distant relationships with a wide range of other interest groups. The particularly strong degree of closeness between Labour and the trade unions seems to have, historically, generated a series of benefits that created a trajectory which is simply hard to leave, both as regards closeness to the traditional associate and the range of organised links. Despite the early end of overlapping organisational structures at the national level, DnA and LO seem, like partners in any fairly happy cohabitation, to have grown attached and become mutually dependent on each other. Meanwhile, the Conservatives and Liberals tradition of a stronger emphasis on the parliamentary groups, makes well-organised extra-parliamentary links with interest groups less pertinent for their party leaderships. Historical legacy and paths might also throw light on why Labour has not followed up the aim of establishing a wide-ranging organised network despite the more limited utility for electoral purposes of the relationship with the unions', and the rest of the labour movements. However, historical constraints seem not able to *generally* explain the seemingly non-instrumental variation in today's *range* of more or less organised links.

For the sake of simplicity, the assumption that current political events might impinge on the relationship as well, was not explored. Yet, it might in conclusion be added that recent developments in other Scandinavian countries have presented DnA with examples of a more positive correlation between electoral results and links with trade unions around the turn of the Millennium. As shown in Allern, Aylott and Christiansen (2007), the Swedish Social Democratic election 'disaster' in 1998, where the party lost votes mainly to the left, was blamed on the unions' lukewarm attitude to the party cause in the campaign. The electoral success in 2002 (39.8 per cent of the vote) was, in contrast, preceded by emphasis on the party-union relationship. Thus, experiences from the primary 'sister party' of Norwegian Labour suggest to DnA's leadership that electoral success might at the present correlate positively with closeness to trade unions, or at least with trade union support. Indeed, the party secretary emphasises that DnA's leadership looked more to Sweden than Denmark, where the party-union link has further weakened, in evaluating the relationship with LO a few years ago (Kolberg 2003 [interview]).

VARIATIONS IN RELATIONSHIPS: CORRESPONDING TO VALUES AND INSTITUTIONALISATION?

Parties are primarily goal-driven organisations, with varying organisational origins, but they also represent collections of norms, routines and understandings. In light of normative institutionalism, the question is whether the deviations from a rational course are related to variation in party-specific values and 'party institutionalisation'. Informed by the normative perspective, original party values may limit the strategic options available to later party leaders: to gain and maintain legitimacy the party leadership avoid means which can be as seen as detrimental to the party's *raison d'être* by its supporters, at least in a party organisation's formative years. Hence, it was first hypothesised that *a party that was originally established independently of well-defined interests is more likely to be marked by relative distance (more or less organised ad hoc contact) from its old associate(s), and a wide range of links, than are parties originally established to promote the interests of a particular social group or cause.* But also that an *institutionalised (old) party tends to have a relatively distant relationship (more or less organised ad hoc contact) from the originally associated interest group(s), and a relatively wide-ranging network of links, compared to new parties established as organisational tools for a particular social group or cause.*

Moreover, parties can be constrained by contemporary normative expectations to parties, but most importantly here, be coloured by the party's own concept of 'appropriate' party-interest group relationships. First, *a party with relatively close relationships with one or more kinds of interest groups tends to emphasise interest representation most, whereas a party characterised by relative distance from the interest-group community tends primarily to promote its governing role.* Fourth, a *party with a relatively wide-ranging network of links with interest groups tends to emphasise its governing role, whilst a party characterised by a relatively narrow range of relationships tends primarily to promote interest representation.* While the former set of hypotheses mainly describe intra-party constraints, the latter set point to accommodation to norms instead of rational goal-seeking. The following sections start by looking at closeness to/distance from traditional associates and other groups, before turning to the range of relations. Finally, the overall pattern of relationships is discussed.

Closeness to Traditional Associates: Constrained by Values, not Institutionalisation

Do differences in the parties' *ideological origins,* in terms of group-orientation, correspond to differences between the Labour Party and the other old parties' closeness to traditional associates, as the first 'normative' secondary hypothesis suggests?

In contrast to the Liberals and the Conservatives, Labour was originally a 'class party' for a particular social group. As described by Duverger's *mass party type,* links with unions was one the party's defining features and a part of the original ideology. So the difference between Labour and the other old parties might reflect that the latter were originally established independently of well-defined interests, while DnA was not. However, the other parties that emerged as a parties for well-defined social segments, for example the Christian People's Party and the Centre Party, have less strong links to their traditional associate today than has the Labour Party. The Centre Party had in fact already weakened its traditional links towards the middle of the twentieth century. Thus, original ideological differences seem to be less influential than the strength of historical connections.

Still, it could be argued that the particular closeness of Labour is related to an ideological constraint as the party-union relationship seems to have served as a specially unifying symbol in the eyes of its supporters. The development of the welfare state was a project that ideologically united the Confederation of Trade Unions and Labour throughout much of the twentieth century. Illustratively, the normative critique from right and left-wing groups of DnA's links with LO has usually been interpreted as no less than an attempt to undermine social democracy (Zachariassen 1966: 7; Martin 1974: 83–4; Bjørgum 1999). In one of DnA's organisational evaluations, the party-union relationship is assessed in the following way: 'The Norwegian Labour Party and the Confederation of Trade Unions have common, basic goals for social development. Historically, this *[consensus]* has formed the basis of a close party-union relationship. This co-operation has influenced the development of essential fields of society during the modern history of Norway' (Arbeiderpartiet 2002a: 19).[210] The relationship between DnA and LO seems to be regarded by some quarters as being a part of the *social democratic project itself.* When commenting on the non-socialist parties' critique of DnA's close relationship with LO, the party secretary argues:

> But they understand that if they can sideline the trade union movement, they will strengthen the social power which they value the most; the market forces. Because a social democratic democracy and trade union democracy is built on a strong popular democracy. And this implies elections, as mentioned earlier, but also political processes at the intersection between the political parties and civil society. (…). It *[the relationship]* bothers them, because it is a power base for the development of social democracy (…). When we choose to keep the links, the goal is to accomplish these two conditions for democracy. That is what this is really about.

Hence, even though cost-benefit calculations are being made, the choice of having particularly strong links with LO and LO Unions is also, at least, presented as connected with the party's *raison d'être*. It appears to be not only one out of many possible means by which the party may efficiently pursue its goals; it also seems as a significant confirmation of the ideological values that keep the organisation together beyond selective incentives. The symbolic and sentimental value of the party-union relationship is still fairly strong (cf. Minkin 1991: 653). To rephrase Minkin (1991: 649), the closeness functions perhaps as a 'public testimony' of the 'hands who gave themselves political voices'. Closeness to LO reflects, at least for factions within the party, what is sometimes referred to as the Labour Party's individual 'soul' (*sjel*). So even if the party leadership wants to abolish old links for the sake of more efficient goal-seeking, they might find it hard to present the decision as 'legitimate'. The party leadership may well have hesitated

210. A similar point was made by DnA leader Jens Stoltenberg when he, as Prime Minister, gave a speech at a conference arranged by the Confederation of Vocational Unions, although he here referred to co-operation with employees' organisations in general – the 'Nordic model' (YS 2005).

to weaken links not only because old organisational habits die hard.[211]

In contrast, the *process of institutionalisation,* i.e. the age, of the party itself seems less significant as regards the closeness to traditional associates. According to Panebianco (1988), a strong degree of institutionalisation of parties implies that the party organisation decreasingly sees itself as the representative of a social group or even an ideology, and gradually becomes more independent of its surroundings. But the variation to be further examined is not about distance of old parties and closeness of new parties emphasising particular group interests. Indeed, the Labour Party is no longer merely the political wing of Norwegian trade unions, but as shown above, the party organisation still partly sees itself as part of a broader 'labour movement'. And to the extent that the Socialist Left Party emerged as a party for a particular social group or cause, it has weaker links today with original associates than Labour.

Do the differences in closeness to particular interest groups, match the parties' more specific views on what role parties are supposed to play in democracy better? Some parties may simply prioritise their image and practice as an 'embedded' organisation more than others, whereas others may view closeness to interest groups as undesirable from a democratic perspective. Traditionally, socialist theory has defined democracy as rule by the working class (Katz 1997: 33). To be sure, social democrats emphasise liberal values like interest pluralism and democratic opposition, but they have continued to define the party's key role in democracy as being the delegate of a majority of the people, workers in particular, in public office (Katz and Mair 1995). Although the Norwegian social democratic party developed to be a pragmatic default party of government, its traditional concept of democracy is based on a certain level of social conflict. A major task of political parties is considered to be interest representation, and DnA still claims in strategy documents that the party's task is to promote, in particular, the common interests of salaried employees. Therefore, it could be argued that DnA's closeness to LO corresponds fairly well to the party's normative view on how parties make democracy work.

The trade unions and the party organisation are together, as in the British case, considered to constitute an *alternative public sphere* in democracy, independent of the occasionally hostile mass media (Myking 1997: 140; Minkin 1991: 649). According to party documents, DnA should be an 'open organisation' which listens to the people, and develops better 'information channels' in order to make sure that 'external signals are expressed by party policy' (Arbeiderpartiet 2002a: 18, my translation). As the party leader argued when commenting on non-socialist parties' normative critique of the relationship: '(...) we do not *tamper with* democracy. We *develop* democracy by making policies which correspond to the needs of ordinary people (...)' (Stoltenberg 2005: 9, my translation). However, in a pluralist society one could question the relevance of strong links with a single kind of

211. Likewise, the Conservatives' relative closeness to the business community might be related to the party's organisational identity The party secretary-general says: 'Our history constrains us, and ideology does. The Conservative Party focuses on civil society, voluntary organisations. I think the party has a lot of such contacts at the local level (....). Ideologically, we concentrate on voluntary organisations and business and industry' (Hole 2003 [interview]).

interest group, as closeness might entail exclusiveness. Indeed, emphasis on interest representation also characterises other Norwegian parties with weaker links to their traditional associates, like the Centre Party (see below). So the alleged accommodation to democratic norms seems not particularly sound.

Closeness to Interest Groups in General: A Question of Origin or Value Accommodation?

As regards the closeness or distance from interest groups in general, the major difference between the Liberals' distance – and the Socialist Left Party comparatively strong links – is still largely unsettled. In light of the hypotheses on parties' ideological origin and age, it does not come as a surprise that a new party historically rooted in anti-establishment groups have stronger links to interest groups than an old liberal party. Also, it could be argued that establishing well-organised links is, to some extent, at odds with the Liberals' *raison d'être*. The Liberal party was not established independently of well-defined interests, but after the foundation of the other centre parties, its orientation towards so-called national interests – and keeping special interests at a distance – became in fact a significant part of the Liberals' ideology. According to the secretary-general in the early 2000s, distance from organised special interests is still seen as 'a part of social liberalism' (Nyhus 2003 [interview]), and thus as a distinguishing feature of the party itself. He argues that the choice is, in certain sense, '(...) contingent upon history (.....). Every time the discussion comes up, we end up with this conclusion' (Nyhus 2003 [interview]). However, the question still is whether virtual detachment from interest groups in general is what liberal ideology implies.

Can differences in normative views throw more light on the issue? It was suggested a party with relatively close relationships with one or more kinds of interest groups tends to emphasise interest representation most, whereas a party characterised by relative distance from the interest-group community tends primarily to promote its governing role. There is no doubt that the Liberals and the Socialist Left do differ in this way. Classical liberal theory distinguishes clearly between the functions of political parties and interest groups (Almond and Powell 1966). Whereas interest groups articulate specific interests, parties are expected to play a brokerage role in democracy (Wright 1971; Katz 1997: 60). In line with the original ideological core, the functional difference between parties and interest groups is today a particular concern in regard to democracy (see Chapter 9). For example, the party's national executive committee has decided to reject financial donations offered by organisations, in order to be independent of organised special interests (Nyhus 2003 [interview]).[212] The secretary-general summarises:

> In recent years, we have gone through a process of consciousness-raising. We should not measure public opinion at all times – we should present a vision (…). We think parties and special interest are to play different roles in democracy. Parties are supposed to provide government by the people (Nyhus 2003 [interview]).

212. In contrast, the Liberals do accept monetary support from individual firms and business people (Liberal Party income accounts 1998–2004).

This notwithstanding, the classical liberal norm in pluralist Western democracies is not full detachment, but primarily avoidance of discrimination between various interest groups in public policy-making (cf. Katz 1997: 60). Hence, it could be argued that the Liberals' distinctive pattern of relationships is more strongly related to the specific ideological identity they consolidated during an historical period where party relations with interest groups meant strong links with particular social segments.

Meanwhile, SV's stronger links, in general, is in line with the general views of Europe's new left parties on parties and democracy. According to a manifesto analysis of parties in eighteen established democracies, the new left and green parties generally devote more attention than all other party families to the topic of democracy in their manifestos, in line with their ideological commitment to inclusion of under-represented groups and popular participation (Kittilson and Scarrow 2003: 62–3). Accordingly, these 'new politics parties' tend to have a 'flat' and highly democratic internal structure (Harmel 2002: 123), and roots in new social movements (Kitschelt 1989). Norway's Socialist Left has adapted to a more mainstream organisational model over time, but party documents show that the party still emphasises the role of providing 'linkage' with civil society and especially with social movements (see Chapter 12). In this perspective, the relative closeness to Norwegian associational life makes sense, even though the electoral benefits thereby provided are not that great in all cases. Certainly, it is possible to interpret SV's links as an accommodation to its normative profile as the advocate of grass roots movements. Thus variation in normative views on parties and democracy seems to throw some, if not much more, light on the major differences as regards the general degree of closeness to interest groups.

Range of Relationships: Constrained by Values or a Matter of Institutionalisation?

The cost-benefit analysis revealed that several old parties have a narrower network of organised links than one would expect, while new parties have generally wide-ranging links. Can this variation be traced back to accommodation to values and institutionalisation?

Above it was argued that Labour's fairly strong links to unions could reflect not only historical constraints, but also ideological ones. Likewise, for a original 'class party', putting other employees' organisations, which were once established *in opposition* to the labour movement, on an almost equal footing with LO and its unions might entail the risk of undermining social democracy *as such* in the view of many party members and leaders. By some, it is perhaps not even considered as a real option. In other words, even if the party leadership actually wanted to weaken the links with LO to increase its openness towards other groups, it runs the risk of being seen as illegitimate by numerous party supporters. However, the fact that the other oldest parties – the Conservatives and the Liberals – have less organised networks of wide-ranging relations suggests that the party's original ideology is not necessarily the key here. Their original ideological core consists of less well-defined group interests than Labour's class party origin.

Looking at the revealed differences, the degree of institutionalisation, i.e. party age, seems at first sight less significant for the range of parties' relations with interest groups. The relatively new Socialist Left Party more closely approximates the pattern of wide-ranging organised links with interest groups than do the three oldest political parties in Norway. Indeed, both the newest parties – SV and FrP – do not differ from old parties in the way the argument of ideological origin and institutionalisation suggested. But does this mean that institutionalisation (in terms of age) and parties' overall relationship with interest group is weakly correlated? The Socialist Left Party is not a brand new party any longer and has itself gone through a period of institutionalisation since the 1960s. SV is today not a pure anti-establishment party for a particular cause (see Chapter 12). Moreover, and most importantly, SV has never had truly close relations with special interest groups, not least in comparison with Labour. However, a clear difference between SV and the old parties was still to be expected according to the literature emphasising ideological origin (cf. Chapters 4 and 5).

Whether the Progress Party's links with interest groups fit into this picture is less clear. Like SV, FrP is not a brand new party any more. Moreover, this party did not emerge as an agent for particular organised interests. But according to Panebianco (1988), parties originally characterised by charismatic leadership will, at the early stage, institutionalise by coming less dependent on the party leader. Pedhazur and Brichta (2002) have questioned this assumption, by arguing that institutionalisation defined as organisation and stabilisation is not incompatible with dependence on strong and highly charismatic leadership. In the Norwegian Progress Party there seems to be an increasing tendency towards organisational autonomy as described by Panebianco (see Chapter 13). Yet, most important here, organised populist right parties were, in any event, not expected to seek resources and legitimacy from external interest groups in their pursuit of office (e.g. Kitschelt 2006). True, FrP is perhaps not a archetypal populist (radical) right party, and the party leader was not originally the conveyor of the message himself as in strongly charismatic parties. However, the fact that a largely populist party with a legacy of weak roots in civil society, which is still marked by a strong party leadership, has organised links with various interest groups came as a surprise in light of the argument emphasising ideological origin. Indeed, the Progress Party points to the old labour movement as a model to learn from in terms of having an external party network.

Finally, the question is *whether the parties' range of relationships match their concept of democracy and parties*, especially if we concentrate again on deliberate attempts to cultivate organised links? Let us start with those parties that have a fairly narrow range of more organised links, Labour and the Conservatives despite apparent usefulness of a more wide-ranging network. True, DnA is characterised by emphasis on interest representation, but in today's pluralist societies, all major parties need to mediate between various groups in order to take account of a sufficient proportion of voter preferences. Interestingly, DnA's own organisational evaluations characterise the labour movement as an insufficient instrument of interest aggregation in the early 2000s:

> (…) political parties cannot, without further discussion, be based on particular social segments and on fixed, permanent loyalty of party support and activity. Compared with earlier times, parties must to a greater extent be based on an open discussion in civil society in order to gain support among less homogenous and fixed voter groups (…). (Labour Party Annual Report 1996–98: 35)

The concept of *Samråd* – 'consultation' – was initiated in order to develop a dialogue with external circles and provide the party with more and different voices (Bjerke 2003 and Bråten 2003 [interviews]). Also the DnA party secretary emphasises that providing democratic linkage requires a different approach than it did throughout most of the twentieth century: 'The Labour Party is today an open party, that's beyond doubt. It is not a closed political culture. In this sense, we break with the historical perspective, the former tradition, which looked at closure as something positive. But that was in another society' (Kolberg 2003 [interview]). However, the cultural change has not resulted in fairly organised links with a wide range of interest groups. Rather, DnA's special relationship with LO appears to slow down such a development. In this sense, there is also some discrepancy between DnA's emphasis on interest representation and its relations with interest groups in politics today. Re-emphasis on core values and on the relationship with LO, following the election shock of 2001, seems to have constrained the democratic argument from intensifying the strategy of systematically seeking contact with various interest groups.

It is also possible to question whether the Conservatives' pattern of relationships actually mirrors the model of democracy typically endorsed by conservatives and liberal parties in pluralist societies. As mentioned above, according to liberal democratic theory, the point is that 'no party should be able to ignore any group completely' (Katz 1997: 60). According to the Conservatives' manifesto, voluntary organisations should preferably be independent of the state and other concentrations of power (Høyre 2005: 11), and the close DnA-LO relationship is often criticised by Conservative Party leaders with reference to democratic norms (see *Dagens Næringsliv* 02.09.2004; *Dagsavisen* 27.09.04). The Conservatives' secretary-general summarises the party's approach as follows:

> We criticize DnA's links with LO, and think these have always included 'return favours' in terms of friendly policy (…). The monetary support is so extensive that it necessarily influences the game of democracy. Interest groups should influence public policy. But parties ought to be critical (Hole 2003 [interview]).

Such critique might of course be used instrumentally, but normative scepticism towards strong links with particular interest groups certainly has long-established roots in the Conservative Party (Sejersted 2003, Willoch 1988: 140). Indeed, the Conservatives are, like Labour, characterised by a wide range of links, if we include all formal and informal ad hoc contact with interest groups. But the more organised links established by the party are not that inclusive in the early 2000s. The party organisation seems to concentrate on the business community outside the Storting. Thus, it seems as if there is (still) a certain tension between the ideological tradition of emphasis on business and trade interests, and the normative view of parties being expected to play a brokerage role between various interests in democracy. Also, most secretaries-general of the non-socialist parties emphasise in particular the special responsibility of political parties to *society as a whole*. Parties are to 'filter' what are defined as special interests, and instead represent comprehensive views and prioritisation (see Hole 2003; Mo 2003; Nyhus 2003; Sundsbø 2003 [interviews]). Hence, again, the correspondence between the range of more organised relations and the normative view seems not particularly strong.

What, then, about the parties characterised by a wider range of more organised links despite limits to usefulness? As shown above, SV does emphasise interest representation, and not primarily the brokerage and governing role. In today's more pluralist society this calls for links with various groups. However, it could be argued that the range of SV's network of organised links is wider than would be expected of an apparently social movement-oriented party in this regard. Likewise, FrP's organised network seems even wider than its normative view on parties and interest groups suggests. Although the ideal of 'critical distance' from special interests is emphasised by the secretary-general of the Progress Party (Mo 2003 [interview]), Frp publicly presents itself as *ombudsmen* for their voters (see *Aftenposten* 23.05.05), and as a new right-wing 'labour party' for 'ordinary people'. In fact, the party leadership has on several occasions pointed to the labour movement as the party's organisational 'role model' (see Chapter 13). The party's organised links with various kinds of employees' organisations matches this role, but FrP's network also includes several other kinds of interest groups. On the whole, we find only some support for the expectation that accommodation to democratic norms explain the deviations from a rational course as regards the range of party relationships with interest groups.

Summary of Analysis

We have noticed that original ideological differences seem to be less influential than the strength of historical connections as regards variation in relations to traditional associates. Still, it could be argued that the particular closeness of Labour is related to an ideological constraint – 'party identity' – which makes the relationship more difficult to weaken. Whereas institutionalisation of the party organisation appears to be of limited importance in this regard: DnA still seems to see itself as part of a broader 'labour movement', while to the extent that the Socialist Left Party emerged as a party for a social group or cause, it has today weaker links with original associates than Labour. Accommodation to the parties' democratic norms seems neither particularly helpful to explain variation in closeness to traditional associates. As far as the general degree of closeness is concerned, we note that original ideological differences might play a (minor) part. The Liberals' general distance – and the relative closeness of the Socialist Left in general – can be traced back to ideological origins. Variation in these parties' normative views on parties and democracy seem, in fact, to be less helpful.

Regarding the range of relations, the analysis suggests that the party's original ideology is not the key to better understand the deviations from an apparently rational course. Moreover, party age – institutionalisation – seems nearly insignificant for the range of parties' relations with interest groups. Both the new parties – SV and FrP – do not differ from old parties in the way this argument suggested. Moreover, it seems as if being a populist entrepreneurial party does not necessarily preclude links with other organisations. Finally, we concluded that despite relevant variation in normative views on parties and democracy, the range of relationships does not seem to strongly correspond to such a 'logic of party appropriateness' – emphasis either on interest representation or on the governing, brokerage role. In any case, the findings make it reasonable to ask to what extent (successful) party institutionalisation involves, or is correlated with, independence from the party surroundings.

Hence, in sum, the hypothesis that a party originally established independently of well-defined interests is more likely to be marked by relative distance (more or less organised ad hoc contact) from its old associate(s), and a wide range of links, than are parties originally established to promote the interests or a particular social group or cause does receive some support. But the variation discussed does not match the expectation that an institutionalised (old) party tends to have a relatively distant relationship (more or less organised ad hoc contact) with the originally associated interest group(s), and a relatively wide-ranging network of links, compared to new parties established as organisational tools for a particular social group or cause very well. Accommodation to normative expectations to parties seems most relevant as far as the general degree of closeness is concerned: to some extent, parties with relatively close relationships with one or more kinds of interest groups tend to emphasise interest representation most, whereas parties characterised by relative distance from the interest-group community tend primarily to promote their governing role fairly well. However, we have not been able to comprehend much better the variation in range of links informed by the normative perspective.

RELATIONS ACCORDING TO INTEREST GROUPS – A NOTE

A complete analysis would also analyse relationships from the viewpoint of the interest groups. It takes two to make a relationship and, in many cases, to divorce after a long-established 'marriage'. Indeed, it is beyond the scope of this project to explore both sides of the party-group dyad. But since the Confederation of Trade Unions – LO – is the only Norwegian interest group involved in what I have termed a true *alliance* with specific party, I will briefly take a look at the DnA-LO relationship from the union point of view.

To begin with, there is little doubt that a basic presupposition for this alliance is LO's choice of (still) acting as a partisan organisation at the national level. Whereas LO considers itself an almost totally political actor, its conservative counterpart, the Confederation of Norwegian Enterprise (NHO), emphasises formal political neutrality more than employers' organisations historically did (see Chapter 6). Other employees' organisations have been established in opposition to LO's partisanship, and new social movement organisations are often sceptical of political parties as institutions in general.

But LO's closeness to the Norwegian Labour Party is certainly not an obvious choice seen from a cost-benefit perspective. DnA's statutes still recommend LO membership, but the number of DnA members has decreased over time (Heidar and Saglie 2002: 35). In fact the closeness between LO and DnA has long been considered an obstacle to attracting white-collar employees to trade unions (Bergh 1987). Many of the collectively affiliated union branches left the party in the 1970s and 1980s (Nyhamar 1990: 23), and potential members considered union membership as equivalent to DnA membership (*LO-Aktuelt* 1996). The rise of white-collar federations like the Confederation of Vocational Unions (YS) and the Confederation of Unions for Professionals (Unio) brought increased competition and rivalry. The proportion of Norwegian employees organised in LO has been shrinking from about 50 per cent to about 30 per cent since the 1950s (Stokke 2000: 7, 17). Thus, LO's strong links with DnA risk alienating more members than they attract.

Interestingly, it was LO and not the party which initiated the abolition of collective membership in the early 1990s (*Aktuelt Perspektiv* 12.09.92), and the LO chair was the one who decided to withdraw temporarily from the DnA executive committee in 2001 after internal pressure from individual unions (see *Befalsbladet* 5/2002). Some unions – like the Electricians' and IT Workers' Union and the Officers' Union of Norway (*El- og IT-forbundet; Befalets Fellesorganisasjon BFO)* – emphasise party-political neutrality in their organisational statutes (EL and IT Statutes, NOF Statutes 2004). According to the Norwegian Election Studies from 1989 and 1993, about 82 per cent of LO's members think that in general 'an employees' federation should be politically neutral' (my translation).[213] Hence, the utility of close relationship with DnA for membership recruitment is indeed much discussed in LO.

Second, DnA's almost total dominance in Norwegian politics does certainly belong to the past. Regular alternation in government suggests that no organisation seeking to influence public policy can depend upon one party only. As a former LO chair concluded in the late 1980s: the long-lasting absence of majority government – and the non-socialist parties' return to office – has stimulated LO to turn to other parties as well (Haraldseth 1989: 127). LO has also opened up more towards other centre-left parties in recent years, for instance, by contributing to the SV election campaign. As in other European countries, associations with incumbent social democrats have become more difficult for unions to justify. In the wake of the decline of Keynesianism, Norwegian governments have also implemented policies painful for trade unions. The agreement(s) developed in the early 1990s involving wage restraint – the 'Solidarity Alternative' – was promoted by the LO leadership after an increase in the unemployment rate (Bergh 1999: 91–2; Hågensen 2004), and resulted in friendly labour market policies, together with a guarantee that major welfare schemes would be maintained (Dølvik and Stokke 1998: 133). But the 'Solidarity Alternative' has also been characterised as a 'gift to private business and industry' by some trade unions (Bergh 1999: 85). Thus, it could be argued that the degree of closeness of DnA to LO is related to the fact

213. The figures have kindly been provided by the Institute for Social Research, Oslo.

that LO's central leadership has continued to deliberately choose responsibility for maintaining economic stability instead of an emphasis on protest and strikes.

However, by the same token, if Labour fails to provide the unions with policy when in office, parts of LO seem willing to opt for the non-partisan strategy of 'seeking out the highest bidder' through weaker and more equal links with different parties. The historical legacy of the labour movement does not appear to constrain the trade unions to the extent that it restrains the party organisation. Hence, the especially close relationship with the Labour Party may be less solid than it seems. Direct access to the party leadership has not given LO an incentive to perfect its ability to communicate *across* the party system. There has probably, over time, been a trade-off between efficiently making use of the links with DnA, and developing the ability to influence others.

CONCLUSIONS

This chapter has attempted to further explore the question of what shapes party relationships with interest groups. A full-blown test of the hypotheses derived from theory on parties and interest groups has not been conducted regarding the case of Norway, but a sound empirical exploration of major differences observed in the relations of Norwegian parties with interest groups has been presented. I started by examining the explanatory utility of the cost-benefit model developed based on general rational-choice theory on political parties: first the issue of relations with individual group categories, and second the patterns of general party relationships with interest groups.[214] Thereafter, I turned to the hypotheses informed by historical and normative institutionalism to explore deviations from the rational course and hereby the relative significance of other, secondary factors.

Although no definite conclusions can be drawn as regards the analytical perspectives *as a whole*, some tendencies have been identified by contrasting the variation described by the hypotheses with the existing differences among parties. Certainly, as expected, hypotheses derived from rational choice theory take us a fair step forward in understanding the major differences revealed by the comparative analysis. Parties do assess their relationships instrumentally, and parties' ways of being linked with interest groups indeed reflect differences in the size of benefits and costs. For example, Labour's fairly strong links with unions does not seem at odds with getting access to public office in the early 2000s. The fact that maintenance of the joint 'Co-operation Committee' between DnA and LO could be combined with the formation of a centre-left coalition in 2005 underscores this observation.

But there are also limits to the correspondence between links, benefits and costs. The cost-benefit balance of DnA *vis-à-vis* LO is certainly fragile. Deviations from a rational course do appear to exist as far as the major differences in relationships, *vis-à-vis* individual group categories and the interest community as a whole,

214. Since links with individual organisations are not explored, the analysis does not take account of the possibility that closeness to an individual group may exist and be useful even if the relationship with the organisation category as a whole is fairly distant and not very advantageous.

are concerned. So other factors and mechanisms do also seem to colour the way Norwegian parties are linked with interest groups in the early 2000s. Above all, the differences among Norwegian parties appear to be connected with differences in historical legacy, at least as regards links with traditional associates and the range of contemporary networks. A long-established history of a close relationship with trade unions seems to restrict the strategic options of today's Labour Party elite. In contrast, the Liberals and the Conservatives, parties which could be described as more or less marked by a certain general distance at the organisational level, have a history of less close relationships with specific groups, and a record of limited extra-parliamentary activity which makes links with interest group less relevant to begin with.

Furthermore, Norwegian parties seem to some extent to accommodate to what we have called institutional norms. In line with Panebianco's specific institutional approach, the original party identity, or ideology, appears, in addition to history, to be what primarily constrains the choices made by party elites, at the expense of pure cost-benefit calculations in relation to individual interest groups. To some extent, traditional core values seem to limit the deliberate choices of party leaders. Party links with interest groups are means by which party leaders might gain and maintain legitimacy, but also make choices that are seen as detrimental to the party's very *raison d'être*.

However, as the case of the Labour Party illustrates in particular, historical legacy and cost-benefit calculations are not necessarily mutually exclusive in a short-term perspective. In fact, it seems probable that *interaction* between several types of factors might have shaped today's relationship patterns: Labour's critical need for restoration after the election disaster of 2001, the members party identity as an original workers' party, the historical legacy of truly strong links with trade unions, perhaps in combination with inspiration from recent political events, like the Swedish Social Democrats experience of a successful party-union alliance in the 2002 general elections. All these factors seem to have contributed to DnA's preference for closeness to the trade unions in the early 2000s.

Finally, we have seen that variation in views on parties and democracy may shed some, if not much, light on deviations as regards the oldest non-socialist parties and others in terms of general degree of closeness. The correlations between emphasised democratic norms and the two relational dimensions appear, however, to be far from strong. The difference regarding range of relations turned out to be particularly difficult to clarify.

In future research, new parties and their relationship with interest groups deserve to receive special attention, not least with regard to the role of ideology. Moreover, the question arises as to whether the new parties, if interested, exploit existing resources in their surroundings more easily, perhaps because they have a less 'sclerotic' organisational structure than old parties (cf. Harmel and Janda 1994: 390). Future studies also need to look into the interest group side of the relationships. The fairly strong links between DnA and LO certainly reflect that the leadership of the trade unions is happy with the exchange of resources as well. As regards the other extreme party case, the Liberals, we should perhaps not forget that this is indeed a small party with a limited central organisation compared to all the other parties studied here. Perhaps, interest groups have not developed routines for links with the Liberals to the extent they have with the major parties. It is not unlikely that weak links are to some extent a matter of organisational capacity and attractiveness outside the Storting over time.

To conclude, the analysis indicates that party-interest group relationships are shaped by both endogenous and exogenous variables in the Norwegian case. As assumed, actor-oriented theory helps us to understand the patterns of relationships better. The hypotheses generated from a 'soft' rational cost-benefit perspective is indeed echoed by the results and takes us a fair step forward. Hence, the analysis does not question the *general usefulness* of this model for the study of parties and interest groups. However, we have nevertheless seen that such relationships are, in real-life, fairly complex affairs. The involved costs and benefits are not always easy to calculate, and deviations from a rational course do indeed exist. Alternative factors, and not least those associated with the historical perspective, enable us to understand more of the variation revealed. Moreover, it turns out that seemingly alternative factors can prove reciprocally reinforcing in some situations. This said, I have not tried to solve the problem of '(...) fitting different motivations and logics of action into a single theory framework' (March and Olsen 2004: 19). The study suggests that future research might incorporate a few more complicating elements into a basically cost-benefit-oriented model yet recalling that the more we give nuance to a 'soft' yet parsimonious rational choice approach, the less generalisable the model is likely to be become.

part five
conclusion

chapter seventeen | political parties and interest groups: between separation and integration

While parties operate within the realms of both public office and civil society, interest groups are primarily societal organisations that seek to influence public decision-making 'from without'. Historically, close relations have existed between particular parties and interest groups, not least in Norway. Parties and interest groups may exist in mutually dependent relationships. When seeking to understand the political parties' role in democracy, exploring their relations with interest groups is of paramount importance.

Nonetheless, the general relationship between parties and interest groups has not been subjected to much empirical research. In recent decades, it has been discussed whether the historically close relationships have eroded. Some have also suggested that parties are today generally characterised by tenuous links into civil society. In particular, it is widely agreed that old alliances like the relationship between social democratic parties and trade unions have declined. But relatively few have actually studied the general party-interest group dyad systematically and in detail. Research on interest groups has tended to concentrate on interaction between interest groups and government agencies and politicians, not political parties as such. Through this book, I have attempted to bridge parts of the gap, starting from the party side of the relationship.

The primary objective has been to improve our knowledge about the nature of the relationships of political parties with interest groups outside public office, and to discover to what extent are parties linked with interest groups today. In order to check that the links revealed are more than symbolic exercises and that they mean more than trivial contact, I have also explored the political significance of party-interest group links. Finally, this research has attempted to throw light on the conditions under which party organisations establish close relations with interest groups, opt for distance or virtual separation, and to resolve the question of when do parties seek links with multiple organisations as opposed to exclusiveness. Empirically, the analysis has been limited to the seven major political parties in Norway after the Second World War: the Conservatives (H), Liberals (V), Christian People's Party (KrF), Centre Party (Sp), Labour Party (DnA), Socialist Left Party (SV) and Progress Party (FrP).

A wide definition of 'interest group' has been applied, one which includes 'traditional' or 'sectional' economic interest groups (like trade unions and business organisations) and 'non-traditional' or 'promotional' interest groups, including non-profit voluntary organisations (like cultural, faith-based and humanitarian organisations), advocacy organisations without members *and* organised parts of social movements (like international solidarity and environmental groups). However, the study has focused on *associational* life: business firms, semi-governmental agencies, professional lobbyists, individuals and latent social groups have been excluded from the analysis.

This last chapter summarises the major findings of the study, outlines the theory implications of the empirical results and offers questions for future research.

CONCEPTUALISATION OF RELATIONSHIPS WITH INTEREST GROUPS

Before embarking on the analysis, it was shown that party relationship with interest groups is a fuzzy concept. Two essential dimensions of the extensiveness of party relationships with interest groups have more or less explicitly been emphasised by the existing scholarly literature on the topic: the *degree of closeness* and the *range of party relationships*. Taken together they depict a party's general configuration of relationships with interest groups: how is the party linked and with what organisations. But no general agreement exists on what it actually means for a party to be involved in relationships with interest groups. 'Aligned', 'interlinked', 'tied' and 'connected' are common terms, but definitions vary significantly and are not always explicit. Scholars often point to links between organisational structures or personnel overlap, links which provide direct or indirect contact or interaction between organisations. However, also transfer of resources and more abstract aspects like ideological overlaps and balance of power are frequently mentioned.

In other words, the relationship of parties with other organisations is a multidimensional phenomenon, which might make it necessary to limit what is meant by 'relationship' in line with the overall purpose of the analysis. Since my aim was not only to describe relationships but also to explain variation in such links, this book has focused on a narrow, sharp concept of relationships. As relevant as finances, ideology and power balance might be, particularly when the starting point is parties as intermediary institutions in democracy, these are qualitatively different from links that provide contact between parties and interest groups. Therefore, I did not treat them as a part of the relationship itself: 'relationship' was defined as links that connect interest groups to the party's members, decision-makers and/or decision-making bodies; links that open up contact and can provide communication about information, know-how, opinions and policy views between parties and interest groups.

Regarding *the degree of closeness* – the strength of links – I argued that instead of concentrating on one kind of link, like collective membership or guaranteed access to decision-making bodies, one should also try to capture other (and weaker) ways in which parties might be linked with interest groups. Otherwise, there is the risk of presenting parties and interest groups as more disconnected than they really are. A threefold distinction was therefore introduced with regard to decreasing degrees of closeness: *overlapping organisational structures*, *inter-organisational links*, and *unorganised (informal) links*. Several kinds of specific links, which are limited to the national level of party organisations, were also specified. A high number of links within the class of overlapping organisational structures and inter-organisational links indicates a higher degree of closeness, but depending on the form. I also made the case for comprehensive analyses that can examine the degree of actual contact, as the lack of well-organised links does not necessarily mean less intense communication in practice. Finally, and ideally, we should examine whether the party elite members actually do initiate some of the meetings themselves. However, as a simplified, summarising device, a typology of six archetypal relationships in terms of closeness was developed. By combining the maximum level of links and the actual frequency of both formal and informal contact, I distinguished between *integration, fictitious integration, alliance, organised ad hoc relation, informal partnership*, and *issue-based contact* (see Chapter 4).

Next, the *range of relationships* with interest groups was defined as a combination of the total number of organisations (the quantitative aspect) and the political variety of interest groups included (the qualitative aspect). In a comparative perspective, such figures are context sensitive, depending on the size of the organisation as a whole. Thus, truly wide-ranging relationships are primarily defined as networks which are not cleavage-based, including links with organisations that may represent several, conflicting sub-cultures and both old and new interest groups. Furthermore, I assumed that there is *a correlation* between the two dimensions: a party with close relationships would tend to have a rather narrow network of links. In this way, a framework for comparative, descriptive studies of the nature of today's political parties' relationships with interest groups was developed.

CLOSENESS AND RANGE: DOES A PREDOMINANT PATTERN EXIST?

The *first* and major question empirically explored in this book is to *what extent political parties in Norway are linked with interest groups at the beginning of the twenty first century:* what characterises the seven major political parties in terms of closeness to or distance from interest groups, and how wide-ranging or narrow are the relationships that exist?

Although the focus of the analysis has been party politics today, the backdrop to the issue is the debate on long-term party change. Existing research indicates that general social and political developments have led to fairly distant relationships with organisations that traditionally have been closely associated with political parties. In other words, it has implicitly been argued that the general incentives for close relationships with special interest groups are relatively weak in the early 2000s. In recent years, some scholars have even maintained that even if long-established links may survive, parties are primarily characterised by closeness to the state. Among other things, the introduction of public subventions to parties, ideological convergence and what is assumed to be the cartelisation of party systems, have made the incentives for party links with interest groups generally weak (Katz and Mair 1995; Katz and Mair 2009).

Existing empirical studies indicate that parties' historically close relationships with certain organisations have declined over time, but that this trend may not be uniform (cf. Padgett and Paterson 1991: 216; Thomas 2001c; Allern *et al.* 2007). The degree to which established parties are today characterised by weaker relations with a broad range of interest groups is a moot point. But the large body of literature emphasising system-level characteristics led us to expect that *political parties tend to have organised but not very strong links – organised ad hoc relationships –*

with a wide range of interest groups today. Alternatively, it was suggested that *parties tend to mostly have distant relations – informal issue-based contact – or to be nearly separated from the interest-group community in general*. Both expectations imply that the *old pattern of close relations with particular interest groups belongs to the past*, and that a *predominant pattern in terms of closeness and range of party relationships exists* in the 2000s. A major aim of this book has been to carefully explore these 'conventional wisdoms' empirically, as regards Norwegian parties.

This said, new parties – that is above all various new (radical and/or populist) right, new left, and green parties – are often identified as probable exceptions to the general rule as these have been established as a reaction to 'old politics'. Also, it has been argued that significant differences are likely to exist *between* the new parties. In sum, the general literature on parties established in the second half of the twentieth century, led us to expect that *these parties are distinctively different from old parties as regards the pattern of relationships with interest groups*. Moreover, it is suggested that new left, green and right parties *are distinctively different from each other:* and while new *left-wing and green parties tend to have informal but significant links – informal partnerships – with social movement organisations, populist radical right and right populist parties were hypothesised to be usually characterised by lack of significant links with interest groups in general.*

Major Findings

By not only taking a 'snapshot', but mapping links at the organisational level from 2000 to 2004, the analysis has taken into account that relationships are not a static phenomenon, and may change abruptly. Organisational-level data and the behaviour and experiences of the top party elites have been examined. On the basis of the triangulation of documentary analysis, in-depth interviews with key informants and a survey among individual elite members, we may conclude that political parties in Norway today are certainly linked with interest groups. Great distance or separation from associational life – from special interest groups, voluntary associations and advocacy organisations – does not characterise Norwegian party organisations in general.

Hence, this research does not support the expectation informed by the party cartelisation thesis that parties are weakly linked into civil society in general. Not only are some of the traditional relations of Norwegian parties still evident, but many parties seem to deliberately *open up* their party organisations to more varied circles, partly in an attempt to compensate for the decline in membership figures. Numerous links to interest groups have been identified, as have links related to opposite sides of both old and new cleavages. In this sense, the findings may echo Yishai's (2001: 670–1) study of Israeli politics, which concludes that established parties have experienced a need to 're-incorporate society into politics' after a period of decline of such links. The main empirical results as regards the more specific features of party-interest group relationships in Norway are summarised in what follows.

On the whole, Norwegian parties tend towards a pattern of not very close and quite wide-ranging relationships with interest groups. No party today is linked by overlapping organisation's structures in terms of, for example, guaranteed representation of external interest groups in executive bodies. But inter-organisational links for contact nonetheless exist. Only one party – Labour – has enduring links like a joint committee and a formal co-operation agreement with any organisation, but numerous parties have routines for inviting external groups to certain party arrangements, including meetings of policy-making committees and the party congress. Parties also arrange dialogue seminars and separate meetings with various organisations. During the manifesto-making process, some sort of active consultation of interest groups is fairly common. At the individual level, a significant proportion of the national elite in all parties are, or have been, officials or staff in one or more interest group although the extent of leadership overlaps is definitely limited. Activism (or a career) in parties and in interest organisations is not mutually exclusive.

However, there are not many organisations with which the parties are linked through extensive regular contact. The most common type of relation thus seems to be one that is not very close. In terms of the typology of relationships, there exist numerous *organised ad hoc relationships,* and if such relationships cannot be found, informal links for contact provide a relationship with many other organisation types. All parties use informal contact as a common way to communicate with other organisations. Finally, numerous links, and relationships related to opposite sides of both old and new cleavages, have been identified.

Thus, we see a degree of homogeneity in support of the first hypothesis but the general tendency is far from strong. Indeed, there are marked differences in terms of closeness to external organisations, between organisation categories and parties. The range of the total network of links is in some cases rather limited, and certain parties have maintained a quite close relationship with their old associate. Some parties – Labour, Centre and Socialist Left – have extensive regular contact with specific organisations through links at the organisational or individual level, and are thus characterised by having *organised alliances* or *informal partnerships* with certain interest groups.

Party links with interest groups that represent old core voters vary significantly. Above all, the Centre Party and the Liberals have much more distant relationships with the social movement organisations from which they emerged than do other parties with similar origins. The Christian People's Party and, above all, the Labour Party are not in the process of inter-organisational divorce from religious organisations or old trade unions, respectively. Previous research has shown that DnA's link with the trade unions had declined by the late 1990s, but its organised relationship with the Confederation of Trade Unions (LO) has been re-consolidated, and perhaps slightly intensified, in recent years.

The Conservatives are a less clear-cut case. The party's inter-organisational links with the employers', business and trade organisations do not appear to be strong, but organised, regular contact with individual businesspeople and companies in relation with fund-raising indicates that such links may be stronger than it seems at first glance. Moreover, omitting financial donations as an indicator of closeness makes the Conservatives seem more weakly connected than would have been the case if we included such 'connections'. With regard to the two 'new' (post-war) parties, the Socialist Left and the Progress Party, we note that the former has maintained fairly close relationships with the trade unions and new social movements – precisely those organisational circles with which the party was associated in the 1960s and 1970s.

The general degree of closeness also varies. The Liberals seem to keep a distance from interest groups in general. This party comes closest to being *virtually separated* from the associational life in Norway at the national level, although no definite conclusions can be drawn due to weak survey material in this case. Labour has particularly close relationships with the trade unions, and together with SV, is the party with generally strongest links at the individual level, but DnA is not among those parties that have the strongest inter-organisational links with interest groups in general. In fact both the Socialist Left and the Progress Party are among those with more organised links with various interest groups.

Moreover, despite links across cleavages, significant differences exist with regard to the parties' strongest links. Parties have closer relationships with particular and different groups, and here a more traditional pattern emerges. Earlier research shows that some of the relationships with old associates, like DnA's links with the trade unions, had declined by the late 1990s, but this study reveals that the Labour Party has thereafter not chosen to further distance the LO and its unions. The Labour Party does not put the old trade unions on an equal footing with other employees' organisations, and its links to business and trade organisations are fairly weak outside Parliament compared to those of other parties. As assumed, a high degree of closeness seems to stimulate exclusiveness: DnA's strategy of both keeping a close relationship with LO *and* establishing wide-ranging relationships appears not that easy in practice. In fact, Labour and the Conservatives have the most wide-ranging networks of links as measured by frequency of both formal and informal contact, but their organised initiatives seem more limited than in the case of several other parties. Thus some of the long-established parties prove to have a narrower range of more organised relationships than often expected.

Hence, contrary to what the contemporary party literature often suggests as regards established democracies in general, a truly *predominant* pattern of relationships with interest groups does not seem to exist among established Norwegian parties. In the early 2000s, DnA prefers to have a quite close relationship with the trade unions, and more distant relations with alternative employees' organisations outside the Storting. Only one party, the Liberals, can be said to seek and to have a very distant, almost separated, relationship in general. In other words, the general societal circumstances that are often argued to call for a specific pattern of relationships, have not lead to considerable homogeneity in party links with the interest-group community in Norway.

Moreover, the variation revealed seems not to systematically correspond to party-related differences *within* the Norwegian social structure and economy. For example, the Centre Party (Sp) has been challenged the most by the employment pattern that has emerged in recent decades, but the party had loosened its links with the Farmers' Union *before* the Second World War. Whereas the Labour Party has also experienced a relatively dramatic decrease in core voters, but nevertheless it keeps a rather close relationship with the trade union movement. By contrast, the new parties – SV and FrP – have somewhat more wide-ranging relationships than would be expected on the basis of the new politics literature. In the case of the Progress Party, the pattern of relationships does certainly not support the conventional wisdom as it provides another example of a networking populist right party (cf. Birenbaum 1992) – beyond 'friendly' anti-establishment groups. Indeed, FrP is shown to have almost as extensive frequent contact with the organised business community and professional organisations as have the Conservatives.

PARTY-INTEREST GROUP RELATIONSHIPS: MORE THAN SYMBOLIC PATTERNS

The *second* major question dealt with in this book was: *what are the consequences of party relationships with interest groups?* Since the aim was not to perform a complete consequence analysis, but to examine critically whether the relations exposed have substantive, political value, I chose to analyse this aspect *before* trying to explain differences along the dimensions of closeness and range of relationships. Do they, as assumed, actually affect the political decisions of party organisations? In theory, old links could be retained mainly for symbolic reasons, whereas new, weaker ones might be equally influential in practice. The analysis had to be content with some fairly crude indicators, but several tentative conclusions could be drawn.

Despite extensive fact-oriented contact, the links of Norwegian parties with interest groups are not trivial. Organisations are given an opportunity to influence the party organisation's policy-making. The contact provided by the links also seems to actually influence the outcome of parties' decision-making processes. Both key informants and individual elite members report that interest groups influence their party to formulate policies that may differ from those it would have developed without such links. Interest groups do not need to take part in standing arrangements in order to have a say; the established weaker links also represent more than legitimising exercises.

However, we also found significant differences among parties which led us to the question of whether the way in which parties are linked with interest groups really matter. Despite a wide range of politically significant links, some were shown to be closer and in practice more influential than others. Those labour market and industry organisations with which the elite tended to have most frequent contact are generally considered to be most important. A major conclusion is that relatively close relationships are more politically significant than more distant ones, but, surprisingly, this tendency is not very strong. This discrepancy could of course reflect normatively biased responses. The sources who attested to weaker degrees of influence also tended to emphasise that parties ought to maintain a distance from special-interest groups. Moreover, the in-depth analysis of the DnA-LO joint 'Co-operation Committee' showed how significant such standing arrangements are, and strengthened the impression that in practice it tempers the extent to which Labour opens up its decision-making for other interest groups.

I have not been able to document the significance of links with *different* kinds of organisations *for each party*. This restriction notwithstanding, we have seen that some organisations in general seem more influential than others. Those labour market and industry organisations with which the party elites generally had most frequent contact are considered to be most important. Despite a wide range of politically significant links, some are closer and in practice more influential than others.

To conclude, variations in the relationships with interest groups seem relevant. Fairly weak links are not merely 'ornamental', symbolic exercises: they affect party decisions, and make a wide range of interest groups politically significant. But it does matter how strongly a party is linked with an interest group; consequently, the dominance of relatively distant relations with interest groups indicates the generally limited significance of links with *individual* organisations today.

EXAMINING VARIATIONS IN RELATIONSHIPS: RELATIVE UTILITY OF A COST-BENEFIT MODEL

Although the focus of this study has been on mapping, describing and categorising patterns of party-interest group relationships, yet another question was addressed: *what can explain differences in this aspect of political parties' organisation and behaviour?* For this third purpose, the literature on parties and interest groups focusing on parties and socio-economic developments, seemed not particularly helpful. Differences in such structures might explain how parties' relationships differ, not least across countries. But even if parties are seen as independent, largely instrumental actors, limited attention is paid to the possible impact of party agency and enduring institutional differences. In order to understand party-interest group relationships better, I made the case for examination of the usefulness of more actor-oriented theory.

The specific aim was to throw more light on the existing variation among Norwegian parties, but embedded in general theoretical statements on political parties. As I presume political parties are largely rational collective actors that aim for political power, the starting point for this part of the analysis was a perspective on party politics which shares a great deal of assumptions with the broader tradition of *rational choice institutionalism.* Here parties and interest groups are seen as involved in exchange relationships, where parties provide legislation and public policy, and interest groups for example votes and monetary support. Informed by transaction-cost economics it was assumed that strong links for contact, and in particular overlapping organisational structures, can be seen as attempts at reducing the transaction costs of exchange and making the mutual provision of resources more reliable for parties and interest groups.

However, since my concern was with the *general* relationship of parties with interest groups, including weaker links and relations with groups that are not necessarily strongly organised themselves, I also discussed under what circumstances different parties (elites) (and interest groups [elites]) will choose differing *degrees of closeness* and addressed the issue of the parties' *range of relationships* separately. Therefore, the analogy of a firm, elaborated and used by Warner (2000) and Quinn (2002, 2003), was not applied in detail. A broader and thus 'softer' cost-benefit model was instead developed. The basic assumption made was that parties seek support from interest groups, but that they calculate whether potential benefits for primary goals of close links compensate for drawbacks like alienating other voter groups. To enable an empirical examination of the utility of this perspective, hypotheses to be explored empirically were derived focusing on the following aspects of party-interest group relationships: First, what can explain that a party chooses to have a close relationship with a specific organisation categories while others prefer a more distant relationship? Second, what can explain variations in parties' overall relationship with interest groups: parties' closeness to/distance from the interest group universe as a whole, and variation in range of party relationships.

In order to reduce the risk of interpretative biases, and as I assume non-instrumental behaviour is not entirely missing in politics, two alternative analytical perspectives to rational choice theory were presented as well. These were generated from the distinguishing features of two other theoretical schools within comparative politics and party research: *historical* and *normative (sociological) institutionalism.* While the former pays particular attention to the historical legacy of party-interest group relationships and interplay with current political events, the latter emphasises parties as collections of values and norms, and suggests that party-interest group relationship would vary according to the parties' original party identity, degree of institutionalisation and its view of the primary role of political parties in democracy. By first presenting these alternatives on their own terms, it was further clarified what parties' behaviour *vis-à-vis* interest groups would *generally* look like if it is not shaped by cost-benefit calculations. Thereafter, specific theory elements of the alternative perspectives was used to identify some *secondary* explanatory hypotheses as regards possible deviations from a rational course. Hence, the *primacy* of the rationalist perspective was emphasised but without entirely dismissing the possible relevance of 'historical' and 'normative' factors. If the general basic assumptions are ignored, the distinction between the three literatures is not watertight.

Major Findings

What has been discussed is far from the whole story, so I have been deliberately cautious about drawing conclusions. The analysis was oriented more towards descriptive than causal inference. However, an empirically sound exploration of major differences between Norwegian parties' relationships with interest groups has been provided. I started by discussing whether the given party's way of being linked with the interest-group community by and large appears to be a rational course, given that party's primary goals and available knowledge of circumstances. The main hypotheses, derived from the general 'soft' cost-benefit model, seem to go a fair way towards throwing light on the observed variation. It has been shown that Norwegian party elites do instrumentally assess their party's relationships in the light of their goals, and that the parties' ways of being linked with the trade unions of LO do correspond to differences in the size of benefits and costs.

For example, the Labour Party's fairly close relationship with interest groups appears to be more useful than often suggested by the party literature suggesting erosion of such links in general.

However, the correspondence between links, benefits and costs seemed not perfect, and the remaining differences to be explained seemed not to be due to variation in primary goals; between seeking office (for its own sake or to implement policy) and being a 'ideologically purist' party. Hence, deviations from a rational course appeared to exist as far as the major differences in relationships, both regarding individual group categories and the interest community as a whole, are concerned. Some parties have stronger links with particular interest groups than a cost-benefit analysis would indicate, whereas others keep their distance even though it would seem that they could benefit from rapprochement to interest groups, or at least links with more organisations.

Next, the analysis moved on to discuss what could explain the deviations from the assumed rational course. First and foremost, I concluded that they seem to be connected with differences in historical legacy, at least as regards links with traditional associates. In particular, a long-established history of close relationships appears to restrict the choices made by today's Labour Party elite. A chain of benefits have probably been created, and it appears risky to change an historical 'winning team' even though a more wide-ranging network of links seems needed. The Liberals and the Conservatives, which could be described as parties more or less marked by a certain general distance at the organisational level, have a history of distance or at least a record of more limited extra-parliamentary activity in general. More specifically, the question was asked if it is the long history of close relations between trade unions and DnA which has made the two sides grow attached in the sense that they have become dependent on their internal division of labour and co-operation.

Furthermore, Norwegian parties seem, to some extent, to additionally accommodate to what we have called institutional norms. In line with Panebianco's specific institutional approach, i.e. the original party identity as expressed by traditional core values and policy views, appear to be what primarily influence the choices made by party elites to the detriment of cost-benefit calculations. In membership parties, leaders come and go, but party activists can be argued to be the 'stewards' of the party's *raison d'être*. In some cases, this is closely associated with either closeness to particular groups, or in fact distance from the interest-group community in general. For example, it seems as even if the Labour Party leadership actually wanted to weaken the links with trade unions to increase its freedom of action and openness towards other groups, it might run the risk of weakening its legitimacy in the eyes of numerous party supporters. The symbolic value of links with unions is strong, and to some extent seen as a part of the social democratic project itself. In a certain sense, the finding can be seen as a parallel to Kitschelt's argument (1994: 58) that the once high degree of class voting has constrained the strategic flexibility in adapting to a changed social structure.

However, the hypothesis that a strong degree of institutionalisation, in terms of organisational routinisation and the development of party as valuable in and of itself, leads to weaker links with external interest groups, whilst newness might imply relatively stronger links if these links originally existed does not receive strong support. In fact, altogether, the findings make it fair to ask to what extent full-scale institutionalisation involves, or is connected with, autonomy from the party surroundings, as Panebianco (1988) suggests. Moreover, contrary to what is often argued by the literature on (radical) right populist parties, the analysis more specifically revealed that the Progress Party attempts to establish a wide network of links with interest groups. In other words, as noted above, we have identified a (new) example of a populist party that enjoys links with organised interests. Indeed, we saw that development of a party organisation based on fairly populist ideology, firm leadership, a relatively high degree of centralisation, and media-orientation does not necessarily preclude emphasis on (ad hoc based) links with interest groups at the national level. Despite the firm analogy used to describe their central organisation, FrP's leadership obviously believes in the usefulness of both extra-parliamentary organisation and contact with the interest-group community.

Variation in views on parties and democracy may also shed some light on the oldest non-socialist parties and others as far as the general degree of closeness. The former have put relatively heavy emphasis on the governing role of parties, whilst social democrats traditionally see articulation of well-defined interests as more important. The Liberals general distance seems connected with a normative view suggesting that having well-organised links with interest groups is incompatible with responsibility to society as a whole. Parties are to 'filter' what are defined as special interests, and instead represent comprehensive views and prioritisation. In contrast, both Labour and the Socialist Left point to the need for channelling specific groups and movements into the political system. However, all together, the correlations between emphasised democratic norms and the two relational dimensions seemed far from strong in this context. The difference regarding the range of relations turned out to be particularly difficult to clarify. So in sum this alleged secondary shaping factor did not prove very important.

Finally, we noted that, as the case of the Labour Party illustrates in particular, historical legacy and cost-benefit calculations are not necessarily mutually exclusive in a short-term perspective and may interact as shaping factors: Labour's critical need for restoration after the election disaster of 2001, the members' party identity as an original workers' party, the historical legacy of truly strong links with trade unions, in combination with inspiration from recent political events – all these factors seem to have contributed to DnA's preference for closeness to the trade unions in the early 2000s. Hence, the question arises as to whether the analysis demonstrates that different logics of actions might co-exist under specific conditions?

To conclude, this research indicates that party-interest group relationships are not simple affairs in Norway. The relationship of Norwegian political parties with interest groups appears to be coloured by both endogenous and exogenous variables. A cost-benefit model is indeed echoed by the results of the empirical analysis of variation. But supplementary factors informed by a historical and normative perspective help us to further understand the revealed patterns of relationships.

LESSONS LEARNED AND SUGGESTIONS FOR FUTURE RESEARCH

What lessons can be learned from the cases of Norwegian parties and interest groups more generally? With a largely unexplored field of research like this one, *any* case will represent a contribution. On the other hand, no definite claims can be made as to whether the results are generalisable beyond Norway. My primary objective has been to map the relationships of major Norwegian parties with interest groups, and to try to understand the variation among the seven parties in focus by examining the relative usefulness of a cost-benefit model. That said, the findings might inform hypotheses that could later be applied to a wider population of cases and in more detailed studies of links between individual parties and specific organisations. Concentration on parties within one specific system has made it possible to study the relationships of parties of various origins and age, and of parties that belong to many different ideological families and vary in their organisational outlook.

In a comparative, international perspective Norway has traditionally provided party researchers with the opportunity to study political developments within a society where the periphery is relatively strong, and a cross-cutting, territorial cleavage exists. Today, the Norwegian political system is less special than it once was. Primarily, a study of parties and interest groups in Norway has given us the chance to further explore how today's political parties are linked into the associational life in a society where such links have been strong historically, and where the social structure and other relevant system-level circumstances do call for the pattern of fairly distant, but wide-ranging relationships. The general socio-economic and cultural developments have been significant by international standards, but there are also features suggesting that this configuration of relations is less likely in Norway. In other words, Norway is probably neither a least-likely nor a most-likely case of party distance from interest groups at the beginning of the twenty-first century.

What, then, are the most interesting findings of this study in light of theories on party organisation and behaviour? What is worth noting with an eye to future research?

The Importance of Specific Definitions and Multiple Indicators

Above all, this study serves as a reminder of the fact that the disintegration of close relationships does not equal separation. Although the organisational structures of parties and interest groups do not overlap, and parties thus are not firmly embedded in associational life, they can nonetheless be quite closely connected with numerous interest groups through other kinds of links. This might seem evident, but the literature sometimes presents the decline of old relationships as the end of party links with the interest-group community.

In contrast, this book has showed that the politically significant exchange of ideas and opinions between parties and interest groups may also take place where inter-organisational links are generally weak. Informal contact is a common way of communicating with interest groups at the elite level in Norway. Perhaps the spread of such recent technological developments as mobile phones and e-mail has facilitated this type of contact? Hence, if one aims to capture interaction between parties and interest groups, a look beyond party statutes and organisational charts is needed.

Also, the book has illustrated how important it is to define carefully what is meant by contested notions such as 'civil society', 'associational life', and 'interest group' when trying to map political party links into society. I chose to apply a wide concept of interest groups, including not only membership organisations for special interests. However, certain delimitations were also made. Poguntke's (2002, 2006) distinction between party-created collateral organisations and externally organised interest groups has underpinned this study, which not only meant that links with ancillary and auxiliary organisations were overlooked. Also, informal groups operating *within* party organisations have been excluded from the analysis. Furthermore, the analysis concentrated on 'associational life', so the links parties have with, for example, individual businesspeople and firms have not been studied here. Interestingly, contact with such groups seems common in the case of the centre-right parties, and suggests that future research should look into an even wider range of collective actors in (civil) society in order to capture all the activities that are relevant to the parties' role as intermediary institutions.

Finally, this study has made clear that national elites in Norwegian parties do interact with interest groups about organisational and political matters, but it has not been systematically examined how interest groups informally may influence parties 'bottom-up'. As Aylott (2003) showed in the case of the Swedish social democratic party, detachment from trade unions was patchier at the local level than at the national level. The fact that Norwegian party members also tend to belong to other organisations suggest that extension of the analysis to the local and mid-level is a major task for future research (Heidar and Saglie 2002), especially in countries where much power is decentralised to lower levels.

The Shaping Factors of Party Relationships with Interest Groups

Another general finding of relevance to the general debate on parties and interest groups is that significant and interesting differences exist among parties exposed to the same social, political and institutional environment.

The Significance of Endogenous Factors and Party Agency

The idea that there is a predominant pattern of party-interest group relationships among (established) parties does not receive much support by this party study, even though we have only looked at parties operating within the same society and state. Thus, the question arises as to how strong is the effect of the socio-structural, political and technological circumstances that characterise established democracies today? Does the literature emphasising system-level trends risk underestimating the potential for variation? Certainly, the party literature referred to does not necessarily ignore the importance of other constraining factors and party agency (Montero and Gunther 2002: 13–5), but only to a limited extent does it thoroughly discuss the potential for variation both across and within countries (see

Kirchheimer 1966; Katz and Mair 1995; Harmel 2002). For example, we may ask whether the enduring, national institutional setting may limit the range of options available to parties.

Also, the assumption that the more shifting parts of the social and institutional structure is likely to affect most political parties equally, within a given country at a particular point in history, is questionable. The study presented in this book clearly illustrates that political parties are, as van Biezen (2003b) has emphasised, autonomous organisations, actors that deliberately *choose* between ways of being linked on an individual basis. Faced by the results of socio-economic change, political developments, and new technology they do not necessarily draw the same conclusions. The surroundings do not always present parties with a clear incentive structure in practice and their evaluation criteria may vary. For example, when systematically comparing the resources provided by the Confederation of Trade Unions to the Labour Party with the potential benefits offered by other groups, the relatively strong links appear as a more rational choice than suggested by general social and political developments. In future research, more attention should also be paid to situational circumstances and the possible impact of specific policy preferences.

More attention should also be paid to the interest-group side of the exchange relationship. Interest groups do not readily choose the option of partisanship and thereby make the threshold for the establishment of close relations generally high. How other organisations respond to today's social, technological and institutional environment is still a largely unexplored question. For example, as regards the Norwegian Liberals' general distance from the interest group community, we should not forget that this is indeed a small party with a limited central organisation compared to all the other parties studied here.

Moreover, this research indicates that future research on a larger number of cases may incorporate a few more elements into a 'soft' rational choice or basic cost-benefit model. Norwegian parties seem not to act only instrumentally when choosing how to be linked into civil society. Two observations are particularly interesting in this regard. To begin with, we have seen that a party may hesitate to weaken significantly its links with the traditionally associated interest groups even though the utility of such closeness for office-seeking purposes may be questioned. The strength of historical links and core values of what seems to be a collective party identity might constrain the party leadership. Next, to a more limited extent, Norwegian party elites also appear to accommodate to what they consider to be the primary task of parties in democracy. Just as members can be recruited in order to make the party appear more legitimate, links with interest groups might be established or avoided to make parties seem like, or actually be, an 'embedded' or 'independent' institution respectively.

Besides, it is, in particular, worth noting for research on a larger number of cases that both the new parties in Norway today have standardised not only their organisations, but also their relationships with interest groups. The Progress Party turned out to be an especially interesting case. For many Norwegians, it is old news that FrP is much more than a loose structure supporting a charismatic party leader.

But even if it is not an archetypal radical right or populist right party, it came as a surprise that FrP is among those that most strongly emphasise having links for contact with interest groups as an organisation. Its populist origin, anti-establishment profile and distinctive 'entrepreneurial' features as a party organisation seems to be not incompatible with organisational routines for contact with various interest organisations. Thus, the study might suggest that the relationship between charismatic leadership, right populist ideology, and party organisational strategies should be further explored in comparative research (cf. Pedhazur and Brichta 2002). Moreover, in future research, it could be interesting to explore whether the new parties exploit existing resources in their surroundings more easily than old parties, perhaps because they have a less 'sclerotic' organisational structure than old parties (cf. Harmel and Janda 1994: 390)? Or could it be that new parties need input from interest groups more than established parties due to capacity constraints if they seek power? Indeed, in Norway they seem even more prone to emphasise a wide range of organised links than do many established parties.

Also, this study reminds us that changing situational circumstance make assessment of the usefulness or desirability of especially strong links an *ongoing and continuous* activity for party elites. The relationship of parties with interest groups is dynamic, and the degree of closeness to specific interest organisations may fluctuate. In other words, the exact degree of closeness observed among Norwegian parties in the early 2000s might to some extent be temporary.

The Enduring Political and Institutional Framework of Party Politics

Although the focus of this research project has been on parties within one country, to some extent the question of how the national institutional setting and state regulations might impinge on the relationship of parties with interest groups has also been addressed. Existing research suggests that variations in this framework have given rise to some significant differences in the development of the relationship between parties and interest groups across countries. In Chapter 5, several alternative propositions were presented to be further explored through comparative research designs across countries. To this proposal, the possible effect of European integration and newness of democracy can certainly be added.

As regards Norway, or Scandinavia, in particular, the comparatively strong degree of corporatism can have made links with the state a regular procedure for interest groups, and perhaps also links with parties more common, but this is still a contested issue. Also, the small size of the Norwegian community probably makes personal overlaps between parties and interest groups somewhat more likely. The cleavage-based profile that emerges when we concentrate on the strongest links of Norwegian parties might well be related to a systemic feature. Although the Norwegian working class has not been divided by religion or ethnicity, party politics in Norway is indeed based on numerous and cross-cutting cleavages. Since the 1960s, old cleavages have declined, but new dimensions of conflict also emerged (see Dalton *et al.* 1984). In recent years, the competition from the New Right and New Left has complicated the pattern of party competition in Norway. Thus, parties that pursue a catch-all strategy certainly risk losing votes to fringe parties, which in turn suggests that the incentives for establishing links with a truly wide range of interest groups is not that great. Moreover, to the extent that electoral competition is based on issue-ownership rather than spatial competition (Budge and Farlie 1983; Green-Pedersen 2007), it could be discussed whether fairly close relationships with specific interest groups like trade unions might be a way to reinforce the party's ownership of issues related to public welfare and redistribution. The need for a more distinct political profile was, certainly, a part of Labour's strategic analysis before the 2005 election.

On the whole, then, this book echoes Harmel's (2002: 133–4) conclusion as regards research on general party organisational change, and Warner's study of the Catholic Church and political parties (2000) in that it seems desirable that work should continue to construct bridges between what are often 'theoretical islands' particularly in this context: emphasis on system-level conditions and trends in society and state, formal political institutions, the cost-benefit calculations of specific parties and other institutional perspectives on party organisations. This said, to what extent and exactly how one should modify a general cost-benefit model is open to debate. Focusing on parties in a single country, this study has emphasised fine distinctions as regards the variation between Norwegian parties. But as previously pointed out, the more we add nuances to a rational choice approach, the less generalisable the model is likely to be.

Consequences of Party Relationships with Interest Groups

The final, major topic addressed by this book has been the possible consequences of party relationships with interest groups. The study suggests that other organisations through weaker links may influence the content of party manifestos and other party-political decisions. In order to assess the political impact of links in detail it is necessary to study the policy-making within specific policy fields.

Also, more systematic insight is needed into the role of interlinked interest groups in candidate selection and electioneering. The tendency observed in recent years of parties to expand their candidacy lists and widen participation during leadership and candidate selection, has opened the leeway for more external interest group influence on this aspect of intra-party politics. In addition, elections have become more complex and unpredictable processes since the heyday of the mass membership party, so there are more opportunities for interest groups to become influential. But the extent to which, and how, they get more involved in elections is still largely unexplored terrain. In all cases, it becomes relevant to ask whether party openness towards external circles may collide with intra-party democracy and affect power relationships *within* the party organisations.

Finally, it is, of course, a task for future research to address the possible impact of party links with interest groups on democracy at large. Recent decades have seen much discussion of the role and importance of political parties in established democracies. Poguntke (2002) has showed that collateral organisations still exist and are positively correlated with the stabilisation of electorates, but in numerous respects 'the golden age' of the mass membership party is over in Europe. It is widely argued that political parties are less able to provide interconnections between mass opinion and public decision than before. More knowledge on party relationships with interest groups may add more pieces to this puzzle.

****

Do parties today prefer fairly distant relationships with various kinds of interest groups or virtual detachment from civil society in general? Based on original and extensive data material, this book has demonstrated that some Norwegian parties still have fairly strong links with their traditional associate, and that many parties have opened up their party organisations to more varied circles in Norway. Equally important, it has been shown that significant differences exist in these party-interest group relationships in terms of both closeness and range. Due to contextual similarities as well as the differences, this should be of interest for others than those particularly interested in Norwegian or Scandinavian politics. So, above all, this study suggests that the widespread hypothesis that party-interest group relations are today wide-ranging but rather distant, or about to wither away, deserves more systematic empirical research across parties and polities. There is a long way from formal integration between parties and interest groups to complete detachment. However, it should also be noted that this book has focused on the relationships at the national level of politics. Such relations do not necessarily connect parties with large groups of the general populace. Hence, it remains to be seen whether the links revealed are an indication of deeper social roots, or mainly indicative of more shallow inter-elitist interaction. And whatever the case might be, how to assess the potential consequences of party links with interest groups at the system level is not straightforward. As illustrated by Norwegian party elites' normative considerations, the relationship of parties with interest groups evokes numerous and contested aspects of democracy.

appendix a: party and interest group documents[215]

Party Documents

Centre Party (Senterpartiet, Sp)

Senterpartiets lover [Centre Party statutes] Available at: <http://www.senterpartiet.no> (accessed spring 2003).

Senterpartiets inntektsregnskap 1998–2004 [Centre Party income accounts 1998–2004] [7 documents]

Senterpartiets årsmeldinger 1977–2004 [Centre Party Annual Reports 1977–2004] [27 documents]

Senterpartiet (1996): *Vi åpner partiets dører: Diskusjonsnotat for fylkesstyrer og lokallagsstyrer fra Senterpartiets hovedorganisasjon August 1996.* Memo from Sp's central organisation.

Senterpartiet (2001): *Innstilling fra Senterpartiets evalueringsutvalg 2001.* Proposal from an internal evauation committee.

Senterpartiet (2003): *Arbeidsplan 2003 for Senterpartiets hovedorganisasjon.* Annual plan for Sp's central organisation.

Senterpartiet (2004a): *Debattutkast til Stortingsvalgprogram for Sp 2 005 – 2009: Vi vil noe med Norge!* Proposal to the internal manifesto debate Online. Available: <http://www.senterpartiet.no//troms/nyhetene/7212/index.shtml> (accessed June 2006)

Senterpartiet (2004b): *Arbeidsplan 2004 for Senterpartiets hovedorganisasjon.* Annual plan for Sp's central organisation.

Senterpartiet (2005): 'Fagforbundet og Senterpartiet med dialogkonferanse: Ansatte som ressurs i utvikling av kommune og offentlige velferdstjenester'. Article Online. Available: <http://www.senterpartiet.no/hovedorg/nyhetene/7840/index.shtml> (accessed February 2005).

Christian People's Party (Kristelig Folkeparti, KrF)

Lover, vedtekter og normallover i Kristelig Folkeparti [Christian People's Party statutes], printed version provided by KrF party headquarters.

Kristelig Folkeparti's inntektsregnskap 1998–2004 [Christian People's Party income accounts 1998] [7 documents]

Kristelig Folkepartis årsmeldinger 1977–2004 [Christian People's Party Biannual Reports 1977–2004] [14 documents]

Politisk program for Kristelig folkeparti 2001–2005 [KrF Election Manifesto 2001–2005]

Bondevik, Kjell Magne (1991): *Foredrag på Kristelig Folkepartis landsstyremøte fredag 13. desember 1991.* Speech at KrF national council meeting, 13 December 1991.

Bondevik, Kjell Magne (2006): *Kristendemokratiet som toneangivende alternativ.* Speech to KrF's local government conference 28 January 2006 Online. Available: <http://www.krf.no/portal/page?_pageid=33,64003&_dad=portal&_schema=PORTAL> (accessed January 2006).

Kristelig Folkeparti (1992): *Kristne Verdier i tjeneste for vårt samfunn*: Et *studie- og samtaleopplegg om fornyelse i KrF.* Party memo.

Kristelig Folkeparti (2004): *Kristendemokratisk manifest* Online. Available: <http://www.krf.no/portal/page?_pageid=33,87414&_dad=portal&_schema=PORTAL> (accessed June 2006).

215. Although this study covers the early 2000s (until 2004), I have consulted older documents for background information. The parties' Annual Reports from the 1990s, 1980s and 1970s are from Knut Heidar's collection, Department of Political Science, University of Oslo. The income accounts were provided by the Constitutional Office of the Storting.

Kristelig Folkerparti (2005): *Kristendemokrati på norsk – en kortversjon* Online. Available: www.krf.no/krfweb/politikk/div_pol_dokumenter/kristendemokratiet_ideologi (accessed January 2005).

Conservatives (Høyre)

Høyres lover [Conservative Party statutes] Online. Available at: <http://www.hoyre.no > (accessed spring 2003).

Høyres Inntektsregnskap 1998–2004 [Conservative Party income accounts 1998–2004] [7 documents]

Høyres årsberetninger 1977–2004 [Conservative Party Annual Reports 1977–2004] [33 documents]

Høyre (2005a): 'Målgrupper', section 1.4 in the Conservatives' Annual Plan for 2001. Excerpt provided through electronic correspondence with Erik Wickstrøm (see above).

Høyre (2005b): 'Joda, Høyre har tett kontakt med næringslivet'. Article Online. Available: <http://www.hoyre.no/Saker/artikkel/2005/1115535139.52/artikkel_print.pt> (accessed June 2005).

Labour Party (Arbeiderpartiet, DnA)

Arbeiderpartiers vedtekter [The Labour Party's Statutes] Available at: <http://www.dna.no> (accessed spring 2003).

Arbeiderpartiets Inntektsregnskap 1998–2004 [Labour Party income accounts 1998–2004] [7 documents]

Arbeiderpartiets beretninger 1981–2004 [Labour Party Biannual Reports 1981–2004] [18 documents]

Referanse- og vedtaksprotokoll: Landsmøtet, Folkets Hus 20.–22. November 1998 [Party Congress Books of Minutes 1998]

Referanse- og vedtaksprotokoll: Landsmøtet, Folkets Hus 9.–12. November 2000 [Party Congress Books of Minutes 2000]

Referanse- og vedtaksprotokoll: Landsmøtet, Folkets Hus 9.–12. November 2002 [Party Congress Books of Minutes 2002]

Samarbeidskomiteens møteprotokoll 1997–2004 [Book of minutes from the 'Co-operation Committee 1997] [8 documents]

Aktuelt Perspektiv (12.09.92): 'Slutt for det kollektive medlemsskapet'.

Andersen, Dag Terje (1995): *Arbeidet i organisasjonen*. Speech to the Norwegian Labour Party's 55th regular congress, 10–12 February 1995.

Arbeiderpartiet (1989): *Forslag til organisasjonsprogram*. Presented to the Labour Party's 52th regular congress 2–5 March 1989.

Arbeiderpartiet (1994): *Mål og strategisk plan 1994. A-info 7/94*. Strategic Plan 1994.

Arbeiderpartiet (1998): *Norges muligheter til å oppfylle forpiktelsene i Kyotoavtalen. By Karsten Jacobsen, Faggruppen for teknologi og miljø*. Memo.

Arbeiderpartiet (1999): *Sosialdemokrati 2000: Arbeiderpartiets programdebatt. Bakgrunn: teknologi og miljø. Arbeiderpartiets utredningsekretariat*. Party Memo.

Arbeiderpartiet (2002a): *Rapport til Arbeiderpartiets landsmøte 2002 fra Dialogforum*. Report presented to the Labour Party's 59th regular congress, 8–10 November 2002.

Arbeiderpartiet (2002b): *Faglig-politisk samarbeid i endring og utvikling*. Resolution passed at Labour Party's 59th regular congress, 8–10 November 2002.

Arbeiderpartiet (2003a): *Organiseringen av det faglig/politiske samarbeidet*. Memo.

Arbeiderpartiet (2003b): *Videreføring av det fagligpolitiske samarbeidet mellom NorskKommuneforbund og Arbeiderpartiet*. Formal co-operation agreement.

Arbeiderpartiet (2005a): 'Gjenvalg og tre nye' Online. Available: <http://www.dna.no/index.gan?id=32514&subid=0> (accessed April 2005).

Arbeiderpartiet (2005b): 'Programkomiteen'. Online. Available: <http://www.dna.no/print.gan?id=20173&subid=0> (accessed September 2005).

Arbeiderpartiet/NEKF/NKF (1997): *Felles innsats for felles mål. Kommunalpolitisk samarbeidsavtale Arbeiderpartiet, Norsk Elektriker og Kraftstasjonsforbund, Norsk Kommuneoforbund*. Formal co-operation agreement.

DnA-LO (1993): *Handlingsplan for Det norske Arbeiderparti og Landsorganisasjonen i Norge før valget i 2003*. Plan of action for DnA and LO before the 1993 general elections.

DnA-LO (2003): *Fagligpolitisk plattform for kommune- og fylkestingsvalget 2003*. Online. Available: <http://www.lo.no/lobasen/Content/1301/1301-fagligpolitiskmanifestvalget2003.pdf> (accessed October 2003)

DnA (17.01.03): *Party and Trade Union Co-operation* Online. Available: <http://www.dna.no/print.gan?id=13611&subid=0&printFriendly=yes> (accessed October 2005).

Gerhardsen, Rune (2002): *Untitled*. Contribution to the Labour Party's 59th regular congress, 8–10 November 2002.

Kolberg, Martin (2002): *Dialogsforums rapport – partiets organisatoriske utvikling*. Speech to the Labour Party's 59th regular congress, 8–10 November 2002.

Kolberg, Martin (2005): *Untitled*. Speech to the Labour Party's 60th regular congress, 9 April 2005.

Stoltenberg, Jens (2005): *Nytt flertall, ny solidaritet*. Opening Speech to the Labour Party's 60th regular congress, 7 April 2005.

Liberals (Venstre)

Vedtekter for Venstre [Liberal Party Statutes] Online. Available: <http://www.venstre.no> (accessed spring 2003).

Venstres inntektsregnskap 1998–2004 [Liberal Party income accounts 1998–2004] [7 documents]

Venstres årsmeldinger 1977–2004 [Liberal Party Annual Reports 1977–2004] [28 documents]

Venstre (2000a): *Ny vår for Venstre*. Report from an internal evaluation committee ('organisassjonsutvalget') to the Party Congress 7–9 April 2000.

Venstre (2000b): *Forslag til vedtak i forbindelse med 'Ny vår for Venstre'*. Proposal in connection with 'Ny vår for Venstre' to the Party Congress 7–9 April 2000.

Progress Party (Fremskrittspartiet, FrP)

Fremskrittspartiets vedtekter [Progress Party statutes] Online. Available: <http://www.frp.no> (accessed spring 2003).

Fremskrittspartiets inntektsregnskap 1998–2004 [Progress Party income accounts 1998–2004] [7 documents]

Fremskrittspartiets årsberetninger 1985–2005 [Progress Party Annual Reports 1985–2005 [17 documents]

Dagsorden og timeplan fra FrPs landsmøte 1997 [Progress Party Congress Agenda 1997]
Dagsorden og timeplan fra FrPs landsmøte 2000 [Progress Party Congress Agenda 1997]
Dagsorden og timeplan fra FrPs landsmøte 2001 [Progress Party Congress Agenda 1997]
Dagsorden og timeplan fra FrPs landsmøte 2002 [Progress Party Congress Agenda 1997]
Dagsorden og timeplan fra FrPs landsmøte 2003 [Progress Party Congress Agenda 1997]

Fremskrittspartiet (2001): *Vil bli regjeringsparti!* Strategic document passed by the Frp National

Council 19–20 February Online. Available: <http://www.frp.no/Strategi/Strategi.html> (accessed January 2001).

Socialist Left Party (Sosialistisk Folkeparti, SV)

The Socialist Left Party's Statutes Online. Available: <http://www.sv.no> (accessed spring 2003

Sosialistisk Venstrepartis inntektsregnskap 1998–2004 [Socialist Left Party income accounts 1998 –2004] [7 documents]

Sosialistisk Venstrepartis beretning 1977–2004 [Socialist Left Party Biannual Reports 1977–2005]

Protokoll fra SVs 14. ordinære landsmøte 8–11 mars 2001 [Books of Minutes from the Socialist Left Party's 15th Regular Congress 8–11 March 2001]

Protokoll fra SVs 15. ordinære landsmøte 6–9 mars 2003 [Books of Minutes from the Socialist Left Party's 15th Regular Congress 6–9 March 2003]

Sosialistisk Venstreparti (1999): *Folkevalgt: Et skoleringshefte for SV's kommunestyre- og fylkestingsrepresentanter*. Pamphlet for training local politicians.

Sosialistisk Venstreparti (2000a): *SVisj: SVprosjekt for visjonær organisasjonsutvikling*. Project Presentation Online. Available: <http://www.sv.no/svisj/prosjektbeskrivelse> (accessed October 2000).

Sosialistisk Venstreparti (2000b): *En solidarisk miljøpolitikk*. Memo from Election Manifesto Committee. Online. Available:<http://www.sv.no/politikk/program/annet.asp> Printed version provided by SV party headquarters in 2003

Sosialistisk Venstreparti (2000c): *Kunnskapssamfunnet*. Memo from Election Manifesto Committee. Online Available: <http://www.sv.no/politikk/program/annet.asp> Printed version provided by SV party headquarters in 2003

Sosialistisk Venstreparti (2000d): *Fred og sikkerhet*. Memo from Election Manifesto Committee. Online. Available: <http://www.sv.no/politikk/program/annet.asp> Printed version provided by SV party headquarters in 2003

Sosialistisk Venstreparti (2000e): *Lesereveiledning*. Memo from Election Manifesto Committee. Online. Available: <http://www.sv.no/politikk/program/annet.asp> Printed version provided by SV party headquarters in 2003

Interest Group Documents

Befalsbladet (5/2000): 'Fagligpolitisk samarbeid'.

Civita (2005): 'Board of Trustees' Online. Available: <http://www.civita.no/english.php?mod=content&id=12> (accessed March 2006).

NOF (2004): Vedtekter for Norges Offiserforbund. Online. Available: <http://www.milnytt.no/default.asp?layout=article&id=81> (accessed autumn 2005).

El and IT Statutes (2004): EL og IT Forbundets vedtekter Online. Available: <http://www.elogit.no/?id=4483&subid=0> (accessed autumn 2005).

Fellesforbundet (2005): 'Vi krever en aktiv industripolitikk'. Online. Available:<http://www.fellesforbundet.no/upload/VALG2005/FFannonse.pdf> (accessed autumn 2005).

Fagforbundet (2005): 'Jeg velger ikke bort jobben min'. Printed in Dagsavisen 10 September 2005.

LO 09.10.05 Online. Available: <http://www.lo.no> (accessed spring 2003).

LO (2005): *Forslag: Den faglige og politiske situasjonen*. LO executive proposal to the 2005 LO Congress Online. Available: <http://www.lo.no/portal/page?_Pageid=56.408198&_dad=portal&_schema=PORTAL> (accessed April 2005).

LO (2000): Beretning 2000 [LO Annual Report 2000]

LO (2001): Beretning 2001 [LO Annual Report 2000]

LO (2002): Beretning 2002 [LO Annual Report 2000]

LO (2003): Beretning 2003 [LO Annual Report 2000]
LO (2004): Beretning 2004 [LO Annual Report 2000]

LO Statutes (2003) Online. Available <http://www.lo.no/portal/page?_pageid=56,1313688&_dad=portal&_schema=PORTAL> (accessed spring 2003).

LO-Aktuelt (1996): 'Ap og LO adskilt'. Issue 20/96.

LO-Aktuelt (06.03.03): 'Det nye solidaritetsalternativet: Kraftige reaksjoner fra LO-forbund' Online. Available: <http://www.lo-aktuelt.no/kunder/lonytt/loaktueltarkiv.nsf/viewHTML/Tekster_Nyheter> (accessed November 2004)

LO-aktuelt (24.06.04): '– Det skal være lov å være FrP'er i LO' Online.Available: <http://www.frifagbevegelse.no/loaktuelt/arkiv_-_lo-aktuelt/article1834719.ece> (accessed June 2004/February 2010)

LO-Aktuelt (08.09.05): 'Venstrevind blant LO-folk' Online. Available: <http://frifagbevegelse.no/stortingsvalget/article1731655.ece> (accessed March 2006

LO-Aktuelt (19.09.05): 'En av fem stemte FrP' Online. Available: <http://frifagbevegelse.no/loaktuelt/nyheter/article1748139.ece> (accessed March 2006) <http://www.lo.no/portal/page?_pageid=56,408198&_dad=portal&_schema=PORTAL> (accessed April 2005).

LO-Aktuelt (20.11.05): 'Truer med å kutte partistøtte' Online. Available: <http://www.frifagbevegelse.no/loaktuelt/arkiv_-_lo-aktuelt/article1834358.ece> (accessed March 2006).

LO-DNA (1996): *Omstilling i statlig virksomhet*. Proposal from joint committee appointed by the 'Co-operation Committee' between LO and DnA.

Milnytt (09.03.02): 'Flere forbund reagerer sterkt mot Gerd-Liv Valla' Online. Available: <http://milnytt.no/default.asp?layout=article&id=582> (accessed September 2004).

NHO (09.09.03): 'Holder fast ved nedtrapping av partistøtten' Online. Available: <http://www.nho.no/printart3973.html> (accessed March 2005).

Valla (2005): DnAs Landsmøte 7.–10. April 2005: *Hilsningstale ved Gerd-Liv Valla*. Speech to the Labour Party's 60th regular congress, 10 April 2005.

YS (2005): 'Ny statsminister varsler ny politikk'. Article Online. Available: <http://www.ys.no/?module=Articles.publicShow;ID=1560;template=pr> (accessed 20 November 2005).

Øverland, Erling (2005): NHOs prioriteringer i valgåret 2005. Speech to the General Assembly of the Confederation of Norwegian Enterprise. Online. Available: <http://www.nho.no> (accessed February 2006)

Electronic Correspondence (with Headquarters of Parties and Interest Groups)

Halvorsen, Anne Gro (2005): *E-mail correspondence with Anne Gro Halvorsen* 8 November 2005.

Heinåli, Bergljot (2005): *E-mail correspondence with Bergljot Heinåli* 9 November 2005.

Hole, Trond Reidar (2005): *E-mail correspondence with Trond Reidar Hole* 21 April 2005.

Jota, Finn (2004): *E-mail correspondence with Finn Jota* 9 August, 10 September 2004.

Jota, Finn (2006): *E-mail correspondence with Finn Jota* 27 June 2006.

Longva, Hilde (2005): *E-mail correspondence with Hilde Longva* 2 November 2005.

Thomassen, Astrid (2003): *E-mail correspondence with Astrid Thomassen* 4 August, 4 September 2003.

Venås, Inger Helene (2005): *E-mail correspondence with Inger Helene Venås* 17 February 2005.

Wickstrøm, Erik (2005): *E-mail correspondence with Erik Wickstrøm* 15 July 2005.

List of Interviewees

Interviewee(s)	Party	Position	Date
Dagfinn Sundsbø	Centre Party	Party secretary-general	06.06.2003
Oddvar Igland	Centre Party	Secretary of Manifesto Committee	18.09.2003
Inger Helene Venås	Christian People's Party	Party secretary-general	11.06.2003
Inger Helene Venås	Christian People's Party	Party secretary-general	24.06.2006*
Dag Eyvind Holhjem	Christian People's Party	Secretary of Manifesto Committee	17.10.2003
Trond Reidar Hole	Conservatives	Party secretary-general	02.06.2003
Lars Andreas Lunde	Conservatives	Secretary of Manifesto Committee	06.11.2003
Beret Bråten	Labour Party	Secretary of Manifesto Committee	18.11.2006
Siri Bjerke	Labour Party	Secretary of Manifesto Committee	10.12.2003
Finn Jota	Labour Party	Party-union adviser (*faglig-politisk rådgiver*)	18.11.2003
Finn Jota*	Labour Party	Party-union adviser(*faglig-politisk rådgiver*)	14.09.2004
Martin Kolberg	Labour Party	Party secretary	18.09.2003
Martin Kolberg	Labour Party	Party secretary	07.08.2004
Geir Rune Nyhus	Liberals	Party secretary-general	05.06.2003
Alfred Bjørlo/Sverre Molandsveen	Liberals	Secretaries of Manifesto Committee	02.10.2003
Geir Mo	Progress Party	Party secretary-general	17.07.2003
Ronny Røste	Progress Party	Secretary of Manifesto Committee	02.08.2003
Bård Vegar Solhjell	Socialist Left Party	Party secretary	30.05.2003
Tor Brostigen	Socialist Left Party	Secretary of Manifesto Committee	19.09.2003
Svein Kiran	Socialist Left Party	Party adviser (former party-union secretary)	20. & 23.06.2005*

* Additional telephone conversation (follow-up).

appendix b: the survey – a methodological note

The questionnaire was sent to all members of the national executive committee and to all relevant party bureaucrats in the seven parties studied here (see Chapter 1 for details). Hence, there is no risk that the results reflect peculiarities in the composition of a sample rather than true characteristics of the party elite population. In other words, the problem of sampling errors is non-existent, and significance tests to estimate probabilities have not been conducted. However, for several reasons, we must nonetheless interpret the results with caution.

First, we must ask whether the non-responses are a problem. The overall response rate is indeed satisfactory (see Chapter 1), but might it be that those who did not reply differ systematically from the others in relevant respects? A noteworthy discrepancy between the population and the respondents is that there are relatively few executive members, with positions in Parliament and government, who replied in the cases of the Conservative Party and the Christian People's Party. One possible explanation is, obviously, that these parties were in power at the time of the research, and cabinet ministers are particularly busy people. On the other hand, it is not clear how this might have influenced the results. The 'under-represented' part of the elite is on the one hand very attractive for interest groups to have contact with, but perhaps also less accessible than the employed party staff. Most important is the fact that national executive members generally tend to be, or have been, officials in interest groups more extensively than employed party staff. The possible implications of this difference will be discussed in due course.

Second, random variation may nonetheless occur.[216] Hence, the question is whether or not the observed differences between respondents from different political parties actually reflect systematic variation. For example, it could be that a specific function, involving special contact with interest groups, was not filled in at a particular party headquarters at the time of the research due to sick leave or reorganisation. This does, of course, also affect the extent to which the results for the individual party are likely to be valid for a longer time perspective. Thus, we need to ask: given a theoretical premise that there is in the population no variation between parties' elites, is the observed variation in contact and personal overlaps with interest groups likely to have occurred by chance? Put differently, only clear differences in percentages should be, and are, reported.

However, intuitively, it seems reasonable to assume that a survey conducted among a small population is more easily influenced by chance than one of a large population. Nonetheless, I must emphasise that the size of the population is not a problem *as such*. The entire top elites of the seven major Norwegian parties have been included in the survey. Since we are dealing with individuals in key positions, the behaviour of every single member can be assumed to matter for the

216. In the social sciences, there are few, if any, deterministic relationships, and mapped elite behaviour can, in theory, be seen as a series of stochastic experiments (cf. Aaberge and Laake 1984; Hellevik 1991; Taylor and Karlin 1998).

party at large. The point is that it is crucial to report all incidents where even a few different answers would have influenced the results, the conclusions, significantly.

A few other methodological issues should also be noted. The first concerns the time horizon and memory. Many questions deal with the respondent's behaviour towards interest groups the past year. This is a common type of construction when mapping contact frequencies of political actors, but we should note that most people find it hard to remember accurately what happened in such a relatively distant past (Haraldsen 1999: 166). Thus, some respondents may not have been able to recall all relevant contact. Nevertheless, in practice applying shorter time horizon was not a viable alternative. A year is needed to cover all major party organisational activities. Furthermore, and importantly, none of the pilot respondents mentioned the time horizon as a problem.

Another matter is the likelihood of respondents overestimating contact. Elite members who have limited contacts will perhaps be less motivated to reply, so that a certain self-selection of those characterised by having frequent contact is possible. Perhaps the differences among parties also reflect an over-representation of responses regarded as desirable by society or the party itself. If the prevalent norm is to have links with civil society (or the opposite), respondents may tend to over-report (or under-report) contact with interest groups. But the survey material is nevertheless a valuable source as a supplement to the data material from the organisational level as long as we follow the general rule of careful interpretation: to look for major tendencies in the survey material, not detailed differences (for further details on the survey material, see Allern 2007).

appendix c: list of organisation categories

Primary-sector organisations

Employers' organisations, business and trade associations (incl. NHO)

LO and LO unions

Employees' and professional organisations outside LO

Christian and missionary organisations

Other religious organisations or communities

Organisations related to non-religious philosophies of life

Temperance organisations

Language associations

Community-centred organisations, related to culture, sport, youth, elderly, hobbies, local environment etc.

Humanitarian and social aid organisations

Internationally-oriented organisations

Organisations in favour of EU membership

Organisations against EU membership

Environmental and conservationist organisations

Women's organisations (housewives' and farmer women's unions)

Immigrant and refugee organisations

Client organisations

Consumer organisations

Other organisations

Note:
LO = Confederation of Trade Unions (Landsorganisasjonen, LO)
NHO = Confederation of Norwegian Enterprise (Næringslivets Hovedorganisasjon, NHO)
EU = European Union

appendix d

Table D1: Share of Labour Party top elite who hold or have held office, are or have been staff members at the national or local levels in various interest groups 2003/2004. Per cent[1]

	Officials		Staff	No positions/ response	Total	N
	Present	Former				
LO and LO unions	15	19	5	61	100	21
Christian organisations	0	0	5	95	100	21
Organisations related to culture, sport, youth, elderly, hobbies etc.	10	5	5	80	100	21
Humanitarian and social organisations	5	0	5	90	100	21
Internationally-oriented organisations	10	5	0	85	100	21
Organisations in favour of EU membership	5	5	5	85	100	21
Organisations against EU membership	0	0	10	90	100	21
Women's and feminist organisations	10	0	0	90	100	21
Immigrant and refugee organisations	5	0	0	95	100	21
Other organisations	5	10	0	85	100	21
Organisations in general (positions in one or more organisations)	63*		19	43	100	21

1 The table is based on two different set of questions, but if a respondent is/has been both official and staff member the answer is registered only in the 'official category'. Due to the choice of an open-question with regard to staff experience, it is not possible to separate no-answers from 'no response', but I have chosen to subtract those who answered that they did have experience as staff but were/had not been officials from the cell of 'no positions' (none).

* Includes elite members who are former/present officials, or both.

Table D2: Share of the Conservatives' top elite who hold or have held office, are/ or have been staff members at the national or local levels in various interest groups 2003/2004. Per cent[1]

	Officials		Staff	No positions/ response	Total	N
	Present	Former				
Employers' organisations, business and trade organisations	0	0	14	86	100	7
Language organisations	0	14	0	86	100	7
Organisations related to culture, sport, youth, elderly, hobbies etc.	14	14	0	72	100	7
Humanitarian and social aid organisations	0	14	0	86	100	7
Organisations in favour of EU membership	14	14	14	58	100	7
Other organisations	14	0	0	86	100	7
Organisations in general (positions in one or more organisations)	43*		14	43	100	7

1 The table is based on two different set of questions, but if a respondent is/has been both official and staff member the answer is registered only in the 'official category'. Due to the choice of an open question with regard to staff experience, it is not possible to separate no-answers from 'no response', but I have chosen to subtract those who answered that they did have experience as staff but were/had not been officials from the cell of 'no positions' (none).

* Includes elite members who are former/present officials, or both.

Table D3: Share of Centre Party top elite who hold or have held office, are/or have been staff members at the national or local levels in various interest groups 2003/2004. Per Cent[1]

	Officials		Staff	No positions/ response	Total	N
	Present	Former				
Primary-sector organisations	0	8	0	92	100	13
Employees' and professional organisations outside LO	8	0	8	84	100	13
Community-centred organisations, related to culture, sport, youth, elderly, hobbies, local environment etc.	15	8	0	77	100	13
Humanitarian and social organisations	0	8	0	92	100	13
Organisation against EU membership	16	23	0	61	100	13
Environmental organisations	0	8	0	92	100	13
Client organisations	8	0	0	92	100	13
Organisations in general (positions in one or more organisations)	61*		0	39	100	13

1 The table is based on two different set of questions, but if a respondent is/has been both official and staff member the answer is registered only in the 'official category'. Due to the choice of an open question with regard to staff experience, it is not possible to separate no-answers from 'no response', but I have chosen to subtract those who answered that they did have experience as staff but were/had not been officials from the cell of 'no positions' (none).

* Includes elite members who are former/present officials, or both.

Table D4: Share of Christian People's Party top elite who hold or have held office, are/or have been staff members at the national or local levels in various interest groups 2003/2004. Per Cent[1]

	Officials		Staff	No positions/ response	Total	N
	Present	Former				
Christian and missionary organisations	0	33	11	56	100	9
Other religious organisations and organised religious communities	11	11	0	78	100	9
Community-centred organisations, related to culture, sport, youth, elderly, hobbies, local environment etc.	0	22	11	67	100	9
Internationally-oriented organisations	0	11	11	78	100	9
Environmental organisations	0	11	0	89	100	9
Client organisations	0	0	11	89	100	9
Organisations in general (positions in one or more organisations)	44*		44	22	100	9

1 The table is based on two different set of questions, but if a respondent is/has been both official and staff member the answer is registered only in the 'official category'. Due to the choice of an open question with regard to staff experience, it is not possible to separate 'no answers' from 'no response', but I have chosen to subtract those who answered that they did have experience as staff but were/had not been officials from the cell of 'no positions' (none).

* Includes elite members who are former/present officials, or both.

Table D5: Share of Socialist Left Party top elite who hold or have held office, are/ or have been staff members at the national or local levels in various interest groups 2003/2004. Per Cent[1]

	Officials		Staff	No positions/ response	Total	N
	Present	Former				
LO and LO Unions	0	17	8	75	100	12
Organisations related to non-religious philosophies of life	0	8	8	84	100	12
Community-centred organisations, related to culture, sport, youth, elderly, hobbies, local environment etc.	8	8	16	68	100	12
Humanitarian and social aid organisations	0	0	8	92	100	12
Internationally-oriented organisations	8	0	0	92	100	12
Organisations against EU membership	25	17	0	58	100	12
Organisations in general (positions in one or more organisations)	58*		17	25	100	12

1 The table is based on two different set of questions, but if a respondent is/has been both official and staff member the answer is registered only in the 'official category'. Due to the choice of an open question with regard to staff experience, it is not possible to separate no-answers from 'no response', but I have chosen to subtract those who answered that they did have experience as staff but were/had not been officials from the cell of 'no positions' (none).

* Includes elite members who are former/present officials, or both.

Table D6: Share of Progress Party top elite who hold or have held office, are/or have been staff members at the national or local levels in various interest groups 2003/2004. Per cent[1]

	Officials		Staff	No positions/ response	Total	N
	Present	Former				
Employees' and professional organisations outside LO	0	8	0	92	100	12
Community-centred organisations, related to culture, sport, youth, elderly, hobbies, local environment etc.	25	8	8	59	99	12
Immigrant and refugee organisations	8	0	0	92	100	12
Organisations in general (positions in one or more organisations)	42**		0	58	100	12

1 The table is based on two different set of questions, but if a respondent is/has been both official and staff member the answer is registered only in the 'official category'. Due to the choice of an open question with regard to staff experience, it is not possible to separate no-answers from 'no response', but I have chosen to subtract those who answered that they did have experience as staff but were/had not been officials from the cell of 'no positions' (none).

* Includes elite members who are former/present officials, or both.

appendix e

Table E1: Total membership figures of major labour market organisations 1955–2004. All membership figures are from the end/turn of the year

Year	LO[1]	YS & AF/ Akademikerne	Other employee org.	Farmers' Union[2]	Smallholders' Union	N entitled to vote
1955	542 105	–	109 346	60 000	20 000	2 298 376
1965[3]	574 295	–	155 676	59 000	*	2 406 866
1975[4]	655 030	71 009	176 934	54 100	6000	2 780 190
1985[5]	768 778	264 264	169 009	65 170	14 500	3 100 479
1995	792 575	464 212	130 634	66 625	12 041	3 311 190
1998	838 628	509 074	140 257	62 800	11 810	3 359 433
2001	796 272	319 544	365 455	59 170	10 651	3 359 433
2002	800 259	328 100	377 636	57 729	9857	3 421 741
2003	838 749	334 308	335 355	57 833	7971	3 421 741
2004	831 464	339 173	339 996	58 958	7921	3 421 741

1 From 1955–1998 the figures are adjusted to transitions of members at the union level (see Stokke 2000). Hence, there is a rupture in the time series for LO in 2001, but not a significant one. Furthermore, the figures include pensioners. Thus, LO's share is over-emphasised in relation to the total number of employees (Stokke 1998: 2000).

2 In 1970, the Farmers' Union ended the practice of separating main members from family members in their files, which explains the increase of membership until the 1990s (Gjerdåker 1995: 298).

3 The figure of the Farmers' Union only includes so-called 'principal members' possessing agricultural areas.

4 The figure of the Farmers' and Smallholders' Union is from 1974, and consists of 'principal members' only.

5 The figure of the Farmers' and Smallholders' Union is from 1986.

* Unknown.

Source: Stokke (2000) and NOS Statistical Yearbook 2001–2004, Steen (1988: 252–253), Gjerdåker (1995: 298) and the headquarters of the Farmers' Union and the Smallholders' Union (Heinåli 2005 and Halvorsen 2005 [e-mail correspondence] – see appendix B).

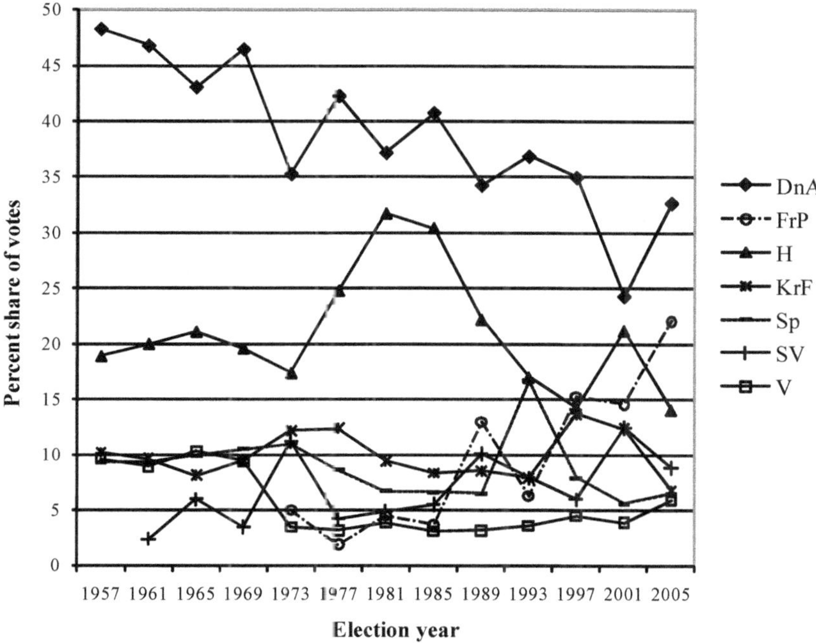

Figure E1: Distribution of votes by party 1957–2005

Source: Statistics Norway (www.ssb.no) and Ministry of Local Government and Regional Development (2005). *Landsoversikt-Stortingsvalget* Online. Available: <http://www.dep.no/krd/html/valgresultat2005/frameset.html> (accessed October 2005)

references

Aaberge, R. and Laake P. (1984): 'Om statistiske teoriar for tolking av data', *Tidsskrift for samfunnsforskning*, 25: 165–86.

Aalberg, T. (2005): 'Norway', *European Journal of Political Research*, 44 (7–8): 1140–6.

Aardal, B. (1991): 'Green Politics: A Norwegian Experience', *Scandinavian Political Studies*, 13 (2): 147–64.

— (1993): *Energi og miljø: Nye stridsspørsmål i møte med gamle strukturer.* Oslo: Institute for Social Research, report no. 15. *Doctoral Thesis*.

— (1999): 'Holdningsprofiler og stemmegivning', in B. Aardal (ed.): *Velgere i 90-årene*. Oslo NKS-forlaget.

— (2000): 'The Religious Factor in Political Life in the Nordic Countries', *Tidsskrift for kirke, religion og samfunn*, 13 (2): 129–39.

— (2003a): 'Velgere i bevegelse', in B. Aardal (ed.): *Velgere i villrede...: En analyse av stortingsvalget 2001*. Oslo: N.W. Damm & Søn.

— (2003b): 'Ideologi og stemmegivning', in B. Aardal (ed.): *Velgere i villrede...: En analyse av stortingsvalget 2001*. Oslo: N. W. Damm & Søn.

— (2007): 'Saker og standpunkter', in B. Aardal (ed.): *Norske velgere: En studie av stortingsvalget 2005*. Oslo: N. W. Damm & Søn.

Aasland, T. (1974): *Fra Landmannsorganisasjon til Bondeparti: Politisk debatt og taktikk i Norsk Landmandsforbund 1896–1920*. Tromsø: Universitetsforlaget.

Allardt, E. (2001): 'Party Systems and Voter Alignments in the Tradition of Political Sociology', in L. Karvonen and S. Kuhnle (eds): *Party Systems and Voter Alignments Revisited.* London: Routledge.

Alldén, L. (1980): *Medlemmene av Sosialistisk Folkeparti: En undersøkelse av medlemsskarens sosiale sammensetning og regionale fordeling 1961–1973*. Oslo: Department of Sociology, University of Oslo. *Thesis*.

Allern, E. H. (2001): *På parti med miljøbevegelsen? En forstudie av norsk politiske partiers forhold til miljøorganisasjonene*. Oslo: NIBR Working Paper 2001:104.

— (2007): *Parties, Interest Groups and Democracy: Political Parties and their Relationship with Interest Groups in Norway*. Oslo: Department of Political Science, University of Oslo. *PhD Thesis*. Oslo: Unipub.

Allern, E. H. and Aylott, N. (2009): 'Overcoming the Fear of Commitment: Pre-electoral Coalitions in Norway and Sweden', *Acta Politica* 44: 259–85.

Allern, E. H. and Heidar, K. (2001): 'Partier og interesseorganisasjoner i Norge', in J. Sundberg (ed.): *Partier och interesseorganisationer i Norden*. Åbo: NORD-serien.

Allern, E. H., Helgesen, M. and Predelli, L. N. (2001): *Mellom konflikt og integrasjon: Evaluering av Kontaktutvalget mellom innvandrere og myndighetene*. Oslo: NIBR Report 2001:11.

Allern, E. H., Aylott, N. and Christiansen, F. J. (2007): 'Social Democrats and Trade Unions in Scandinavia: The Decline and Persistence of Institutional Relationships', *European Journal of Political Research* 46 (5): 607–35.

Allern, E. H., Aylott, N. and Christiansen, F. J. (2010): *Scenes from a Marriage: Social Democrats and Trade Unions in Scandinavia*. CVPA Working Paper February 2010. Copenhagen: University of Copenhagen.

Allern, E. H. and Saglie, J. (2008): 'Between Electioneering and "Politics as Usual": The Involvement of Interest Groups in Norwegian Electoral Politics', in D.Farrell, D. Schmitt-Beck and R. Schmitt-Beck (eds): *Non-Party Actors in Electoral Politics: The Role of Interest Groups and Independent Citizens in Contemporary Election Campaigns.* Baden-Baden: Nomos Verlag.

Allern, E. H., Bay, A.-H. and Saglie, J. (2009): 'Velferdspolitisk konsensus og elitesamarbeid? Partiprogrammer og politikkutforming på 2000-tallet', in A.-H. Bay, A. W. Pedersen and J. Saglie (eds): *Når velferd blir politikk. Partier, organisasjoner og opinion.* Oslo: Abstrakt forlag.

Almond, G. A. and Powell, G. B. (1966): *Comparative Politics: A Developmental Approach*. Boston, MA: Little, Brown.

Andersen, J. G. and Bjørklund, T. (1990): 'Structural Changes and New Cleavages: the Progress Parties in Denmark and Norway', *Acta Sociologica,* 33 (3): 195–217.

— (2000): 'Radical Right-wing Populism in Scandinavia: From Tax Revolt to Neo-liberalism and Xenophobia', in P. Hainsworth (ed.): *The Politics of the Extreme Right: From the Margins to the Mainstream*. London: Pinter.

Andersen, S. (1997): *Case-studier og generalisering: Forskningsstrategi og design*. Bergen: Fagbokforlaget.

Andersen, Ø. (1999): *Organisasjonsdeltakelse i Norge fra 1983 til 1997*. SSB report 1999/34. Oslo/Kongsvinger: Statistics Norway.

Andeweg, R. (1999): 'Parties, Pillars and the Politics of Accommodation: Weak or Weakening Linkages? The Case of Dutch Consociationalism', in K. R. Luther and K. Deschouwer (eds): *Party Elites in Divided Societies*. London: Routledge.

Anthonsen, M., Lindvall, J. and Schmidt-Hansen, U. (forthcoming): 'Social Democrats, Unions and Corporatism: Denmark and Sweden Compared', *Party Politics*.

Arter, D. (1999): *Scandinavian Politics Today*. Manchester: Manchester University Press.

— (2001) (ed.): *From Farmyard to City Square? The Electoral Adaptation of the Nordic Agrarian Parties*. Aldershot: Ashgate.

— (2003): 'Scandinavia: What's Left is the Social Democratic Welfare Consensus', *Parliamentary Affairs*, 56: 75–98.

Atkinson, A. B. (1999): 'The Distribution of Income in the UK and OECD Countries in the Twentieth Century', *Oxford Review of Economic Policy*, 15 (4): 56–75.

Aylott, N. (2003): 'After the Divorce: Social Democrats and Trade Unions in Sweden', *Party Politics*, 9 (3): 369–90.

Barney, D. D. and Laycock, D (1999) 'Right-Populists and Plebiscitary Politics in Canada', *Party Politics* 5 (3): 317–339.

Bates, R. H., Greif, A., Levi, M., Rosenthal, J.-L. and Weingast, B. R. (1998): *Analytic Narratives*. Princeton, NJ: Princeton University Press.

Bátora, J. (2006): *Dipl@macy.com or Diplomacy.gone? Foreign Affairs in the Information Age*. Oslo: Department of Political Science, University of Oslo. *PhD Thesis*.

Baumgartner, F. R. and Leech, B. (1998): *Basic Interests: The Importance of Groups in Politics and in Political Science*. Princeton NJ: Princeton University Press.

Beer, S. (1965/1982): *Modern British Politics: Parties and Pressure Groups in the Collectivist Age*. New York: W. W. Norton.

Berg, S. L. (2003): *Samling om verdier – en studie av Kristelig Folkeparti 1969–2001*. Oslo: Department of Political Science. *Thesis*.

Berger, S. (ed.) (1981): *Organizing Interests in Western Europe: Pluralism, Corporatism and the Transformation of Politics*. Cambridge: Cambridge University Press.

Bergh, T. (1987): *Storhetstid*, volume 5 in E. Bull, A. Kokkvoll and J. Sverdrup (eds): *Arbeiderbevegelsens historie i Norge*. Oslo: Tiden Norsk Forlag.

— (1999): 'Solidaritetsalternativet – typisk LO?', in T. Bergh, S. Halvorsen, S.-A. Larsen, M. Hegna, L.-A. Jensen, T. A. Johansen, L. Langangen, E. Lorenz and E. A. Terjesen (eds): *Arbeiderhistorie 1999: Årbok for Arbeiderbevegelsens arkiv og bibliotek*. Oslo: Arbeiderbevegelsens arkiv og bibliotek.

Berglund, F. (2003): 'Valget i 2001 – skillelinjemodellens endelikt?', in B. Aardal (ed.): *Velgere i villrede...: En analyse av stortingsvalget 2001*. Oslo: N.W. Damm & Søn.

— (2007): 'Nye sosiale skiller: Sektor teller, ideologi avgjør', in B. Aaardal (ed.): *Norske velgere: En studie av stortingsvalget 2005*. Oslo: N.W. Damm & Søn.

Berglund, S. and Lindström, U. (1978): *The Scandinavian Party System(s)*. Lund: Studentlitteratur.

Berry, J. M. (1997): *The Interest Group Society*. New York: Addison Wesley Longman.

— (2002): 'Validity and Reliability Issues in Elite Interviewing', PS*Online*. Available at <http://www.apsanet.org> (accessed December 2002).

Betz, H.-G. (1998): 'Introduction', in H.-G. Betz and S. Immerfall (eds): *The New Politics of the Right: Neo-populist Parties and Movements in Established Democracies*. New York: St. Martin's Press.

Beyers, J. (2008): 'Policy Issues, Organisational Format and the Political Strategies of Interest Organizations', *West European Politics*, 31 (6): 1188–211.

Beyers, J., Eising, R. and Mahoney, W. (2008): 'Researching Interest Group Politics in Europe and Elsewhere: Much We Study, Little We Know', *West European Politics*, 31 (6): 1103–128.

Bille, L. and Christiansen, F. J. (2000): *Parties and Interest Organizations in Denmark 1960–98*. Presented at the Southwestern Social Science Association conference, Galveston, TX. *Conference paper*.

Bilstad, K.-A. (1994): 'Konfliktstruktur og partiavstand', in K. Heidar and L. Svåsand (eds): *Partiene i en brytningstid*. Bergen: Alma Mater.
Bindekrantz, A. (2005): 'Interest Group Strategies: Navigating Between Privileged Access and Strategies of Pressure', *Political Studies,* 53: 694–715.
Bjørgum, J. (1999): 'Arbeiderpartiet og LO', in T. Bergh, S. Halvorsen, S.-A. Larsen, M. Hegna, L.-A. Jensen, T. A. Johansen, L. Langangen, E. Lorenz and E. A. Terjesen (eds): *Arbeiderhistorie 1999: Årbok for Arbeiderbevegelsens arkiv og bibliotek*. Oslo: Arbeiderbevegelsens arkiv og bibliotek.
Bjørklund, T. (1983a): 'Fra lokalparti til landsparti', in O. Garvik (ed.): *Kristelig Folkeparti mellom tro og makt*. Oslo: J. W. Cappelens Forlag.
— (1983b): 'Kvinnepartiet med menn i toppen', in O. Garvik (ed.): *Kristelig Folkeparti mellom tro og makt*. Oslo: J. W. Cappelens Forlag.
— (1984): 'Den krympende velgerflokk', in O. Grepstad and J. Nerbøvik (eds): *Venstres hundre år*. Oslo: Gyldendal Norsk Forlag.
— (2001): 'Hvor godt egnet er "skillelinjemodellen" til å forklare norske velgeres partivalg i tidsrommet 1945–1997?', *Tidsskrift for samfunnsforskning*, 42 (1): 31–63.
Bjørklund, T. and Andersen, J. G. (2002): 'Anti-Immigration Parties in Denmark and Norway: The Progress Parties and the Danish People's Party', in M. Schain, A. Zolberg and P. Hossay (eds): *Shadows over Europe: The Development and Impact of the Extreme Right in Western Europe*. New York: Palgrave Macmillan.
Bjørklund, T. and Hagtvet, B. (1981): 'De bleknede skillelinjer – Arbeiderkultur og motkultur som bølgebrytere mot Høyre', in T. Bjørklund and B. Hagtvet (eds.) *Høyrebølgen: epokeskifte i norsk politikk?* Oslo: Aschehoug, 1981.
Bjørklund, T. and Hellevik, O. (1988): 'De grønne stridsspørsmål i norsk politikk', *Politica,* 20 (1): 414–31.
Bjørnson, Ø. (1990): *På klassekampens grunn*, volume 2 in A. Kokkvoll and J. Sverdrup (eds): *Arbeiderbevegelsens historie i Norge*. Oslo: Tiden Norsk Forlag.
Blom, I. (1984): 'En liten ondskap?', in O. Grepstad and J. Nerbøvik (eds): *Venstres hundre år*. Oslo: Gyldendal Norsk Forlag.
Blom-Hansen, J. and Daugbjerg, C. (eds) (1999): *Magtens organisering: Stat og interesseorganisationer i Danmark*. Århus: Forlaget Systime.
Blyth, M. and Katz, R. (2005): 'From Catch-all Politics to Cartelization: The Political Economy of the Cartel Party', *West European Politics*, 28 (1): 33–60.
Borgatti, S. P. and Everett, M. (1997): 'Network Analysis of 2-Mode Data', *Social Networks,* 19: 243–69.
Bortne, Ø., Grenstad, G., Selle, P. and Strømsnes, K. (2001): *Norsk miljøvernorganisering mellom stat og lokalsamfunn*. Oslo: Det Norske Samlaget.
Broder, D. (1972): *The Party's Over: The Failure of Party Politics in America*. New York: Harper and Row.
Budge, I. and Farlie, D. (1983): 'Party Competition – Selective Emphasis or Direct Confrontation? An Alternative View with Data', in H. Daalder and P. Mair (eds): *Western European Party Systems*. Beverly Hills, CA: SAGE.
Budge, I. and Laver, M. (1993): 'The Policy Basis of Government Coalitions: A Comparative Investigation', *British Journal of Political Science* 23 (4): 499–519.
Bull, E. (1985): *Arbeiderklassen blir til*, volume 1 in E. Bull, A. Kokkvoll and J. Sverdrup (eds): *Arbeiderbevegelsens historie i Norge*. Oslo: Tiden Norsk Forlag
Carter, E. (2005): *The Extreme Right in Western Europe*. Manchester: Manchester University Press.
CCS – London School of Economics' Centre for Civil Society (2004): *Definition of Civil Society* (http://www.lse.ac.uk/collections/CCS/introduction.htm)
Chhibber, P. K. (1999): *Democracy Without Associations: Transformation of the Party System and Social Changes in India*. Ann Arbor, MI: University of Michigan Press.
Christensen, D. A. (1992): *Bondeparti, Distriktsparti eller Folkeparti; Ei komparativ analyse av fornyinga av bondepartia i Noreg og Sverige*. Bergen: Department of Comparative Politics, University of Bergen. *Thesis*.
— (1996): 'The Left-Wing Opposition in Denmark, Norway and Sweden: Cases of Euro-phobia'?, *West European Politics,* 19 (3): 525–46.
— (2001): 'The Norwegian Agrarian-Centre Party: Class, Rural or Catchall Party?', in D. Arter (ed.): *From Farmyard to City Square? The Electoral Adaptation of the Nordic Agrarian Parties*. Aldershot: Ashgate.

— (2005): 'Senterpartiene i Norge og Sverige', in M. Demker and L. Svåsand (eds): *Partiernas århundrade: fempartimodellens oppgang och fall i Norge og Sverige.* Stockholm: Santérus Förlag.

Christensen, D. A. and Midtbø, T. (1998): 'Leaders and Activists in Scandinavian Left Socialist Parties: Still Pressure from Below?', in D. A. Christensen (ed): *Venstresosialistisk EU politikk: Ei analyse av Sosialistisk Venstreparti i Noreg, Vänsterpartiet i Sverige og Socialistisk Folkeparti i Danmark 1973–1997.* Bergen: Department of Comparative Politics, University of Bergen. *Doctoral Thesis.*

Christiansen, P. M. and Rommetvedt, H (1999): 'From Corporatism to Lobbyism? Parliaments, Executives, and Organized Interests in Denmark and Norway', *Scandinavian Political Studies*, 22 (3): 195–220.

Ciegler, A. J. and Loomis, B.A. (eds) (2002): *Interest Group Politics.* Washington DC: CQ Press.

Coase, R. H. (1937): 'The Nature of the Firm', *Economica*, New Series IV, November, 386–405.

Cohen, W. M. and Levinthal, D. (1990) 'Absorptive Capacity: A New Perspective on Learning and Innovation', *Administrative Science Quarterly*, 35 (1990): 128–52.

Conway, M., Connor Green, J. and Currinder, M. (2002): 'Interest Group Money in Elections', in A. J. Ciegler and B. A. Loomis (eds): *Interest Group Politics.* Washington, DC: CQ Press.

Coxall, B. (2001): *Pressure Groups in British Politics.* Harlow: Longman.

Dalton, R. J. (1994): *The Green Rainbow: Environmental Groups in Western Europe.* New Haven, CT: Yale University Press.

— (2002a): *Citizen Politics: Public Opinion and Political Parties in Advanced Industrial Democracies.* New York: Chatham House Publishers/Seven Bridges Press.

— (2002b): 'The Decline of Party Identifications', in R. J. Dalton and M. P. Wattenberg (eds): *Parties Without Partisans: Political Change in Advanced Industrial Democracies.* Oxford: Oxford University Press.

Dalton, R. J.; Flanagan, S. C. and Beck P. A. (1984): *Electoral Change in Advanced Industrial Democracies: Realignment or Dealignment?* Princeton, NJ: Princeton University Press.

Dalton, R. J.; Kuechler, M. and Bürklin, W. (1990): 'The Challenge of New Movements', in R. J. Dalton and M. Kuechler (eds): *Challenging the Political Order: New Social and Political Movements in Western Democracies.* Cambridge: Polity Press.

Dalton, R. J.; McAllister, I. and Wattenberg, M. P. (2002): 'The Consequences of Partisan Dealignment', in R. J. Dalton and M. P. Wattenberg (eds): *Parties Without Partisans. Political Change in Advanced Industrial Democracies.* Oxford: Oxford University Press.

Danielsen, R. (1964): *Tidsrommet 1870–1908*, volume 2 in C. J. Hambro, J. S. Worm-Müller, K.Bjørnstad and S. Steen (eds): *Det Norske Storting gjennom 150 år.* Oslo: Gyldendal.

— (1984): *Borgerlig oppdemningspolitikk 1918–1940,* volume 2 in *Høyres Historie.* Oslo: J. W. Cappelens Forlag.

Daugbjerg, C. and Marsh, D. (1998) 'Explaining Policy Outcomes: Integrating the Policy Network Approach with Macro-level and Micro-level Analysis', in D. Marsh (ed.): *Comparing Policy Networks: Policy Networks in Theoretical and Comparative Perspective.* Milton Keynes: Open University Press.

Demker, M. and Svåsand, L. (2005) 'Den nordiska fempartimodellen. En tilfällighet eller et fundament?', in M. Demker and L. Svåsand (eds): *Partiernas århundrade: fempartimodellens oppgang och fall i Norge og Sverige.* Stockholm: Santérus Förlag.

de Lange, S. (2008): *From Pariah to Power: The Government Participation of Radical Right-Wing Populist Parties in West European Democracies.* Antwerp: Department of Political Science, University of Antwerp. PhD Thesis.

Denver, D. (1988): 'Britain: Centralized Parties with Decentralized Selection', in M. Gallagher and M. Marsh (eds): *Candidate Selection in Comparative Perspective: The Secret Garden of Politics.* London: SAGE.

Dexter, L. A. (1970): *Elite and Specialized Interviewing.* Evanston, IL: Northwestern University Press.

Diani, M. (1992): 'The Concept of Social Movement', *The Sociological Review* 40 (1): 1–25.

Diani, M. and McAdam, D. (eds) (2003): *Social Movements and Networks: Relational Approaches to Collective Actions.* Oxford: Oxford University Press.

Dillman, D. A. (2000): *Mail and Internet Surveys: The Tailored Design Method.* New York: John Wiley & Sons.

DiMaggio, P. J. and Powell, W. W. (1983): 'The Iron Cage Revisited: Institutional Isomorphism and Collective Rationality in Organizational Fields', *American Sociological Review*, 48 (2): 147–60.

DiMaggio, P. J. and Powell, W. W. (1991): in P. J. DiMaggio and W. W. Powell (eds): *The New Institutionalism in Organizational Analysis*. Chicago, IL: University of Chicago Press.

Downs, A. (1957): *An Economic Theory of Democracy*. New York: Harper & Row.

Duverger, M. (1954/1972): *Political Parties. Their Organization and Activity in the Modern State*. London: Methuen.

– (1968): *Sociologie Politique*. Paris: Presses Universitaires France.

– (1972): *Party Politics and Pressure Groups: A Comparative Introduction*. New York: Crowell.

Dølvik, J. E. and Stokke, T. A. (1998): 'Norway: The Revival of Centralised Concertation', in A. Ferner and R. Hyman (eds): *Changing Industrial Relations in Europe*. Oxford: Blackwell.

Eatwell, R. (2000): 'The Rebirth of the "Extreme-Right" in Western Europe?', *Parliamentary Affairs*, 53: 407–25.

Egeberg, M. (1981): *Stat og organisasjoner: Flertallstyre, partsstyre og byråkrati i norsk politikk*. Oslo: Universitetsforlaget.

Ekeberg, J. O. and Snoen, J. A. (2001): *Kong Carl: En uautorisert biografi om Carl I. Hagen*. Oslo: Kagge.

Eliassen, K. A. (1971): *Fagbevegelsen og de sosialdemokratiske partier*. Bergen: University of Bergen, Department of Sociology. *Thesis*.

Elvander, N. (1980): *Skandinavisk arbetarrörelse*. Stockholm: LiberFörlag.

– (2002): 'The Labour Market Regimes in the Nordic Countries: A Comparative Analysis', *Scandinavian Political Studies*, 25: 117–37.

Epstein, L. E. (1967): *Political Parties in Western Democracies*. London: Pall Mall.

Ersson, S. (2005): 'Den yttre vänstern i Norge och Sverige', in M. Demker and L. Svåsand (eds): *Partiernas århundrade: fempartimodellens oppgang och fall i Norge og Sverige*. Stockholm: Santérus Förlag.

Espeli, H. (1999): *Lobbyvirksomhet på Stortinget: Lange linjer og aktuelle perspektiver med hovedvekt på næringsinteresser og næringspolitikk*. Oslo: Tano Aschehoug.

Evanson, R. K. and Magstadt, T. M. (2001): 'The Czech Republic: Party Dominance in a Transitional System', in C. S. Thomas (ed.): *Political Parties and Interest Groups: Shaping Democratic Governance*. Boulder, CO: Lynne Rienner.

Fischer, F. (1990): *Technocracy and the Politics of Expertise*. London: SAGE.

Flote, E. A. (2008): *Framstegsrørsla: For fagorganiserte flest? Framstegspartiets syn på LO og arbeidslivspolitikk 1973–2007*. Bergen: Department of Archaeology, History, Cultural Studies and Religion, University of Bergen. *Thesis*.

Foss, V. (2005): *Det norske Arbeiderparti: fra masseparti til catch-all parti?* Oslo: Department of Political Science, University of Oslo. *Thesis*.

Foster, J. and Muste, C. (1992): 'The United States', in D. Butler and A. Ranney (eds): *Electioneering: A Comparative Study of Continuity and Change*. Oxford: Clarendon Press.

Franklin, M. N., Mackie,T. T. and Valen, H. (eds) (1992): *Electoral Change: Responses to Evolving Social and Attitudinal Structures in Western Countries*. Cambridge: Cambridge University Press.

Fuglum, P. (1989): *Én skute, én skipper: Gunnar Knudsen som statsminister 1908–10 and 1913–20*. Trondheim: Tapir.

Galenson, W. (1968): 'Scandinavia', in W. Galenson (ed.): *Comparative Labor Movements*. New York: Russell & Russell.

Garvik, O. (1983): 'Et parti blir født', in O. Garvik (ed.): *Kristelig Folkeparti mellom tro og makt*. Oslo: J. W. Cappelens Forlag.

Gerring, J. (2007): *Case Study Research: Principle and Practice*. Cambridge: Cambridge University Press.

Gjerdåker, B. (1995): *Bygdesamfunn i omveltning 1945–1996*. Volume 1, *Hundre år for bygd og bonde 1896–1996*. Oslo: Landbruksforlaget.

Goldstone, J. A. (2004): 'More Social Movements or Fewer? Beyond Political Opportunity Structure', *Theory and Society*, 33: 333–65.

– (2003): *States, Parties, and Social Movements*. Cambridge: Cambridge University

Press.
Grant, W. (2003): 'Interest Groups', in I. McLean and A. McMillan (eds): *Concise Oxford Dictionary of Politics. Oxford Reference Online*. Oxford University Press. Oslo University. 17 March 2006: <http://www.oxfordreference.com/views/ENTRY.html?subview=Main&entry=t86.e652>
Green-Pedersen, C. (2007): 'The Growing Importance of Issue Competition: The Changing Nature of Party Competition in Western Europe', *Political Studies,* 55: 586–606.
Grepstad, O. and Rattsø, J. (1986): 'Venstre grønne greiner', *Nytt Norsk Tidsskrift,* 3 (1): 38–51.
Gulbrandsen, T.; Engelstad, F., Klausen, T. B., Skjeie, H., Teigen, M. and Østerud, O. (2002): *Norske makteliter*. Oslo: Gyldendal Akademisk.
Gundersen, F. (1991): 'Utviklingstrekk ved norsk miljøbevegelse', *Sosiologi i dag,* 2: 12–35.
Gundersen, F. (1996): 'Framveksten av den norske miljøbevegelsen', in K. Strømsnes and P. Selle (eds): *Miljøvernpolitikk og miljøvernorganisering mot år 2000*. Oslo: Tano Aschehoug.
Gunther, R. and Diamond, L. (2001): 'Types and Functions of Parties', in L. Diamond and R. Gunther (eds): *Political Parties and Democracy*. Baltimore, MD: Johns Hopkins University Press.
Haaversen-Westhassel, O. (1984): *Norsk eliteforskning: en studie av sammensetningen av sentralstyrene i Høyre, Arbeiderpartiet og Sosialistisk Folkeparti/Sosialistisk Venstreparti i etterkrigstiden*. Oslo: Department of Political Science, University of Oslo. *Thesis*.
Hadenius, A. (1984): 'Att belägga motiv', in A. Hadenius, R. Henning and B. Holmström (eds): *Tre studier i politiskt beslutsfattande*. Stockholm: Almquist and Wiksell.
Hainsworth, P. (2000): 'Introduction: the Extreme Right', in P. Hainsworth (ed.): *The Politics of the Extreme Right: From the Margins to the Mainstream*. London: Pinter.
Hall, P. A. and Taylor, R. C. R. (1996): 'Political Science and the Three New Institutionalisms', *Political Studies,* 44 (5): 936–57.
Hallenstvedt, A. and Trollvik, J. (1993: eds): *Norske organisasjoner*. Oslo: Fabritius.
Halvorsen, T. (2000): 'Mobilisering for modernisering: LO og arbeidet for produktivitetsøkning i norsk industri etter 1945', in I. Bjørnhaug, Ø. Bjørnson and T. Halvorsen . (eds): *I rettferdighetens navn: LO 100 år – historiske blikk på fagbevegelsens meningsbrytninger og veivalg*. Oslo: Akribe.
Haraldsen, G. (1999): *Spørreskjemametodikk etter kokebokmetoden*. Oslo: Ad Notam Gyldendal.
Haraldseth, L. (1989): 'Det faglige-politiske felleskapet', in R. Hirsti (ed.): *Gro – midt i livet*. Oslo: Tiden Norsk Forlag.
Harmel, R. (2002): 'Party Organizational Change: Competing Explanations?', in K. R. Luther and F. Müller-Rommel (eds): *Political Parties in the New Europe*. Oxford: Oxford University Press.
Harmel, R. and Janda, K. (1994): 'An Integrated Theory of Party Goals and Party Change', *Journal of Theoretical Politics,* 6 (3): 259–87.
Harmel, R. and Svåsand, L. (1993): 'Party Leadership and Party Institutionalization: Three Phases of Development', *West European Politics,* 16: 67–88.
— (1997): 'The Influence of New Parties on Old Parties' Platforms: The Cases of the Progress Parties and Conservative Parties of Denmark and Norway', *Party Politics,* 3 (3): 315–40.
Harrison, M. (1960): *Trade Unions and the Labour Party*. London: Allen & Unwin.
Heidar, K. (1981): 'The Norwegian Federation of Trade Unions', English version of chapter in S. Mielke (ed.) (1983): *Handbuch der Internationalen Gewerkschaftsbewegung*. Opladen: Leske Verlag.
— (1988): *Partidemokrati på prøve*. Oslo: Universitetsforlaget.
— (1993): 'The Norwegian Labour Party: "En attendant l'Europe"', in R. Gillespie and W. Paterson (eds): *Rethinking Social Democracy in Western Europe*. London: Frank Cass.
— (1994): 'The Polymorphic Nature of Party Membership', *European Journal of Political Research,* 25: 61–86.
— (2004): 'Parties and Party Systems', in K. Heidar (ed.): *Nordic Politics: Comparative Perspectives*. Oslo: Universitetsforlaget.
— (2005): 'Norwegian Parties and the Party System: Steadfast and Changing', *West European Politics*, 28 (4): 807–33.

Heidar, K. and Saglie, J. (1994): 'Mot mediepartier? Partienes organisasjonsstrategier på 1990-tallet', in K. Heidar and L. Svåsand (eds): *Partiene i en brytningstid*. Bergen: Alma Mater.
Heidar, K. and Saglie, J. (2002): *Hva skjer med partiene?* Oslo: Gyldendal Akademisk.
— (2003): 'Predestined Parties? Organizational Change in Norwegian Political Parties', *Party Politics*, 9 (2): 219–39.
— (2004): 'Kristenfolket – noe for seg selv i norsk politikk?', in O. G. Winsnes (ed.): *Tallenes tale 2003: Perspektiv og statistikk på kirke*. Trondheim: Tapir Akademisk.
Helgesen, V. (ed.) (1995): *Partiet, makten og staten.* Oslo: Høyres hovedorganisasjon.
Hellevik, O. (1991): *Forskningsmetode i sosiologi og statsvitenskap*. Oslo: Universitetsforlaget.
Hermansson, K. B. (2004): *Partikulturer: Kollektiva självbilder och normer i Sveriges riksdag*. Uppsala: Uppsala Universitet. *Doctoral Thesis*.
Hernes, G. (1991): 'The Dilemmas of Social Democracies: The Case of Norway and Sweden', *Acta Sociologica,* 34 (4): 239–60.
Hopkin, J. and Paolucci, C. (1999): 'The Business Firm Model of Party Organization: Cases from Spain and Italy', *European Journal of Political Research*, 35: 307–39.
Howell, C. (2001): 'The End of the Relationship Between Social Democratic Parties and Trade Unions?', *Studies in Political Economy,* 65: 7–37.
Hrebenar, R. J., Benedict, R. C. and Burbank, M. J. (1999): *Political Parties, Interest Groups and Political Campaigns*. Boulder, CO: Westview.
Høybråten, D. (1985): 'Idéparti og hjertesaksparti (1973–1983)', in O. J. Sæter (ed.): *Kristelig Folkepartis historie 1933–1983. Samling om verdier*. Oslo: Valo.
Hågensen, Y. (2004): *Gjør din plikt, krev din rett.* Oslo: Aschehoug.
Ignazi, P. (1992): 'The Silent Counter-Revolution: Hypotheses on the Emergence of Extreme Right-Wing Parties in Europe', *European Journal of Political Research,* 22: 3–34.
— (1996): 'The Crisis of Parties and the Rise of New Political Actors', *Party Politics,* 2 (1): 549–66.
— (2003): *Extreme-Right Parties in Western Europe*. Oxford: Oxford University Press.
ILO (International Labour Office) (2002a): *Key Indicators of the Labour Market. Third Edition.* Geneva: International Labour Office.
— (2002b): *World Labour Report 1997–98: Industrial Relations, Democracy and Social Stability*. Online.<http://www.ilo.org> (accessed June 2005).
Inglehart, R. (1971): 'The Silent Revolution in Europe: Intergenerational Change in Post-Industrial Societies', *American Political Science Review*, 65 (4): 991–1017.
— (1977): *The Silent Revolution: Changing Values and Political Styles among Western Publics*. Princeton, NJ : Princeton University Press
— (1990): *Cultural Shift in Advanced Industrial Society*. Princeton, NJ: Princeton University Press.
Inglehart, R. and Norris, P. (2004): *Sacred and Secular. Religion and Politics Worldwide.* Cambridge: Cambridge University Press
Ippolito, D. S. and Walker, T. G. (1980): *Political Parties, Interest Groups and Public Policy: Group Influence in American Politics*. Englewood Cliffs, NJ: Prentice-Hall.
Ivarsflaten, E. (2008): 'What Unites Right-Wing Populists in Western-Europe? Re-Examining Grievance Mobilization Models in Seven Successful Cases', *Comparative Political Studies*, 41 (1): 3–23.
Jordan, G. and Maloney, W. A. (2001): 'Britain: Change and Continuity Within the New Realities of British Politics', in C. S. Thomas (ed.): *Political Parties and Interest Groups: Shaping Democratic Governance*. Boulder, CO: Lynne Rienner.
Kaartvedt, A. (1984): *Drømmen om borgerlig samling*, volume 1 in *Høyres Historie*. Oslo: J.W. Cappelens Forlag.
Kaid, L. L. and Holtz-Bacha, C. (eds) (1995): *Political Advertising in Western Democracies: Parties & Candidates on Television*. Thousand Oaks, CA: SAGE.
Kalyvas, S. N. (1996): *The Rise of Christian Democracy in Europe*. Ithaca, NY: Cornell University Press.
Karvonen, L. (1994): 'Christian Parties in Scandinavia: Victory over the Windmills?, in D. Hanley (ed.): *Christian Democracy in Europe: A Comparative Perspective*. London: Pinter.
Karvonen, L. and Kuhnle, S. (eds) (2001): *Party Systems and Voter Alignments Revisited.* London: Routledge.
Kasa, S. (2000): 'Policy Networks as Barriers to Green Tax Reform: The Case of CO_2-Taxes in

Norway', *Environmental Politics,* 9 (4):104–22.
Kassalow, E. M. (ed.) (1963): *National Labor Movements in the Postwar World.* Evanston, IL: Northwestern University Press.
Katz, R. S. (1987): 'Party Government and Its Alternatives', in R. S. Katz (ed): *Party Government: European and American Experiences.* Berlin and New York: Walter de Gruyter.
— (1997): *Democracy and Elections.* New York: Oxford University Press.
— (2001): 'Are Cleavages Frozen in the English-speaking Democracies?', in L. Karvonen and S. Kuhnle (eds): *Party Systems and Voter Alignments Revisited.* London: Routledge.
— (2002): 'The Internal Life of Parties', in K. R. Luther and F. Müller-Rommel (eds): *Political Parties in the New Europe: Political and Analytical Challenges.* Oxford: Oxford University Press.
Katz, R. S. and Mair, P. (1992): 'Introduction: The Cross-National Study of Party Organizations', in R. S. Katz and P. Mair (eds): *Party Organizations: A Data Handbook.* London: SAGE.
— (1993): 'The Evolution of Party Organizations in Europe: Three Faces of Party Organization', *American Review of Politics,* 14: 593–617.
— (eds) (1994): *How Parties Organize: Change and Adaptation in Party Organizations in Western Democracies.* London: SAGE.
— (1995): 'Changing Models of Party Organization and Party Democracy: The Emergence of the Cartel Party', *Party Politics* 1 (1): 5–28.
— (1996): 'Cadre, Catch-all or Cartel? A Rejoinder', *Party Politics,* 2 (4): 525–34.
— (2002): 'The Ascendancy of the Party in the Public Office: Party Organizational Change in Twentieth-Century Democracies', in R. Gunther, J. R. Montero and J. J. Linz (eds): *Political Parties. Old Concepts and New Challenges.* Oxford: Oxford University Press.
— (2009): 'The Cartel Party Thesis; A Restatement', *Perspectives on Politics,* 7 (4): 753–66
Key, V. O. (1942/1964): *Politics, Parties, and Pressure Groups.* New York: Thomas Y. Crowell.
King, A. (1969): 'Political Parties in Western Democracies', *Polity,* 2: 111–41.
King, G., Keohane, R. O. and Verba, S. (1994): *Designing Social Inquiry: Scientific Inference in Qualitative Research.* Princeton, NJ: Princeton University Press.
Kirchheimer, O. (1966): 'The Transformation of the Western European Party Systems', in J. LaPalombar and M. Weiner (eds): *Political Parties and Political Development.* Princeton, NJ: Princeton University Press.
Kirchner, E. J. (1988a): 'Introduction', in E. J. Kirchner (ed.): *Liberal Parties in Western Europe.* Cambridge: Cambridge University Press.
— (1988b): 'Western European Liberal Parties: Developments Since 1945 and Prospects for the Future', in E. J. Kirchner (ed.): *Liberal Parties in Western Europe.* Cambridge: Cambridge University Press.
Kitschelt, H. P. (1986): 'Political Opportunity Structures and Political Protest: Anti-Nuclear Movements in Four Democracies', *British Journal of Political Science,* 16: 57–85.
— (1988): 'Left-Libertarian Parties: Explaining Innovation in Competitive Party Systems', *World Politics,* 40 (2): 194–234.
— (1989): *The Logics of Party Formation. Ecological Politics in Belgium and West Germany.* Ithaca, NY: Cornell University Press.
— (1994): *The Transformation of European Social Democracy.* Cambridge: Cambridge University Press.
— (1995): *The Radical Right in Western Europe.* Ann Arbor, MI: University of Michigan Press.
— (2000): 'Citizens, Politicians, and Party Cartellization: Political Representation and State Failure in Post-industrial Societies', *European Journal of Political Research,* 37: 149–79.
— (2006): 'Movement Parties', in R. S. Katz and W. Crotty (eds): *Handbook of Party Politics.* London: SAGE.
Kittilson, M. C. and Scarrow, S. E. (2003): 'Political Parties and the Rhetoric and Realities of Democratization', in B. E. Cain, R. J. Dalton and S. E. Scarrow (eds): *Democracy Transformed? Expanding Political Opportunities in Advanced Industrial Democracies.* Oxford: Oxford University Press.

Kjellberg, A. (1998): 'Sweden: Restoring the Model?' in A. Ferner and R. Hyman (eds): *Changing Industrial Relations in Europe*. Oxford: Blackwell.

Klarén, K. (2000): *Det socialdemoratiska mötet med miljøfrågan. Integreringen av det miljöpolitiska idéelementet hos de socialdemokratiska partierna i Danmark, Norge och Sverige*. Bergen: Department of Comparative Politics. *Thesis*.

Knutsen, O. (1989): 'The Priorities of Materialist and Post-Materialist Values in the Nordic Countries – a Five-Nation Comparison', *Scandinavian Political Studies,* 12(3): 221–43.

— (1990): 'The Materialist/Post-materialist Value Dimension as a Party Cleavage in the Nordic Countries', *West European Politics,* 13 (2): 258–74.

— (1997): 'From Old Politics the New Politics: Environmentalism as a Party Cleavage', in K. Strøm and L. Svåsand (eds): *Challenges to Political Parties: The Case of Norway*. Ann Arbor, MI: University of Michigan Press.

— (1998a): 'Expert Judgements of the Left-Right Location of Parties: A Comparative Longtudinal Study', *West European Politics* 21 (2): 63–94.

— (1998b): *Social Class, Sector Employment and Gender as Political Cleavages in the Scandinavian Countries: A Comparative Longitudinal Study, 1970–95*. Oslo: Department of Political Science, University of Oslo, Research Report no. 2/1998.

— (2004a): *Social Structure and Party Choice in Western Europe: A Comparative Longtudinal Study*. New York: Palgrave Macmillan.

— (2004b): 'Voters and Social Cleavages', in K. Heidar (ed.): *Nordic Politics: Comparative Perspectives*. Oslo: Universitetsforlag.et.

Koelble, T. A. (1987): 'Trade Unionists, Party Activists, and Politicians: The Struggle for Power over Party Rules in the British Labour Party and the West German Social Democratic Party', *Comparative Politics*, 19 (3): 253–66.

— (1992): 'Recasting Social Democracy in Europe: A Nested Games Explanation of Strategic Adjustment in Political Parties', *Politics & Society* 20 (1): 51–70.

Koole, R. (1994): 'The Vulnerability of the Modern Cadre Party in the Netherlands', in R. S. Katz and P. Mair (eds): *How Parties Organize*. London: SAGE.

— (1996): 'Cadre, Catch-all or Cartel?', *Party Politics,* 2 (4): 507–23.

Korsvold, B. O. (1974): *Kristelig Folkeparti 1945–1949*. Oslo: Department of History, University of Oslo. *Thesis*.

Kriesi, H. and van Praag Jr., P. (1987): 'Old and New Politics: The Dutch Peace Movement and the Traditional Political Organizations', *European Journal of Political Research,* 15: 319–46.

Kristinsson, G. H. (1991): *Farmers' Parties. A Study in Electoral Adaptation*. Reykjavík: Félagsvísindastofnun.

Krouwel, A. (2003): 'Otto Kirchheimer and the Catch-All Party', *West European Politics,* 26 (2): 23–40.

— (2006): 'Party Models', in R. S. Katz and W. Crotty (eds): Handbook of Party Politics. London: SAGE.

Kuhnle, S.; Strøm, K. and Svåsand, L. (1986): 'The Norwegian Conservative Party: Setback in an Era of Strength', *West European Politics,* 9 (3): 448–71.

Kunkel, C. and Pontusson, J. (1998): 'Corporatism versus Social Democracy: Divergent Fortunes of the Austrian and Swedish Labour Movements', *West European Politics,* 21 (2): 1–31.

Kvale, S. (1996): *Interviews: An Introduction to Qualitative Research Interviewing*. London: SAGE.

Kvavik, R. B. (1976): *Interest Groups in Norwegian Politics*. Oslo: Universitetsforlaget.

LaPalombara, J. and Weiner, M. (eds) (1966): *Political Parties and Political Development*. Princeton, NJ: Princeton University Press.

Laver, M. (1997): *Private Desires, Political Action: An Invitation to the Politics of Rational Choice*. London: Sage Publications.

Lawson, K. (1980): 'Introduction', in K. Lawson (ed.): *Political Parties and Linkage: A Comparative Perspective*. New Haven, CT: Yale University Press.

— (1988): 'When Linkage Fails', in K. Lawson and P. H. Merkl (eds): *When Parties Fail*. Princeton, NJ: Princeton University Press.

— (2002): 'Introduction: Parties and NGOs in the Quest for Global Democracy', *International Political Science Review,* 23 (2): 131–3.

Lawson, K. and Merkl, P. H. (eds) (1988): *When Parties Fail*. Princeton, NJ: Princeton University Press.

Lazarsfeld, P. and Barton, A. H. (1951): 'Qualitative Measurement in the Social Sciences: Classifications, Typologies and Indices', in D. Lerner and H. D. Lasswell (eds): *The Policy Sciences: Recent Developments in Scope and Method*. Stanford, CA: Stanford University Press.

Leiphart, J. Y. and Svåsand, L. (1988): 'The Norwegian Liberal Party: From Political Pioneer to Political Footnote', in E. J. Kirchner (ed.): *Liberal Parties in Western Europe*. Cambridge: Cambridge University Press.

Leirfall, J. (1989): *I storm og stille: blad frå minneboka*. Oslo: Samlaget.

Levitsky, S. (2009): 'Institutionalization: unpacking the concept and explaining party change', in D. Collier and J. Gerring (eds): *Concepts and Method in Social Science: The Tradition of Giovanni Sartori*. New York: Routledge.

Lijphart, A. (1971): 'Comparative Politics and the Comparative Method', *American Political Science Review*, 65:682–93.

— (1999): *Patterns of Democracy: Government Forms and Performance in Thirty-Six Democracies*. New Haven, CT: Yale University Press.

Lijphart, A. and Crepaz, M. M. L. (1991): 'Corporatism and Consensus in Eighteen Countries: Conceptual and Empirical Linkages', *British Journal of Political Science*, 21: 235–56.

Lindström, U. (2005): 'De socialdemokratiska partierna', in M. Demker and L. Svåsand (eds): *Partiernas århundrade: fempartimodellens oppgang och fall i Norge og Sverige*. Stockholm: Santérus Förlag.

Lipset, S. M. (1994): 'The Social Requisites of Democracy Revisited: 1993 Presidential Address', *American Sociological Review*, 59 (1): 1–22.

Lipset, S. M. and Rokkan, S. (1967): 'Cleavage Structures, Party Systems and Voter Alignments: An Introduction', in S.M. Lipset and S. Rokkan (eds): *Party Systems and Voter Alignments: Cross-National Perspectives*. New York: Free Press.

Listhaug, O. (1997): 'The Decline of Class Voting', in K. Strøm and L. Svåsand (eds): *Challenges to Political Parties: The Case of Norway*. Ann Arbor, MI: University of Michigan Press.

Listhaug, O., Huseby, B. and Matland, R. (1995): 'Valgatferd blant kvinner og menn: 1957 – 1993', in N. Raaum (ed.): *Kjønn og politikk*. Oslo: TANO.

Lomeland, A. R. (1971): *Kristelig Folkeparti blir til*. Oslo: Universitetsforlaget.

Lorenz, E. (1972): *Arbeiderbevegelsens historie 1789–1930: En innføring*. Oslo: Pax.

Lucardie, P. and ten Napel, H.-M. (1994) 'Between Confessionalism and Liberal Conservatism: The Christian Democratic Parties of Belgium and the Netherlands', in D. Hanley (ed.), *Christian Democracy in Europe: A Comparative Perspective*. London: Pinter.

Luther, K. R. and Deschouwer, K. (eds) (1999): *Party Elites in Divided Societies*. London: Routledge.

Luther, K. R. (1999): 'A Framework for the Comparative Analysis of Political Parties and Party Systems in Consociational Democracy', in K. Luther, R. Deschouwer and K. Deschouwer (eds): *Party Elites in Divided Societies*. London: Routledge.

Lægreid, P. and Roness, P. G. (1997): 'Political Parties, Bureaucracies, and Corporatism', in K. Strøm and L. Svåsand (eds): *Challenges to Political Parties: The Case of Norway*. Ann Arbor, MI: University of Michigan Press.

Løke, E. and Pape, A. (2004): *LO i offentlig sektor: Fra vekst og hegemoni til omstilling og konkurranse*. Oslo: Fafo Report 437.

Lønnå, E. (2000): 'En feministisk opposisjon til Arbeiderpartiet', in K. E. Eriksen, S. Halvorsen, S. A. Hansen, M. Hegna, L.-A. Jensen, L. Langangen and E. A. Terjesen. (eds): *Arbeiderhistorie 2000: Årbok for Arbeiderbevegelsens arkiv og bibliotek*. Oslo : Arbeiderbevegelsens arkiv og bibliotek.

Mackie, T. T. and Rose, R. (1991): *The International Almanac of Electoral History*. Washington, DC: Congressional Quarterly Inc.

Madeley, J. (1994): 'The Antinomies of Lutheran Politics: The Case of Norway's Christian People's Party', in D. Hanley (ed.): *Christian Democracy in Europe: A Comparative* Perspective. London: Pinter.

— (2000): 'Reading the Runes: The Religious Factor in Scandinavian Electoral Politics', in D. Broughton and H.-M. ten Nape (eds): *Religion and Mass Behaviour in Europe*. London: Routledge.

Madsen, R. (2001) *Motstraums: Senterpartiets historie 1959–2000*. Oslo: Det Norske Samlaget.

Mahoney, C. and Baumgartner, F. (2008): 'Converging Perspectives on Interest Group Research in Europe and America', *West European Politics*, 31 (6): 1103–28.

Mair, P. (1994): 'Party Organizations: From Civil Society to the State', in R. S. Katz and P. Mair (eds): *How Parties Organize: Change and Adaptation in Western Democracies*. London: SAGE.

— (1995): 'Political Parties, Popular Legitimacy and Public Privilege', *European Politics,* 18: 40–57.

— (1997): *Party System Change: Approaches and Interpretations*. Oxford: Oxford University Press.

Mair, P. and van Biezen, I. (2001): 'Party Membership in Twenty European Democracies, 1980–2000', *Party Politics,* 7 (1): 5–21.

Maisel, S. L. and Berry, J. M. (2010): *The Oxford Handbook of American Political Parties and Interest Groups*. Oxford: Oxford University Press.

Malmstrøm, C. (2005): 'Folkepartiet och Venstre – liberala partier i Sverige och Norge', in M. Demker and L. Svåsand (eds): *Partiernas århundrade: fempartimodellens oppgang och fall i Norge og Sverige.* Stockholm: Santérus Förlag.

March, J. and Olsen, J. P. (1984): 'The New Institutionalism: Organizational Factors in Political Life', *American Political Science Review*, 78 (3): 734–49.

— (1989): *Rediscovering Institutions: The Organizational Basis of Politics*. New York: Free Press.

— (1995): *Democratic Governance*. New York: Free Press.

— (2004): *The Logic of Appropriateness*. Working Paper 04/09. Oslo: Arena – Centre for European Studies, University of Oslo.

Marsh, D. (ed.) (1998): *Comparing Policy Networks: Policy Networks in Theoretical and Comparative Perspective.* Milton Keynes: Open University Press.

Marsh, D. and Rhodes, R. A. W. (eds) (1992): *Policy Networks in British Government.* Oxford: Clarendon.

Martin, P. G. (1974) 'Strategic Opportunities and Limitations: The Norwegian Labor Party and the Trade Unions', *Industrial and Labor Relations Review,* 28: 75–88.

Maurseth, P. (1987): *Gjennom kriser til makt*, volume 2 in A. Kokkvoll and J. Sverdrup (eds): *Arbeiderbevegelsens historie i Norge*. Oslo: Tiden Norsk Forlag.

Mavrogordatos, G. Th. (2009): 'Models of Party-Interest Group Relations and the Uniqueness of the Greek Case'. Presented at the ECPR Joint Sessions of Workshops, Lisbon 14–19 April 2009. *Conference paper*.

McLean, I. (1987): *Public Choice: An Introduction.* Oxford: Basil Blackwell.

McLean, I. and McMillan, A. (eds) (2003): *The Concise Oxford Dictionary of Politics.* Oxford University Press 2005. *Oxford Reference Online*. Oxford University Press. Oslo University. <http://www.oxfordreference.com/views/ENTRY.html?subview=Main&entry=t86.e203> (accessed 18 April 2006)

McMenamin, I. (2004): 'Parties, Promiscuity and Politicisation: Business-political Networks in Poland', *European Journal of Political Research,* 43: 657–76.

Melve, J. (1999): *Venstresosialistiske partistrategiar: Ein analyse av den strategiske åtferda til Vänsterpartiet i Sverige, Socialistisk Folkerparti i Danmark og Sosialistisk Venstreparti i Noreg*. Bergen: Department of Comparative Politics, University of Bergen. *Thesis.*

Mershon, C. (2002): *The Costs of Coalition*. Stanford, CA: Stanford University Press.

Meyer, J. W. and Rowan, B. (1977): 'Institutionalized Organizations: Formal Structure as a Myth and Ceremony', *American Journal of Sociology,* 83 (2): 340–63.

Michels, R. (1911/1962): *Political Parties*. New York: Collier.

Millen, B. (1963) 'The Relationship of the Norwegian Labor Party to the Trade Unions', in E. M. Kassalow (ed.): *National Labor Movements in the Postwar World.* Evanston, IL: Northwestern University Press.

Miller, G. (2000): 'Rational Choice and Dysfunctional Institutions', *Governance: An International Journal of Policy and Administration,* 13 (4): 535–47.

Minkin, L. (1991): *The Contentious Alliance: Trade Unions and the Labour Party*. Edinburgh: Edinburgh University Press.

Mjeldheim, L. (1984): *Folkerørsla som vart parti: Venstre frå 1880åra til 1905*. Bergen: Universitetsforlaget.

— (1978): *Parti og rørsle: Ein studie av Venstre i landkrinsane 1906–1918*. Oslo:

Universitets forlaget.

Moe, E. (1984): 'På vei til Røros', in O. Grepstad and J. Nærbøvik (eds): *Venstres hundre år*. Oslo: Gyldendal Norsk Forlag.

Montero, J. R. and Gunther, R. (2002): 'Introduction: Reviewing and Reassessing Parties, in R. Gunther, J. R. Montero and J. J. Linz (eds): *Political Parties: Old Concepts and New Challenges*. Oxford: Oxford University Press.

Morlino, L. (1998): *Democracy Between Consolidation and Crisis: Parties, Groups, and Citizens in Southern Europe*. Oxford: Oxford University Press.

Mudde, C. (2007): *Populist Radical Right Parties in Europe*. Cambridge: Cambridge University Press.

Müller, W. (2000): 'Political Parties in Parliamentary Democracies: Making Delegation and Accountability Work', *European Journal of Political Research* 37: 309–33.

— (2002): 'Parties and the Institutional Framework', in K. R. Luther and F. Müller-Rommel (eds): *Political Parties in the New Europe*. Oxford: Oxford University Press.

Müller, W. and Strøm, K. (1999): 'Conclusions: Party Behaviour and Representative Democracy', in W. Müller and K. Strøm (eds): *Policy, Office or Votes? How Political Parties in Western Europe Make Hard Decisions*. Cambridge: Cambridge University Press.

Müller-Rommel, F. (1989): *New Politics in Western Europe: The Rise and Success of Green Parties and Alternative Lists*. Boulder, CO: Westview.

— (1990): 'New Political Movements and New Political Parties', in R. Dalton and M. Kuechler (eds): *Challenging the Political Order: New Social and Political Movements in Western Democracies*. Cambridge: Polity Press.

Myking, I. (1997): *Konstituering av politisk kapital: organisasjonsutviklingsprosessen i Arbeiderpartiet 1990–93*. Bergen: Department of Sociology, University of Bergen. Thesis.

Narud, H. M. and Strøm, K. (forthcoming): 'Norway: An Unconstrained Polity', in T. Bergman and K. Strøm (eds): *Democratic Institutions in Decline?* Ann Arbor: University of Michigan Press.

Nassmacher, K.-H. (ed.) (2001): *Foundations for Democracy: Approaches to Comparative Political Finance*. Baden-Baden: Nomos.

Nerbøvik, J. (1984): 'På leit etter venstrelina (1984–1935)', in O. Grepstad and J. Nerbøvik (eds): *Venstres hundre år*. Oslo: Gyldendal Norsk Forlag.

Neumann, S. (1956): 'Toward a Comparative Study of Political Parties', in S. Neumann (ed.): *Modern Political Parties*. Chicago, IL: University of Chicago Press.

Nielsen, Ø. (2002): 'Spis eller bli spist', commentary in *Dagsavisen*, 16 October 2002.

Nordby, T. (2000): *I politikkens sentrum. Variasjoner i Stortingets makt 1814–2000.* Oslo: Universitetsforlaget.

NOU (government white paper) 2004: 25: *Penger teller, men stemmer avgjør. Om partifinansiering, åpenhet og partipolitisk fjernsynsreklame* [Money counts, resources decide: On party finance, openness and party political TV advertising].

Nyhamar, T. (1990): *Nye utfordringer*, volume 6 in A. Kokkvoll and J. Sverdrup (eds): *Arbeiderbevegelsens historie i Norge*. Oslo: Tiden Norsk Forlag.

Ohman Nielsen, M.-B. (2001): *Bondekamp om markedsmakt: Senterpartiets historie 1920–1959*. Oslo: Det Norske Samlaget.

Oliver, P. E. and Myers, D. J. (2003): 'Networks, Diffusion, and Cycles of Collective Action', in M. Diani and D. McAdam (eds): *Social Movements and Networks: Relational Approaches to Collective Actions*. Oxford: Oxford University Press.

Olsen, J. P. (2009): 'Change and continuity: an institutional approach to institutions of democratic government', *European Political Science Review* 1 (1): 3–32.

Olson, M. (1971): *The Logic of Collective Action: Public Goods and the Theory of Groups*. Cambridge, MA: Harvard University Press.

Opdahl, I. L. (1976): *Kristelig Folkeparti blir landsparti*. Bergen: Department of History, University of Bergen. *Thesis*.

Osa, M. (2003): 'Networks in Opposition: Linking Organisations Through Activists in the Polish People's Republic', in M. Diani and D. McAdam (eds): *Social Movements and Networks: Relational Approaches to Collective Actions*. Oxford: Oxford University Press.

Ot. prp. (parliamentary bill) nr. 84 (2004–2005): Om lov om visse forhold vedrørende de politiske partiene (partiloven). [On the Law Concerning Certain Conditions Regarding Political

Parties (the 'Party Law')]
Padgett, S. and Paterson, W. (1991): *A History of Social Democracy in Postwar Europe*. London: Longman.
Panebianco, A. (1988): *Political Parties: Organizations and Power*. Cambridge: Cambridge University Press.
Pedahzur, A. and Brichta, A. (2002): 'The Institutionalization of Extreme Right-wing Charismatic Parties: A Paradox?', *Party Politics* 8 (1): 31–49.
Pedersen, K. (2003): *Party Membership Linkage: The Danish Case.* Copenhagen: Department of Political Science, University of Copenhagen. *PhD Thesis.*
Pedersen, M. (1979): 'The Dynamics of European Party Systems: Changing Patterns of Electoral Volatility', *European Journal of Political Research,* 7 (1): 1–26.
— (1989): 'En kortfattet oversigt over det danske partisystemets udvikling', *Politica,* 21: 265–78.
Pelizzo, R. (2003): *Cartel Parties and Cartel Party Systems*. Baltimore, MD: Department of Political Science, Johns Hopkins University. *PhD Thesis.*
Peters, G. (1999): *Institutional Theory in Political Science: The 'New Institutionalism'*. London: Continuum.
Pharr, S. J.; Putnam, R. D. and Dalton, R. J. (2000): 'A Quarter Century of Declining Confidence', *Journal of Democracy,* 11 (2): 5–25.
Piazza, J. (2001): 'De-linking Labour: Labour Unions and Social Democratic Parties under Globalization', *Party Politics,* 7 (4): 413–35.
Pierre, J.; Svåsand, L. and Widfeldt, A. (2000): 'State Subsidies to Political Parties: Confronting Rhetoric with Reality', *West European Politics*, 23 (3): 1–24.
Pierson, P. (2000): 'The Limits of Design: Explaining Institutional Origins and Change', *Governance: An International Journal of Policy and Administration,* 13 (4): 475–99.
Poguntke, T. (1993): 'New Politics and Party Systems: The Emergence of a New Type of Party?' *West European Politics,* 10 (1): 76–88.
— (1998): 'Party Organizations', in J. W. van Deth (ed.): *Comparative Politics: The Problem of Equivalence*. London: Routledge.
— (2000): *Parteiorganisation im Wandel. Gesellschaftliche Verankerung und organisatorische Anpassung im europäischen Vergleich*. Wiesbaden: Westdeutscher Verlag.
— (2002): 'Parties without Firm Social Roots? Party Organisational Linkage', n K. R. Luther and F. Müller-Rommel (eds): *Political Parties in the New Europe: Political and Analytical Challenges*. Oxford: Oxford University Press.
— (2006): 'Political Parties and Other Organizations', in R. S. Katz and W. Crotty (eds): *Handbook of Party Politics*. London: SAGE.
Predelli, L. N. (2003): *Uformelle veier til makt: Om minoritetskvinners politiske innflytelse*. Oslo: Makt og demokratiutredningen, Report no. 60.
Puhle, H.-J. (2002): 'Still the Age of Catch-allism? Volksparteien and Parteienstaat in Crisis and Re-equilibration', in R. Gunther, J. R. Montero and J. J. Linz (eds): *Political Parties: Old Concepts and New Challenges*. Oxford: Oxford University Press.
Quinn, T. (2002): 'Block Voting in the Labour Party', *Party Politics,* 8 (2): 207–26.
— (2003): *Modernising the Labour Party: Organisational Change since 1983*. London: Palgrave Macmillan.
Ragin, C. C. (1987): *The Comparative Method: Moving beyond Quantitative and Qualitative Strategies*. Berkley, CA: University of California Press.
— (1994): *Constructing Social Research*. Thousand Oaks, CA: Pine Forge.
Rawson, D. W. (1969): 'The Life-span of Labour Parties', *Political Studies,* 17 (3): 313–33.
Repstad, P. (2002): *Dype, stille, sterke, milde: religiøs makt i dagens Norge*. Oslo: Gyldendal Akademisk.
Richard, H. and Demker, M. (2005): 'Religion och politik i Norge och Sverige: Kd och KrF, in M. Demker and L. Svåsand (eds): *Partiernas århundrade: fempartimodellens oppgang och fall i Norge og Sverige.* Stockholm: Santérus Förlag.
Riker, W. (1982): *Liberalism against Populism*. Prospect Heights, IL: Waveland.
Ringdal, N. and Sæter, O.J. (1985): 'KrF-innslag i regjeringen Borten (1965–1969)', in O. J. Sæter (ed.): *Kristelig Folkepartis historie 1933–1983. Samling om verdier*. Oslo: Valo.
Rokkan, S. (1966): 'Norway: Numerical Democracy and Corporative Pluralism', in R. A. Dahl (ed.): *Political Oppositions in Western Democracies*. New Haven, CT: Yale University Press.
— (1967): 'Geography, Religion, and Social Class: Crosscutting Cleavages in Norwegian

Politics', in S. M. Lipset and S. Rokkan (eds): *Party Systems and Voter Alignments: Cross-National Perspectives*. New York: Free Press.
— (1998): 'Interesseorganisasjoner i dansk politik. Traditioner og problemstillinger', in K. Ronit (ed.): *Interesseorganisationer i dansk politikk*. Copenhagen: Jurist- og økonomforbundets forlag.
Rohrschneider, R. (2002): 'Mobilizing versus Chasing: How Do Parties Target Voters in Election Campaigns?', *Electoral Studies*, 21: 367–82.
Rothstein, B. (1992): 'Labour Market Institutions and Working Class Strength', in S. Steinmo, K. Thelen and F. Longstreth (eds), *Structuring Politics: Historical Institutionalism in Comparative Politics*. Cambridge: Cambridge University Press.
Rozell, M. J.; Wilcox, C. and Madland D (2006): *Interest Groups in American Campaigns. The New Face of Electioneering*. Washington, D.C: CQ Press.
Rovde, O. (1995): *I kamp for jamstelling 1896–1945*. Volume 1 in *Hundre år for bygd og bonde 1896–1996*. Oslo: Landbruksforlaget.
— (2000): 'Bonde-, småbrukar- og arbeiderørsla – i konflikt og samarbeid', in K. E. Eriksen, S. Halvorsen, S. A. Hansen, M. Hegna, L.-A. Jensen, L. Langangen and E. A. Terjesen (eds): *Arbeiderhistorie 2000: Årbok for Arbeiderbevegelsens arkiv og bibliotek*. Oslo: Arbeiderbevegelsens arkiv og bibliotek.
Sabatier, P. (1994): 'Introduction', in H.-D. Kingemann, R. Hofferbert and I. Budge (eds): *Parties, Policies and Democracy*. Boulder, CO.: Westview.
Saglie, J. (1994): 'Partimedlemmer og politisk avstand', in K. Heidar and L. Svåsand (eds): *Partiene i en brytningstid*. Bergen: Alma Mater.
— (2002): *Standpunkter og strategi: EU-saken i norsk partipolitikk, 1989–1994*. Oslo: Department of Political Science, Institute for Social Research, and Pax Forlag.
Salvesen, T. L.-S. (2003): 'Hva er et Arbeiderparti', commentary in *Klassekampen,* 5 May 2003, electronic edition Online<http://www.Klassekampen.no/kk/index.php/news/home/artical_categories/kommentarer/2003/may/hva_er_et_arbeiderparti>
Sartori, G. (1976): *Parties and Party Systems: a Framework of Analysis. Volume I*. Cambridge: Cambridge University Press.
Sartori, G. (1993): 'Totalitarianism, Model Mania and Learning from Error', *Journal of Theoretical Politics,* 5 (1): 5–22.
Scarrow, S. (1996): *Parties and their Members: Organizing for Victory in Britain and Germany*. Oxford: Oxford University Press.
Scarrow, S. (2002a): 'Parties without Members? Party Organization in a Changing Electoral Environment', in R. J. Dalton and M. P. Wattenberg (eds): *Parties without Partisans: Political Change in Advances Industrial Democracies*. Oxford: Oxford University Press.
— (ed.) (2002b): *Perspectives on Political Parties: Classic Readings*. New York: Palgrave Macmillan.
Schattschneider, E. E. (1942): *Party Government*. New York: Rinehart.
— (1960): *The Semisovereign People: A Realists' View of Democracy in America*. New York: Holt, Rinehart and Winston.
Schlesinger, J. A. (1984): 'On the theory of Party Organization', *Journal of Politics*, 46 (2): 369–400.
— (1991): *Political Parties and the Winning of Office*. Ann Arbor, MI: University of Michigan Press.
Schmitt, R. (1989): 'Organizational Interlocks between New Social Movements and Traditional Elites: the Case of the West German Peace Movement', *European Journal of Political Research,* 17: 583–98.
Schmitter, P. (2001): 'Parties Are Not What They Once Were', in L. Diamond and R. Gunther (eds): *Political Parties and Democracy*. Baltimore, MD: Johns Hopkins University Press.
Schneider, F. and Naumann, J. (1982) 'Interest groups in democracies – How influential are they?', *Public Choice* 38 (3) 281–303.
Schwartz, M. (2005): 'Linkage Processes in Party Networks', in A. Römmele, D. M. Farrell and P. Ignazi (eds): *Political Parties and Political Systems: The Concept of Linkage Revisited.* Westport, CT: Praeger.
Scott, J. (2000): 'Rational Choice Theory', in G. Browning, A. Halcli and F. Webster (eds): *Understanding Contemporary Society: Theories at the Present.* London: SAGE.
Scott, J. and Marshall, G. (2006): *A Dictionary of Sociology.* Oxford University Press

2005. *Oxford Reference Online*. Oxford University Press. Oslo University. 18 April 2006 Online. <http://www.oxfordreference.com/views/ENTRY.html?subview=Main&entry=t88.e264>
Sejersted, F. (2003): *Opposisjon og posisjon: Høyres historie 1945–1981*. Oslo: Pax.
Selle, P. (1997): 'Parties and Voluntary Organizations: Strong or Weak Ties?', in K. Strøm and L. Svåsand (eds): *Challenges to Political Parties: The Case of Norway*. Ann Arbour, MI: University of Michigan Press.
Selle, P. and Tranvik, T. (2004): 'Civil Society in Transition', in K. Heidar: *Nordic Politics: Comparative Perspectives*. Oslo: Universitetsforlaget.
Selznick, P. (1957): *Leadership in Administration: A Sociological Interpretation*. New York: Harper and Row.
Shefter, M. (1977): 'Party and Patronage: Germany, England and Italy', *Politics & Society*, 7: 403–51.
Simon, H. (1985): 'Human Nature in Politics: The Dialogue of Psychology with Political Science', *American Political Science Review*, 79 (2): 293–304.
Sjöblom, G. (1968): *Party Strategies in a Multiparty System*. Lund: Studentlitteratur.
— (1980): 'Some Problems in the Study of Party Strategies' in L. Lewin, and E. Vedung (eds): *Politics as Rational Action. Essays in Public Choice and* Policy Analysis. Dordrecht : Reidel.
Skjeie, H. (1999): *Vanens makt. Styringstradisjoner i Arbeiderpartiet*. Oslo: ad Notam Gyldendal.
Solheim, E. (1999): *Nærmere*. Oslo: Millennium.
Steen, A. (1988): *Landbruket, staten og sosialdemokratene*. Oslo: Universitetsforlaget.
Stokke, T. A. (1998): *Utmeldinger i LO-forbundene på 1990-tallet*. Oslo: FAFO Report 256.
— (2000): *Organisasjonsgrader i norsk arbeidsliv 1945–1999*. FAFO Working Paper 2000 no. 10.
Strand, A. (2005): 'Historisk sus i Folkets Hus', commentary in *Dagsavisen*, 30 May 2005.
Strøm, K. (1990): 'A Behavioural Theory of Competitive Political Parties', *American Journal of Political Science* 34 (2): 565–98.
Strøm, K. and Svåsand, L. (1997): 'Political Parties of Norway: Facing the Challenges of a New Society', in K. Strøm and L. Svåsand (eds): *Challenges to Political Parties: The Case of Norway*. Ann Arbor, MI: University of Michigan Press.
Strøm, K. and Müller, W. (1999): 'Political Parties and Hard Choices', in W. Müller and K. Strøm (eds): *Policy, Office or Votes? How Political Parties in Western Europe Make Hard Decisions*. Cambridge: Cambridge University Press.
Strømsnes, K. (2001): *Demokrati i bevegelse*. Bergen: Report/LOS-senteret R0111. *Doctoral Thesis*.
Strømsnes, K. and Selle, P. (1996): 'Miljøvernpolitikk og miljøvernorganisering', in K. Strømsnes and P. Selle (eds): *Miljøvernpolitikk og miljøvernorganisering mot år 2000*. Oslo: Tano Aschehoug.
Sundberg, J. (ed.) (2001): *Partier och interesseorganisationer i Norden*. Copenhagen: Nordisk Minsterråd.
— (2003): *Parties as Organized Actors: The Transformation of the Scandinavian Three-Front Parties*. Helsinki: Finnish Society of Sciences and Letters.
Svensson, T. and Öberg, P. (2002): 'Labour Market Organisations' Participation in Swedish Public Policy-Making', *Scandinavian Political Studies*, 25 (4):295–315.
Svåsand, L. (1990): 'Organisasjonsstrukturen i norske politiske partier', in G. Djupsund and L. Svåsand (eds): *Partiorganisasjoner: Studier i strukturer og prosesser i finske, norske og svenske partier*. Åbo: Åbo Academy Press.
Svåsand, L. (1992): 'Norway', in R. S. Katz and P. Mair (eds): *Party Organizations: A Data Handbook*. London: SAGE.
— (1994): 'Fra mangfold til standardisering: Om utformingen av partienes organisasjoner', in K. Heidar and L. Svåsand (eds): *Partiene i en brytningstid*. Bergen: Alma Mater.
— (1998a): 'Scandinavian Right-Wing Radicalism', in H.-G. Betz and S. Immerfall (eds): *The New Politics of the Right: Neo-populist Parties and Movements in Established Democracies*. New York: St. Martin's Press.
— (1998b): 'The Centre-Right Parties in Norwegian Politics: Between Reformist Labor and Radical Progress', in F. L. Wilson (ed.): *The European Centre-Right at the End of the 20th Century*. Basingstoke: Macmillan.
Svåsand, L.; Strøm, K. and Rasch, B. E. (1997): 'Change and Adaptation in Party Organization', in K. Strøm and L. Svåsand (eds): *Challenges to Political Parties: The Case of*

Norway. Ann Arbor, MI: University of Michigan Press.

Svåsand, L. and Wörlund, I. (2005): 'Partifremvekst og partioverlevelse: Fremskrittspartiet og Ny Demokrati', in M. Demker and L. Svåsand (eds): *Partiernas århundrade: fempartimodellens oppgang och fall i Norge og Sverige*. Stockholm: Santérus Förlag.

Sæter, J. (1985): 'KrFs særpreg – Samling om verdier (Et tilbakeblikk)', in O.J. Sæter. (ed.): *Kristelig Folkepartis historie 1933–1983. Samling om verdier*. Oslo: Valo.

Sæter, J.; Venås, K. E. and Åsheim, J. (1985): 'Med kurs for regjeringssamarbeid (1975–65)', in O.J. Sæter. (ed.): *Kristelig Folkepartis historie 1933–1983. Samling om verdier*. Oslo: Valo.

Taggart, P. (1995): 'New Populist Parties in Western Europe', *West European Politics*, 18 (1): 34–51.

Takvam, M. (2002): *Arbeiderpartiets fall*. Oslo: Tiden Norsk Forlag.

Taylor, A. J. (1993): 'Trade Unions and the Politics of Social Democratic Renewal', in R. Gillespie and W. E. Patterson (eds): *Rethinking Social Democracy in Western Europe*. London: Frank Cass.

Taylor, H. M. and Karlin, S. (1998): *An Introduction to Stochastic Modeling*. San Diego, CA: Academic Press.

Terjesen, E. A. (1995): *Fellesskap og likeverd*, volume 2 in *Norsk Kommuneforbund 75 år*, Oslo: Tiden Norsk Forlag.

— (1999): 'Respekt og selvrespekt: Perspektiver på fagbevegelsens historie', in T. Bergh, S. Halvorsen, S.-A. Larsen, M. Hegna, L.-A. Jensen, T. A. Johansen, L. Langangen, E. Lorenz and E. A. Terjesen (eds): *Arbeiderhistorie 1999*. Oslo: Arbeiderbevegelsens Arkiv og bibliotek.

Thelen, K. (1999): 'Historical Institutionalism in Comparative Politics', *Annual Review of Political Science*, 2: 369–404.

Thelen, K. and Steinmo, S (1992): 'Historical Institutionalism in Comparative Politics', in S. Steinmo, K. Thelen and F. Longstreth (eds): *Structuring Politics: Historical Institutionalism in Comparative Politics*. Cambridge: Cambridge University Press.

Thomas, C. S. (ed.) (2001a): *Political Parties and Interest Groups: Shaping Democratic Governance*. Boulder, CO: Lynne Rienner.

— (2001b): 'Preface', in C. S. Thomas (ed.): *Political Parties and Interest Groups: Shaping Democratic Governance*. Boulder, CO: Lynne Rienner.

— (2001c): 'Studying the Political Party-Interest Group Relationship', in C. S. Thomas (ed.): *Political Parties and Interest Groups: Shaping Democratic Governance*. Boulder, CO: Lynne Rienner.

— (2001d): 'The United States: The Paradox of Loose Party-Group Ties in the Context of American Political Development', in C. S. Thomas (ed.): *Political Parties and Interest Groups: Shaping Democratic Governance*. Boulder, CO: Lynne Rienner.

— (2001e): 'Toward a Systematic Understanding of Party-Group Relations in Liberal Democracies', in C. S. Thomas (ed.): *Political Parties and Interest Groups: Shaping Democratic Governance*. Boulder, CO: Lynne Rienner.

Torgersen, U. (1962): 'The Trend towards Political Consensus: The Case of Norway', *Acta Sociologica*, 6: 159–72.

— (1984): 'Interesseorganisasjonene og partilivet', *Nytt Norsk Tidsskrift*, 1 (4):44–54.

Tranvik, T. and Selle, P. (2005): 'State and Citizens in Norway: Organisational Society and State-Municipal Relations', *West European Politics*, 28 (4): 852–71.

Tranøy, T. (2007): *Vallas fall*. Oslo: Manifest

Tresselt, T. (1977): *Reorganiseringen og reaktiviseringen av Høyre 1945*. Bergen: Department of History, University of Bergen. *Thesis*.

Truman, T. (1980): 'The Australian Labor Party and the Trade Unions: Linkage as Penetration and Reaction', in K. Lawson (1980): *Political Parties and Linkage: A Comparative Perspective*. New Haven, CT: Yale University Press

Uhrwing, M. (2001): *Tillträde i maktens rum. Om interesseorganisationer i miljöpolitisk beslutsfattande*. Göteborg Studies in Politics, 70: Gidlunds förlag (Hedemora)/ *Doctoral Thesis*.

Urwin, D. (1997): 'The Norwegian Party System from the 1880s to the 1990s', in in K. Strøm and L. Svåsand (eds): *Challenges to Political Parties: The Case of Norway*. Ann Arbor, MI: University of Michigan Press.

Valen, H. (1992): *Valg og politikk – et samfunn i endring*. Oslo: NKS-forlaget.

— (1999): 'Kapittel 5', in B. Aardal (ed.): *Velgere i 90-årene*. Oslo: NKS-forlaget.

— (2001): 'Sentrum-periferi motesentingen. – En saga blott?', in B. Aardal (ed.): *Velgere i villrede...: En analyse av stortingsvalget 2001*. Oslo: N. W. Damm & Søn.

Valen, H. and Katz, D. (1964): *Political Parties in Norway: A Community Study*. Oslo: Universitetsforlaget.

Valla, G.-L. (2007): *Prosessen*. Oslo: Cappelen

van Biezen, I. (1998): 'Building Party Organizations and the Relevance of Past Models: The Communist and Socialist Parties in Spain and Portugal', *West European Politics*, 21 (2): 32–62.

— (2003a): *Political Parties in New Democracies: Party Organization in Southern and* East-Central Europe. Basingstoke : Palgrave Macmillan

— (2003b): 'The Place of Parties in Contemporary Democracies', *West European Politics*, 26 (3): 171–84.

— (2005): 'On the Theory and Practice of Party Formation and Adaptation in New Democracies', *European Journal of Political Research*, 44: 147–74.

van Biezen, I., Mair, P. and Poguntke, T. (2009): 'Going, Going,……Gone? Party Membership in the 21st Century'. Presented at the ECPR Joint Sessions of Workshops, Lisbon 14–19 April 2009. *Conference paper*.

van Kersbergen, K. (1994): 'The Distinctiveness of Christian Democracy', in D. Hanley (ed.): Christian Democracy in Europe: A Comparative Perspective. London: Pinter.

van der Heijden, H.-A. (2002): 'Political Parties and NGOs in Environmental Politics', *International Political Science Review*, 23 (2): 131–3.

von Beyme, K. (1985): *Political Parties in Western Democracies*. Aldershot: Gower.

Vasaasen, Ø. (1990): *Dannelsen av Sosialistisk Venstreparti – forhandlingene om samarbeid og samling på venstresiden 1969–75*. Oslo: Department of Political Science, University of Oslo. *Thesis*.

Verge, T. (2009): 'Competition, Penetration or Collaboration: The Development of Party Linkages and Strategies towards Civil Society in Spain'. *Unpublished paper*.

Volkens, A. and Klingemann, H.-D. (2002): 'Parties, Ideologies and Issues: Stability and Change in Fifteen European Party Systems 1945–1998', in K. R. Luther and F. Müller-Rommel (eds): *Political Parties in the New Europe*. Oxford: Oxford University Press.

Wallerstein, M. and Western, B. (2000): 'Unions in Decline? What Has Changed and Why', *Annual Review of Political Science*, 3: 355–77.

Ware, A. (1979): *The Logic of Party Democracy*. London: Macmillan.

— (1996): *Political Parties and Party Systems*. Oxford: Oxford University Press.

Warner, C. M. (2000): *Confessions of an Interest Group. The Catholic Church and Political Parties in Europe*. Princeton, NJ: Princeton University Press.

— (2003): 'Strategies of an Interest Group: The Catholic Church and Christian Democracy in Postwar Europe, 1944–58', in T. Kselman, and J. A. Buttigieg (eds): *European Christian Democracy*. Notre Dame, IN: University of Notre Dame Press.

Weber, M. (1978, G. Roth and C. Wittich, eds): *Economy and Society: An Outline of Interpretive Sociology*, volume 1. Berkeley, CA: University of California Press.

Webb, P. D. (1992): *Trade Unions and the British Electorate*. Aldershot: Dartmouth.

— (1994): 'Party Organizational Change in Britain: The Iron Law of Centralization?' in R. S. Katz and P. Mair (eds): *How Parties Organize*. London: SAGE.

Widfeldt, A. (1999): 'The Nordic Centre Parties: Immune to the Catch-all Bug?' Presented at the XII Nordic Political Science Association Meeting, Uppsala, 19–21 August 1999. *Conference Paper.*

Widfeldt, A. (2000): 'Scandinavia: Mixed Success for the Populist Right', *Parliamentary Affairs,* 53: 486–500.

— (2005): 'De konservative partierna i Norge och Sverige: Høyre och Högern/Moderata samlingspartiet', in M. Demker and L. Svåsand (eds): *Partiernas århundrade: fempartimodellens oppgang och fall i Norge og Sverige*. Stockholm: Santérus Förlag.

Williamson, O. E. (1979): 'Transaction-Cost Economics: The Governance of Contractual Relations', *Journal of Law and Economics,* 22 (2): 233–61.

Williamson, O. E. and S. G. Winter (1993): *The Nature of the Firm: Origins, Evolution and Development*. New York: Oxford University Press.

Willoch, K. (1988): *Minner og meninger*. Oslo: Schibsted.

Wilson, G. (1990): *Interest Groups*. Oxford: Blackwell.

Wolinetz, S. B. (1991): 'Party System Change: The Catch-all Thesis Revisited', *West European*

Politics, 14 (1): 113–28.
— (2002): 'Beyond the Catch-All Party: Approaches to the Study of Parties and Party Organization in Contemporary Democracies', in R. Gunther, J. R. Montero and J. J. Linz (eds): *Political Parties: Old Concepts and New Challenges*. Oxford: Oxford University Press.
Wollebæk, D. and Selle, P. (2002): *Det nye organisasjonssamfunnet: Demokrati i omforming*. Bergen. Fagbokforlaget.
Wright, W. E. (1971): 'Comparative Party Models: Rational-Efficient and Party Democracy', in W. Wright (ed.): *A Comparative Study of Party Organization*. Columbus, OH: C.E. Merrill.
Yin, R. (1994): *Case Study Research: Design and Methods*. Thousand Oaks, CA: SAGE.
Yishai, Y. (1991): *The Land of Paradoxes: Interest Politics in Israel*. Albany, NY: State University of New York Press.
— (2001): 'Bringing Society Back In: Post-Cartel Parties in Israel', *Party Politics*, 7 (6): 667–87.
Yoho, J. (1998): 'The Evolution of a Better Definition of Interest Group and Its Synonyms', *Social Science Journal*, 35 (2): 231–43.
Young, L. (1996): 'Women's movement and Political Parties: A Canadian-American Comparison', *Party Politics*, 2 (2): 229–50.
Zachariassen, A. (1966): *Det kollektive medlemskap*. Oslo: Tiden.
Øidne, G. (1984): 'Om noen politiske flaskehalser', in O. Grepstad and J. Nerbøvik (eds): *Venstres hundre år*. Oslo: Gyldendal Norsk Forlag.
Østby, H. (1997): 'Media in Politics: Channels, Arenas, Actors, Themes', in K. Strøm and L. Svåsand (eds): *Challenges to Political Parties: The Case of Norway*. Ann Arbor, MI: University of Michigan Press.
Østerud, Ø. (2005): 'Introduction: The Peculiarities of Norway', *West European Politics*, 28 (4): 705–20.
Østerud, Ø. and Selle, P. (2006): 'Power and Democracy in Norway: The Transformation of Norwegian Politics', *Scandinavian Political Studies*, 29 (1): 25–46.
Åsheim, J. and Sæter, J. (1985): 'Nytt parti i nødsår (1933–1945)', in O. J. Sæter. (ed.): *Kristelig Folkepartis historie 1933–1983. Samling om verdier*. Oslo: Valo.

index

F

G

H

I

M

Q

R

T

U

www.ingramcontent.com/pod-product-compliance
Lightning Source LLC
Chambersburg PA
CBHW072044020426
42334CB00017B/1388

* 9 7 8 0 9 5 5 8 2 0 3 6 6 *